WOMEN, RELIGION, AND THE ATLANTIC WORLD
(1600–1800)

Women, Religion, and the Atlantic World (1600–1800)

Edited by Daniella Kostroun and Lisa Vollendorf

Published by the University of Toronto Press in association with the
UCLA Center for Seventeenth- and Eighteenth-Century Studies and
the William Andrews Clark Memorial Library

www.utppublishing.com
Printed in Canada

ISBN 978-0-8020-9906-8

Printed on acid-free paper

Library and Archives Canada Cataloguing in Publication

Women, religion, and the Atlantic world (1600–1800) / edited by Daniella
Kostroun and Lisa Vollendorf.
(UCLA Center/Clark series)
Includes bibliographical references and index.
ISBN 978-0-8020-9906-8

1. Women and religion – Atlantic Ocean Region – History – 17th century.
2. Women and religion – Atlantic Ocean Region – History – 18th century.
3. Women – Religious life – Atlantic Ocean Region – History – 17th century.
4. Women – Religious life – Atlantic Ocean Region – History – 18th century.
5. Atlantic Ocean Region – Religion – 17th century.   6. Atlantic Ocean Region
– Religion – 18th century.   7. Atlantic Ocean Region – Social conditions –
17th century.   8. Atlantic Ocean Region – Social conditions – 18th century.
I. Vollendorf, Lisa   II. Kostroun, Daniella J., 1970–   III. William Andrews
Clark Memorial Library   IV. University of California, Los Angeles. Center for
17th- & 18th-Century Studies   V. Series: UCLA Clark Memorial Library series

BL458.W652 2009   200.82′09182109032   C2009-900974-9

This book has been published with the help of a grant from the UCLA Center
for Seventeenth- and Eighteenth-Century Studies.

University of Toronto Press acknowledges the financial support for its
publishing activities of the Government of Canada through the Book
Publishing Industry Development Program (BPIDP).

University of Toronto Press acknowledges the financial assistance
to its publishing program of the Canada Council for the Arts and the
Ontario Arts Council.

Contents

Acknowledgments

We have accumulated numerous intellectual and personal debts during the preparation of this volume. First and foremost, we are grateful to the authors, whose knowledge and commitment made this book possible. We also thank Peter Reill, director of UCLA's Center for Seventeenth and Eighteenth Century Studies, for his support of the original colloquium and of this publication. The Center's activities are at the heart of seventeenth- and eighteenth-century scholarship in southern California and made possible our initial incursions into Atlantic studies. The staff at the William Andrews Clark Memorial Library and, in particular, Suzanne Tatian have supported this project with efficiency and grace. The meticulous anonymous readers for the University of Toronto Press improved the manuscript immeasurably; we acknowledge our debt to them with humility and gratitude. The staff members at University of Toronto Press have been extraordinarily supportive. We take this opportunity to thank Ronald Schoeffel, Anne Laughlin, Richard Ratzlaff, and Curtis Fahey for their professional, humane approach to academic publishing. We also want to thank graduate students Karl Lindner and Sarah Babovic for their help as research assistants. Finally, on a more personal note, we wish to thank our colleagues and our home institutions (Indiana University – Purdue University Indianapolis and California State University, Long Beach) for their support of our scholarly activities.

We dedicate this volume to our contributors, who made the project possible.

Contributors

Joan Cameron Bristol is associate professor of history at George Mason University. She is the author of *Christians, Blasphemers, and Witches: Afro-Mexican Ritual Practice in the Seventeenth Century* (University of New Mexico Press, Diálogos series, 2007) as well as articles and book chapters on gender, curing, and Afro-Mexican history.

Tracy Brown is assistant professor of anthropology at Central Michigan University, in Mount Pleasant. She is the author of numerous essays on Pueblo ethnohistory and is currently at work on a book-length manuscript about Pueblo constructions of gender and sexuality in the eighteenth century.

Barbara B. Diefendorf is professor of history at Boston University. Author of *From Penitence to Charity: Pious Women and the Catholic Reformation in Paris* (Oxford University Press, 2004), *Beneath the Cross: Catholics and Huguenots in Sixteenth-Century Paris* (Oxford University Press, 1991), and *Paris City Councillors: The Politics of Patrimony* (Princeton University Press, 1983), she co-edited with Carla Hesse *Culture and Identity in Early Modern Europe (1500–1800)* (University of Michigan Press, 1993). Her current research focuses on Catholic activism in late sixteenth- and seventeenth-century France.

Martha Few is associate professor of colonial Latin American history at the University of Arizona. She is author of *Women Who Live Evil Lives: Gender, Religion and the Politics of Power in Colonial Guatemala* (University of Texas Press, 2002) and has published several articles and book chapters on the history of chocolate in Guatemala, accounts of miraculously healed children in New Spain, and the use of medical autopsies during sixteenth-century epidemics in colonial Mexico. Her current book projects include *All of Humanity: Colonial Guatemala and New World Medical Cultures before the Smallpox Vaccine,* and, with Zeb Tortorici, *Centering Animals: Writing Animals into Latin American History.*

Amy M. Froide is associate professor of history at the University of Maryland, where she teaches courses in early modern British history and European women's history. She is the co-editor, with Judith M. Bennett, of *Singlewomen in the European Past, 1250–1800* (University of Pennsylvania Press, 1999) and the author of *Never Married: Singlewomen in Early Modern* England (Oxford University Press, 2005). She currently is working on a study of female investors during England's financial revolution, c. 1680–1750.

Daniella Kostroun is assistant professor of history at Indiana University – Purdue University Indianapolis. She is currently working on a book provisionally entitled 'Undermining Obedience: Louis XIV and the Port Royal Nuns.' She has written several articles examining early modern feminism, women and religion, and the political culture of absolutism.

J. Michelle Molina is assistant professor of history at Northwestern University. She has published several articles on Jesuit spiritual practices and the resulting forms of subjectivity operative in the early modern Catholic imaginary. An article that explores how Jesuit techniques of the self informed Mexican women's letters to their confessors was published recently in the journal *History of Religions.* She is at work on a book-length manuscript tentatively titled 'The Jesuit Ethic and the Spirit of Global Expansion.'

Rachel Sarah O'Toole is assistant professor of the colonial Andes and the early modern African Atlantic in the History Department at the University of California, Irvine. She has published articles in *Text* regarding indigenous-African relations as well as the laws and practices related to race and identity in colonial Peru in *The Americas: Journal of Colonialism and Colonial History* and *Social Text.*

Bianca Premo is associate professor of history at Florida International University in Miami. She is the author of *Children of the Father King: Youth, Authority and Legal Minority in Colonial Lima* (University of North Carolina, 2005), is co-editor of *Raising an Empire: Children in the Early Modern Iberia and Colonial Latin America* (Diálogos, University of New Mexico, 2007), and has written several articles and book chapters on Peruvian children, gender, and Spanish colonial law.

Stacey Schlau is professor of Spanish and women's studies at West Chester University, Pennsylvania. Her books include *Approaches to Teaching Sor Juana Inés de la Cruz,* co-edited with Emilie Bergmann (Modern Language Association, 2007); *Spanish American Women's Use of the Word: Colonial through Contemporary Narratives* (University of Arizona Press, 2001); the critical edition of *Viva al siglo, muerta al mundo: Obras escogidas de María de san Alberto (1568–1640)* (University Press of the South, 1998); and *Untold Sisters: Hispanic Nuns in Their Own Works,* co-authored with Electa Arenal (University of New Mexico Press, 1989; 2nd ed., 2009). In addition, she has published numerous articles on seventeenth- through twentieth-century Hispanic women writers, especially on narrative.

Jon Sensbach is professor of history at the University of Florida, with specialties in early America, African American, and religious history. He is the author of *Rebecca's Revival: Creating Black Christianity in the Atlantic World* (Harvard University Press, 2005) and *A Separate Canaan: The Making of an Afro-Moravian World in North Carolina, 1763–1840* (University of North Carolina Press, 1998). His current research explores the interplay of religious cultures in the early American south.

Ulrike Strasser is associate professor of history and affiliate faculty in Women's Studies and Religious Studies at the University of California, Irvine. She is the author of the award-winning monograph *State of Virginity: Gender, Religion and Politics in an Early Modern Catholic State* (University of Michigan Press, 2004, paper 2007). Strasser also co-edited *Gender, Kinship, Power: A Comparative and Interdisciplinary History* (Routledge, 1995) and has published on questions of gender and global history. Her current book project focuses on the activities and writings of German Jesuits who worked in the Philippines and Oceania.

Lisa Vollendorf is professor of Spanish and chair of the Department of Romance, German, Russian Languages and Literatures at California State University, Long Beach. Author of *The Lives of Women: A New History of Inquisitional Spain* (Vanderbilt University Press, 2005) and *Reclaiming the Body: María de Zayas's Early Modern Feminism* (University of North

Carolina Press, 2001), she has edited *Literatura y feminismo en España* (Icaria, 2006) and *Recovering Spain's Feminist Tradition* (Modern Language Association, 2001). Her current projects include 'Cervantes and His Women Readers'; 'Approaches to Teaching Cervantes's Don Quixote' (with James A. Parr); and 'Theorizing the Ibero-American Atlantic' (with Harald Braun).

WOMEN RELIGION AND THE ATLANTIC WORLD
(1600–1800)

Introduction

DANIELLA KOSTROUN AND LISA VOLLENDORF

In the early eighteenth century, an African slave named Mariana reportedly spoke to white men 'with such authority about what she has read in the Bible that they cannot open their mouths against her.' Through religion, Mariana found the voice and authority to confound European slaveholders with the hypocrisies inherent in the slave system. A few decades earlier, in Mexico City, the elite Creole nun Sor Juana Inés de la Cruz denounced 'stupid men' ('hombres necios') for a sexual double standard that judged women harshly. Sor Juana also echoed the Spanish Carmelite Saint Teresa of Avila's theological writings when she went so far as to argue for women's right to teach and preach the tenets of Catholicism. As Sor Juana endeavoured to expose the gendered hypocrisies of Catholic culture, a young woman in colonial Lima successfully petitioned the ecclesiastical courts to grant her an annulment. María Teresa de Saénz's petition claimed that her mother had threatened to kill her if she did not marry at the age of fourteen. Using a mechanism created by the colonial system, Saénz challenged her parents' and, more specifically, her mother's control.

Temporal, geographical, class, and racial differences separate Mariana, Sor Juana, and María Teresa, yet together the women give us a glimpse into the complex interplay between religion, gender, and authority in the early modern Atlantic world.[1] The essays in this volume examine these and other European, indigenous, Creole, African, and mestiza women's interactions with shifting paradigms of Protestantism, Catholicism, Judaism, and syncretic beliefs throughout the Atlantic basin. As suggested by the examples of Mariana, Sor Juana, and María Teresa, cultural, intellectual, religious, and economic history comes to bear throughout the essays, as do questions of class, status, power, and authority. The essays investigate the impact of the early modern Atlantic world's changing cultural landscape on slaves and free people, migrants and natives, nuns, wives, widows, mothers, and singlewomen.

The book has its roots in a colloquium sponsored by UCLA's Center for Seventeenth and Eighteenth Century Studies at the William Andrews Clark Memorial Library. The original colloquium led to many surprising discoveries of commonalities across boundaries of nation, class, religion, and ethnicity, and left the participants eager to explore convergences and differences via a broader rubric. The collaboration that ensued brought our contributors into conversation with one another about the promises and pitfalls of Atlantic Studies, and its relationship to women's and gender studies in our numerous respective subfields.

In casting the project within the Atlantic framework, we seek to transcend the limitations of binaries of Old versus New worlds, Catholicism versus Protestantism, or indigenous people versus Europeans. Instead, we aim to examine the changes created by the movement of people, ideas, objects, and beliefs in the shared spaces of the Atlantic. As many historians and literary scholars know, Atlantic Studies rests on the premise that the Atlantic basin forms a community bound by economic, political, and cultural ties.[2] With its roots in the economic and political history of the early twentieth century, the discipline has gained new ground as centres, seminars, journals, and degree programs have been established throughout North America. This activity has coincided with an increasing number of scholars from a wider range of humanistic fields turning their attention to this area of study, whose vitality was made evident with the creation of the journal *Atlantic Studies: Literary, Cultural, Historical Perspectives* (2004).[3] The journal focuses on 'historical, cultural, and literary issues arising within the new disciplinary matrix of the circumatlantic world.'[4] As this statement suggests, the journal invites examinations of the shared space of the Atlantic community, which is linked by the exchange of goods, labour, ideas, and culture. In this regard, it reflects a field that welcomes large- and small-scope studies of the circulation of people, ideas, and objects throughout the Atlantic basin.[5] It also promises a re-evaluation of many assumptions rooted in research on the Columbian exchange, the industrial era, European-based empires, and such broader themes as the black, red, and white Atlantics (as categorized through slavery, revolutions, and settlement of the Americas).[6] At its best, the enterprise aspires to foster a transcultural dialogue among scholars of Europe, the Americas, and Africa.

Increasingly, scholars have had to contend with challenges put to the concept of the Atlantic community. Many of those challenges question whether that community was unique in any significant sense. Some have charged that claims of Atlantic 'exceptionalism' have facilitated a political or neo-imperialistic agenda to redefine Europe or the 'West' so as to include the Americas. These criticisms seem most valid when we look at the Atlantic from a perspective of trade routes and empire building, which have served as the focal point for much research to date. William O'Reilly has addressed critics who characterize Atlantic Studies as a 'neo-colonial, politically correct attempt at re-writing European history with some "other bits" given deferential treatment' and 'a weak attempt to replace national histories with global methods.'[7] In responding to such criticism, O'Reilly acknowledges the legitimacy of some of the charges and emphasizes the need for research to focus on the complexity of the Atlantic system. His engagement with Atlantic Studies critics speaks to a larger dynamic in the field. Indeed, seen from the perspective of the growing number of critics, one might say that Atlantic Studies has reached a crossroads. To preserve its self-legitimizing claim that the Atlantic forms a unique, bounded community, the field needs to re-evaluate many of its fundamental critical assumptions.

Our project allows us to begin assessing the critiques of Atlantic exceptionalism by highlighting the legitimacy of women's and gender studies as it relates to the articulation, practice, and definition of religion in the various times and spaces that constitute the early modern and colonial Atlantic. We cannot escape the reality that Atlantic Studies grows out of a focus on empire and economics, but, by building on the fine research done by others whose work is pushing similar boundaries, we aim to map new ways of examining the cultural components of the Atlantic world and their impact on individuals, groups, and societies throughout that space.

Whereas Atlantic Studies has at its origin an emphasis on economic forces that linked Europe and the Americas, our essays rely on historical, literary, and anthropological methodologies to add a cultural and gendered emphasis to existing research in cultural, intellectual, and social history. Our book places gender and religion at the centre of analyses about the Atlantic world. Relying on historical, literary, and anthropological methodologies, the essays add to the body of research defined broadly as Atlantic Studies. Through both macro- and micro-level interpretations, the book aims to engage self-identified Atlanticists as well as scholars of women's and gender studies vis-à-vis three primary goals.

First, we aim to break down boundaries of nation-bound inquiry by placing women, gender, and religion at the centre of current dialogues about a shared Atlantic space. Second, our analyses urge other scholars to attend to the promising ways a focus on women, gender, and religion engages, challenges, and, perhaps, expands the rubric of the Atlantic community into a more global perspective. Third, in analysing women, religion, and gender across national, ethnic, class, and religious lines, we hope to create the basis for a community of scholars who will continue to push the boundaries of their respective disciplines as well and to redefine the limits of Atlantic, women's, and gender studies.

By analysing the flows of ideas, peoples, and things and the impact of those exchanges on individuals and groups, this book encourages a dialogue about the role played by women, gender, and religion within and across local, national, and international boundaries during the period 1600–1800 in the Atlantic basin. The urgency of the project grows from the resistance to placing women or gender at the centre of analysis that we perceive among numerous Atlantic Studies seminars, degree programs, and conferences held over the past decade. For example, none of the Atlantic History seminars offered at Harvard since the inception of the program in 1996 has focused on women or gender. Similarly, no articles in *Atlantic Studies* to date have been gender-studies oriented, whereas military, political, and economic history have received what we view as perhaps more than their due share. While acknowledging the contributions of these venues to the development of Atlantic Studies, we nonetheless find it surprising that, in light of the impact of both religion and women's studies since the 1970s, there has been no sustained effort to question what we can learn about the Atlantic world through the lens of women, gender, and religion.[8]

While the absence of women, gender, and religion might make sense in light of the economic and political origins of Atlantic Studies, our call for a focus on these themes stems from the belief that the methods and tradition of critical inquiry emerging from women's studies and the study of religion are particularly well suited to answer O'Reilly's and others' call for research that focuses on the complexity of the Atlantic world system. From the beginning, women's studies distinguished itself by interrogating established narratives and literary canons in search of the 'hidden' agency and voices of women. Over the past few decades, this interrogation has led to a re-evaluation of the basic assumptions and research methodologies of many major fields in the humanities and social sciences, and has ushered in the field of gender studies.

Crucial to the entire Atlantic world in the sixteenth through eighteenth centuries in particular was the politics of religion. Examinations of religious institutions, beliefs, and practices in turn force a critique of the standard categories of race, class, and gender. Religion creates a category of identity sometimes independent of these three and can provide people with sources of motivation and agency in its own right.[9] Religion also forces us to reconceptualize space in ways that perhaps more closely mirror people's experiences of the early modern world. Since politics and religion often were closely linked in the period, confessional boundaries had real significance, and delimiting sacred and profane also held great importance for individuals and communities. On a related note, Keith Luria has argued that the very definition of self in the era was different, since many people imagined themselves living in 'territories of grace' as much as within political or geographical boundaries.[10] These are just some examples of the ways a focus on religion opens our eyes to alternative, non-political ways of imagining space, the very concepts to which many individuals across ethnic and religious lines adhered before the rise of the modern nation-state.

Our call for critical inquiry into the Atlantic world through the lens of women, gender, and religion is indebted to scholars who have already made important contributions to Atlantic Studies in exactly this fashion. The twenty-first century has seen numerous landmark studies that have examined the imbrication of spiritual beliefs, practices, and gender dynamics. Recent scholarship articulates this agenda vis-à-vis the Atlantic as a space of contact, change, and continuities. Susan Dinan and Deborah Meyers's *Women and Religion in Old and New Worlds* (2001) examines women's experiences of religion, primarily through a social-history framework. Taking a thematic approach, Nora Jaffary's volume, *Gender, Race, and Religion in the Colonization of the Americas* (2007), inserts race into the mix and is structured around 'four salient topics in the history of women's experiences in the colonization of the New World: the colonial frontier, women's relationships to Christian institutions, race mixing, and female networks.'[11] Several other volumes explore these topics in the context of empire, slavery, and authority in the colonial era. Without making explicit reference to the Atlantic diaspora, this second group of publications is characterized by its interest in probing the realities of those affected by colonization, slavery, and expansion, as seen in Mary E. Giles's *Women in the Inquisition: Spain and the New World* (1999); Allan Greer and Jodi Bilinkoff's *Colonial Saints: Discovering the Holy in the Americas* (2003); David Barry Gaspar and Darlene Clark Hine's *Beyond*

Bondage: Free Women of Color in the Americas (2004); and John Smolenski and Thomas J. Humphrey's *New World Orders: Violence, Sanction, and Authority in the Colonial Americas* (2005).[12]

Publications by individual scholars who have trained their eye on gender and religion in the Europe and the Americas also have broken new ground. Among dozens of recent publications that examine the complicated relationship between colonial era gender codes and religious and sexual practices, the following stand out: Jodi Bilinkoff's *Related ·Lives: Confessors and Their Female Penitents* (2005); Sharon Block's *Rape and Sexual Power in Early America* (2006); Kathryn Burns's *Colonial Habits: Convents and the Spiritual Economy of Cuzco, Peru* (1999); Silvia Frey and Betty Wood's *Come Shouting to Zion: African-American Protestantism in the American South and British Caribbean to 1830* (1998) and *From Slavery to Emancipation in the Atlantic World* (1999); Jacqueline Holler's *Escogidas Plantas: Nuns and Beatas in Mexico City, 1531–1601* (2005); and Kathleen Myers's *Neither Saints nor Sinners: Writing the Lives of Spanish American Women* (2001). The contributors to the present volume also have a distinguished list of publications that have added to the growing body of research on early modern and colonial gender studies.[13] This corpus makes it clear that we need to take stock of Atlantic Studies and examine where the field stands in light of these new developments.

The organization and methodology that inform *Women, Religion, and the Atlantic World (1600–1800)* are indebted to these and other scholars whose work engages the Atlantic community using methodologies of women's and religious studies. Like much of the existing research on the Atlantic world, the present volume focuses on the migration of ideas and people that resulted in transactional, dynamic relationships among and between people and institutions. All of this scholarship acknowledges that the watershed events of European exploration and expansion of empire through slavery, trade, and settlement profoundly influenced everyday people's experiences, lives, and identities.[14] We explicitly engage expressions of belief, authority, and gender throughout the Atlantic basin as a means of deciphering how individuals negotiated the changing realities into which they migrated, were born, or were forcibly placed.

By highlighting individuals' negotiations of institutions, belief systems, and local culture, we build on the groundbreaking work of Joan Wallach Scott, Merry Wiesner-Hanks, Judith Bennett, Mary Nash, and other influential feminists who have put forth convincing arguments about gender and experience as analytical categories. Our project also grows out of Caroline Walker Bynum's work on women's religious expression

and Natalie Zemon Davis's publications on early modern culture.[15] As
suggested by this list, our scholarship is based on a tradition of feminist
critique and is deeply indebted to these and other analyses of gender,
religion, and history. Joan Kelly-Gadol's question in 1977 – 'Did women
have a Renaissance?' – also influences our work, as new understanding
of women's lives in early modern and colonial contexts continues to cast
doubt on whether accepted temporal periodization and geographical
demarcations make sense when we accumulate bodies of knowledge
about gender and other previously understudied analytical categories.[16]
More than three decades after Kelly-Gadol provoked extensive debate,
the women's Renaissance is understood to have been both extraordinarily limited, as she argued, and a foundational period for women's intellectual history.[17] We take these and other scholars who have enriched
the field as role models for their successful incursions into previously
gender-blind disciplines. Their scholarship conclusively demonstrates
the impact that a focus on women and gender can have on received notions of truth, history, and experience.

In spite of an earlier – and persistent – focus on economic, political,
and military history, scholars of women, gender, and religion should feel
at home in Atlantic Studies: it promises to level the analytical playing
field in ways that mirror the attention given to race, class, status, gender, and sexual difference by those whose work is grounded in women's
and gender studies. Similarly, we invite those who self-identify as Atlanticists to embrace the methodologies, theories, and topics brought to
the table by those working in women's and gender studies. In its most
expansive and, from our perspective, interesting manifestation, Atlantic
Studies provides a framework for examining the cultural, political, religious, economic, and social interactions and experiences of individuals
and groups. This description should appeal to scholars working in the
women's studies tradition, which uses similar language to argue for the
validity and importance of gender as a category of analysis.

Women, Religion, and the Atlantic World (1600–1800) provides an outline for refining our collective understanding of the Atlantic community.
While we invite readers to find connections among the essays, we do not
advance a strictly comparative approach to women, gender, and religion
in the Atlantic basin. Rather, we advocate a methodological approach dependent both on microhistory and on women's studies. In this sense, we
support Lara Putnam's articulation of the links between Atlantic Studies
and microhistory.[18] We agree with Putnam's endorsement of the micro
approach as a means of developing macro understandings of the com-

plexities of the Atlantic world, and we also see women's studies as a fruit-ful model for probing questions of alliances and community. The eleven essays that follow thus take a micro approach to the study of women, gender, and religion and use that approach to probe broader structures and notions of community. Collectively, the essays provide a model for an interrogation of Atlantic Studies as viewed through the promising integration of women's and religious studies into the broader field.

In terms of that interrogation, it would be impossible to represent all religious beliefs, ethnic groups, class issues, colonialists, and indigenous people in one volume. We want to emphasize from the outset that our coverage does not intend to be comprehensive. We address European, transatlantic, and indigenous paradigms and particularities, but we do not, for instance, devote an essay to the Anglo-American colonies. Islam, too, is absent from these pages, even though the history of many minor-ity groups, such as the descendants of Islamo-Arab Iberians known as *moriscos,* has yet to be fully integrated into the fabric of the early modern world.[19] The line-up of contributors is weighed heavily towards histo-rians, with one anthropologist and two literary scholars in the fray. In taking a step towards providing a model for interdisciplinary, gender-focused analyses of the Atlantic basin, the volume makes a methodologi-cal argument for the benefits of a more incisive, self-conscious focus on women, gender, and religion across the disciplines. Similarly, we hope to build sensitivity to the ways a focus on women, gender, and religion can both complicate and enrich studies of individuals and groups, religious institutions and spiritual practices, and macro- and micro-level consid-erations of an Atlantic community. Collectively, our work as historians, anthropologists, and literary scholars is enriched by this conversation, which encourages us to transcend disciplinary and national boundaries in an effort to define more clearly our terms of engagement with the historical concepts and peoples we study.

Part One, 'Theoretical Reflections on Women and Religion from an At-lantic Perspective,' challenges current understandings of religion, par-ticularly Catholicism and Protestantism, throughout the Atlantic. The essays in this section examine some of the larger questions related to the geographical expansion of European religions and their impact on individuals throughout Europe and the Americas. The importance of religion in Europe and in the contact zones that emerged in the Ameri-cas cannot be overstated, since the export of religious institutions, ideologies, and frameworks had an enduring impact on individuals and societies on both sides of the Atlantic. If we are to speak of an Atlantic community at all, the cultural components of those contact zones must be considered. Religious change in early modern Europe was inextricably linked to empire, nation building, and grabs for power, as can be traced in the expulsions of Jews and Muslims from Iberia, the Protestant and Catholic Reformations, and the establishment of the Church of England. The expulsions led to thousands of forced conversions and displacements of Sephardic and Islamic Iberians, and prompted some Jews and *conversos* to try their luck in Africa and across the Atlantic. The Tridentine decrees mandating the cloistering of religious women cut some religious communities off from their livelihoods yet opened up opportunities for engagement with education and reform, as seen in the influential case of Teresa of Avila's Discalced Carmelites.

Barbara Diefendorf begins Part One with an analysis of Teresian reform, female spirituality, and other facets of the Catholic Reformation that had lasting effects throughout the Catholic Atlantic. In 'Rethinking the Catholic Reformation: The Role of Women,' Diefendorf probes the limitations of the accepted scholarly interpretation of the Council of Trent as an adverse event for female spirituality. The essay delineates the uneven application of post-Tridentine reform and shows that, while the cloistering mandated by the council had negative economic effects on women by robbing them of earnings as teachers, nurses, and prayer givers, its role as an isolating and regressive force has been sorely overstated in much of the scholarship. The permeability of the cloister, as studied extensively by Italianists and Hispanists, is taken up here as a key factor in understanding the relationships between cloistered women and their surrounding societies.

In exposing blind spots regarding women in the early modern Catholic world, Diefendorf argues for reconsideration of received views towards religion and spirituality. Rather than assume that women were placed in convents, we should more self-consciously interrogate potential spiritual motivations, for instance. We also should question the scholarly biases (prevalent in francophone and anglophone studies in particular) that presume active orders to be more interesting – and therefore more worthy of study – than contemplative orders. Diefendorf sets the stage for the rest of the volume when she calls for an examination of a wider variety of sources as a means of contextualizing belief and spirituality within a larger framework of religious, social, and political climates.

Amy Froide takes up Diefendorf's call for attention to women's spirituality vis-à-vis cultural politics in 'The Religious Lives of Singlewomen in the Anglo-Atlantic World: Quaker Missionaries, Protestant Nuns, and Covert Catholics.' Froide debunks the myth of English exceptionalism with regard to female religious communities in the seventeenth century. Emphasizing the pan-European and transatlantic nature of those communities, she argues that Englishwomen built on personal experience and second-hand knowledge of women's communal living throughout the Christian West. Using Atlantic world models, they created the basis for Quaker, Catholic, and Protestant communities. Like Diefendorf's inquiry into Catholicism, Froide's dismantling of assumptions about English spirituality implicitly calls upon scholars of the Atlantic world and of women's history to devote more attention to the process of contact between women of different nationalities and religious traditions. Froide also articulates a methodological point for scholars of women and gender. Whereas much other research ignores singlewomen – including the 'ever married' and the 'never married' – Froide legitimizes these women as a category of individual who must be studied if we are to come to a full understanding of the economies, societies, and religious configurations of the early modern Atlantic world.[20] The evidence regarding singlewomen uncovered by Froide and other scholars suggests that more research should be done to deepen our understanding of the roles played by these women in the Atlantic world.

The emphasis on cross-cultural, transatlantic fertilization of women's emotional and intellectual lives seen in Amy Froide's work on Englishwomen is expanded to include the Iberian empire in Lisa Vollendorf's essay on women's cultural and intellectual history in the early modern and colonial Hispanic worlds. In 'Transatlantic Ties: Women's Writing in Iberia and the Americas,' Vollendorf examines evidence of women's textual production as a means of probing strategies of self-representation in early modern and colonial culture. Evidence of women's manipulation of dominant ideas about Christian femininity and piety links secular and religious writers throughout the Iberian Atlantic. Common rhetorical strategies and thematic similarities in women's writing from the period raise the question of how women experienced the culture of control throughout the Iberian empire and the extent to which they had knowledge of other women's writing both within and outside convent walls. Vollendorf echoes Diefendorf's focus on the significant impact of religion on models of piety, communal living, and women's opportunities in leadership, education, religion, and mercantile economies. Like Diefen-

dorf and Froide, she investigates the history of experience and the limitations of the sources we can use to decipher that history.

The first trio of essays thus pushes scholars to reconsider the limitations of current inquiry into early modern and colonial cultural and
social history. By drawing on research that crosses national and religious lines, Diefendorf, Froide, and Vollendorf collectively argue for a
reconceptualization of methodologies used to decipher early modern
and colonial experiences as inflected by gender and religion. Individual
and group expressions of piety took different forms in the Catholic and
Protestant traditions probed in these essays. The essays also expose the
pitfalls of remaining within national or even religious boundaries when
considering gender history. Together, the essays call for more broadly
Atlanticized considerations of women's history.

The second section of the book, 'Negotiating Belief and Ethnicity in
the Atlantic Basin,' builds on the methodological overviews presented
in Part One by examining the often conflictive and not always successful
negotiations between indigenous and marginalized people and dominant groups and institutions throughout the Atlantic world. During the
era under consideration, the consequences of contact rippled throughout the Atlantic, as native peoples, African slaves, and European immigrants intermingled, intermarried, and interacted in complex and
not always predictable ways. The essays in this section explore questions of identity, belief, and spiritual expression at local and community
levels with a focus on the role of ethnic difference. The Atlantic diaspora's racial and ethnic diversity is highlighted, with all of the essays focusing on tensions between a European-imposed sense of order
(as expressed through law, economic structures, and religion) and the
challenges put to that order by everyday people's experiences of the
colonial Atlantic world. Individuals' experiences of colonial society are
examined in terms of interactions and ideologies that affected the ra-
cially and ethnically diverse population throughout the Atlantic basin.
The four essays in Part Two engage notions of community and alliances
that have been investigated by scholars of Atlantic Studies. In many instances, allegiances and boundaries shifted and changed in response
to colonial structures and ideologies, which in turn had a surprising
impact on the practices and beliefs of both colonists and those they
sought to control.

In an examination of the abundant archives of the Moravians, Jon
Sensbach turns our attention to the interplay between race, gender, and

religion among Africans in the Atlantic world. In 'Prophets and Helpers: African American Women and the Rise of Black Christianity in the Age of the Slave Trade,' Sensbach studies the embrace of Protestantism by free and enslaved Africans in the Dutch West Indies. The analysis challenges current periodization of African American activism in Christianity (currently ascribed to nineteenth-century preachers such as Rebecca Cox Jackson, Jerena Lee, and Sojourner Truth) by revealing women's active roles as evangelizers and teachers within the Moravian church as early as the 1730s. Focusing on displaced Africans and European missionaries, Sensbach engages migration as a central feature of the Atlantic world experience. People, ideas, and institutions migrated – either forcibly or freely – during the early modern and colonial periods.[21] The impact of those migrations is apparent in the mixing of free blacks and whites in the Danish West Indies and, poignantly, in the story of the Afro-Moravian Rebecca, a free slave who worked for the Moravians and married a free white man. The link between Africans' religion and mobility, between spirituality and freedom, is one that has not been sufficiently explored for this early period. By focusing on the pioneering Moravians, Sensbach encourages a reconsideration of the roots of the black Protestant international movement.

Sexual, gender, religious, and racial politics of the Atlantic world converge in the next essay. Rachel Sarah O'Toole's '"The Most Resplendent Flower of the Indies": Making Saints and Constructing Whiteness in Colonial Peru' examines the drama that unfolded around a case of possession by a black devil in late-seventeenth-century Peru. The critical role played by the construction of race and gender throughout the Atlantic is at the centre of O'Toole study of clerics' responses to women's spirituality. Her analysis questions clerics' investments in women's religious experience while revealing that colonial whiteness was a contested category. By considering European definitions of demonic possession and mystic experience as they were expressed in a colonial setting, O'Toole shows how colonial anxieties about Africans and authority played out in highly racialized ways. This analysis of sexuality, spirituality, and sexual violence highlights the fears of black masculinity that played a role in the imagination of Europeans who had never crossed the Atlantic as well as in everyday life in colonial society.

J. Michelle Molina and Ulrike Strasser propel the analysis of the Atlantic in two directions in their study of Jesuit hagiography written about the Asian-Mexican holy woman Catarina de San Juan. 'Missionary Men and the Global Currency of Female Sanctity' challenges scholars to rethink the connections between early modern Catholicism across both the Atlantic and the Pacific. The analysis expands the boundaries of the Atlantic world through a focus on a South Asian–born slave whose spiritual experiences as a free woman in Puebla, Mexico, gained renown among Jesuit clerics and other inhabitants of that colony. Echoing Sensbach's focus on Protestant evangelism, Molina and Strasser consider the global imperative of Jesuit evangelism and how the role of both German and Iberian missionary expansion into the Pacific by way of New Spain complicates any consideration of the Atlantic diaspora.

Molina and Strasser also emphasize the import of gender studies as they relate to men's experiences. While Atlantic Studies analyses often centre on domains of life in which men are primary actors, the scholarship rarely examines the cultural dynamics that code these domains as male. Building on recent work on the relationship between spiritual biographers and their subjects, Molina and Strasser use practices of devotional writing as a means of locating different struggles for manhood on the colonial grid, variously expressed as the desire for martyrdom or aspirations to be published among natural philosophers.[22] In the process, they push the boundaries of the analytic constructs of colonialism and Catholicism and suggest new ways to study the early stages of European expansion as an Atlantic-focused enterprise whose impact also was felt in the Pacific.

In 'Patriarchs, Petitions, and Prayers: Intersections of Gender and *Calidad* in Colonial Mexico,' the last essay of Part Two, Joan Cameron Bristol turns to many of the questions about authority, identity, and difference that are addressed in other essays in this section. Bristol's focus is the overlap of gender and racial dynamics in Inquisition cases involving Afro-Mexicans. Relying on the concepts of 'calidad' (status or quality) and genealogy (defined by whether one had 'pure blood'), Bristol argues that individual authority depended on numerous factors, including skin colour, occupation, lineage, personal relationships, gender, and status as free person or slave. Afro-Mexican resistance to and manipulation of colonial ideologies of race, gender, and power demonstrate a complex interplay between people of the non-dominant classes and a dominant ideology that strove to disempower them. Wives who pointed the finger at husbands and slaves and servants who accused masters and mistresses of ill treatment exemplify attempts to parrot the Inquisition's own ideas about authority and hierarchy. Borrowing Steve J. Stern's designation of such strategies as 'pluralizing the patriarchs,' Bristol examines how such tactics were used to varying degrees of success by marginalized people (slaves, mestizos, and Afro-Mexicans) and other supposedly inferior individuals (women) to assert power within the colonial religious system.[23] Her analysis of gender and authority dissects the rhetorical strategies by which individuals belonging to non-dominant races and classes attempted to assert authority within the parameters imposed by religious institutions and other colonizing mechanisms of power in New Spain. In doing so, Bristol emphasizes that European beliefs about non-Europeans often resulted in unforeseen, manipulative responses by mixed-race and non-white people who sought authority and redress in the Atlantic basin. By examining the interactions of peoples of various nationalities, ethnicities, and religious affiliations, Bristol and other authors in this section encourage readers to rethink the geographic, intellectual, and social realities of the Atlantic world during the early modern era.

The interplay between belief systems and authority as expressed by individuals and collective entities in the early modern and colonial contexts resulted in syncretism, unpredictable alliances, and new forms of knowledge that forged increasing links among the people and places of the Atlantic basin. As seen in the examples of evangelism by Moravians and Jesuits and complex views on race and difference on behalf of mestizo and African colonial subjects, the flow of ideas and peoples across the Atlantic resulted in individuals and groups forging new ways of interacting with a rapidly changing world.

The third section of the volume, 'Authority and Identity in the Catholic Atlantic,' focuses on the negotiation of authority within that world. All four of its essays highlight how individuals in various locations throughout the Atlantic found themselves articulating defences of their own beliefs and reshaping those beliefs in response to the world around them.

Martha Few puts the interplay between the beliefs of the marginalized and those of the colonizers into relief in 'Atlantic World Monsters: Monstrous Births and the Politics of Pregnancy in Colonial Guatemala.' Examining the link between colonial medical practice and religious imperialism, Few explores cultural continuities and disjunctures between early modern Europe and colonial Guatemala. She analyses official Catholic Church responses to unusual pregnancies and births as a means of identifying the emerging syncretism that came to influence religious expression, medical practice, and political power in Guatemala. Such arguments trace a two-way circulation of ideas by which European ideas about wonder and specifically about monstrous births became imbued with Mesoamerican ideas about pregnancy and childbirth. As Catholic Spaniards sought to provide explanations for conjoined twins, 'half-toad' babies, and other birth-defect or stillbirth-related phenomena, indigenous ideas about deformity and wonder influenced their interpretations to such an extent that, in the end, syncretism prevailed. Few thus uses religion and gender to decipher links between women's bodies, local and native knowledge, and the colonial project.

Stacey Schlau's essay, 'A Judaizing "Old Christian" Woman and the Mexican Inquisition: The "Unusual" Case of María de Zárate,' analyses the story of a Creole tried for practising Judaism in mid-seventeenth-century New Spain. Born to Spanish parents and laying claim to Old Christian lineage, in 1636 Zárate married an Andalusian Crypto-Jew, Francisco Botello, who was burned at the stake as punishment for his unrepentant embrace of Judaism. Schlau's examination of how a troubled family dynamic could lead to denunciation and death reveals disturbing interplay between race, class, gender, and religion in colonial Mexico. As a literary scholar, Schlau is particularly attuned to the ideology that informs inquisitorial documents, and her analysis makes explicit the complexity of narrative voice, ideological imperative, and formulaic discourse in the production of such records. Examining Zárate's life story and self-defence as well as witnesses' depositions and inquisitors' responses, Schlau reveals the means by which interpersonal allegiances dissolved in inquisitional settings, in which dominant, often oppressive ideologies regarding race, class, religion, gender, and status were mobilized by defendants and witnesses alike.

Tracy Brown engages questions of movement and community in her analysis of Pueblo men and women in colonial New Mexico. 'A World of Women and a World of Men?: Pueblo Witchcraft in Eighteenth-Century New Mexico' examines the gendered uses of sorcery among Pueblos as a means of deciphering indigenous people's access to different social spheres. The focus on sorcery allows Brown to explore motivations for sorcery as they were informed by gender, status, and ethnicity. By positioning male and female uses of sorcery at the centre of her analysis, Brown investigates intra- and inter-community conflict, showing that the Pueblo forged networks of interdependence among themselves and across class and ethnic lines. Yet many of those relationships were fraught with conflict. Brown examines that conflict and raises questions about the gendered exercise of power and uses of knowledge among both the Pueblo and the Spanish in colonial New Mexico. The exploration of Pueblo-Spanish relations focuses our attention on the negotiation between Catholic orthodoxy and everyday practices throughout the Atlantic. In Europe and abroad, the church's ability to control beliefs, emotions, and actions was regularly challenged by people of all creeds and castes.

Such challenges – to local, global, and even parental authority – form the basis of Bianca Premo's 'The Maidens, the Monks, and Their Mothers: Patriarchal Authority and Holy Vows in Colonial Lima, 1650–1715.' In this analysis of gender and family politics as reflected in ecclesiastical court records, Premo examines the negotiation between the ideal of patriarchy and the realities of life in South American colonies. Through a focus on testimonies rendered by individuals forced to marry against their will, Premo argues that we cannot fully understand gender power unless we consider the interplay between the mechanisms that informed colonial society – secular and canonical law, European and indigenous cultures – and the lived, colonial experience in which women and many others exercised authority. In exercising their right to appeal unwanted marriages, colonial subjects of different races and social standing requested the help of Spanish authorities in settling intergenerational family conflict. The analysis shows that Lima inhabitants resisted colonial attempts to impose laws that would allow families to disinherit daughters who married against their parents' will. By the same token, many youth appealed their parents' decisions, using the mechanism provided by the ecclesiastical court to request annulment of such unions. In deciphering the appeals, Premo finds that patriarchal authority often was curbed in favour of children's rights, and she also uncovers evidence for mothers' influential role in arranging marriages for the next generation. In this light, the exercise of patriarchal authority is revealed to work in conjunction with other factors, such as free will, local custom, and family dynamics. As such, patriarchal authority must be understood as fluid within the context of colonial Lima: that is, in a context in which church doctrine and local beliefs constantly interacted, women and children had more access to the exercise of power than we might otherwise assume.

Premo's essay concludes the volume with an emphasis on questioning the rubrics with which scholars have approached gender studies and cultural history within the Atlantic basin. Like all of the essays, hers lays bare some of the blind spots of current scholarship and urges a reconsideration of the definitions and frameworks used to study early modern Europe and the colonial Americas, pointing to what we can learn from casting our research questions in terms of the broader Atlantic basin.

Shifting the focus to women, gender, and religion complicates the ways that some scholars have attempted to view allegiance and space in the Atlantic basin. Consider Stacey Schlau's example of the condemned Old Christian María de Zárate, who seems to have practised Judaism as a Crypto-Jew. Even as the boundary between 'Jew' and 'Christian' had little measurable meaning in the context of colonial Mexico, the shifting familial dynamic that resulted in inquisitional accusations and the execution of Zárate's husband reveals that no fixed ideas about family or community can be counted on within such a destabilized context. As with the case of Jon Sensbach's Afro-Moravian evangelist, Rebecca, the notion of community implicitly involves a notion of shared experience, yet also the necessary consideration of inclusion and exclusion in that world.

The alliances in these instances fall along surprising lines. Whereas Rebecca preached to enslaved fellow Africans, she married across race lines. Similarly, Zárate took in a mixed-race foster son who turned against her, so she declared him a 'mestizo dog' and a disgrace to her family. These are just two of numerous examples that suggest that further inquiry into the shifting allegiances among and between women and their communities will help scholars come to a more expansive understanding of the tenuous – yet paradoxically sometimes very stable – networks and allegiances that provided lifelines for many women and led many others into peril.

Similarly, in arguing for a self-conscious integration of gender and religion into the broader field of Atlantic studies, the essays in this volume illustrate that a combined rubric of gender and religion helps expand the usual 'Atlantic' world (as defined by the major European colonizing powers) to include missionaries in Asia, refugees from India, and freed slaves who migrated of their own accord to Germany. This in turn suggests that the migratory patterns and cultural imbrications of the broader community with the Atlantic diaspora need to be more fully explored. This line of inquiry should encourage more scholars to leave behind divisions between Europe and the Americas in favour of nuanced analyses of how individuals experienced that broader community as they travelled to new places or as new institutions, laws, and ways of life emerged. In this respect, the role of female migration and the geography of the Pacific emerge as two arenas for future investigation.

Our final claim remains more of an invitation than an argument. Just as we encourage scholars of the Atlantic basin to reconsider the role of women, gender, and religion in their own research, we also urge scholars of women, gender, and religion to take this 'global' turn. Although we were not entirely convinced of the promises of this turn when we began, as women's studies scholars we now are firmly convinced that the next frontier of Atlantic World studies is not just topical but methodological. Women, gender, and religion cannot simply be added and stirred into the mix. Instead, scholars engaged with Atlantic Studies need to recognize that the field's strength lies in the promise it holds for pushing the boundaries of interdisciplinarity. Women's studies has a proven ability to uncover new sources, overturn received knowledge, and open up new lines of inquiry. In this fundamental sense it has much to offer scholars of the Atlantic world. Indeed, the interdisciplinary, transgeographical, and expansive claims of Atlantic Studies run the risk of devolving into mere lip service if we do not bridge the divide that continues to leave scholars of women and gender on the margins of the field.

As editors of this project, we would like to conclude by emphasizing the intellectual rewards that such interdisciplinary projects can bring. The initial colloquium we organized with the support of UCLA's Center for Seventeenth and Eighteenth Century Studies and the William Andrews Clark Memorial Library in 2004 has led to a collaboration that has improved our work and changed our perspectives on questions related to women's and religious studies. Speaking across national, geographic, ethnic, religious, and disciplinary lines that often define and, we would argue, constrain humanities scholarship, we have become increasingly aware of similarities among the men, women, and historical phenomena studied by all of the scholars in this volume. Moreover, we have become deeply committed to probing convergences and divergences across the disciplines as a means of broadening our own research. It is in this spirit of collaboration and enrichment that we invite readers to consider the promise offered by forging a closer relationship between scholars of women, gender, and religion and those whose work grows out of other disciplines related to the Atlantic diaspora. We hope that the stories and analyses offered up in the essays that follow provide a roadmap for that collaboration.

Notes

1 Mariana's story is taken from Jon Sensbach's essay in this volume. Also see C.G.A. Oldendorp, *History of the Mission of the Evangelical Brethren on the Caribbean Isalnds of St. Thomas, St. Croix, and St. John*, ed. Johann Jakob Bossard

(Barby, 1777), trans. Arnold R. Highfield and Vladimir Barac (Ann Arbor: University of Michigan Press, 1987), 412–13. Sor Juana and María Teresa de Saénz are discussed, respectively, by Lisa Vollendorf and Bianca Premo, in the present volume.

2 The field is indeed vast, so we point readers to recent scholarship that provides succinct overviews: Bernard Bailyn, *Atlantic History: Concepts and Contours* (Cambridge, Mass.: Harvard University Press, 2005); Thomas Benjamin, Timothy D. Hall, and David E. Rutherford, eds., *The Atlantic World in the Age of Empire* (New York: Houghton Mifflin, 2001); Jorge Cañizares-Esguerra and Erik Seeman, eds., *The Atlantic in Global History* (New York: Prentice Hall, 2006); Donna Gabbacia, 'A Long Atlantic in a Wider World,' *Atlantic Studies: Literary, Cultural, and Historical Perspectives*, 1, no. 1 (2004): 1–27; Richard Kagan and Geoffrey Parker, eds., *Spain, Europe, and the Atlantic World: Essays in Honour of John H. Elliott* (Cambridge: Cambridge University Press, 1995); William O'Reilly, 'Genealogies of Atlantic History,' *Atlantic Studies*, 1, no. 1 (2004): 66–84; Carla Gardina Pestana, *The English Atlantic in an Age of Revolution, 1640–1661* (Cambridge, Mass.: Harvard University Press, 2004); and Timothy J. Shannon, *Atlantic Lives: A Comparative Approach to Early America* (New York: Pearson Longman, 2004).

3 In addition to the gender- and religion-focused research cited in this Introduction, the diversity of the post-2000 humanistic turn in Atlantic Studies is exemplified by the following publications: Ida Altman, *Transatlantic Ties in the Spanish Empire: Brihuega, Spain, & Puebla, Mexico, 1560–1620* (Stanford, Calif.: Stanford University Press, 2000); Rebecca Ann Bach, *Colonial Transformations: The Cultural Production of the New Atlantic World, 1580–1640* (New York: Palgrave Macmillan, 2000); Philip Beidler and Gary Taylor, eds., *Writing Race across the Atlantic World, 1492–1789* (New York: Palgrave Macmillan, 2002); Lauren Benton, *Law and Colonial Cultures: Legal Regimes in World History, 1400–1900* (Cambridge: Cambridge University Press, 2002); Russell Bourne, *Gods of War, Gods of Peace: How the Meeting of Native and Colonial Religions Shaped Early America* (New York: Harcourt, 2002); Emily Clark, *Masterless Mistresses: The New Orleans Ursulines and the Development of a New World Society, 1727–1834* (Chapel Hill: University of North Carolina Press, 2007); Kimberly Gauderman, *Women's Lives in Colonial Quito: Gender, Law, and Economy in Spanish America* (Austin: University of Texas Press, 2003); Carla Gerona, *Night Journeys: The Power of Dreams in Transatlantic Quaker Culture* (Charleston: University of Virginia Press, 2004); John Gillis, *Islands of the Mind: How the Human Imagination Created the Atlantic World* (New York: Palgrave Macmillan, 2004); Allan Greer, *Mohawk Saint: Catherine Tekakwitha and the Jesuits* (Oxford and New York: Oxford University Press, 2005); Nich-

ols Griffiths and Sue Peabody, *Slavery, Freedom, and the Law in the Atlantic World: A Brief History with Documents* (New York: Bedford St. Martin's Press, 2007); Nicholas Griffiths and Fernando Cervantes, eds., *Spiritual Encounters: Interactions between Christianity and Native Religions in Colonial America* (Lincoln: University of Nebraska Press, 1999); Sheryllynne Haggerty, *The British-Atlantic Trading Community, 1760–1810: Men, Women, and the Distribution of Goods* (London: Brill, 2006); Kirsten Ibsen, *Women's Spiritual Autobiography in Colonial Spanish America* (Gainesville: University Press of Florida, 1999); Colin Kidd, *The Forging of Races: Race and Scripture in the Protestant Atlantic World, 1600–2000* (Cambridge: Cambridge University Press, 2006); Ann M. Little, *Abraham in Arms: War and Gender in Colonial New England* (Philadelphia: University of Pennsylvania Press, 2006); Jane E. Mangan, *Trading Roles: Gender, Ethnicity, and the Urban Economy in Colonial Potosí* (Durham, N.C.: Duke University Press, 2005); Jane T. Merritt, 'Cultural Encounters along a Gender Frontier: Mahican, Delaware, and German Women in Eighteenth-Century Pennsylvania,' *Pennsylvania History,* 67 (autumn 2000): 503–32; Bernard Moitt, *Women and Slavery in the French Antilles, 1635–1848* (Bloomington: Indiana University Press, 2001); Ann Marie Plane, *Colonial Intimacies: Indian Marriage in Early New England* (Ithaca, N.Y.: Cornell University Press, 2000); Susan Sleeper-Smith, *Indian Women and French Men: Rethinking Cultural Encounter in the Western Great Lakes* (Amherst: University of Massachusetts Press, 2001); and Stephanie Wood, *Transcending Conquest: Nahua Views of Spanish Colonial Mexico* (Oklahoma City: University of Oklahoma Press, 2003).

4 *Atlantic Studies,* http://www.tandf.co.uk/journals/journal.asp?issn=1478–8810&linktype=1. As editors Maria Lauret, Bill Marshall, and David Murray highlight in the special *Atlantic Studies* volume of 2007 on the French Atlantic, this volume was the first to focus primarily on cultural and literary history, 'thus beginning to fulfill the journal's original intention of widening the Atlantic Studies paradigm from history to the arts and social sciences' ('The French Atlantic,' Editorial, *Atlantic Studies,* 4, no. 1 [2007]: 1–4, 2).

5 O'Reilly argues in favour of Atlantic Studies, highlighting the core issues of 'state, economy and culture' and affirming that all three concepts bind the Atlantic community in interconnective webs ('Genealogies of Atlantic History,' 69).

6 See Donna Gabbacia, 'A Long Atlantic in a Wider World,' *Atlantic Studies,* 1, no. 1 (2004): 1–27. For research that puts these ideas into practice, see T.H. Breen and Timothy Hall, *Colonial America in an Atlantic World: A Story of Creative Interaction* (New York: Pearson Longman, 2004); Jorge Cañizares-Esguerra, *Puritan Conquistadors: Iberianizing the Atlantic, 1550–1700* (Stanford, Calif.: Stanford University Press, 2006), and *Nature, Empire, and Nation:*

Explorations of the History of Science in the Iberian World (Stanford, Calif.: Stanford University Press, 2006); Christine Daniels and Michael V. Kennedy, eds., *Negotiated Empires: Centers and Peripheries in the Americas, 1500–1820* (New York: Routledge, 2002); Donna J. Guy and Thomas E. Sheridan, eds., *Contested Ground: Comparative Frontiers on the Northern and Southern Edges of the Spanish Empire* (Tucson: University of Arizona Press, 1998); Kenneth Mills and Anthony Grafton, eds., *Conversion: Old Worlds and New* (Rochester, N.Y.: University of Rochester Press, 2003); Elizabeth W. Kiddy, *Blacks of the Rosary: Memory and History in Minas Gerais, Brazil* (College Station: Penn State University Press, 2005); Nicole Delia Legnani, *Titu Cusi: A 16th Century Account of the Conquest* (Cambridge, Mass.: Harvard University Press, 2006); Jane Landers and Barry M. Robinson, eds., *Slaves, Subjects, and Subversives: Blacks in Colonial Latin America* (Albuquerque: University of New Mexico Press, 2006); Matthew Restall, *Beyond Black and Red: African-Native Relations in Colonial Latin America* (Albuquerque: University of New Mexico Press, 2005); David J. Silverman, *Faith and Boundaries: Colonists, Christianity, and Community among the Wampanoag Indians of Martha's Vineyard, 1600–1871* (Cambridge: Cambridge University Press, 2005); Marta V. Vicente, *Clothing the Spanish Empire: Families and the Calico Trade in the Early Modern Atlantic World* (New York: Palgrave Macmillan, 2006); and Angela Woollacott, *Gender and Empire* (New York: Palgrave Macmillan, 2006).

7 O'Reilly, 'Genealogies of Atlantic History,' 69.

8 Merry Wiesner-Hanks, *Women and Gender in Early Modern Europe* (Cambridge: Cambridge University Press, 1993), 3.

9 Susan Rosa and Dale Van Kley, 'Religion and the Historical Discipline: A Reply to Mack Holt and Henry Heller,' *French Historical Studies,* 21, no. 4 (1998): 611–29, 616.

10 Keith Luria, *Territories of Grace: Cultural Change in the Seventeenth-Century Diocese of Grenoble* (Berkeley: University of California, 1991), available online at http://ark.cdlib.org/ark:/13030/ft6n39p11n/. Luria's excellent introduction probes the intersections of culture and religion in the early modern world. For a consideration of these issues vis-à-vis questions of co-existence, see his more recent *Sacred Boundaries: Religious Coexistence and Conflict in Early-Modern France* (Washington, D.C.: Catholic University of America Press, 2005).

11 Nora E. Jaffary, 'Introduction: Contextualizing Race, Gender, and Religion in the New World,' in *Gender, Race, and Religion in the Colonization of the Americas* (Burlington, Vt.: Ashgate, 2007), 1–11, 2. We want to express our gratitude to Nora Jaffary for generously sharing her Introduction and Afterword with us while her book was in press.

12 Also see Merry Wiesner-Hanks, 'The Voyages of Christine Columbus,' *World History Connected,* July 2006, <http://worldhistoryconnected.press.uiuc. edu/3.3/wiesner-hanks.html> (9 March 2008); and Eyda Merediz and Nina Gerassi-Navarro, 'Introduction: Confluencias de lo transatlántico y lo latino-americano,' in Nina Gerassi-Navarro y Eyda M. Merediz, eds., *Otros estudios transatlánticos. Lecturas desde lo latinoamericano. Revista Iberoamericana, 75, no. 228 (2009).*

13 Our contributors' publications on women and religion include Joan Bristol, *Christians, Blasphemers, and Witches: Afro-Mexican Ritual Practice in the Seventeenth Century* (Albuquerque: University of New Mexico Press, Diálogos series, 2007); Barbara Diefendorf, *From Penitence to Charity: Pious Women and the Catholic Reformation in Paris* (Oxford: Oxford University Press, 2004); Martha Few, *Women Who Live Evil Lives: Gender, Religion, and the Politics of Power in Colonial Guatemala* (Austin: University of Texas Press, 2002); Daniella Kostroun, 'A Formula for Disobedience: Jansenism, Gender and the Feminist Paradox,' *Journal of Modern History,* 75 (September 2003): 483–522; Bianca Premo, *Children of the Father King: Youth, Authority, and Legal Minority in Colonial Lima* (Chapel Hill: University of North Carolina Press, 2005); Electa Arenal and Stacey Schlau, with translations by Amanda Powell, *Untold Sisters: Hispanic Nuns in Their Own Works* (Albuquerque: University of New Mexico Press, 1989); Jon Sensbach, *Rebecca's Revival: Creating Black Christianity in the Atlantic World* (Cambridge, Mass.: Harvard University Press, 2005); Amy Froide, *Never Married: Singlewomen in Early Modern England* (Oxford: Oxford University Press, 2005); Ulrike Strasser, *State of Virginity: Gender, Religion, and Politics in an Early Modern Catholic State* (Ann Arbor: University of Michigan Press, 2004); Lisa Vollendorf, *The Lives of Women: A New History of Inquisitional Spain* (Nashville, Tenn.: Vanderbilt University Press, 2005).

14 Nicholas Canny and Anthony Pagden's pioneering *Colonial Identity in the Atlantic World, 1500–1800* (Princeton, N.J.: Princeton University Press, 1989) remains important for its analysis of issues of identity formation and its contribution to the shift towards culture in Atlantic Studies. Also, see Karen Anderson, *Chain Her by One Foot: The Subjugation of Native Women in Seventeenth-Century New France* (New York: Routledge, 1993); Kenneth J. Andrien, *Andean Worlds: Indigenous History, Culture, and Consciousness under Spanish Rule* (New Mexico: University of New Mexico Press, 2001); Jorge Cañizares-Esguerra, *How to Write the History of the New World: Histories, Epistemologies, Identities in the Eighteenth-Century Atlantic World* (Stanford, Calif.: Stanford University Press, 2001); Magali M. Carrera, *Imagining Identity in New Spain: Race, Lineage, and the Colonial Body in Portraiture and Casta Paintings* (Austin: University of Texas Press, 2003); Susan E. Klepp, Farley Grubb,

and Anne Pfaelzer de Ortiz, eds., *Souls for Sale: Two German Redemptioners Come to Revolutionary America* (College Station: Penn State University Press, 2006); Sabine MacCormack, *On the Wings of Time: Rome, the Incas, Spain, and Peru* (Princeton, N.J.: Princeton University Press, 2006); Helen C. Rountree, *Pocahontas, Powhatan, Opechancanough: Three Indian Lives Changed by Jamestown* (Charleston: University of Virginia Press, 2005); and Linda Sturtz, *Within Her Power: Propertied Women in Colonial Virginia* (New York: Routledge, 2002).

15 The influence of Bynum's work is discussed by Barbara Diefendorf in the first essay of our volume. See Bynum's *Fragmentation and Redemption: Essays on Gender and the Human Body in Medieval Religion* (New York: Zone Books, 1991); and *Holy Feast and Holy Fast: The Religious Significance of Food to Medieval Women* (Berkeley and Los Angeles: University of California Press, 1987). Natalie Zemon Davis's influence on early modern studies has been theoretical, topical, and methodological. See, for example, 'Iroquois Women, European Women,' in Margo Hendricks and Patricia Parker, eds., *Women, 'Race,' and Writing* (London: Routledge, 1994), 96–118; *Society and Culture in Early Modern France: Eight Essays* (Stanford, Calif.: Stanford University Press, 1975); and *Women on the Margins: Three Seventeenth-Century Lives* (Cambridge, Mass.: Harvard University Press, 2005).

16 All of the work by these scholars has engaged feminist methodological questions. The following publications in particular have been influential in our thinking about the topic: Judith Bennett, 'Feminism and History,' *Gender and History*, 1, no. 2 (1989): 251–72; Joan Kelly-Gadol, 'Did Women Have a Renaissance?' in Renate Bridenthal and Claudia Koonz, eds., *Becoming Visible: Women in European History* (Boston: Houghton Mifflin, 1977), 148–52; Mary Nash, 'Two Decades of Women's History in Spain: A Reappraisal,' in Karen Offen et al., eds., *Writing Women's History: International Perspectives* (Bloomington: Indiana University Press, 1991), 381–415; Joan Wallach Scott, *Gender and the Politics of History*, rev. ed. (New York: Columbia University Press, 1999 [1988]); and Merry Wiesner-Hanks, *Gender in History* (London: Blackwell, 2001). Also, see Kathleen Canning, 'Feminist History after the Linguistic Turn: Historicizing Discourse and Experience,' *Signs*, 19, no. 2 (1994): 368–404. For an accessible summary of gender history, see Laura Lee Downs, *Writing Gender History* (Oxford: Oxford University Press, 2005).

17 In addition to scholarship by our contributors and the work cited throughout our volume, the University of Chicago series 'Other Voice in Early Modern Europe' has been an important venue for revising our understanding of women's role in early modern European culture. As of 2009, the series is being published by the University of Toronto Press. Other important contri-

butions include: P. Renée Baernstein, *A Convent Tale: A Century of Sisterhood in Spanish Milan* (New York and London: Routledge, 2002); Frances Dolan, *Whores of Babylon: Catholicism, Gender, and Seventeenth-Century Print Culture* (Ithaca, N.Y.: Cornell University Press, 1999); Kelley Harness, *Echoes of Women's Voices: Music, Art, and Female Patronage in Early Modern France* (Chicago: University of Chicago Press, 2005); Amy Leonard, *Nails in the Wall: Catholic Nuns in Reformation Germany* (Chicago: University of Chicago Press, 2005); Phyllis Mack, *Visionary Women: Ecstatic Prophecy in Seventeenth-Century England* (Berkeley: University of California Press, 1992); Allyson Poska, *Women and Authority in Early Modern Spain: The Peasants of Galicia* (Oxford: Oxford University Press, 2005); Anne Jacobson Schutte, *Aspiring Saints: Pretense of Holiness, Inquisition, and Gender in the Republic of Venice, 1618–1750* (Baltimore: Johns Hopkins University Press, 2001); Alison Weber, *Teresa of Avila and the Rhetoric of Femininity* (Princeton, N.J.: Princeton University Press, 1989); and Merry Wiesner-Hanks, *Christianity and Sexuality in the Early Modern World: Regulating Desire, Reforming Practice* (New York: Routledge, 2000). Also, see Stephanie Tarbin and Susan Broomhall's edited collection, *Women, Identities, and Communities in Early Modern Europe* (Burlington, Vt.: Ashgate, 2008).

18 Lara Putnam, 'To study the Fragments/Whole: Microhistory and the Atlantic World,' *Journal of Social History*, 49, no. 3 (2006): 615–30. In particular, see her argument about Atlanticists' lack of honesty (or awareness) about the imbrication of their field with microhistory.

19 Two recent publications strive to redress this gap: L.P. Harvey, *Muslims in Spain, 1500–1614* (Chicago: University of Chicago Press, 2005), and Mary Elizabeth Perry, *The Handless Maiden: Moriscos and the Politics of Religion in Early Modern Spain* (Princeton, N.J.: Princeton University Press, 2005).

20 See Judith M. Bennett and Amy M. Froide, eds., *Singlewomen in the European Past, 1250–1800* (Philadelphia: University of Pennsylvania Press, 1999).

21 Important work in this field includes Klaus Bade, *Migration in European History*, trans. Allison Brown (Malden, Mass.: Blackwell, 2003); Nicholas Canny, ed., *Europeans on the Move: Studies on European Migration, 1500–1800* (Oxford: Oxford University Press, 1994); Sylvia R. Frey and Betty Wood, eds., *From Slavery to Emancipation in the Atlantic World* (New York: Frank Cass, 1999); Tamar Herzog, *Defining Nations: Immigrants and Citizens in Early Modern Spain and Spanish America* (New Haven, Conn.: Yale University Press, 2003); Wim Klooster and Alfred Padula, eds., *The Atlantic World: Essays on Slavery, Migration, and Imagination* (Upper Saddle River, N.J.: Pearson/Prentice Hall, 2005); Rebecca Larson, *Daughters of Light: Quaker Women Preaching and Prophesying in the Colonies and Abroad, 1700–1775* (New York: Alfred A. Knopf, 1999); Leslie Page Moch, *Moving Europeans: Migration in Western Europe since*

1650, 2nd ed. (Bloomington: Indiana University Press, 2003); and Pamela Scully and Diana Paton, *Gender and Slave Emancipation in the Atlantic World* (Durham, N.C.: Duke University Press, 2005).

22 Recent scholarship focused on masculinity includes Jodi Bilinkoff, *Related Lives: Confessors and their Female Penitents (1450–1750)* (Ithaca, N.Y.: Cornell University Press, 2005); Bilinkoff, 'Francisco Losa and Gregorio Lopez: Spiritual Friendship and Identity Formation on the New Spain Frontier,' in Allan Greer and Jodi Bilinkoff, eds., *Colonial Saints: Discovering the Holy in the Americas* (New York: Routledge, 2003), 115–28; Elizabeth Rhodes, 'Join the Jesuits, See the World: Early Modern Women in Spain and the Society of Jesus,' in *The Jesuits, II: Cultures, Sciences, and the Arts, 1540–1773*, edited by John W. O'Malley et al. (Toronto: University of Toronto Press, 2005), 33–47; Ulrike Strasser, '"The First Form and Grace": Ignatius of Loyola and the Reformation of Masculinity,' in Scott Hendrix and Susan Karant-Nunn, eds., *Masculinity in the Reformation Era*, Sixteenth Century Essays and Studies Series, editor-in-chief Ray Mentzer (Kirksville, Mo.: Truman State University Press, 2008), 45–70.

23 Steve J. Stern, *The Secret History of Gender: Men, Women, and Power in Late Colonial Mexico* (Chapel Hill, N.C.: University of North Carolina Press, 1995), 99–103.

PART I

Theoretical Reflections on Women and Religion from an Atlantic Perspective

chapter one

Rethinking the Catholic Reformation: The Role of Women

BARBARA B. DIEFENDORF

From Lima to Vienna and Montreal to Naples, hundreds of new convents placed walls around tens of thousands of women in the sixteenth and seventeenth centuries. These walls have tended to dominate discussion of women's role in the great expansion of Catholic religious life that occurred in the early modern era. Convent walls loomed especially large in accounts of the Catholic Reformation written in the 1970s and 1980s, when they were commonly depicted as solid edifices erected by male clerics to constrain weak and unruly women and to spare their families the cost of an expensive marriage. A parallel and related theme made the picture all the more bleak by suggesting that the requirement for strict cloistering (*clausura*) imposed on female religious by the Council of Trent ran directly contrary to women's own desire for an active apostolate as catechists, teachers, or nursing sisters. Like all generalizations, these contain at least a grain of truth, and yet recent research has shown just how deceptive such sweeping claims can be. Scholars have come to realize that even the highest convent walls were not sealed but remained porous; even tightly cloistered nuns remained members of families and a presence in the city. If some religious women did find their ability to work in the community constrained by the rules of *clausura*, others found ways to engage in an active apostolate in spite of these rules. Focusing less on convent walls and more on what went on within these walls, scholars have offered new insights not only into women's spirituality and spiritual authority but also into their role as patrons and administrators of religious institutions. A new picture of the richness and diversity of early modern women's religious experience is coming into view.

The product of numerous case studies of individual convents, congregations, and cities, this picture is emerging only piecemeal. More a collage than a painting or tapestry, its textures betray the contrasting and sometimes clashing approaches of historians, art historians, and literary scholars. Its outlines and patterns are appearing unevenly – here sharp and distinct, there muted and blurred – across the broad canvas of the Atlantic world. The overall design is as yet unclear; new attempts to generalize would be premature. Indeed, one thing recent studies have shown is just how much the history of an institution could be influenced by local particularities – by the charisma of a founding nun, or the enthusiasm with which the local bishop took up his charge of church reform, or the property laws and politics of a given city or region. This chapter is thus not an attempt at a new synthesis. Nor does it attempt a comprehensive survey of recent writings on Catholic women's piety and religious life in the early modern Atlantic world. This literature is too large and rapidly growing to survey in the space of an article. My ambitions are more modest. I want to point to some of the more intriguing results of recent research in a variety of disciplines, delineate the broader questions raised by these studies, and encourage more comparative and cross-disciplinary inquiry on this basis. Principally, I want to reinforce a tendency that I believe is already under way: to look at early modern women's religious experience not uniquely through the lens of gender but also more broadly within the context of the social, religious, and cultural values of the age.

The chapter will begin by re-examining the strict cloistering imposed by the Council of Trent. How did religious women react to this requirement, and what did it mean in practice for them? A second section will take up the questions of women's spirituality and the spiritual authority they exercised in the convent and the world. A third and final section will look at the influence of temporal issues like property laws and family ambitions on early modern nuns and convents. That is to say, I will look first at the convent walls, then within these walls, and finally at their relationship to the city, and society, that surrounded them.

My examples range geographically from colonial Chile, Mexico, and Quebec to Paris, Munich, and Rome. This range is justified by the institutional and spiritual commonalities between colonial and metropolitan Catholicism in the early modern Atlantic world. Disparities in the social, economic, and political conditions in these various settings may make direct comparisons risky, but transcending the geographical and disciplinary borders that traditionally divide scholarship into disparate fields helps bring to light traits common to Catholic women's experience across Europe and the Americas. The rough wooden stockades that walled the convents of Quebec may have looked very different from the high stone walls and belvederes of aristocratic convents in Naples, but the questions of how nuns lived within these walls and how they related to the world outside them are pertinent to both settings. New World nuns lived by the same rules as their European sisters; they also read very much the same spiritual literature and aspired to imitate the same saints' lives, however different their material situations. Moreover, with few exceptions, convents in the Americas served local elites in the same way European convents traditionally did. Debates over whether to allow indigenous girls the high status implicit in being brides of Christ reflect European attitudes about class and status and not just ethnic or racial prejudices specific to the Americas.[1] This chapter will thus look at both differences and similarities in how religious women in different early modern settings responded to common challenges to their vocation and faith.

Convent Walls and the Demand for Clausura

As Elizabeth Lehfeldt points out in *Religious Women in Golden Age Spain*, 'the prevailing historiography of female religiosity in the early modern era pivots on the Council of Trent's enclosure decree.'[2] More specifically, it is the combination of the Tridentine decree prohibiting professed nuns from exiting the cloister with two further rules handed down in 1566, extending the rule of strict cloistering to include female tertiaries and barring from the cloister anyone except a community's professed nuns, that encapsulates what Lehfeldt terms the Catholic Reformation's 'restrictive climate for religious women.'[3] Indeed, it can be argued that the 1566 rulings had a bigger impact on religious life than the decree issued at Trent. As early as 1298, the papal directive Periculoso had mandated strict active enclosure for professed nuns, and the rule was reiterated in periodic, if largely regional, reforms.[4] Enclosure had never, however, been demanded of female tertiaries, who took only simple vows, lived at home or in open communities, and did nursing or charitable work in their towns. Moreover, while there had sometimes been lapses in observance of the active enclosure historically required of professed nuns, the principle of passive enclosure, which forbade entry to all outsiders, was more frequently ignored. Enforcing passive enclosure would require nuns to divest themselves of their lay servants, cease educating girls within their walls, and forbid entry to lay benefactors accustomed

to using the convents for private retreats. The rules of strict enclosure
thus not only had an impact on the character of religious life but also
threatened the financial underpinnings of communities dependent on
income from teaching or nursing and on the generosity of patrons who
expected entry to the cloister as recompense for their gifts.

There is good reason, then, to stress the significance of the Tridentine era decrees for religious women. Convent walls did enclose religious
women more securely after Trent. At the same time, it is important not
to exaggerate the negative impact of these decrees by assuming that they
imposed an abrupt and radical change on the character of religious life.
Recent research shows that enforcement of the decrees varied widely.
However much the Catholic Church wanted to be a centrally directed
and centralizing institution, the implementation of its decrees depended on the will and spirit of local ecclesiastical and secular authorities.
The timing, pace, and thoroughness of Catholic reforms differed greatly
from place to place on account of their disparate political situations and
the character of the individuals who assumed leadership roles.

It may be true, as Gabriella Zarri asserts, that Italian bishops 'undertook reform with zeal' in the wake of the Council of Trent, but in many
other parts of Europe the Tridentine reforms were only slowly implemented and erratically enforced.[5] In the Spanish Netherlands, for example, many convents remained uncloistered half a century later.[6] The
sisters continued to go out into local homes to provide nursing care and
pray for the dying and dead. At least one archbishop moderated his demand for strict enclosure of religious women when he recognized that
attempting to force the many active congregations of nursing sisters in
his diocese into the cloister might undermine the Catholic allegiance of
the entire community. The proximity of the Dutch Republic made the
danger of apostasy a far more compelling concern than it would have
been to Italian bishops.[7] Yet, even on the Italian peninsula, some bishops undertook rigorous reform movements very early in the sixteenth
century while others lagged behind and only slowly and incompletely enforced the reforms decreed at Trent, whether because of a personal lack
of enthusiasm for the changes or because of resistance on the part of
local communities. In some dioceses, charismatic clerics intent on both
religious revival and reform drew women into their orbit and inspired
them to take an increased role in parish life through new confraternities and charitable activities and to found new religious communities. In
others, reform was imposed from above with less of an attempt to inspire
popular support.

Secular authorities could also encourage (or discourage) enforcement of the decrees on religious enclosure if they chose. Ulrike Strasser
has shown how state-building princes and reforming clerics collaborated
to overcome resistance on the part of female religious and force enclosure on two communities in Munich. Through the protection of Duke
Albrecht V, these open communities survived the first pressures to accept enclosure in the 1570s and 1580s, only to be forced into the cloister
by Albrecht's grandson Maximilian I in the 1620s. Unlike Albrecht V,
who was willing to maintain the status quo on account of the services the
communities had traditionally offered his family, Maximilian I was determined to impose order and discipline on his domains in the midst of the
turmoil of the Thirty Years' War.[8] Nevertheless, the fact that enclosure
was imposed only some sixty years after the Council of Trent underscores
the extent to which enforcement of the Tridentine decrees depended
on local circumstances.[9] Only when the interests of lay and religious authorities coincided could these decrees be effectively enforced.

In many cases, moreover, authorities had to surmount not just nuns'
resistance to the demand for strict enclosure but also opposition mus-
tered on their behalf by the powerful families to which they belonged.
Mary Laven's study of Venetian nuns shows how pressure from local
elites could result in the relaxation of reforms they considered too strictly enforced.[10] Venetian nuns' freedom to leave their convents to visit
families and friends was curtailed, but they still received visitors freely,
kept up with local gossip, and engaged in other worldly pastimes. Laven
might have found a somewhat different story if she had looked at the
newer and more austere orders founded in Venice, such as the Angelics,
instead of focusing on convents traditionally favoured by the Venetian
patriciate. Yet it remains true that, in many Old and New World cities,
aristocratic convents resisted attempts at strict reform. As in Venice, active enclosure (the requirement that nuns not leave the cloister) was
in general far better enforced than passive enclosure (the prohibition
against secular persons entering the convent). In the Clarist Convent de
la Plaza in Santiago de Chile, for example, professed nuns owned houses
within the convent compound and shared them with a variety of servants, nieces, and other lay women. Kathleen Ann Myers describes one
seventeenth-century nun, Ursula Suárez, as sharing her house (*celda*)
and garden with 'as many as eleven women, ranging from a small tod-
dler to servants and several women who lived with Ursula nearly thirty
years.' Myers also points out, that, although Ursula had taken a vow of
poverty, 'the interpretation of it was obviously quite lax since [in her

autobiographical writings] she talks of amassing luxury items through the generosity of her *devotos*.' These were lay men who visited her and from whom both she and the convent reaped rewards. Among Ursula's gifts were 'silver platformed shoes,' dresses, and funds to help pay for the remodelling of her 'cell.'[11]

To judge from the current literature, Ursula's convent was far more worldly than most, both in its tolerance for male visitors and in the nature of the gifts nuns were allowed to receive. However, comparative data are sorely lacking. With few exceptions, scholars have paid more attention to the internal workings of the Catholic Reformation's austere new orders than to the persistence of relaxed or unreformed houses. Still, there is good evidence that nuns in many convents continued to receive personal allowances above and beyond the dowry required to enter a convent, and that they used this money to pay for personal luxuries that violated both their vows of poverty and the monastic principle of the common life. Furnishing their cells to suit personal taste and hiring servants to provide private meals in their apartments, nuns in many convents replicated the status hierarchies of the secular world. As Helen Hills discovered in studying aristocratic convents in Naples, church authorities made 'intermittent attempts' to regulate the luxury in which nuns lived, but the power of the families to which the nuns belonged was such that these efforts were never very firmly or consistently applied.[12]

If high social standing helped some religious women escape the rigours of strict enclosure, it worked against others, as Renée Baernstein has shown in her study of Milan's Angelics. Asking why the city's Ursulines escaped the Tridentine order for enclosure with Carlo Borromeo's aid, while the Angelics were forced to abandon their apostolic mission and become a traditional cloistered order in 1552, Baernstein identifies as a key factor the Ursulines' 'low social profile – most Ursulines came from a humble background.' Their modest spiritual ambitions also helped 'keep them out of the public eye.' The Angelics, by contrast, had a high social profile on account of the relatively large number of elite women who either joined as members or lived with them as lay associates. They also attracted attention on account of their very public apostolate, their close association with the male congregation of Barnabites, and the charismatic leadership exercised by one of their members.[13] I will return to the question of spiritual claims later in this chapter. For the time being, it is the correlation between high social standing and the enforcement of strict enclosure that is relevant.

This correlation is evident in many New and Old World settings. In

Spanish America, for example, the possibility of becoming a black-veiled choir nun was limited almost exclusively to Spanish and *Criolla* women from rich and prominent families, and strict active enclosure was seen as a necessary protection for the honour of these virginal brides of Christ in a frontier society, even if the convents were sometimes lax about allowing servants, children, and benefactors into the cloister.[14] Convents were not, however, the only possible venue for a religious life in Spanish America. From Chile to Mexico, informally founded *beaterios* and *recogimientos* (retreat houses) allowed those women who were unable to afford the high dowries demanded by convents to live pious lives of seclusion or service without taking religious vows.[15] These institutions served a variety of functions. Many of the *beaterios* offered classes to poor Spanish and mestiza girls, while *recogimientos* served as places of voluntary retreat for married women whose husbands were absent, for mestizas desiring to assimilate to Spanish ways, and for *Criollas* whose vulnerable personal situation suggested that they might otherwise fall into prostitution. *Recogimientos* could also be used to incarcerate women who violated traditional social mores, but their most important function was to provide a safe and respectable existence for women whose family circumstances did not permit either marriage or the veil. Colonial authorities recognized the utility of these institutions and, as a consequence, were not inclined to force their inhabitants to formalize their structures or submit to the strict cloistering required of professed nuns.

In many parts of Europe too, informally organized groups of women ran schools, opened shelters for widows and orphans, tended the sick, and provided other services without submitting to the formalities of religious vows. Organized by devout widows with private means or small groups of single women, most of these communities remained small in scale and escaped censure by not affiliating with a religious order, by not taking any vows, and by not making the outward displays of dress and behaviour that would have marked their members as religious. Because they provided services, these women were far from invisible in their local societies and often worked with the approval and even collaboration of church officials.[16] As we have seen, Carlo Borromeo himself allowed Milan's Ursulines to avoid formal vows and enclosure so that they could carry out the educational mission he intended for them.

The same was true for Ursuline communities founded in a number of cities across Italy and France, at least initially. Gradually, however, these communities transformed themselves from open congregations whose members took only simple vows to enclosed convents of professed nuns.

For this reason, the Ursulines have often been held up as prime examples of the pressures placed on uncloistered women by the Council of
Trent. Recent research, however, has revealed a more complex process
of change. Some communities did accept cloistering only reluctantly;
others embraced this change as a way of fusing the prestigious vocation
of contemplative nuns with their active apostolate as schoolteachers.
This was the case for the Paris community, whose (female) founders and
initial members believed they had thereby adopted a higher form of religious life.[17] Pressure from ecclesiastical superiors was, moreover, only
one reason for adopting enclosure and not necessarily the most important one. As Laurence Lux-Sterritt points out, 'the Ursulines hoped to
recruit from amongst the ranks of influential and wealthy families, to secure their patronage and to benefit from their connections in spheres of
power.' The targeted families, however, had no desire to see 'one or several daughters join an indigent congregation of no approved status.'[18]
The Ursulines' own ambitions thus led them into the cloister as surely as
the demands made by reforming prelates.

Local elites may have been acting on many of the same assumptions
about women's innate fragility and the need to protect their honour as
the clerics who drew up the Tridentine decrees when they identified enclosure as a necessary part of religious life, but they were also motivated
by property concerns. A daughter who became a professed nun received
a dowry from her family but after her vows was officially 'dead to the
world.' She had no further inheritance rights or claims on her family's
estate. But what was the situation of a woman who took only simple, annual vows – or no vows at all – and lived in a community with no official
standing or rules? What demands might she later return to make? These
questions worried propertied families, who preferred to settle their
daughters into situations that avoided such uncertainties. The Ursulines'
transition from open communities to enclosed convents was thus bound
up in complex ways with family strategies and cultural values and was not
simply the result of new rules imposed by church prelates at Trent.

Similar concerns were behind the Visitandines' transition from open
communities to enclosed convents. It has seldom been noticed, however,
that in consenting to this change, François de Sales and Jeanne de Chan-
tal insisted on maintaining – as essential to the Visitandines' purpose –
the right of lay women to enter the cloister for religious retreats. In other
words, they accepted the principle of active but not of passive enclosure.
In this way, the nuns of the Visitation, like the Ursulines, found a way to
combine an apostolic vocation instructing women and guiding them in
their devotions with a cloistered state.[19]

But, even as some open congregations were adopting the 'more per-fect state' of cloistered nuns, other uncloistered communities with mis-sions in the world continued to exist, and at least in France and New France new ones were being founded. The story of how Vincent de Paul and Louise de Marillac protected the uncloistered status of the Daugh-ters of Charity they sent out into the community as 'servants of the poor' by organizing them as a simple confraternity, delaying seeking formal recognition, and not allowing them to take even private, annual vows has been frequently told.[20] But the Daughters of Charity are just the most famous of the new active congregations of uncloistered nurses, catechists, and teachers that took shape in seventeenth-century France and Quebec.[21] Against a background of the Tridentine requirement of strict cloistering for religious women, these active congregations can look quite novel, especially the Daughters of Charity, who went about the community in small groups and even entered and worked in the homes of the poor. And yet many of their activities –teaching poor girls, shelter-ing girls deemed to be in peril, offering lay women a place for spiritual reflection and retreat, and attempting to rehabilitate prostitutes – were being performed elsewhere by pious lay women through *beaterios, re-cogimientos,* conservatories, and other specialized institutions.

Although it has been customary to categorize women's religious voca-tions in binary fashion as either active or contemplative, it seems more useful to envision a continuum of feminine devotion that extended from lay *dévotes* who dedicated their lives to funding and delivering charity at one pole to the most reclusive contemplative orders at the other, with informally organized households of women serving as teachers but tak-ing no vows, active congregations living a common life but going into the world as their work required, and cloistered orders offering classes or delivering retreats to lay women arrayed in between. This broad spec-trum of institutional and non-institutional structures offers a better rep-resentation of the ways in which pious women adapted their vocations to accommodate the church's requirements as well as their own desires after Trent than a simple active/contemplative divide.

Inside the Walls: Spirituality and Spiritual Authority

This diversity of vocations naturally corresponded to a variety of spiritual priorities and inclinations. When open communities were forced into enclosure, the sisters' reactions ranged from resistance to wholehearted acceptance. As Ulrike Strasser has documented for two Munich convents, some inmates refused to learn to pray the breviary or comply in other

ways with new practices of communal life, yet others were attracted to
the contemplative life and eager to adopt the sorts of reforms they had
read about in Teresa of Avila's life and works.[22] Those who welcomed
the new regime appear to have been in the minority in the convents
Strasser studied, but why should women who had chosen one sort of
life have welcomed the forced change to a very different one, especially
when it not only restricted their movements and radically changed their
daily routine but also seriously threatened their ability to earn a living
by cutting them off from their previous practice of tending the sick and
praying for the dead in people's homes? The change must have been
very disruptive to those who had it forced upon them. Moreover, it was
particularly disruptive to women of modest means, who could not afford
the dowries the new convents required and, unless they entered as lay
sisters and spent their lives doing the convent's heavy work, lost a viable
alternative to married life.

It would nevertheless be wrong to conclude from this and other examples of communities forced into the cloister that Tridentine Catholicism
was primarily characterized by the thwarting of an 'active' spiritual mission on women's part.[23] Interpreting early modern spirituality in terms
of a binary opposition between 'active' and 'contemplative' impulses is
even less helpful. Recent research has shown that the same interiorized
and mystical tendencies existed among Mary Ward's English Ladies, Ursulines, and members of other congregations with a mission in the world
as among nuns in the most austere contemplative convents.[24] *Beates* and
the pious lay women who founded charity hospitals and dedicated their
lives to good works frequently displayed the same characteristics.[25] This
should not be surprising. The spirituality expressed by all of these wom-
en has its roots in the same body of late medieval devotional texts and
saints' lives. As a result, they often employed the same penitential practices and bodily mortifications as well.

To be sure, there are important differences between women with a
calling to reclusive prayer and women with a calling to evangelize in
the world. The latter took as their model the evangelical Jesus – healer,
teacher, and friend to the poor – in a way that contemplatives did not,
and they looked for God in those they served. My intention is not to
gloss over these differences but rather to point to common foundations,
or contexts, in which the particular spiritual values of individuals and
groups, their regional differences, and their changes over time can be
better charted. It is useful to recognize that the women with an apostolic calling did not despise or reject traditional monastic values. On

the contrary, as Laurence Lux-Sterritt has written of the English Ladies, 'when they abandoned the ideal of monastic life and the serenity of private devotion in order to labor as evangelists in the world, their vocation became their cross.' The French Ursulines, too, understood 'their catechetic vocation as an act of self-denial and religious altruism.'[26] Religious women working on the New World frontier were especially given to expressing their mission in tropes of mystical immolation and an intense desire for martyrdom.[27] Very real dangers, isolation, and a sense of venturing into the great unknown encouraged this, as did the sense that 'by bringing the Gospel message to distant lands, they were actively furthering the course of salvation history.'[28] These women were indeed participating in a new vocation and a great venture, and yet the tropes through which they understood and expressed this vocation cast it back into a traditional mould. At least this was true at the beginning. More work also needs to be done to understand how the spirituality of nuns with an active vocation changed over time in both Old and New World settings.

The same is true of contemplative nuns in both traditional orders and the austere new orders associated with the Catholic Reformation. Craig Harline suggested more than a decade ago that studies of women in the Catholic Reformation tended to favour women with active religious vocations, in large measure because 'modern sensibilities about practicality and utility can lead one to sympathize more with actives than with contemplatives.'[29] Scholars found it easier to admire women who were fighting to lead independent lives and doing good in their community than recluses whose lives passed in religious ceremonies and meditative prayer. They also, as Kathleen Myers and Amanda Powell have suggested, lacked sympathy for women whose achievements were made 'not in resistance to but rather through extensive participation in the orthodox religious world of the Catholic Church and its hierarchies.'[30] This tendency to neglect or disparage traditional contemplative convents is waning as scholars better appreciate both the important roles that contemplative houses continued to play and the rapid multiplication of new foundations across Europe and the Americas in the sixteenth and seventeenth centuries.[31]

As a consequence, orthodox spirituality is getting more attention; so is the collaboration – and not just resistance – that occurred between nuns and their spiritual directors. Whereas an earlier generation of scholars frequently cited Teresa of Avila's youthful desire to run away and missionize the Muslims as evidence of a frustrated apostolic fervour, scholars

now show a stronger appreciation for just how central religious enclosure was to Teresa's concept of the ideal religious life. The publication
of an increasing number of writings by nuns has also helped show how
Teresa's enthusiastic praise for the joys of the cloistered life influenced
not just the Discalced Carmelite order that she founded but also a number of other reformed orders founded on the model of her rule.[32] It is
only natural that many of the women who looked to Teresa, the most
widely admired and imitated religious reformer of her era, for religious
enlightenment and adopted her counsels on prayer should have aspired
to experience these pleasures for themselves.

This influence can be identified not just in the frequent references to
Teresa in the writings of seventeenth-century nuns but also in conventual art. The Carmelites of Pontoise, the second French convent of the
reformed order of Teresa of Avila's Discalced Carmelites, still possess a
seventeenth-century painting that vividly illustrates the passage from the
concluding chapter of Teresa's *Book of Foundations* in which she describes
the great joy felt by the nuns 'when we find ourselves at last in a cloister
which can be entered by no one from the world.'[33] Borrowing Teresa's
metaphor of nuns as fish who can live only in the 'streams of the waters
of their Spouse,' the painting depicts Joseph lifting a fish from the water
and handing it to the baby Jesus, seated on the lap of his mother Mary,
who passes another fish to Saint Teresa, who in turn places it in a stream
of fresh water flowing from Jesus' heart. Naive in execution, the large
painting (roughly 1.5 × 2 metres) offers a daily reminder of the Carmelites' joyous acceptance of their reclusive vocation.

It is significant, moreover, that the painting's iconographic program
was drawn up by one of the nuns. Other paintings at Pontoise also show a
very original iconography. Illustrating the visions the French Carmelites'
founder Barbe Acarie experienced in her final years, which she spent as
a lay sister in the Pontoise convent, they suggest a much more intimate
and personal bond between the Pontoise nuns and their founder than is
evident in the far grander art that decorated both church and cloister in
the Paris convent of the Incarnation, the Carmelites' first French foundation.[34] When combined with written sources, these artworks testify
to very different spiritual climates in these neighbouring convents and
even to a certain competition between them over who represented the
more authentic Teresian heritage.[35] More comparative work needs to
be done to explore such variations in the way a common religious heritage could be expressed under different circumstances and in different
locales.

If variations in orthodox spirituality still remain in many respects un-explored, recent scholarship displays a greater effort to understand and explain some of the more difficult – and less appealing – dimensions of early modern spirituality, including the bodily mortifications and peni-tential practices adopted by large numbers of devout lay women and nuns. Caroline Bynum's studies of the ways in which medieval women mystics used their penitential practices to achieve religious transcen-dence have fundamentally reshaped our understanding of the role of the body in medieval mysticism.[36] Some scholars have criticized Bynum for assuming that women had a 'natural' propensity towards somatiza-tion of religion and for being motivated by the desire to 'write a positive and even a triumphant history of the (fore)mother(s).' 'Is it possible,' asks Marie-Florine Bruneau, 'to rehabilitate the female mystics of the past, together with their ailing bodies, in a positive way as Bynum does, without lapsing into the celebration and the essentialization of women's suffering? ... Is female mysticism a possible space for the disruption of the patriarchal order, or, as Sarah Beckwith puts it, does it "exist to act out rigorously ... [the patriarchal order's] most sexist fantasies"?'[37] These questions, however provocative, misstate Bynum's essential purpose, which is to examine the religious meaning of the women's penitential practices and not their social consequences. Unlike Bynum, Bruneau fails to ask what the women themselves might have felt they gained from their asceticism – whether, in their own minds, they achieved a transcen-dence and union with God that gave meaning to the practices. Instead, she limits her interest to the social dimensions of bodily mortifications, asking whether they served to subvert or to reinforce the patriarchal or-der and whether we should celebrate the women who practised them on this account. Women are depicted as having only the options of re-sistance or cooptation, and the value of their behaviour is calculated according to whether or not *we* can celebrate it – not in terms of the meaning it gave to *their* lives.

A more penetrating criticism of the attention the *Vitae* of early mod-ern religious women often give to self-torture and bodily mortifications rests in the observation that these practices assume a far greater role in male-authored biographies than in women's autobiographical writings. Two reasons have been suggested for this: first, that 'it was this side of sanctity rather than abstract spiritual values that most appealed to the "passion for the outlandish" of the baroque reading public'; second, that the male clerics who authored these accounts were attempting to coerce women into using their bodies as the measure of their worth by focusing attention on 'those who most flamboyantly abused their bodies.' This is a troubling thought, especially if followed to its logical conclusion: 'With women's energies engaged in self-monitoring and self-destruction, control over their bodies – and their minds – was ensured at all times.'[38]

But was women's attempt to gain sanctity through their bodies merely a negative, self-destructive phenomenon? I cannot agree. I remain revolted by the penitential excesses of some of the women whose practices I examine in *From Penitence to Charity* and disturbed by their intense focus on renunciation of self-will. By deliberately choosing self-abasement, humiliation, and obedience, they indeed seem to reinforce every gender stereotype. I do not believe, however, that these women mortified their bodies because it was somehow innate to their feminine nature or because these practices were foisted on them by men who took pleasure in humiliating them or keeping them in a subordinate role. I remain convinced that they deliberately chose these practices because they saw heroic asceticism as a viable path to religious enlightenment. This path was consistently gendered as male, and yet it remained open to women. They could not enjoy the sacerdotal role of the priest or travel as missionaries to foreign lands, but they could undertake the quest for heroic asceticism in the expectation that, through the destruction of self-will, they might be infused with the will of God.

I would argue, moreover, that women who successfully pursued this path of ascetic self-discipline were paradoxically empowered by it. Evaluating every potential act in terms of God's will, they cultivated powers of discernment that ultimately allowed them to make their own judgment of what God's will might in any situation be. Schooling in ascetic self-denial could produce individuals who were both confident in their intimate knowledge of the will of God and moved by an apostolic desire to serve. As such, it served as unexpectedly good preparation for the careers of such women as Marie de la Trinité Sévin, who founded nine Carmelite convents during her fifty years of religious life. Although moved to take the veil by a powerful contemplative vocation, Sévin was forced by the circumstances of the Carmelites' swift expansion in France to spend much of her time organizing building projects, negotiating with city officials and donors, selecting novices, and tending to the thousand and one administrative details that went into the establishment of each new convent – just as Teresa had done in Spain.[39]

It is true that interiorization and self-scrutiny could also lead to intense questioning and self-doubt – even to accusations of demonic possession or pretense of sanctity. Moshe Sluhovsky's *Believe Not Every*

Spirit makes a compelling argument for the close connection between the practices of self-scrutiny, or examination of conscience, encouraged in the convents of the Catholic Reformation, and the rash of cases of demonic possession that broke out at this time.[40] Sluhovsky's argument focuses particularly on the spread of passive forms of mysticism whose practitioners sought union with God through complete passivity and abandonment to divine love. Both theologians and less learned spiritual directors (priests, but also prioresses and novice mistresses) warned that such seekers of spiritual perfection could expect to be tested and potentially deceived by demons on their spiritual journey. The challenge thus became to identify the good spirits from the bad, and to exorcise the malignant ones. Because of deeply ingrained attitudes – associations between women and flesh and a long-standing belief in women's innate sinfulness as daughters of Eve – this process was inevitably a gendered one. Male clerics subjected the spiritual states, visions, and prophecies of their female penitents to increasingly rigorous scrutiny, and more and more often their diagnosis was a negative one, with the afflicting spirits being pronounced malevolent and not divine.

As Sluhovsky observes, many cases ultimately diagnosed as demonic possession – including some of the mass possessions in convents – began as a vague sort of 'spiritual restlessness,' with none of the physical symptoms or behaviours associated with possession by demons. These characteristic behaviours emerged only *after* the diagnosis of demonic possession was made. Already fearful about their interior state, women accepted the diagnosis and, perhaps unconsciously, began to act out the behaviours expected of demoniacs. And yet the afflicted women were not simply victims of a misogynistic clergy but rather actively participated in the process of searching out and evaluating the movements of their souls. This last point is important; much of the earlier literature tends to portray demoniacs either as passive victims of clerical manipulation or as artful, self-promoting schemers without even considering the possibility that these women might have been serious, if troubled, seekers after spiritual truth. By contrast, Sluhovsky's argument gives women agency both as concerned spiritual directors and as spiritually afflicted individuals seeking to make sense of their afflictions. The argument also, by extension, helps explain why so many pious early modern women, even among those engaging in thoroughly orthodox spiritual pursuits, feared being led astray by demonic spirits.[41] This fear can be read as an unfortunate, but natural, by-product of the very intensification and internalization of spirituality that the Catholic renewal provoked.

Can my thesis that women were empowered by ascetic self-discipline and the internalization of their faith be reconciled with the seemingly contradictory argument that these same or related practices led to self-doubt? It can if we look more closely at the spiritual guidance that religious women received and the ways in which it served to reinforce either confidence or self-doubt. The accusations of feigned piety studied by Anne Schutte and other scholars show just how important a spiritual director's interpretation of the spiritual states and 'movements' described by his penitents could be. Like Sluhovsky, Schutte observes that this scrutiny was gendered – women were presumed to be more likely to be deceived or deceivers than men. It was also socially discriminatory. The 'little women' from the lower social orders were presumed to be more ignorant and easily deluded that those higher on the social ladder.[42] On the other hand, religious women were far from being simple victims of repressive scrutiny on the part of suspicious and misogynistic clergy. As Jodi Bilinkoff has shown, many male confessors admired and learned from the spiritually gifted women they directed, even to the point of constructing their own identities in terms of their interactions with these women.[43] The relationship was by no means uni-directional. Moreover, as the dialogues in María de San José Salazar's *Book for the Hour of Recreation* demonstrate, early modern nuns were by no means uniformly accepting of spiritual directors who insisted that they should engage in only the most humble sorts of spiritual practices because their womanly nature made them weak, ignorant, and easily deceived. María refutes these notions with a gentle mockery. She also goes on to show how much spiritual guidance the nuns gained from one another, not just from the male superiors ostensibly charged with the cure of their souls.[44]

Women's roles as spiritual guides is an aspect of early modern religious life that has received too little attention. Certainly the Parisian sources that I know best show women playing a much larger role in shaping their religious environment than we might expect. They show religious women playing an almost sacerdotal role as spiritual guides and counsellors to their fellow nuns and also to lay women, and even men, who came to seek advice in the convent parlours.[45] And yet women's role as spiritual directors remains little explored.[46] Even a casual reading of primary and secondary sources brings to light examples of prioresses and novice mistresses who played an important role in the spiritual formation of their daughters, of convents that lay people regularly visited for spiritual advice, and of *beates* with a reputation for wise counsel. More systematic study of this phenomenon, which is evident on the farthest reaches of the American frontiers as well as throughout Europe, would be useful.

It is tempting to suspect that Italian and Hispanic clerics, with their suspicion of illuminism and inquisitorial machinery, were more controlling of women's spirituality and inclined to repressive measures than the French clerics who directed the convents I studied, but only close comparative study can demonstrate this conclusively. Parisian women may have had unusual latitude because local mores placed fewer restrictions on women's behaviour than Italian and Spanish cultures did. There is reason to believe these patterns were common to France as a whole, because many provincial houses of the new religious orders were founded by nuns who served their novitiate in Paris, but we lack adequate comparative data on other parts of Europe or the Americas. We also need to take into consideration the biases imposed by the sources. Inquisition records have great appeal as historical sources. They give us a level of detail few other sources provide and even allow us a relatively trustworthy reconstruction of the protagonists' voices, if we are careful to factor out biases produced by inquisitors' methods of collecting and producing evidence.[47] By definition, however, cases that came before the Inquisition represent deviations from the norm. They also, by definition, foreground the repressive machinery of the church and the imbalance in the power relationship between the male inquisitor and his female penitent. These records can teach us a lot, but they do have inherent biases and limits. They give only glancing insights into ordinary practices of piety and spiritual leadership exercised by religious women and offer a very different picture of the relationship between pious women and the Catholic clergy than appears in such other sources as pious biography.[48]

Pious biography must also be handled carefully, of course, but its biases are very different, since the author's intentions were hagiographic and prescriptive rather than sceptical and denunciatory. There has been excellent recent scholarship showing how autobiographies written originally at a confessor's demand have been reworked by male biographers to disseminate their own, normative social and religious values in place of their female subject's. It is enlightening to see how even minor omissions and changes in emphasis could work to silence a woman's authentic voice and bring her behaviour and ideas into conformity with approved female roles.[49] Nevertheless, it is important to recognize that women, too, tended to record their lives in normative terms, partly because this was what was expected of them by the confessors who authorized or demanded them to write, and also because saints' lives and hagiography made up such an important part of what they read and heard that they consciously and unconsciously sought to make their own lives conform to these models. We should not, moreover, assume that conforming one's life to a saintly model was just a literary device or way to avoid the inquisitor's scrutiny.[50] Early modern Catholicism was fundamentally imitative, both in its prescription to imitate Christ and in its expectation of ritual and doctrinal conformity. We can scour women's autobiographical writings for signs of originality, or resistance to superiors' demands, but we should not measure their lives by these criteria alone, not if we wish to understand early modern women within the context of their complex value system and not our own.

The Cloister in the World

Two themes emerge with particular importance from recent scholarship concerning the relationship between convents and the larger society of which they were a part. The first is the close ties that nuns retained with their families despite the convent's high walls and rules of enclosure. The second is the important role played by women themselves as founders of religious institutions and shapers of religious culture in early modern times.

As Mary Laven has shown, the imposition of Tridentine reforms in Venice put an end to the freedom with which outsiders entered the cloister and nuns exited it but did not succeed in walling the nuns off from worldly visitors and entertainments, or even in squelching the penchant of some nuns for political intrigue. 'The directives of the Counter-Reformation had certainly left their mark on conditions in the nunnery,' concludes Laven, 'but they had not succeeded in severing religious women from the society in which they were so firmly embedded.'[51] Although using very different sorts of evidence, Helen Hills makes a similar point about the aristocratic convents of Naples. 'Families did not give up daughters who became nuns,' she observes; 'instead the convent became another space to be inscribed by those families.'[52] Analysing the architecture and patronage of these convents, Hills convincingly demonstrates that their aristocratic inhabitants competed to claim a dominant place for themselves – and by extension for their families – through the high walls, towers, and belvederes they constructed over the city. And, if the art and decoration of convent churches proudly showed the arms and names of the convent's patrons, it also focused attention on the grilles that concealed the nuns, thereby emphasizing their privileged status as brides of Christ.[53]

Even in convents far more observant than was apparently common in Venice or Naples, the close connections nuns maintained with family members allowed them to serve as conduits for information and, in some cases, as political actors behind the scene. Renée Baernstein shows, for example, how Paola Antonia and Agata Sfondrati quite deliberately used their position as prioresses of Milan's Angelics to benefit their family's social and political ambitions. They even served as family treasurers, collecting and disbursing funds for male relatives from the convent's parlour.[54] At the same time, they shaped a new and aristocratic culture for the Angelics through their introduction of more elaborate ritual, patronage of the arts and music, and adoption of elegant habits and manners. This satisfied their personal inclinations but also served family ambitions by enhancing the Sfondratis' reputation at Milan's Spanish court. As Baernstein observes, 'the close interweaving of family and ecclesiastical resources was a common technique, and one in which women could play a powerful role, contributing actively to the "team game" of family advancement.'[55]

The letters that Jeanne de Jésus Séguier wrote while prioress of the Carmelite convent of Pontoise to her brother, French chancellor Jean Séguier, show that French nuns could play the same game. Jeanne did not hesitate to offer her brother advice when it was rumoured that Anne of Austria intended to replace him as chancellor after the death of Louis XIII.[56] Once his position was again secure, she returned to her previous pattern of using her numerous letters to intercede for friends who needed the chancellor's help in one way or another. Most of the letters requested his intervention in the legal affairs of private individuals, but several pleaded for a reduction of taxes for the entire town of Pontoise on account of the 'extreme misery' to which France's costly participation in the Thirty Years' War had reduced the town by the 1640s.[57] Although a cloistered nun, Jeanne did not think to work good solely through her prayers. She used her family connections unselfconsciously in order to help her friends and, through their good will, to aid her convent and order and, by her own estimation, to serve God.

Of course, not all Carmelite prioresses had Jeanne's powerful political connections, but there is good evidence that, in spite of their strict seclusion, many interacted with their local communities in a variety of ways. Using knowledge gained through their lay porteress's contacts in the community but also their own conversations in the convent parlour (or 'locutory'), they sent food to the poor in times of famine, prepared ointments and other medicines for the sick, and counselled lay people troubled in their daily lives or in their souls. As Alison Weber has pointed

out, when a prioress developed too great a reputation as a healer or
came to be viewed by the surrounding community as a 'living saint,' this
could provoke jealousies and factionalism within the cloister. 'Convent
permeability was not natural or structural,' Weber reminds us, 'but politically charged and potentially divisive.'[58] This is true; we need to pay
close attention to the ordinary sorts of interactions that developed between cloistered nuns and their secular neighbours, family members,
and friends but also to the actions and events that disrupted ongoing
relationships and provoked tensions either inside the cloister or between
nuns and their superiors.

One frequent source of tension concerned the possibility for secular
individuals to penetrate walls of all but the very most reclusive convents.
I have already noted the tendency for active cloistering to be far better
observed than the passive cloistering intended to keep all but professed
nuns out. These rules generally were observed when it came to preventing men from entering the cloister, but they were often ignored when
it came to lay women – especially benefactresses to whom the convent
owed a debt of gratitude. Even the founders of the austere new Catholic Reformation orders, although moved to make their gifts by admira-
tion for the nuns' pious reclusion, wanted to participate in this reclusion
through frequent visits and sometimes lengthy retreats. And, although
church authorities tried at various times to eliminate or at least limit
these privileges, in many places they more often ended up closing their
eyes to the problem because they feared cutting off a crucial source of
patronage and funding.[59]

The importance of women's patronage of Catholic Reformation institutions is still incompletely explored. Art historians have thus far made
the greatest contributions and have productively enlarged their domain
from building programs, iconography, and the like to encompass also
the legal and personal situations of the donors, their spirituality and formative spiritual influences, and their awareness of and personal ties to
one another.[60] As Marilyn Dunn has pointed out, 'many noblewomen
who were inclined toward a religious life were pressured by their families
into marriages of political and social alliance. Only later in their lives, often in their widowhood, were these women able to pursue their religious
goals.'[61] These goals could include entering religious orders themselves,
but they could also take the form of endowing convents and taking an
active role in their construction and decoration.

More systematic and comparative study of this important subject
is needed. Women founded all but two of the forty-eight new female

religious communities created in Paris during the first half of the seventeenth century. What little data I have found on other cities suggest that this was also true elsewhere. Secular women established most of the twenty-six convents that existed in Seville by the seventeenth century. They also founded eighteen of twenty-two convents in Mexico City and six of the eight convents created in Lima between 1558 and 1650.[62] But it is not just numbers that matter. Marie-Madeleine Chauvigny de la Peltrie, the lay founder of the Ursulines of Quebec, actually came to the New World to supervise personally this foundation. In order to do so, she made a second and fictive marriage (she was widowed at twenty-two) and sued her family to recover her dowry.[63] La Peltrie's venturesome spirit may have been unique, but she was far from the only woman who fought for her property rights so as to use the money for religious purposes that her family did not approve.

We need to know more about such women and about the property laws that both limited and determined their opportunities. These laws differed significantly in different parts of Europe and the Americas. Scholars have convincingly argued that a tightening of inheritance laws in favour of primogeniture limited the funds available for daughters and younger sons in Italian families, resulting in fewer marriages and more religious professions.[64] 'Surplus daughters' do not appear to have been sent to convents at the same rate in France and Spain, by contrast, and the colonizers of New Spain were initially unwilling even to found convents because it would remove potential brides from the marriage market. The pressures in New Spain were clearly demographic – there were too few Spanish and *Criolla* women by comparison with men. But inheritance laws also played into the story, and in complex ways. In colonial Mexico, women's right to property could stand in the way of both marriage and a religious profession. If the family's wealth was landed, a girl's father or brother might choose to keep her unmarried at home rather than to risk losing his hacienda in order to provide the dowry needed for either marriage or a convent.[65] Again, more comparative work is needed to understand how women's place in family strategies differed according to the laws and customs of different locales. What is clear is that the church did not pay for the many new religious communities founded during the Catholic Reformation. Individual donors did, and many of these donors were women. We need to know more about who these women were, what motivated them, and how they paid for their foundations. But we need also to recognize the broader truth that the Catholic Reformation was not just a top-down affair implemented by reforming prelates and clerics. It was fundamentally dependent on individual initiatives that worked also from the bottom up.

Conclusion

Recent research has shown early modern women's spiritual practices and beliefs as authentic products of personal conviction, and not mere by-products of either socio-political forces or the beliefs and actions of secular and religious men. Some women undoubtedly were placed in convents against their will, and some of these women spent miserable lives rebelling against their misfortune (just as some of their sisters given in marriage against their will rebelled against their misfortune), but constraint and rebellion do not characterize the dominant mood of early modern religious life. Convent walls were never so high that nuns were cut off from continued contact with family members; those continuing relationships often proved productive for individuals on both sides of the wall. Women took part alongside – and often in advance – of men in a spiritual revival that inclined them both to fund new religious communities and to join them.

Many of the new communities were traditional in form and austere in practice. Teresa of Avila's advocacy for strictly reformed contemplative convents was enormously influential, but her spirituality must be seen as both a symptom and a cause of a broader spiritual current advocating rejection of worldly pastimes and associations as the only sure path to God. This was neither the naive religious enthusiasm depicted by Catholic Reformation scholars half a century ago nor the repressed and repressive male-imposed piety that figures in much of the literature published a quarter century later. The intensely interiorized piety of the Catholic Reformation is now better understood in both its orthodox expressions and its more extreme manifestations of penitential piety and demonic possession. That said, our understanding of women's role in the Catholic Reformation nevertheless remains incomplete. We need to expand our horizons both literally and figuratively for the study of women religious in the early modern Atlantic world. We need more comparative work, so as to comprehend better the pace and character with which different aspects of church reform and spiritual renewal were taken up in different locales. We also need more studies of daily life in women's religious communities, of women's leadership within these communities, and of their attempts both to spread old and to invent new forms of community life. When we have done this, the old narratives of a male-directed Catholic

Reformation that pit men against women will be replaced by more nuanced histories that encompass the initiatives of lay and religious women
to fulfil their spiritual needs in the complex social and cultural contexts
of European and colonial societies.

Notes

1 Asunción Lavrin, 'Indian Brides of Christ: Creating New Spaces for Indigenous Women in New Spain,' *Mexican Studies/Estudios Mexicanos*, 15 (1999):
   225–60. There were no rules against admitting native women to religious
   professions in New France, but little effort was made to recruit them. Nor
   do the Indians appear to have wanted to adapt to European culture in the
   way that religious vocations would have required. See Allan Greer, *Mohawk
   Saint: Catherine Tekakwitha and the Jesuits* (Oxford and New York: Oxford University Press, 2005), 113.
2 Elizabeth A. Lehfeldt, *Religious Women in Golden Age Spain: The Permeable
   Cloister* (Aldershot, U.K.: Ashgate, 2005), 175.
3 Ibid., 175.
4 Ibid., 106–8, on the broader response to *Periculoso;* 108–36, on attempts to
   apply it in medieval Spain.
5 Gabriella Zarri, 'From Prophecy to Discipline, 1450–1650,' in Keith Botsford, trans., and Lucetta Scaraffia and Gabriella Zarri, eds., *Women and Faith:
   Catholic Religious Life in Italy from Late Antiquity to the Present* (Cambridge,
   Mass.: Harvard University Press, 1999), 83–112, 103.
6 Craig Harline, *The Burdens of Sister Margaret* (New York: Doubleday, 1994), 11;
   idem, 'Actives and Contemplatives: The Female Religious of the Low Countries before and after Trent,' *Catholic Historical Review*, 81 (1995): 541–68.
7 Craig Harline and Eddy Put, *A Bishop's Tale: Mathias Hovius among his Flock
   in Seventeenth-Century Flanders* (New Haven, Conn., and London: Yale University Press, 2000), 235–36.
8 Ulrike Strasser, *State of Virginity: Gender, Religion, and Politics in an Early Modern Catholic State* (Ann Arbor: University of Michigan Press, 2004), 72–82
   and 120–3. See also idem, 'Bones of Contention: Cloistered Nuns, Decorated Relics, and the Contest over Women's Place in the Public Sphere of
   Counter-Reformation Munich,' *Archiv für Reformationsgeschichte /Archive for
   Reformation History*, 90 (1999): 254–88, 261–7.
9 Strasser, *State of Virginity*, 154–63.
10 Mary Laven, *Virgins of Venice: Broken Vows and Cloistered Lives in the Renaissance
   Convent* (New York: Viking, 2003), 204.

11 Kathleen Ann Myers, *Neither Saints Nor Sinners: Writing the Lives of Women in Spanish America* (Oxford and New York: Oxford University Press, 2003), 119–21. See also Kristine Ibsen, *Women's Spiritual Autobiography in Colonial Spanish America* (Gainesville: University Press of Florida, 1999), 7–9, which cites a number of recent works on living conditions in the convents of Spanish America.

12 Helen Hills, *Invisible City: The Architecture of Devotion in Seventeenth-Century Neapolitan Convents* (Oxford and New York: Oxford University Press, 2004), 115–17.

13 P. Renée Baernstein, *A Convent Tale: A Century of Sisterhood in Spanish Milan* (New York and London: Routledge, 2002), 53–4 and 72–3.

14 A few poorer women whose families were unable to pay the high dowries required of choir nuns might be taken in free of charge if the convent's founder made this a requirement in the original donation, but such girls were inevitably selected from the ranks of well-born families whose finances had suffered but bloodlines had not. Girls of lower status could enter only as white-veiled lay sisters or servants. Amaya Fernández Fernández et al., *La mujer en la conquista y la evangelización en el Perú (Lima 1550–1650)* (Lima: Pontificia Universidad Católica del Perú, 1997), especially 133–4. For the debate over Indian women and religious vocations, see Lavrin, 'Indian Brides of Christ.' A few women of mixed blood (mestizas) were admitted to convents in Peru and New Spain, but only with the consent of authorities and, apparently, at a higher dowry than those of pure Spanish descent.

15 Ibsen, *Women's Spiritual Autobiography*, 4. Nancy van Deusen, *Between the Sacred and the Worldly: The Institutional and Cultural Practice of Recogimiento in Colonial Lima* (Stanford, Calif.: Stanford University Press, 2001), identifies eleven such institutions in seventeenth-century Lima (by comparison with ten convents) and discusses their evolving purposes.

16 An excellent case study is Monica Chojnacka, 'Women, Charity and Community in Early Modern Venice: The Casa delle Zitelle,' *Renaissance Quarterly*, 51 (1998): 68–91. Counter-examples can, of course, be cited. Nicholas Terpstra, 'Mothers, Sisters, and Daughters: Girls and Conservatory Guardianship in Late Renaissance Florence,' *Renaissance Studies*, 17 (2003): 201–29, shows how several informal institutions founded by women for the protection of vulnerable girls in Florence were gradually transformed into convents under male direction. Terpstra nevertheless emphasizes the complexity of this lengthy transformation; it did not occur simply as a reaction to the Council of Trent.

17 Barbara B. Diefendorf, *From Penitence to Charity: Pious Women and the Catholic Reformation in Paris* (New York and Oxford: Oxford University Press, 2004), 124–30.

18 Laurence Lux-Sterritt, *Redefining Female Religious Life: French Ursulines and English Ladies in Seventeenth-Century Catholicism* (Aldershot, U.K.: Ashgate, 2005), 41–2. See also Linda Lierheimer, 'Preaching or Teaching: Defining the Ursuline Mission in Seventeenth-Century France,' in Beverly Mayne Kienzle and Pamela J. Walker, eds., *Women Preachers and Prophets through Two Millennia of Christianity* (Berkeley and Los Angeles: University of California Press, 1998), 212–26, on the pressures that convinced many Ursuline congregations to accept cloistering.

19 Diefendorf, *From Penitence to Charity,* 174–83.

20 Most recently, by Susan Dinan in *Women and Poor Relief in Seventeenth-Century France: The Early History of the Daughters of Charity* (Aldershot, U.K.: Ashgate, 2006).

21 Local studies make it clear how important the inclinations of the bishop and other supervising clergy were in permitting or forbidding the creation of uncloistered congregations. For the contrasting situations in Paris and New France, for example, see Diefendorf, *From Penitence to Charity,* 210–26; Leslie Choquette, '"Ces Amazones du Grand Dieu": Women and Mission in Seventeenth-Century Canada,' *French Historical Studies,* 17 (1992): 627–55, 646–53; and Dominique Deslandres, *Croire et faire croire: Les missions françaises au XVIIe siècle* (Paris: Fayard, 2003), 356–89.

22 Strasser, *State of Virginity,* 127–32.

23 Among other works, see Ruth Liebowitz, 'Virgins in the Service of Christ: The Dispute over an Active Apostolate for Women during the Counter-Reformation,' in Rosemary Ruether and Eleanor McLaughlin, eds., *Women of Spirit: Female Leadership in the Jewish and Christian Traditions* (New York: Simon and Schuster, 1979), 131–52; and Elizabeth Rapley, *The Dévotes: Women and Church in Seventeenth-Century France* (Montreal and Kingston: McGill-Queen's University Press, 1990).

24 Lux-Sterritt, *Redefining Female Religious Life,* 155–77, especially 168–75; also, Querciolo Mazzonis, *Spirituality, Gender, and the Self in Renaissance Italy: Angela Merici and the Company of St. Ursula (1474–1650)* (Washington, D.C.: Catholic University of America Press, 2007), on the spirituality of the Ursulines' founder. See also recent scholarship on the mystical tendencies of French Ursuline Marie Guyart de l'Incarnation, including Raymond Brodeur, ed., *Femme, mystique et missionnaire: Marie Guyart de l'Incarnation: Tours, 1599–Québec, 1672* (Quebec: Les Presses de l'Université de Laval, 2001); Marie-Florine Bruneau, *Women Mystics Confront the Modern World: Marie de l'Incarnation (1599–1672) and Madame Guyon (1648–1717)* (Albany: State University of New York Press, 1998); and Anya Mali, *Mystic in the New World: Marie de l'Incarnation (1599–1672)* (Leiden: E.J. Brill, 1996).

25 *Beates* (*beatas* in Spanish) was the term applied in Hispanic cultures to 'holy

women' who adopted a religious life of prayer and service without joining a
convent. They sometimes had affiliations with a religious order.

26 Lux-Sterritt, *Redefining Female Religious Life*, 189.
27 Deslandres, *Croire et Faire Croire*, 294–5.
28 Mali, *Mystic in the New World*, 170.
29 Harline, 'Actives and Contemplatives,' 566.
30 Kathleen A. Myers and Amanda Powell, eds. and trans., María de San José,
    *A Wild Country out in the Garden: The Spiritual Journals of a Colonial Mexican
    Nun* (Bloomington: Indiana University Press, 1999), xxi.
31 In Paris alone, more than 60 per cent of the 48 new religious communities
    founded in the first half of the seventeenth century belonged to traditional
    contemplative orders. Diefendorf, *From Penitence to Charity*, 135–7.
32 The dialogue form adopted in María de San José Salazar's *Book for the Hour
    of Recreation,* edited by Alison Weber and translated by Amanda Powell
    (Chicago: University of Chicago Press, 2002), proves especially effective at
    revealing the various ways in which Teresa's teachings and personal example
    could be interpreted even within the Carmelite tradition.
33 Teresa of Jesus, *The Complete Works of Saint Teresa of Jesus,* edited and trans-
    lated by E. Allison Peers (London: Sheed and Ward, 1946), 3: 203.
34 The paintings were put on display in the Musée Tavel-Delacour in Pontoise
    in connection with the celebration with the convent's 400th anniversary in
    2004–5. Christian Olivereau, ed., *Les collections du Carmel de Pontoise: Un patri-
    moine spirituel à découvrir* (Paris: Éditions Créaphis, 2004).
35 Barbara B. Diefendorf, 'Franciser les carmélites espagnoles: la compétition
    entre Paris et Pontoise pour l'héritage thérésien' (unpublished paper
    presented at the École des Hautes Études en Sciences Sociales, Paris, May
    2006).
36 Caroline Walker Bynum, *Holy Feast and Holy Fast: The Religious Significance of
    Food to Medieval Women* (Berkeley and Los Angeles: University of California
    Press, 1987); and idem, *Fragmentation and Redemption: Essays on Gender and
    the Human Body in Medieval Religion* (New York: Zone Books, 1991).
37 Bruneau, *Women Mystics Confront the Modern World,* 10–13, citing Sarah
    Beckwith, 'A Very Material Mysticism: The Medieval Mysticism of Margery
    Kempe,' in David Aers, ed., *Medieval Literature: Criticism, Ideology and History*
    (Brighton, U.K.: Harvester, 1986), 34–57, 36.
38 Ibsen, *Women's Spiritual Autobiography,* 73–5, citing José Antonio Maravall's
    Cultural del barroco: Análisis de una estructura histórica, 4th ed. (Barcelona:
    Ariel, 1986).
39 Diefendorf, *From Penitence to Charity,* 65–76 and 116.
40 Moshe Sluhovsky, *Believe Not Every Spirit: Possession, Mysticism, & Discernment
    in Early Modern Catholicism* (Chicago: University of Chicago Press, 2007).

41 María de San José Salazar's *Book for the Hour of Recreation,* 42–61, illustrates
   well the tendency to attribute all temptations to the devil's battle against
   pure souls.
42 Schutte, *Aspiring Saints,* 42–59.
43 Jodi Bilinkoff, *Related Lives: Confessors and Their Female Penitents, 1450–1750*
   (Ithaca, N.Y.: Cornell University Press, 2005).
44 María de San José Salazar, *Book for the Hour of Recreation.*
45 Diefendorf, *From Penitence to Charity,* 149–60; also idem, 'Discerning Spirits:
   Women and Spiritual Authority in Counter-Reformation France,' in Margaret Mikesell and Adele Seeff, eds., *Culture and Change: Attending to Early
   Modern Women* (Newark, Del.: University of Delaware Press, 2003), 241–65.
46 An exception is Patricia Ranft, *A Woman's Way: The Forgotten History of Women
   Spiritual Directors* (New York: Palgrave, 2001). Alison Weber, 'Spiritual Administration: Gender and Discernment in the Carmelite Reform,' *Sixteenth
   Century Journal,* 31 (2000): 123–46, gives a good account of how Spanish
   Carmelites lost the ability to choose their own confessors and assume an
   important role in directing the conscience of other nuns, but we know little
   about the situation in other orders. In addition, Weber's 'The Partial Feminism of Ana de San Bartolomé,' in Lisa Vollendorf, ed., *Recovering Spain's
   Feminist Tradition* (New York: Modern Language Association of America,
   2001), 69–87, shows that reactions to this loss of authority differed even
   among Spanish Carmelites.
47 Among recent works that make excellent use of Inquisition records are
   Cecilia Ferrazzi, *Autobiography of an Aspiring Saint,* edited and translated by
   Anne Jacobson Schutte (Chicago: University of Chicago Press, 1996); Mary
   Giles, *Women in the Inquisition: Spain and the New World* (Baltimore: Johns
   Hopkins University Press, 1999); Myers, *Neither Saints Nor Sinners;* Schutte,
   Aspiring Saints; idem, 'Inquisition and Female Autobiography: The Case
   of Cecelia Ferrazzi,' in Monson, *The Crannied Wall,* 105–18; and Lisa Vollendorf, *The Lives of Women: A New History of Inquisitional Spain* (Nashville,
   Tenn.: Vanderbilt University Press, 2005).
48 See, for example, the new understanding of the mutuality that could develop in the confessor/penitent relationship that Jodi Bilinkoff has drawn
   from the study of pious biography. Bilinkoff, *Related Lives;* idem, 'Confessors, Penitents, and the Construction of Identities in Early Modern Avila,'
   in Barbara B. Diefendorf and Carla Hesse, eds., *Culture and Identity in Early
   Modern Europe (1500–1800)* (Ann Arbor: University of Michigan Press, 1993),
   83–102, and idem, 'Confession, Gender, Life-Writing: Some Cases (Mainly)
   from Spain,' in Katharine Jackson Lualdi and Anne T. Thayer, eds., *Penitence
   in the Age of Reformations* (Aldershot, U.K.: Ashgate, 2000), 168–83.
49 See, for example, Ibsen, *Women's Spiritual Autobiography;* E. Ann Matter, 'The

Personal and the Paradigm: The Book of Maria Domitilla Galluzzi,' in Monson, *The Crannied Wall*, 87–102; and Myers, *Neither Saints Nor Sinners*. Strasser, 'Bones of Contention,' makes a similar demonstration of the differences between the manuscript diaries of the Pütrich sisters and the chronicle published by a male cleric a century later.

50 Alison Weber, *Teresa of Avila and the Rhetoric of Femininity* (Princeton, N.J.: Princeton University Press, 1990), and Carole Slade, *St. Teresa of Avila: Author of a Heroic Life* (Berkeley and Los Angeles: University of California Press, 1995), have offered penetrating insights into the way Teresa's rhetoric was shaped by her fear of the Inquisition. At the same time, they show that there was much more to her writing than this and that she borrowed from a number of different literary genres. Teresa's literary skills were unparalleled, however; many women who recorded their lives at their confessor's demand did so in more directly imitative ways.

51 Laven, *Virgins of Venice*, 204.

52 Hills, *Invisible City*, 118.

53 As Hills points out, 'conventual architecture relies not only on separation, exclusion, and hierarchies of access. It also depends to an unusual degree on what Foucault termed "the optics of power" – the control of sight lines, the deliberate granting or stinting of visual access, and carefully contrived asymmetrical viewing patterns.' Ibid., 18.

54 Baernstein, *A Convent Tale*, 138–44.

55 Ibid, 144.

56 Jeanne de Jésus Séguier, *Lettres à son frère, chancelier de France (1643–1668)*, edited by Bernard Hours (Lyon: Centre André Latreille, 1992), 20–8 (letters 8–16).

57 Ibid., 40 and 42–3 (letters 34 and 36).

58 Alison Weber, 'Locating Holiness in Early Modern Spain: Convents, Caves, and Houses,' in Joan E. Hartman and Adele Seeff, eds., *Structures and Subjectivities: Attending to Early Modern Women* (Newark, Del.: University of Delaware Press, 2007), 52–74, 58.

59 Diefendorf, *From Penitence to Charity*, 160–7.

60 See, for example, Carolyn Valone, 'Women on the Quirinal Hill: Patronage in Rome, 1560–1630,' *Art Bulletin*, 76 (1994): 129–46; idem, 'Roman Matrons as Patrons: Various Views of the Cloister Wall,' in Monson, *The Crannied Wall*, 49–72; and idem, 'Architecture as a Public Voice for Women in Sixteenth-Century Rome,' *Renaissance Studies*, 15 (2001): 301–27. Also, Marilyn Dunn, 'Piety and Patronage in Seicento Rome: Two Noblewomen and Their Convents,' *Art Bulletin*, 76 (1994): 644–63; idem, 'Nuns as Art Patrons: The Decoration of S. Marta al Collegio Romano,' *Art Bulletin*, 70 (1988): 451–77; and Hills, *Invisible City*.

61 Dunn, 'Piety and Patronage in Seicento Rome,' 644.
62 Mary Elizabeth Perry, *Gender and Disorder in Early Modern Seville* (Princeton, N.J.: Princeton University Press, 1990), 76 and 78; Ibsen, *Women's Spiritual Autobiography*, 6; and Fernández Fernández, *La mujer en la conquista y la evangelización en el Perú*, 134.
63 Deslandres, *Croire et faire croire*, 361.
64 See, for example, Hills, *Invisible City*, 35; Laven, *Virgins of Venice;* Jutta Gisela Sperling, *Convents and the Body Politic in Late Renaissance Venice* (Chicago: University of Chicago Press, 1999).
65 Myers and Powell, *A Wild Country out in the Garden*, 261–2.

chapter two

The Religious Lives of Singlewomen in the Anglo-Atlantic World: Quaker Missionaries, Protestant Nuns, and Covert Catholics

AMY M. FROIDE

In 1673 Richard Allestree, the author of the popular conduct book *The Ladies Calling,* had some words of advice for never-married women, or, as he liked to call them, those 'calamitous creatures' who had 'failed' to marry. Allestree told these women to 'addict themselves to the strictest virtue and piety, [so that] they would give the world some cause to believe, 'twas not their necessity, but their choice which kept them unmarried, that they were pre-engaged to a better amour, espoused to the spiritual bridegroom; and this would give them among the soberer sort, at least the reverence and esteem of matrons.'[1] The women to whom Allestree recommended a life of piety were by no means a small group in late-seventeenth-century England. The numbers of never-married English-women had been rising over the seventeenth century and in most towns at least a third of adult women were single. Referred to as 'spinsters' or 'singlewomen,' they had become an acknowledged female group as well as a topic of societal concern.[2] Contemporaries worried about and debated how women who had presumably failed to become wives and mothers should employ themselves. Most commentators echoed All-estree (and exhibited their class bias) by suggesting that singlewomen should practise a life of religious retirement rather than one of active business or trade.

Such advice did not much help English singlewomen. The model of female religiosity in Protestant England was one that focused on the mother as religious instructor to her children and the mistress of the household as religious exemplar to the family. This Protestant paradigm excluded singlewomen, in contrast to Catholic countries that offered the religious vocation of a celibate nun to never-married women who either were called to this vocation or simply needed an alternative to marriage. As the numbers of English singlewomen increased, several authors suggested that it might be time for England to bring back nunneries, albeit in a Protestant form. Mary Astell, Clement Barksdale, Edward Chamberlayne, and George Wheler all penned schemes for Protestant colleges or houses of retirement.[3] Their voices were drowned out, however, by the fierce anti-Catholicism that flared up in England in the wake of political crises in the late seventeenth century.

Historians have assumed that, despite the proposals of writers like Mary Astell, religious communities never materialized for English singlewomen in the early modern period. This chapter will show that this notion is incorrect. I argue that never-married women created various modes of religious life that required them to reach out across the Channel and the Atlantic to emulate female religious institutions and connect with religious women in Europe and North America. In particular, I examine three forms of religious community created by English singlewomen in the seventeenth and eighteenth centuries. The first form of community was established by pairs of female Quakers who pursued an active form of religiosity through itinerant preaching in both the British Isles and the British colonies in North America. The second type of community was created by Mary Wandesforde, who endowed a house for Anglican singlewomen in the city of York. And the third model of communal life was exemplified by covert Catholic followers of the reformer Mary Ward, who established secret nunneries in York and the London suburb of Hammersmith. On the one hand, these women obeyed Allestree's suggestion that never-married women should devote themselves to piety. On the other, the religious vocations these women actually forged were based much more on models of female authority and female-centred piety than anything male commentators such as Allestree would have ever advocated or even imagined.

Female Quakers as Preachers and Missionaries

Scholars have aptly documented the important role of women in seventeenth- and eighteenth-century Quakerism and the relatively enlightened views the sect held on the participation of women as religious leaders, preachers, and decision makers.[4] Rebecca Larson also has emphasized the transatlantic character of the Quaker faith, noting that no 'religious group had closer transatlantic ties' than Quakers before the American Revolutionary War. Quaker writings and itinerant preachers circulated the Atlantic to maintain these ties. Both male and female preachers spread the Quaker faith throughout England, Wales, and Ireland, as well as Britain's North American and Caribbean colonies. Women were noted for being pioneering missionaries in areas such as New England and the southern colonies. Their numbers were impressive; Larson estimates that there were between 1,300 and 1,500 female Quaker ministers in the Anglo-American Atlantic community.[5]

Female Quaker preachers were a diverse lot, ranging in age and social status. Nevertheless, transatlantic travelling and preaching were not necessarily compatible with wifely and motherly duties. A good proportion of female Quaker preachers deferred marriage and childbearing, or were widowed, or never married. The Quaker faith condoned and even encouraged women to put religion before the traditional roles of wife and mother. In advocating a religious, in addition to a marital, vocation for women, Quakerism particularly validated single females. Female preachers who never married did not find themselves bereft of emotional and material companionship; the Quakers required female missionaries to travel and work in same-sex pairs. The bonds that female Friends formed with one another were often as important as those they might form with spouses; and sometimes these relationships even took the place of spousal ones.

The female minister Mary Capper provides an example of how female Quakers crafted a form of religious community that particularly appealed to singlewomen. She also illustrates how religious vocations led to the migration of never-married women throughout the Atlantic world. Mary Capper was born in Rugley, Staffordshire, in 1755 to a family of the middling sort.[6] She and her nine siblings were raised in the Church of England. A serious, intelligent, and pious youth, by age twenty-one Capper was corresponding with her brother Jasper, who had moved to London and converted to Quakerism. In 1776 Mary Capper's ill health led her to France. On her way she stopped in London and stayed with Jasper. It is there that Capper attended her first Quaker meeting, and, tellingly, she was especially pleased by one of the female preachers. She then continued on to France. Evidently searching for a religious home (in both senses of the word), Capper contemplated a stay at a convent. But she was dissuaded from convent life because the food was spare and pensioners (those who paid to lodge in a convent) had to rise at five in the morning and take part in prayers. She also disliked the ceremony of the Mass and the idleness produced by the multiple saints' days.

Mary Capper's narrative is typical of its genre in that it focuses on the sufferings she encountered during her conversion to the Quaker faith. Back in England, Capper grew more interested in the sect, which caused her parents to disown her and forbid her to live with them. Even though Capper was now twenty-six years of age, she was not married and her parents still exercised enough control over her life that they ordered her to live with her brother James. Although a rector in the established church, James Capper was perhaps more sympathetic to his sister's religious struggles than his parents would have wished. He asked Mary to attend his congregation but did not require her to receive the Eucharist. A year later, Mary Capper went to live with another brother, William, and served as his housekeeper for six years. Now in her early thirties, she made a bid for independence and began to attend Quaker meetings regularly. Capper's religious struggle ended in her decision to choose God over her parents. Her mother wrote that she would never accept another letter from her daughter, whom she declared to be under a 'strong, enthusiastic delusion.'

At the age of thirty, Mary Capper entered fully into the Society of Friends. It is evident that her conversion was by no means a rushed one. Soon after, she began to speak as a minister in meetings. Capper mentions a man to whom she had formed a 'strong attachment,' and, although her narrative becomes terse here, it seems she expected to marry him. It was not to be, however, for his religious faith did not prove strong enough; 'although it nearly cost her her life,' she broke off the relationship. Capper's turn away from marriage meant that she remained single for her ninety-one-year-long life. Around the same time Capper rejected marriage, her father died and she reconciled with her mother. Rebecca Capper wrote to her daughter that 'whilst you remain single, I would have you to look upon my habitation, so long as I live, as your fixed and settled home.' Mary hastened to that home and cared for her mother until she died in 1793. It is no coincidence that, within the year, she embarked on her career as an itinerant preacher. At age thirty-eight, Mary was free of family duties and able to devote her life to her religion. The path she chose was an active one.

In 1794 Mary Capper met one of the most important people in her life, a Quaker preacher named Mary Beesley. She and Beesley embarked on the first of many religious travels together, the first being to Wales. For the next five years, Mary Capper divided her time between travelling and ministering with her partner Mary Beesley and staying with fam-

ily members to help care for her nieces and nephews. She also resided
frequently with Mary Beesley. Capper viewed her ministry as one of companionship and partnership rather than a solitary religious career. At a
Birmingham Quaker meeting in 1799, she noted wistfully that she felt
'solitary, having no companion in the ministry.'

In 1800 Capper's partnership with Beesley was threatened when the
latter received a marriage proposal from a fellow Quaker named James
Lewes. The marriage did take place but had much less effect on the wom-
en's companionship than we might expect. Capper continued to reside
with Beesley and the two maintained their travel and ministry together.
Writing to a friend in 1807, Mary Capper said: 'Since Mary Beesley's marriage, I have been mostly with her. Such a quiet retreat, with her.' One
would think the two women were living a life of female religious retirement except for the presence of Beesley's husband, James Lewes. Significantly, Capper portrayed Lewes as the third wheel in this arrangement
rather than herself. A year later, James Lewes died and Mary Capper was
soon writing of herself and Mary Beesley: 'We returned to *our* habitation
at Trosnant; it is a quiet retreat, but we miss the dear head of the family.'
The two women continued to live together and by 1811 were residing in
the small town of Leominster.

Two years later, Mary Beesley died and a twenty-year partnership ended. Beesley had been Mary Capper's closest companion throughout her
life and Capper had been Beesley's partner for twice as long as the latter's husband. The year after her dear friend and partner's death, Capper began to refer to her own old age. Nevertheless, she continued her
itinerant ministry until 1825, when she seems to have retired at the age
of seventy. In some of these later travels, Capper continued to travel and
preach in female company, with a new companion named Hannah Evans. After a thirty-year career as a Quaker female preacher, Mary Capper survived another twenty years after her retirement, dying at the age
of ninety-one. As Richard Allestree had suggested, she chose a life of
religion since she had not engaged in marriage and childrearing. But
her preaching, ministering, travelling, and residence with female companions were most likely not the religious life that commentators like
Allestree had envisioned.

Not all female Quaker preachers remained single for their entire lives
like Mary Capper, but many deferred marriage until their late thirties,
forties, and even fifties. Marrying later meant that these female Quakers also bypassed childbirth. When they did finally wed, they attached
great importance to their female relationships and manipulated their

marriage arrangements to further their religious vocations. Catherine Payton Philips provides an example of how one Englishwoman did this.[7] Payton Phillips was called into the Quaker ministry at the young age of eighteen and for the next fifty years, until her death in 1794, she kept busy travelling and preaching. In the twelve-year period between 1749 and when she married in 1762, Payton Phillips visited Wales, western and southwestern England, London, Ireland, northern England, and Scotland. She then spent over two and a half years in North America, travelling the Carolinas, Pennsylvania, New York, Rhode Island, Massachusetts, and Connecticut. Recrossing the Atlantic, she went again to Dublin, travelled throughout England and Wales, and made a trip to Holland.

Payton Phillips's memoirs reveal that she obviously enjoyed her religious vocation and preferred it to the more normative life of an early modern singlewoman. The difference between these religious and social roles made her defensive when recalling her mission to America in the 1750s. Payton Phillips said that she and her companion Mary Peisley did not stay abroad 'longer than usual' compared to other Friends who had made such visits: 'Whatever some loose spirits might suggest respecting our long absence from home ... we did not travel for pleasure, or to gratify a roving or curious disposition.' This statement sounds even more doubtful when read alongside the resentment she felt when she returned home and was expected to take up family responsibilities. In 1760 she said: '[She was] endeavoring to discharge my duty in domestic cares a greater weight whereof than heretofore rested upon me since my sister's marriage; through which, and my brother's continued indisposition, my way in leaving home was straightened; yet I know not that any clear manifestation of duty was omitted; although sometimes it was discharged with difficulty.' Two years later Payton Philips lamented that 'a load of domestic concerns devolved on me.'[8]

Ironically, Payton Philips escaped her duties and burdens through marriage, which one would presume to be full of familial responsibilities. She did so suddenly, after forty-five years of singleness. Her memoirs offered little by way of explanation, noting merely that she had not wed earlier because 'my mind had been, and was under strong restrictions in regard to entering into the marriage state, should I be solicited thereto; for as it appeared that for a series of years I should be much engaged in traveling for the service of truth, I feared to indulge thoughts of forming a connection, which from its encumbrances, might tend to frustrate the intention of Divine wisdom respecting me. This caution tended to keep me reserved in my conduct, towards such as might be likely to entertain views beyond friendship.'

Payton Philips made it plain that she attached more value to her religious career than to the normative path of marriage, so why was she willing to marry at the age of forty-five, while she was still ministering? By taking a spouse, Payton Philips escaped the duty of caring for her natal household because she had now formed one of her own. In addition, because she married around the age of menopause, Payton Philips never had children during her thirteen-year marriage; therefore, she had to care only for her husband and herself. How much she even had to do that is uncertain, since she continued to preach and travel with female companions after marrying, except for one ten-month period that she noted 'was the longest period I remember to have been *confined* [emphasis added].' Payton Philips was an enterprising and independent woman who used both the single and the married state to ensure a continued enjoyment of freedom and career. She married only when she could do so on her terms, and even then she continued to enjoy the independence women usually found only while single.

Payton Philips was not a rarity among female Quaker preachers. Larson's sample of fifty-six women (of the 1,300–1,500 who were transatlantic ministers between the years 1700 and 1775) includes five women who never married and thirteen more who married but had no children.[9] In other words, 30 per cent of these female preachers did not have husbands or children, leaving them more time to preach and travel. Of the thirty-eight women who married and had children, many did so past the normative age of marriage. On average, Englishwomen married in their early to mid-twenties in the first half of the eighteenth century. By contrast, twenty-one of the Quaker preachers who married did so at age twenty-eight or older. The breakdown of these ages is even more interesting, with eight women marrying between ages twenty-eight and thirty-four, another ten between ages thirty-five and thirty-nine, and three between ages forty and forty-five. It is striking just how many female Quaker preachers married late in life and thus either had small families or no children at all. These women's lifestyle decisions made religious travels and bonds with other female preachers possible for long periods of their lives.

The religious community fashioned by female Quakers was geographically broad and female-centred. Single, married but often childless, and widowed Quaker women practised and promoted their faith by travelling the Atlantic world in pairs. In an era when not many women, especially non-elite ones, expected to travel internationally, religion allowed Quaker women to do so. This observation is not meant to discount the piety of these women, but rather to highlight the connection between faith and freedom and to explain why itinerant preaching was particularly appealing to independent women.

An Anglican Community for Singlewomen

While female Quaker preachers dedicated themselves to a religious life based on public speaking and itinerant preaching, Anglican women (those who belonged to the Protestant Church of England) often advocated a life of religious retreat and retirement. The gentlewoman Elizabeth Hastings, for example, lived a life of pious retreat on her estate at Ledstone, never marrying and seldom leaving home. Her engagement with the outside world mostly involved contributing to charitable causes and interacting with other single pious women such as herself. Among her friends was the more famous Mary Astell, who pursued a more active model of Anglican religiosity. Astell ran a charity school and wrote a number of religious-minded works, the most famous of which was a treatise calling for the establishment of Protestant institutions of religious retirement for singlewomen. Men such as Daniel Defoe attacked Astell's ideas as papist-leaning, and, for some time, historians assumed that no such institutions ever came to fruition.[10]

In fact, however, Mary Wandesforde, a genteel singlewoman whose life spanned the late seventeenth and early eighteenth centuries, did establish an Anglican religious community for singlewomen.[11] A devout Anglican, she moved away from her family's estate in rural Yorkshire to the provincial city of York in order to pursue her religion. Anglican women in early modern England did not have the option of a full-time religious vocation available to them, but Wandesforde did not let that stop her. Instead, she created such a vocation for herself. Packing up her belongings, which included a picture of the Virgin Mary, she rented lodgings in York's cathedral close. There she became a part of the religious circle attached to York Minster and its archbishop. Wandesforde took advantage of the power that genteel women like herself had by using her money in the service of the church. Even today, a visitor to York's cathedral can admire the striking black and gilded iron gates marking the entrance to the choir. Few know, however, that the gates were the gift of Mary Wandesforde to her beloved York Minster.

While Mary Wandesforde's pious gifts were by no means rare among the devout Anglican women of her day, she did leave a much more unique legacy. In her will of 1725 she bequeathed an estate that included a mortgage worth £1,200 and an additional £1,200 in South Sea Company stock 'for the use of ten poor gentlewomen who were never married, and shall be of the religion which is taught and practised in the Church of England as by law established, who shall retire from the hurry and noise of the world into a religious house or Protestant retirement, which shall be provided for them.'[12] Recognizing the lack of an Anglican vocation for singlewomen such as herself, Wandesforde created one. She set up what, in her words, was a Protestant retirement. As we shall see, her male contemporaries believed it to be nothing less than a Protestant nunnery. To oversee her scheme, Wandesforde named four trustees: the archbishop of York, two canons at the Minster, and her nephew John Wandesforde, the rector of Kirklington. Mary Wandesforde was shrewd: by naming such powerful male clergy as trustees, she implicated them in her scheme and thereby acquired their blessing on and protection for it. Mary Wandesforde's family was less than impressed by her piety and fought against the establishment of her Protestant home for singlewomen. Wandesforde's nephew contested her will in the Court of Chancery, claiming that, as heir-at-law, he had the right to inherit her estate. After much legal wrangling, in 1737 the court upheld Mary Wandesforde's will and paved the way for her Anglican female community. Nevertheless, the judge did not scruple to amend the will by ordering that only women over the age of fifty might inhabit the house. The justice said he did this to ensure that the house would not be perceived as a nunnery. By defining the institution as a home for elderly singlewomen, however, he ignored Wandesforde's original intent. In the records from this point onward, the Wandesforde house is referred to as a 'charity,' or by the locals in York as the 'Old Maid's hospital,' names that altered the religious aim of Wandesforde's establishment.[13]

Yet Mary Wandesforde's vision was not completely erased. Her retirement facility for singlewomen began to be built in 1739. An attractive Georgian-style house was erected in the western suburb of St Marys, York. Still standing today, the house also continues as a home for unmarried women. Staying true to Mary Wandesforde's original intent, only Anglican singlewomen lived in the home until as recently as 1999, when the Archbishopric of York took the controversial step of allowing widows to live there. But divorced women and any who are Catholic, Methodist, or any other sort of non-Anglican Protestant continue to be turned away. The house is still divided into two-room apartments for ten to twelve singlewomen, although private bathrooms were introduced (as late as the 1960s) and stoves have replaced the original open hearths. Two communal rooms were originally built along with the private apartments. One was a sitting room that still features a prominent picture of the founder. (Her image also appears in a bust that adorns the pediment above the front door to the home.) The other communal room was a chapel. This room and a clergyman who was hired to celebrate communion once a week were the primary vestiges of Wandesforde's vision of religious retirement for singlewomen. The trustees added additional requirements as well.

For instance, the trustees required all prospective inhabitants of the home to prove mature age, gentle birth, financial need, and good standing in the Church of England. Advanced age was critical to the trustees so that the Mary Wandesforde house would not be confused with a nunnery. Prospective female inhabitants had to provide certificates from the parishes of their birth that attested to their age and parentage. Some of the women also produced poignant tales of disease, deformity, and misfortune to explain why they were in need of charity even though they came from good families. Other never-married women went to great lengths to prove their genteel status – naming all of the peers and gentlemen to whom they were related. The petition of Sarah Priestly, which she made in November 1751, reflects the concerns of the trustees: 'The petition of Sarah Priestly Humbly Sheweth That your Petitioner is a Gentlewoman by birth, daughter of John Priestly of the City of York, merchant, was never married, has never had child or children, has lived all along in constant communion with the Church of England, established by law, is aged upwards of 50 years, is in needy and necessitous circumstances, not having sufficient for my support without the benefit of Mrs. Wandesforde's charity. Therefore your petitioner desires to be admitted.'[14] Priestly's petition was witnessed and attested to by ten prominent local men. She evidently fit all the requisite criteria and was admitted accordingly.

The trustees also established specific rules of conduct for the singlewomen who lived in the Wandesforde house. The idea of a group of never-married women living alone was a concern to these men. They put in place a system of surveillance to assuage their worry, appointing a clergyman who not only conducted daily church services according to Wandesforde's will but also kept an eye on the female inhabitants. Additionally, the trustees required one of the gentlewomen to lock 'the court gate leading to the street and the out [front] doors to the house and take the keys into her room and secure them till the morning.' Each week the key to the door rotated to a new inmate, who would sleep with it under her pillow to ensure that none of her fellow singlewomen could sneak out at night. The poor gentlewomen were not 'upon any pretence whatsoever to be absent from their lodgings after the hour of nine o'clock at night [in winter] nor after the hour of ten o'clock at night [in summer].' The women were not allowed to admit any person into their rooms overnight except in case of sickness. In other words, trustees averse to giving the impression that the Wandesforde house was a nunnery nonetheless created rules that echoed the enclosure movement advocated for Catholic nuns on the continent and the Americas, as discussed by Barbara Diefendorf in her contribution to this volume.[15]

The trustees also wrote specific rules for the house that reflected its religious nature. These rules stated that 'ten maiden gentlewomen shall be elected and placed in the Hospital by a majority of the votes of Trustees and receive each the stipend of ten pounds yearly.' And they ordered that 'the poor maiden gentlewomen shal [sic] to the best of their endeavors be of pious godly chast [sic] and virtuous behaviour neither offensive to each other by scolding and brawling calumny and slander strife and contention and if they offend in any of these particulars they shall be expelled and removed from all the benefit of the Hospital by any three trustees or more.' In addition, the 'poor gentlewomen elected and admitted into the Hospital shall attend prayers there daily except in case of sickness or of leave of absence by one trustee or more under the penalty of one penny to be deducted for each and every omission of that duty from their half years stipend ... And on such days as they have not prayers at the Hospital they shall not fail under the like penalty to attend the publick worship of God either at the parish church or at the Cathedral.' The women were expected to draw up a monthly list of those fellow inmates who had failed to attend daily prayer and present it to the chaplain.[16] It is significant that, despite the worries that the home might be mistaken for a nunnery, the only duties required of the singlewomen in the Wandesforde house were attendance at religious services and prayers.

Notwithstanding such measures and the required testimonies of Anglican piety, some women did not meet the high standards set for them. The trustees evicted one of the original inmates from the house relatively soon after her arrival for drunkenness and disorderly behaviour. They also removed another singlewoman (Rebecca Moore) upon learning that she had conceived and borne an illegitimate child in her youth. The child apparently died young, and, although Moore had lived an upright life for the next thirty years, she was asked to leave the house. The trustees did give her the option of leaving of her own accord and they did not make her story public. Nonetheless, the message was clear that they did not intend the Wandesforde home to serve as a Magdalen house for reformed prostitutes or penitent singlewomen who had lost their moral compass.

This analogy to a Magdalen house is telling. The English largely denied unmarried women the option of communal living so common in continental European countries. In addition to convents, there was a tradition in countries like Italy and Spain of establishing Catholic-sponsored institutions such as Magdalen houses for reformed prostitutes, *casa delle zitelle* for at-risk single girls, and orbatello (asylums) for widows. Another option for singlewomen in France and the Low Countries since the Middle Ages had been to join *beguinages,* or semi-religious houses where unmarried women lived and worked together without having to take vows.[17] The Wandesforde house, however, stands out as perhaps the only Protestant communal experiment in early modern England. (There do not seem to have been any similar experiments in colonial British America.) While Richard Allestree had advocated a religious life for never-married women, he had imagined it as a solitary one. But Mary Wandesforde transformed this religious life into a collective endeavour that she may have modelled on continental forms of female religious community.

Covert Catholic Nunneries

Wandesforde's Anglican community was an attempt to recover a religious vocation for women that had been lost in England with the Reformation. Another group of English singlewomen also set out to re-establish female religious communities, but these women did so under England's old religion. After the state-led Reformation of the 1530s, women who wanted to devote themselves to a monastic life had no legal option in England. This led thousands of Catholic women to leave their homes, families, and country to profess in religious houses on the continent during the early modern period.[18] In the early seventeenth century, a Catholic Englishwoman named Mary Ward established a new order, which she envisioned as a female counterpart to the Jesuits. Since Catholicism was illegal in England, she and her followers originally founded their communities on the continent. In the second half of the seventeenth century, Ward's

Institute of the Blessed Virgin Mary (IBVM) even established covert nunneries in England, although she herself had died before this homecom-
ing came to pass.[19] The IBVM convents in England were part of a larger
European, Catholic community as well as a larger movement of Catholic
singlewomen who were debating the ways that they could serve God.
Similar to the Ursulines, Ward's followers were an active, teaching order.
Nevertheless, the IBVM nuns differed from the Ursulines in that they
rejected enclosure and did not send missionaries across the Atlantic in
the early modern period. The Ursulines founded convents in French
colonial America where they taught native Americans in Quebec and accepted African nuns into their convent in New Orleans.[20] For the IBVM
nuns, however, bringing convent life back to England was enough of a
missionary endeavour for the time being.

    The Catholic convents established covertly in England in the 1670s
and 1680s served both Catholic women who wished to profess as nuns
in England as well as the wider Recusant community (i.e., those who
'recused' themselves from attending Church of England services) in
England. Two of these nunneries were founded by Frances Bedingfield.
She founded the first at Hammersmith sometime after 1669, and then
shortly thereafter a second in York. After Bedingfield left Hammersmith,
the direction of the community fell to Cecilia Cornwallis, a young woman who had entered the Hammersmith Convent at the age of nineteen.
The Hammersmith establishment survived clandestinely by posing as a
girls' boarding school. Not only did education supply a respectable front
for these nuns, it also helped them to recruit future members, most notably from the broader Recusant community. These secret (and not so
secret) Catholics sent their daughters to be educated by the nuns and
often sent money as well. More than a few of these boarders eventually
joined the religious communities in Hammersmith and York as permanent residents.

    Although the boarding school helped to facilitate recruitment, un-
fortunately, for the women of Hammersmith, recruiting remained a
constant challenge. Many singlewomen were hesitant to risk living out
their days in a secret, illegal life. The Hammersmith community also suffered from anti-Catholic raids in 1680 and again in 1780. By the 1780s,
the convent was down to a few members and in 1795 the almost empty
convent was turned over to a community of Benedictine nuns who had
fled the continent in the wake of the French Revolution. In a touch of
irony, a convent established by English nuns, who almost two hundred
years earlier had fled Protestant England for Catholic countries such as

France, now served as an English refuge for French Catholic nuns fleeing religious persecution.

Mother Frances Bedingfield's other convent at York, the Bar Convent, was ultimately more successful than the one at Hammersmith and is still in existence today. She purchased the property for the Bar Convent in 1686 and established a community capable of sustaining around ten professed women. The financial status of Bedingfield's two clandestine nunneries can be gleaned from her will of 1691. There, she represented herself as nothing more than an ordinary spinster: 'I, Frances Bedingfield of Hammersmith, co. Middlesex, spinster.' She then stated: 'To Mrs. Cecily Cornwallis my dear friend I give my dwelling house and gardens that I have in Hammersmith with all money, plate, household goods of bedding, pewter, linen and all other furniture belonging, with all debts due to me from the parents of children which have been there educated.' Similarly, 'to my beloved niece Mrs. Dorothy Bedingfield I give my dwelling house and gardens which I have in the city of York with all money, plate, household goods of bedding, pewter, linen and all other furniture belonging, with all debts due to me from the parents of children which have been there educated.'[21] Hidden behind Bedingfield's description of herself as a 'spinster' and her unremarkable-sounding bequest of property and instructions to a close friend and relative was the reality of a mother superior ensuring the continuance of two convents and religious schools, as well as naming her two chosen successors.

The neighbours referred to the nuns at York as the 'Ladies of the Bar' – supposedly just a group of gentlewomen residing together in a house immediately outside York's city walls at Micklegate Bar (gate). The women were known to practise an activist piety of feeding the poor, caring for the sick, and keeping a school for girls. But, apart from a few instances, the York community seems to have accepted them and turned a blind eye to their murky status. The nuns made it easier for the surrounding community to accept them by purposefully keeping their condition unclear. For instance, they wore gray gowns, caps, and hoods instead of religious habits. This clothing may have intentionally suggested the status of widows, the most independent marital status for an Englishwoman. In the same vein, the portrait of Mother Cecilia Cornwallis, one of the founding members of both the Hammersmith and Bar convents, shows a woman clearly in the dress of a seventeenth-century widow. To hide their religious character further, the members were allowed to keep a private purse, called 'spending money,' so that friends on the outside would not think them different from other gentlewomen. Also, in the eighteenth century it was not yet safe to use the titles 'mother' and 'sister,' even in the house, so the pupils always addressed the nuns as 'Madam.' In similar fashion, the Georgian façade and a second roof discreetly hid the domed Catholic chapel inside. Not until the 1790s, when the government lifted the penal codes against Catholics, could the gray-garbed Ladies of the Bar admit who they really were.

Before that time, burial was the moment that exposed the women the most. Without a Catholic church or cemetery, the women were buried in the local parish churchyard. The registers of Holy Trinity Church in Micklegate list the burials of 'a gentlewoman,' a 'Mrs. Raquet,' and Dorothy Stansfield at 'Madame Paston's.' Despite such titles, these women were all nuns under Mother Dorothy Bedingfield alias Paston. But by 1720 Mrs Clifton 'from the nunnery' and Mrs Cornwallis 'Roman' are listed in the burial registers. At a time when Catholicism was still illegal, it seems that the nature of the house and its female inhabitants had become an open secret.[22]

Under the rubric of the Catholic religion, the 'Ladies of the Bar' created a community that took in a variety of unmarried women. Not only did professed nuns live at Bar Convent, but a number of women found refuge there as boarders, lay sisters, and pupils. For instance, the York widow Dame Mary Hungate died in 1749 while boarding at the convent. She left the nuns her furniture, crucifix, and other belongings. In 1738 Mary Metcalfe, the daughter of a gentlewoman who boarded in the house with her maid for many years, was professed as a nun. Lay sisters such as Anne Mason, Elisabeth Tasker, and Fanny Audas lived and worked at the convent for long periods of time. Mason, known as 'Nanny,' was well beloved by the community where she lived for forty-nine years. Tasker worked in the kitchen and when she died she bequeathed her entire estate of about £100 to the mother of the convent. Audas worked specifically with the sick who came to the convent to be nursed and for cures. She also served as a porteress and collected rents from the estates of some professed gentlewomen. Since the Ladies of the Bar were not subject to enclosure, the need for women like Fanny Audas as well as her tasks reflected their social status rather than their inability to venture into the world.

In addition to boarders and lay sisters, a large number of young singlewomen came to the convent to receive an education from the nuns. In 1710 there were forty-three young gentlewomen boarding in the house, and that did not include the day scholars. In the mid-1700s as many as 128 pupils were admitted during the fourteen-year tenure of Mother Esther Conyers. And in the 1760s the convent was renovated and enlarged

to provide better facilities for the fifty to eighty children who were en-
rolled in the boarding school. Some of these pupils were like Elizabeth
Atkinson, who stayed on after her schooling and professed as a nun.[23]

The nuns of Bar Convent not only provided a community for themselves and for other sorts of singlewomen in early modern England, they
also served a maternal role by providing a home to the wider Recusant
community in the north of England. For many years during the eighteenth century, the convent's chapel was the only place where Catholics
could receive the sacrament in York. The chapel remained open to the
Catholic public into the nineteenth century. Catholic gentry contributed
money to the convent and the chapel, and especially to their rebuilding
in the 1760s. Because the nuns were not enclosed and were passing as
gentlewomen, this meant that they could also freely receive and return
visits. This made their house a place for Catholics in the north to gather.
And their school was the only one in northern England for Catholic
girls. By forming a religious community, then, the nuns of Bar Convent
also met the religious needs of others of like mind. Although they were
singlewomen who had eschewed marriage and family themselves, they
served as religious mothers and caregivers to a larger Recusant family.

Defiant in the face of anti-Catholic sentiment and sometimes outright
harassment in the 1690s and 1740s, the covert Catholic nuns at Hammersmith and York persevered in their unlawful religious vocations and
prohibited religious communities. When Allestree recommended a religious life to women who never married, he probably never imagined a
resurgence of illegal Catholic nunneries. He certainly did not mean for
religion to serve as the justification for rebellious behaviour on the part
of England's never-married women.

Conclusion

Despite their denominational differences, the Quaker, Anglican, and
Catholic women discussed here all shared some striking similarities in
how they viewed religious life for singlewomen. First, each of the religious traditions to which these women belonged provided singlewomen
with a space of their own, an activity to which they could devote their
lives, a sense of community, and a modicum of religious authority. Female Quaker preachers, the Anglican Mary Wandesforde, and covert
Catholic nuns all gravitated towards and created models of female religious community. Secondly, these women all enjoyed a degree of religious autonomy and the ability to control their own spirituality. Thirdly,

these disparate women conceived of single female piety in a variety of ways but often fixed on an active rather than contemplative or passive mode. Lastly, and perhaps most significantly, these singlewomen all looked beyond England for their models of religious opportunities. English singlewomen both shaped and were shaped by a larger Atlantic world of female religiosity. Quaker singlewomen travelled the Atlantic world, Mary Wandesforde pioneered a form of religious community for Anglican singlewomen that would have looked familiar to women on the continent, and Catholic nuns defied the law by bringing back to England a form of convent life that was readily available in Europe and in the New World. To some degree, situating English singlewomen within this larger European and Atlantic context is the only way to make sense of their actions and religious experiences. In this instance, 'English exceptionalism' is not the rule.

Notes

1 *The Ladies Calling* (London, 1673), pt. 2, 3–4.
2 See my book *Never Married: Singlewomen in Early Modern England* (Oxford: Oxford University Press, 2005).
3 Mary Astell, *A Serious Proposal to the Ladies,* 4th ed. (London, 1701; repr. New York: Source Book Press, 1970); Clement Barksdale, *A Letter Touching a Colledge of Maids, or, a Virgin Society* (London, 1675); Edward Chamberlayne, *An Academy or Colledge, wherein Young Ladies and Gentlewomen May at a Very Moderate Expense Be Duly Instructed in the True Protestant Religion, and in All Vertuous Qualities That May Adorn That Sex* (London, 1671); George Wheler, *A Protestant Monastery* (London, 1698).
4 Phyllis Mack, *Visionary Women: Ecstatic Prophesy in Seventeenth-Century England* (Berkeley: University of California Press, 1992), and Rebecca Larson, *Daughters of Light: Quaker Women Preaching and Prophesying in the Colonies and Abroad 1700–1775* (New York: Alfred A. Knopf, 1999).
5 Larson, *Daughters of Light,* 8–9, 26, 63.
6 My discussion of Mary Capper's religious career is based on William and Thomas Evans, ed., 'A Memoir of Mary Capper, Late of Birmingham. A Minister of the Society of Friends,' *The Friends Library,* 12 (Philadelphia, 1848). 'A Memoir of Mary Capper' was produced after her death. Capper's friend Katherine Backhouse was authorized by the Quaker leadership to create a memoir out of Capper's journals and papers. This meant that much of the account was in Capper's own words, although the account of her childhood

was written from the hindsight of her eighties. Capper died in 1845 at the age of ninety-one and her memoir left off a decade prior to her death. It was probably widely disseminated since the Quakers used the written word to strengthen their ministry and so produced and disseminated memoirs of the Quaker faithful.

7 William and Thomas Evans, ed., 'Memoirs of the Life of Catharine Philips,' *The Friends Library,* 11 (Philadelphia, 1847). The Quaker minister Catharine Philips wrote her own narrative. Her memoirs were largely based on a journal she kept from age twenty-two to sixty, while the account of her youth came from memory and that of her death was provided by the testimony of Friends.

8 Ibid., 188, 231, 247, 253, 261.

9 This analysis of marital status is my own. I have used Larson's list of transatlantic female Quaker preachers for the sample. See Larson, *Daughters of Light,* 305–18, appendix 1, which provides short biographies of fifty-six female ministers in the transatlantic Quaker community during the period 1700–75. Larson refers to these years as the 'high point' of transatlantic Quaker culture, which ended with the American Revolution (ibid., 12, 63).

10 Ruth Perry, *The Celebrated Mary Astell: An Early English Feminist* (Chicago: University of Chicago Press, 1986); Astell, *A Serious Proposal to the Ladies;* Bridget Hill, ed., *The First English Feminist: Reflections upon Marriage and Other Writings by Mary Astell* (New York: St Martin's Press, 1986); idem, 'A Refuge from Men: The Idea of a Protestant Nunnery,' *Past & Present* 117 (1987): 107–30.

11 My discussion of Mary Wandesforde is based on Hardy B. M'Call, *Story of the Family of Wandesforde of Kirklington and Castlecomer* (London, 1904); P.M. Tillot, ed. *The Victoria History of the Counties of England. A History of Yorkshire. The City of York* (London: Oxford University Press, 1961), 426; the records of Wandesforde's house, held by the Borthwick Institute of Historical Research (hereafter BIHR); my own visits to the Wandesforde house; and interviews with the present inhabitants.

12 'The Autobiography of Mrs. Alice Thornton of East Newton, co. York,' *Surtees Society,* 62 (Durham, 1875), 323–4. Mary Wandesforde's will is reproduced in the appendix. Alice Thornton was born a Wandesforde and was Mary's aunt.

13 BIHR, Records of the Wandesforde Hospital, DR.WH 3.

14 Ibid., 5.

15 Ibid., 4.

16 Ibid.

17 Sharon Farmer, '"It Is Not Good That [Wo]man Should be Alone": Elite

Responses to Singlewomen in High Medieval Paris'; and Monica Chojnacka, 'Singlewomen in Early Modern Venice: Communities and Opportunities.' Both in Judith M. Bennett and Amy M. Froide, eds., *Singlewomen in the European Past, 1250–1800* (Philadelphia: University of Pennsylvania Press, 1999), 82–105, 217–35. Also, Sherrill Cohen, *The Evolution of Women's Asylums since 1500: From Refuges for Ex-Prostitutes to Shelters for Battered Women* (Oxford: Oxford University Press, 1992).

18 See Claire Walker, *Gender and Politics in Early Modern Europe: English Convents in France and the Low Countries* (New York: Palgrave, 2003).

19 My discussion of York's Bar Convent and the Hammersmith Convent is based on Sister M. Gregory Kirkus, 'The History of Bar Convent' and 'The Institute after 1645' (both of these sources are pamphlets written by the Bar Convent archivist and are available at the Bar Convent archives); J.S. Hansom, 'The Nuns of the Institute of Mary at York from 1677 to 1825,' *Catholic Record Society,* 4 (London, 1907), 353–67; Johanna Harting, 'Catholic Registers of Hammersmith, Middlesex, 1710–1838,' *Catholic Record Society,* 26 (London, 1926), 58–130; and Henry James Coleridge, ed., *St Mary's Convent Micklegate Bar York* (London: Burns and Oates, 1887).

20 Natalie Zemon Davis, *Women on the Margins: Three Seventeenth-Century Lives* (Cambridge, Mass.: Harvard University Press, 2005); and Emily Clark, *Masterless Mistresses: The New Orleans Ursulines and the Development of a New World Society, 1727–1834* (Chapel Hill: University of North Carolina Press, 2007).

21 Coleridge, *St Mary's Convent,* 78–9.

22 Ibid., 117–18.

23 Ibid., 149–62.

chapter three

Transatlantic Ties: Women's Writing in Iberia and the Americas

LISA VOLLENDORF

In 1614 Mexican nun Francisca de Miranda (b. late 1500s) claimed she was cured from a near fatal illness by miraculous intervention of the Spanish founder of the Discalced Carmelites, Teresa of Avila (1515–82), who had been dead for twenty-two years.[1] Across the Atlantic, in 1646, the Portuguse Dominican nun Sor Violante do Ceo (1601–93) wrote a poem declaring female friendship more valuable than the 'silver and gold of Arabia and Potosí.'[2] A third event takes us back to the Americas: Colombian Poor Clare Gerónima Nava y Saavedra (1669–1727) had a mystical vision of travelling to Asia to convert souls to Catholicism.[3] These cases from the Iberian Atlantic point to the role women played in defining, imagining, and expanding the influence of Catholic culture beyond the confines of Europe in the early modern period. In conjunction with the legacies of other secular and religious women from both continents, the examples provide a framework for probing the religious, cultural, and intellectual links between women in Iberia and the Americas.

This chapter examines those links by focusing on female textual production in the Hispanic diaspora in order to decipher women's representations of life in Iberia and colonial Spanish America. To the extent possible, women from Portugal are included, particularly since that country formed part of Spain's imperial enterprise between 1580 and 1640.[4] The analysis focuses on rhetorical strategies, thematic elements, and affective and experiential dimensions of women's texts. As such, it investigates the promises and limitations of the sources that provide the key to unlocking that history. The entry of women into the realm of cultural production in Spain and Spanish America is used as a point of departure for more fully understanding the roles played by gender and religion throughout the Iberian and Ibero-American Atlantic.

Gender Politics in Spain, Portugal, and Spanish America

Spain's imperial age has been well studied in terms of political, social, and cultural impact, yet the nuns' stories remind us that the Iberian Atlantic is less well understood in terms of its effects on women. Contact between Europeans and indigenous Americans significantly changed life on both continents, as expulsions, forced conversions, relocations, and the arrests of tens of thousands of individuals altered the lives of Jews, Muslims, and Catholics throughout the Hispanic diaspora. Women across class and ethnic lines were affected as a group, particularly as the Purity of Blood Statutes (1449–1547) complicated questions of religious and ethnic identity by racializing the population and positioning women as a threat to the social fabric. Genealogy became linked to identity, status, and privilege through official policy that aimed to categorize all Spaniards as New Christians (converts to Catholicism or their descendants) or Old Christians (those of Catholic lineage). The statutes had the curious effect of unifying women as a group to be controlled. Women of diverse backgrounds and circumstances found themselves under pressure to comply with rigid gender roles in the ethnically, religiously, and politically complex landscape of early modern Spain and, subsequently, Spanish America. While many new identities emerged out of the nation-building, inquisitorial culture of the period, women arguably were positioned as the group that posed the single most important threat to a homogenous Catholic state.[5] Indeed, regardless of background, class, or beliefs, women were viewed as sexually and, therefore, genealogically dangerous.

In spite of the cultural shift that dramatically redefined gender codes in the period, women's stories have been left out of many early modern and colonial histories.[6] Moreover, women's experiences of life in the Iberian Atlantic have been difficult to decode as a result of the paucity of written sources produced by women and the lack of attention to the existing sources that trace women's words. Yet emerging research on women in Iberia and Spanish America has made clear that bringing women's concerns and experiences to bear on the historiography of the Iberian Atlantic significantly alters our understanding of that geographic and cultural space for the early modern and colonial periods.

Recent research on the Iberian and Latin American Atlantic suggests that women found opportunities for engagement with the public sphere in the emerging mercantile, urban economy and for education and community in the many convents founded in the Counter-Reformation and colonial periods. Spanish women had property and dowry rights that women in other parts of Europe did not: partible inheritance, rather than primogeniture, gave all legitimate heirs the legal right to equal parts of an estate.[7] The high numbers of men leaving for the Americas also opened opportunities for women shopkeepers, printers, and guild members.[8] Old and New Christian women ran schools, convents, and small businesses in Spain. They worked as vendors, seamstresses, and healers, and often made a living based on a combination of these activities. Noblewomen influenced political decisions and marital allegiances among the most powerful families in Europe.[9] From inside and outside convents, they functioned as community leaders, educators, and reformers. *Conversas* and *moriscas* – descendants of Jews and Muslims – played key roles in keeping their cultures alive. Whereas women in *converso* culture were educated by their family members, both conversas and moriscas transmitted religious customs and knowledge to their children.[10]

Similarly, we have examples of both mestiza (of mixed indigenous and European stock) and *Criolla* (descendants of Europeans born in the Americas) who successfully inserted themselves into convent leadership structures and gained reputations as writers, leaders, and major players in colonial societies.[11] Among hundreds of such examples, Kathryn Burns (in *Colonial Habits: Convents and the Spiritual Economy of Cuzcu, Peru*) has found extensive evidence of women's economic participation in colonial society. Similarly, Silvia Arrom (in *Women of Mexico City 1790–1857*) has argued that the Bourbonic incorporation of women into education and the economy was possible because of the participation of women in those sectors during the colonial era. Furthermore, Octavio Paz recognized early on that 'a notable characteristic of Sor Juana's family is the independence, fortitude, and energy of the women.'[12]

In conjunction with the previous scholarship, emerging evidence of the involvement of conversas, moriscas, mestizas, and Criollas in the workings of the private, public, and religious spheres of Spain and the Americas highlights the importance of including women in any discussion of the Iberian Atlantic. Such analyses overwhelmingly show that women across class, ethnic, and religious lines made significant contributions to early modern and colonial cultures in more ways than previously had been traced or even imagined. The diversity of religious beliefs and ethnic backgrounds of the citizens of the Iberian Atlantic also underlines the importance of framing any discussion of the shared Atlantic space in terms of the wide range of experiences people had of inquisitional culture and the emerging mercantilist economic order on both continents. The life of a noblewoman at court necessarily was different from that of a morisca slave, a lower-class nun of the white veil, or a *beata* (lay religious woman), for example. Moreover, given that mixed-race, indigenous, and African women outnumbered the Criolla and Spanish nuns they served in Spanish America, convents differed significantly on both sides of the Atlantic.[13]

Until recently, it was nearly impossible to decipher women's experiences of the diverse manifestations of imperial Spanish culture throughout the early modern and colonial periods since most research had been based on legal, political, and cultural texts produced by men. Yet the scholarship on women's literary history in early modern Iberia and colonial Spanish America has resulted in numerous studies focused on women's texts. Dozens of women writers from Spain, Spanish Portugal (1580–1640), and Spanish America have been brought to light in recent years.[14] This body of literature shows that dominant histories about the early modern and colonial periods have misrepresented and miscomprehended the roles and experiences of women in the Iberian Atlantic world. Interpretations of women as home-bound bystanders on the sidelines of change and upheaval have been replaced by nuanced studies about women's participation in the economic, political, and cultural landscapes of the early modern and colonial Hispanic world. Furthermore, the emerging corpus of early modern texts produced by and about women in Iberia and colonial Latin America reveals striking thematic similarities related to gender, religion, and self-representation among texts produced by women during the period.

During the foundational period of Hispanic women's writing, texts written by women and those that transcribe or interpret women's words show a surprising coherence of rhetorical strategies and thematic focus. Characterized by the entry of dozens of women into the writing sphere, the shift occurred in Spain between 1580 and 1700. In the Americas, the colonization process, including slightly later dates for en masse convent foundations, led to a later time frame for women's first collective engagement with the written word. Whereas a handful of colonial American women's texts exists from before 1680, the bulk can be traced to the period between that date and 1800.[15]

On both sides of the Atlantic, the revolution that occurred with regard to women's educational and literary engagement was bolstered by

humanism and the Counter- Reformation.[16] Whereas humanism emphasized education, albeit of a limited sort, for women in order to create
better wives and mothers among Spanish citizenry, the boom in convent
foundations that followed the Council of Trent gave more women access
to education within convent walls than ever before had been possible in
Iberia and, later, the Catholic diaspora. The Counter-Reformation also
brought renewed emphasis on the practice of confession, which in turn
led to more spiritual autobiographies and biographies presenting intimate details of religious women's lives.

The Counter-Reformative impulse to spiritual instruction, full confession, and thoughtful engagement with the word of God is best exemplified by the highly influential author and nun Teresa of Avila. Well
before her canonization in 1622, the Dicalced reformer had an impact
on women in Iberia and, indeed, throughout the Catholic world in ways
that she probably did not foresee.[17] In imitation of her popular spiritual,
instructional, and autobiographical writings, Iberian and Latin American women often turned to the written word at the mandate of confessors and as a means of expression. Thus, a tripartite confluence of
humanist advocacy for women's education, the validation of full confession as a means of performing exemplary Catholicism, and the model
of Teresa of Avila as a writer-reformer paved the way for secular and religious women's engagement with the written word inside and outside
the convent setting. Indeed, hundreds of nuns' texts are available today,
though most have not been studied in depth. Also, beginning in the late
sixteenth century, a few Iberian secular women participated in literary
culture and positioned themselves as successful authors whose work was
read by women and men alike. Subsequently, seventeenth-century Spain
saw its first cohort of secular women write plays, novellas, and poetry for
literary salons and the general public.[18]

In the Americas, the impulse to write was linked explicitly to the religious impulse that helped to justify – in the minds of many – the colonization process. With a ban on the publication of secular fiction that
loosened only in the nineteenth century and was nullified upon independence from Spain, writers in the colonies might be seen as having
been limited to participating in a republic of letters fully devoted to the
evangelical mission of the empire.[19] The ban reminds us that women's
intellectual and cultural history in the Iberian Atlantic must be situated
in terms of the homogenizing, nation-building, Catholic discourse of
early modern empires. Emphasis on gender codes in the cultural politics
of the era influenced individual women's representations of themselves

in texts as diverse as Inquisition and legal depositions, poetry, prose fiction, plays, letters, autobiography, and biography. The deployment of such codes occurs in texts produced by women of different class, ethnic, and national backgrounds, thus leading us to probe further the role of gender in representation and experience for women in the Iberian diaspora during the age of empire.

   It is difficult to decipher whether gender influenced women's experiences more or less than other identity markers – such as ethnicity, class, and religious belief and practice – since we have access only to textual representations of those experiences. Yet, by analysing rhetorical strategies and themes in texts produced by women (such as literature and autobiography) or texts that reproduce or interpret women's words (such as depositions, spiritual biographies, and sermons), we can begin to understand the expectations that women had of their intended audiences. Only then can we reconstruct an approximation of the experiences women had of the controlling culture so famously propagated throughout the empire. Likewise, thematic and rhetorical similarities found in women's texts produced throughout Iberia and the Americas reaffirm the need for a transatlantic approach to women's cultural history.

The Boom in Women's Writing: Iberia (1580–1700)

Influenced by Mother Teresa's successes as reformer and bolstered through the educational apparatus provided by the numerous convent foundations after the Council of Trent, women in late-sixteenth-century Iberia had more access to the written word than ever before. During her lifetime, Teresa of Avila redefined female monasticism through religious reform and extensive textual production. After her death in 1582, she became a spiritual and intellectual model for countless women throughout Europe and the Americas.[20] The links between Mother Teresa's popularity, women's education, and convent foundations is crucial for an understanding of literacy and female monasticism in the era: without the example of Mother Teresa, many women would not have been legitimized to write. Likewise, her texts would not have gained such widespread popularity if women did not read and integrate her ideas into their own expressions and experiences of Catholicism and convent life.

   As the example of Teresa of Avila suggests, the Counter-Reformation convent quickly became the primary institution for women's education throughout Spain, Portugal, and the Iberian Atlantic. Although we are only beginning to appreciate the scope and importance of women's participation in literary culture, and issues such as manuscript circulation and familial literary production have not yet been studied at length, numerous women writers from the period are known to us today.[21] Most lived in convents and only a minority wrote for literary salons or the book market. The convent emerges as a crucial site for women's educational and literary history, given that most female textual production occurred within that setting on both sides of the Iberian Atlantic. While most nuns wrote for religious audiences, some addressed a broader public. Women outside convent walls produced fiction for the emerging book market; plays to be performed in the public theaters; and testimonies, auto/biographies, treatises, conduct manuals, poetry, and letters. Convent and other texts were destined for a range of readers that included noblewomen and men, inquisitors, confessors, convent sisters, family members, and friends.

Table 1 presents more than fifty of the early modern Iberian women whose work as cultural actors is traceable today through their texts. The table delineates the genres cultivated by women and describes the contexts in which the authors lived and wrote. The handful of sixteenth-century writers known to have been active before the entrance of women in larger numbers into the writing field are included here to give an indication of the dearth of traceable activity before the 1580–1700 period.[22] Given the fast rate at which research in the field of early modern women's literary history continues to evolve, the list is not comprehensive. Instead, it provides an overview of women from early modern Spain and Portugal, which was under Spanish control between 1580 and 1640, and aims to highlight women who have been studied in recent scholarship on women's literary and intellectual history as well as those whose work remains understudied.[23]

Table 1. Women's textual production in Iberia (1500–1700)[24]

Name	Description
Abarca de Bolea, Ana Francisca (1602–1680s)	Cistercian nun in the Real Monasterio de Santa María in Huesca; of Aragonese noble stock; poet; author of fiction and non-fiction, including the pastoral novel *Vigil and Octavary of Saint John the Baptist* (Vigilia y octavario de San Juan Bautista, 1679).
Agreda, María de Jesús de (Madre) (1602–65)*	Conceptionist nun; author of *The Mystical City of God* (La mística ciudad de Dios, 1670); spiritual adviser and correspondent of King Philip IV.

Table 1.   (*Continued*)

Name	Description
Ana de Jesús (Sor) (b. late 1500s)	Nun in Convento de la Encarnación in Granada; author of *Birth and Upbringing of doña Isabel de Avalós, Also Known as Isabel de la Cruz, and Other Nuns' Vidas from the Same Convent* (Nacimiento, y crianza de Doña Isabel de Avalos, y por otro nombre Isabel de la Cruz … con algunas vidas de otras religiosas, 1629).
Ana de San Bartolomé (Madre) (1549–1626)*	Discalced Carmelite; close associate of Teresa of Avila; self-trained scribe; beatified in 1917; author of *vida*, letters, and *Defense of Teresian Inheritance* (Defensa de la herencia teresiana, 1621–3).
Angela María de la Concepción (Sor) (b. 1600s)	Trinitarian Recollect nun; author of *Spiritual Waters for New Plants* (Riego espiritual para nuevas plantas, 1686).
Azevedo, Angela de (c. 1600–?)	Lisbon-born playwright; served in Philip IV's court.
Beatriz de Jesús (Sor) (d. 1636)	Born Beatriz Ovalle y Ahumada. Niece of Teresa of Avila. Prioress of Convento de Santa Ana in Madrid. Author of letters.
Bernal, Beatriz (b. 1500s)*	Born in Valladolid; author of chivalric novel *Don Cristalián of Spain* (Don Cristalián de España, 1545).
Buesso, Eugenia (b. 1600s)	Author of *Account of the Running of the Bulls in the Imperial City of Zaragoza in Honor of His Majesty* (Relación de la corrida de toros, que la Imperial ciudad de Zaragoza hizo en obsequio a Su Alteza, Zaragoza, 1669).
Caro Mallén de Soto, Ana (c. 1600–?)*	Professional playwright and poet; author of *Valor, Affront, Woman* (*Valor, agravio y mujer*) and *Count Partinuplés* (El conde Partinuplés).
Carvajal, Mariana de (c.1610–?)*	Author of novella collection *Christmas in Madrid* (Navidades de Madrid, 1663); widow and mother of nine.
Carvajal y Mendoza, Luisa de (1566–1614)*	Noblewoman of Mendoza family; author of poems, letters, and prose. Died in England.
Castro y Egas, Ana (b. late 1500s?)	Author of biography of Philip III: *Eternity of the King don Philip III, Our Lord, the Pious* (Eternidad del Rey don Felipe Tercero, Nuestro Señor, el Piadoso, 1629).
Catalina de Jesús (Sor) (1639–77)	Poor Clare nun; wrote autobiography; founded a girls' school.

Table 1. (*Continued*)

Name	Description
Cecilia del Nacimiento (Sor) (1570–1646)*	Discalced Carmelite nun; writer and translator.
Cerda y Sandoval, Catalina de la (Condesa de Lemos) (1580–1648)	Daughter of Catalina de Zúñiga y Sandoval and Duke of Lerma, Francisco Gómes de Sandoval y Rojas. Entered Convento de Franciscanas Descalzas de Santa Clara de Monforte in 1633 upon widowhood. Took name of Catalina de la Concepción. Author of letters.
Cueva y Silva, Leonor de la (b. 1600s)	Author of plays and poetry.
Enríquez de Guzmán, Feliciana (b. 1500s)	Playwright from Seville who wrote *Tragicomedy* (Tragicomedia) and *The Sabeos Gardens and Fields* (Los jardines y campos Sabeos, 1624).
Erauso, Catalina de (1592?–1650)*	Basque nun who left convent; lived as a man in Latin America; returned to Europe; received dispensation from pope to live as a man; some believe her to be author of *The Lieutenant Nun* (Vida i sucesos de la monja alférez), which was discovered only in the eighteenth century and perhaps is a forged memoir. She died in the Americas.
Estefanía de la Encarnación (Sor) (1597–1665)	Poor Clare nun; author of her *vida*, which she illustrated beautifully.
Feliciana de San José (Madre) (b. late 1500s?)	Discalced Carmelite in Zaragoza; author of *Instruction of Religious Women* (Instrucción de religiosas, 1654).
Ferreira de Lacerda, Bernarda (Sor) (1595 or 1596–1644)	Discalced Carmelite in Lisbon's San Alberto convent; poet and chronicler; author of *Liberated Hispania* (Hespaña libertada, 1618) and *Solitudes of Buzaço* (Soledades de Buzaço, 1634).
Francisca de los Apóstoles (b. 1539)*	Established community of *beatas* with her sister, Isabel, and was tried by Inquisition; author of letters.
Francisca de Santa Teresa (Sor) (1654–1709)	Trinitarian Discalced nun; poet; author of numerous plays and colloquies.
Guevara, María de (b. 1600s–1683)*	Noblewoman, biographer, author of advice manuals.
Hipólita de Jesús y Rocaberti (Madre) (b. 1600s)	Dominican nun, author of spiritual treatises.

Table 1.   (*Continued*)

Name	Description
Inés del Santísimo Sacramento (Madre) (b. 1500s)	Augustinian Recollect in Convento de San Juan Bautista de la villa de Arenas; collaborated with Isabel de Jesús to write that nun's life story: *Life Account of the Venerable Mother Isabel de Jesús* (Vida de la venerable madre Isabel de Jesús).
Isabel de Jesús (Madre)* (1586–1648)	Joined Augustinian Recollect convent upon widowhood; illiterate; dictated her autobiography to Inés del Santísimo Sacramento.
Isabel de la Madre de Dios (Sor) (1614–87)	Augustinian Recollect; niece of Isabel de Jesús; wrote *Manifestations* (Manifestaciones)*;* founder of convents in Serradilla and Calzada de Oropesa.
Jerónima de la Ascensión (Sor) (b. 1600s?)	Poor Clare nun in Tudela de Navarra; possible author of *Spiritual Exercises* (Exercicios, 1661)
Liaño, Isabel de (b. 1500s)	Author of epic poem in honour of Saint Catherine of Siena published in Valladolid, 1604.
Lucía de Jesús (Sor) (1601?–1653)	Author of *vida; beata,* Madrid.
Magdalena de Jesús (Sor) (b. late 1600s)	Poor Clare nun in Pamplona; author of *Orders and Rules for the Convent of Our Mother Saint Clare of the City of Pamplona* (1722).
Magdalena de San Jerónimo (Madre) (b. 1500s)	Jeronymite nun; author of treatise on women's prisons titled *Reason and Form of the Galley and Royal House* (Razón y forma de la galera y casa real, 1608).
Manuel, Bernarda (c. 1616–?)	Merchant-class mother convicted of judaizing. Author of self-defence for Inquisition case.
Marcela de San Félix (Sor) (1605–88)*	Discalced Trinitarian; playwright; poet; daughter of Lope de Vega.
María de la Antigua (Sor) (1566–1617)*	Poor Clare in Villa de Marchena; author of her *vida* and of *Disenchantment of Religious Men and Women* (Desengaño de religiosos, 1678).
María de la Ascensión (Sor) (d. 1679)	*Beata* in Madrid in the order of Nuestra Señora del Carmen. Subject of *vida* with possible autobiographical excerpts.
María de San Alberto (Madre) (1568–1640)*	Discalced Carmelite; author; translator; highly skilled humanist.

Table 1.   (*Continued*)

Name	Description
María de San José Salazar (Madre) (1548–1603)*	Discalced Carmelite; prolific writer who worked with Teresa of Avila; author of *Book for the Hour of Recreation* (Libro de recreaciones).
Mariana de Jesús (Sor) (b. late 1500s)	Franciscan nun in Convento de San Antonio, Trujillo; author of *Pure Mirror of the Life, Death, and Resurrection of Christ* (Espejo purísimo de la vida, muerte, y resurrección de Christo, 1617).
Mariana Francisca de los Angeles (Madre)(1637–97)	Born Mariana Francisca Blázquez Merino. Founder of Convento de Carmelitas Descalzas de Santa Teresa de Jesús in Madrid. Author of her *vida*.
Mariana de San José (Madre) (1568–1638)	Born Mariana de Manzanedo Maldonado. Augustinian nun in Monasterio de la Encarnación in Madrid. Wrote her *vida*.
María de Santa Isabel (Sor) (a.k.a. Marcia Belisarda) (b. 1600s?)*	Conceptionist nun in Convento real de la Concepción in Toledo; wrote lyrical and spiritual poetry under pseudonym of Marcia Belisarda; her work was not published during her life.
Meneses, Juana (b. 1600s)	Author of *Alerting of the Soul, to the Dream of Life* (Despertador del Alma, al Sueño de la Vida, Lisbon, 1695). Wrote under pseudonym Apolinario de Almada.
Meneses, Leonor de (c. 1620–64)	Lisbon-born author of novella collection *The Firmest Disdained One* (El desdeñado más firme, 1665).
Morillas Sobrino, Cecilia (1539–81)	Educated her nine children, who included María de San Alberto and Cecilia del Nacimiento, with a focus on humanism and art.
Navas, María de(1666–?)	Actress born in Milan and active in Spanish theatre; probably not the author of the short biography attributed to her: *Manifestation of María de Navas, the Actress* (Manifesto de María de Navas, la comedianta, Lisbon, 1695).
Nieto de Aragón, María (b. 1600s?)	Poet; author of celebratory poem dedicated to her friend Violante de Ribera y Pinta and written for Philip IV's wedding to Mariana de Austria: *Nuptial Song for the Happy Nuptials of the King, our Lord* (Epitalamio a las felicíssimas bodas del rey nuestro señor, n.d.)

Table 1. (*Continued*)

Name	Description
Orozco y Luján, María de (1635–1709)	*Beata* who wrote some 3,000 letters.
Ossorio, Constanza (c. 1565–1637)	Cistercian nun in Convento de Santa María de las Dueñas, Seville; author of advice manual for clerics: *Garden of the Celestrial Spouse* (Huerto del celestial esposo, 1686).
Padilla Manrique, Luisa María de (1590–1646)	Noblewoman; author of instructional treatises for the nobility.
Pinelo, Valentina (b. 1500s)	Augustinian nun in Convento de San Leandro, Sevilla; author of biography of Saint Anne: *Book of the Praises and Excellencies of the Glorious Saint Anne* (Libro de las alabanzas y excelencias de la gloriosa Santa Anna, 1601).
Ramírez de Guzmán, Catalina Clara (1611– after 1633)*	Noblewoman; prolific poet who wrote about domestic, familial, and social themes.
Sabuco, Oliva (1567–?)*	Philosopher and author of natural-science treatises in Latin and Spanish, including *New Philosophy of Human Nature Not Known and Not Reached by the Ancient Philosophers That Improves Human Life and Health* (Nueva Filosofía de la Naturaleza del Hombre, no conocida ni alcanzada por los grandes Filósofos antiguos, la cual mejora la Vida y la Salud humana, Madrid, 1587).
Sallent, Mariana (Sor) (b. 1600s)	Poor Clare nun; poet; author of *Life of Our Seraphic Mother Saint Clare* (Vida de nuestra seráfica madre Santa Clara, Zaragoza, 1700).
Sallent, Teresa (Sor) a (unknown)	Mariana Sallent's sister. Author of poem that appears in Sor Mariana's *Life of Our Seraphic Mother Saint Clare.*
Souza, Joana Theodora de (Sor) (b. late 1600s)	Playwright born in Lisbon who lived in Lisbon's Monasterio de la Rosa; author of one known play, *The Great Prodigy* (El gran prodigio, n.d.)
Teresa de Jesús (Santa) (1515–82)*	A.k.a. Saint Teresa of Avila; founder of Discalced Carmelite order; influential mystic, reformer, and writer.
Teresa de Jesús María (Sor) (1592–?)	Discalced Carmelite who wrote about convent life.

Table 1.   (*Concluded*)

Name	Description
Valle de la Cerda, Teresa (b. late 1500s)	Aristocratic founder of Benedictine convent of La Encarnación Bendita de San Plácido; author of letters written to Inquisition during her trial for demonic possession and false revelations.
Vela y Cueto, María (Sor) (1561–1617)	Cistercian nun; author of her *vida*.
Violante de la Concepción (Sor) (Dates unknown)	Discalced nun in Convento de Carmen de las Descalzas, Granada; author of an account (relación) written for confessor, probably in the seventeenth century.
Violante do Ceo, (Sor) (1601 or 1607–93)	Dominican nun from Lisbon's Monasterio de la Rosa; bilingual poet; author of *Lusitanian Parnassus* (Parnaso lusitano, posthumously published 1733).
Zayas y Sotomayor, María de (1590–?)*	Popular novella author; poet; playwright; author of *Enchantments of Love* (Novelas amorosas y ejemplares, 1637); *Disenchantments of Love* (Desengaños amorosos, 1647); and *Friendship Betrayed* (Traición en la amistad, 1620s or 1630s).
Zúñiga y Sandoval, Catalina de la (d. 1628)	Lady-in-waiting to Ana de Austria. Married Fernando Ruiz de Castro Andrade y Portugal, VI Count of Lemos. Author of letters.

*Asterisk indicates authors available either partially or entirely in English translation

In addition to surveying women's textual production in early modern Spain and Portugal, this partial list of women whose texts have survived provides a guideline for understanding literacy at a time when no formal educational systems existed for women. It demonstrates that the wealthy and noble classes valued female education within convents, and, as will be discussed, within converso culture. Notoriously difficult to estimate, women's literacy for the period 1550–1700 recently has been recalculated to range from 0 per cent in rural areas to as high as 40 per cent in urban settings. In formulating such statistics, which differ significantly from the highest mark of 25 per cent previously attributed to urban women, Pedro Cátedra and Anastasio Rojo have argued convincingly that previous measures of literacy, based solely on the ability to sign one's name, reveal little about individuals' relationship to the written word because reading and writing were taught as separate skills.[25] Similarly, inventories of women's libraries suggest that aristocratic women owned, whether or not they read, religious texts (including devotional and prayer books), fiction (for example, Boccaccio and the anonymous *Amadis of Gaul)*, philosophy (such as Aristotle), and recipe books.[26] Women of less wealth also owned books, thus suggesting that the ability to read, if not to write, was valued across a larger swath of the population than we previously could measure. Indeed, Cátedra and Rojo describe reading as a skill that allowed young women access to certain trades and to higher social status. They also provide evidence of literate wives having illiterate husbands. The emphasis on teaching women across class lines to read suggests the possibility that female literacy may have been viewed as an advantage when contracting marriage.[27]

The diversity of texts owned by women finds its complement in the wide range of texts produced by women. Broadly speaking, texts by women or those that purport to represent women's words were produced both inside and outside the convent for literary, political, spiritual, and personal reasons. Such texts were written for both *intramuros* and *extramuros* readers. Other venues in which texts were created include inquisitional tribunals (which generated depositions, trial records, and the occasional first-person autobiographical text) and the legal framework of the courts (both secular and ecclesiastical), in which women's claims and arguments appear as part of the records. In many cases, including inquisitional, legal, and even hagiographical texts, scribes and biographers controlled the presentation of women's stories. Questions of control, access, and representation are thus extraordinarily complicated for this corpus of mediated texts.

Traditional literature (such as drama, poetry, and prose fiction) also presents its own set of generic conventions. In terms of extramuros literary production, Spain had few women who published their work for the book market in the early modern period, and all of them came from the wealthy, if not aristocratic, classes. The group includes Spain's first known professional woman writer, poet and playwright Ana Caro Mallén de Soto (c. 1600–?), who was commissioned to produce work for the city of Seville. Three prose fiction writers published novella collections: Mariana de Carvajal (c.1610–?), Leonor de Meneses (c. 1620–64), and María de Zayas y Sotomayor (1590–?). Moreover, five women (Azevedo, Caro, Cueva y Silva, Enríquez de Guzmán, and Zayas) also wrote dramatic texts that seem to have been intended for public performance. With few examples preceding them – only a handful of women are known to

have written for public consumption in the sixteenth century – these
women constitute the first cohort to bring women's writing to the Spanish public.

Like their sisters throughout Europe, this group worked within and
against a literary tradition that excluded and often denigrated women.
Perhaps operating with an awareness of each other's work and bound by
a desire to insert women's issues into literary tradition, they fashioned
self-consciously female-centred texts and participated in the evolving
debate on the worth and ability of women by rewriting literary history
to include women.[28] Of the works produced for the public stage or the
book market by these novelists and dramatists, every known text ad-
dresses what today we might call 'women's issues' – marriage, motherhood, sexuality, friendship – as well as anxiety about authorship. With
few exceptions, women's relationships dominate the plots and thematics
of much of this literary production.[29] Critics almost unanimously agree
that, while the authors worked within the literary conventions of their
time, they also brought a distinctive, if not decidedly female, perspective
to bear on discourse otherwise controlled by men.[30]

A striking example of this female perspective is the woman-centred
revision of the Don Juan myth in Ana Caro's play *Valor, Affront, Woman*,
in which a female protagonist cross-dresses to take vengeance upon her
infamous spurned lover. In fashioning herself into a man, the main character also mimics the language of conquest and successfully competes
with Don Juan for the love of another woman. Similarly, María de Zayas
explicitly engages violence against women in *Enchantments of Love* and
Disenchantments of Love, a popular two-volume novella collection that de-
nounces women's lack of access to the justice system and to education.
The *Disenchantments* in particular showcases the mistreatment of women
by men. After numerous female characters fall victim to their male relatives and lovers, the protagonist, Lisis, retreats to a convent with her
mother and a friend. Such an ending would have come as a surprise to
seventeenth-century readers, since novella collections almost inevitably
culminated with marriages. Yet the narrator hails the resolution as the
best possible outcome because the protagonist refuses to 'subject herself
to anyone.'[31] The emphasis on women's lives and experiences in Zayas
is echoed by the theme of female friendship and the aesthetic of domes-
ticity in Mariana de Carvajal's novella collection, *Christmas in Madrid,*
which takes place in the lavishly decorated home of a recently widowed
mother.[32] Both collections emphasize female networks, as suggested by
the women's withdrawal to the convent in Zayas's *Disenchantments* and by

Carvajal's depiction of widows working together to arrange successful marriages for their children.

The focus on women in nearly every female-authored play and fictional text written for the stage or the book market during the late sixteenth and seventeenth centuries provides a core of issues and strategies of representation that can help us examine other examples of women's self-representation in the period. Book-market literature can be used to make an initial assessment of the influence of gender on women's strategies, ideologies, and, in some cases, personal experience. Tropes of humility – what Barbara Diefendorf describes in the present volume as the 'rhetoric of submission' – abound in the texts. Zayas and Carvajal, for instance, both position themselves as women writers in their prefaces, calling on readers to forgive the errors of their 'scribbles' (Zayas) or the 'abortion of their limited wit' (Carvajal) and urging them to read the texts in spite of their female identities.[33]

The reliance on humility as a primary mode of expression draws on the writing strategies of Teresa of Avila, who relied heavily on colloquialisms, self-denigrating statements, and claims to ignorance. Alison Weber's analysis of the Discalced Carmelite's unusual writing style as a self-consciously manipulative 'rhetoric of femininity' has effected a major shift in our understanding of Mother Teresa's brilliant autobiographical texts and theological treatises.[34] As suggested by Diefendorf in her contribution to the present volume, Weber's revolutionary work has helped scholars understand the strategies at work in other Catholic women's texts. Certainly, Saint Teresa's daughters throughout the Iberian Atlantic used that rhetorical strategy to draw on Christian piety and femininity.[35] This in turn provided a legitimate position from which women could present their work to readers.

In combination with women fiction writers' focus on female allegiances and affective lives, the sophisticated discursive strategies afforded women an authorized stance from which they could speak and write. Whether the emphasis on humility was more prevalent in Hispanic women's writing than in other literary or religious traditions has not yet been studied. We do know, though, that throughout the Catholic world, women writers employed rhetorical strategies such as those used by Teresa of Avila. Indeed, in spite of the varied circumstances in which convent, Inquisition, and secular records and texts were produced, women who wrote or whose words were recorded in those contexts often relied on a specifically Christian conceptualization of female identity as a means to legitimate themselves as intellectuals.

Transatlantic Ties: Women's Writing in Spanish America (1600–1800)

The connections between Saint Teresa and her sisters across the Atlantic can best be understood in terms of their shared religious context, since almost all Spanish American women's writing that is known to us was produced in convents or by women with religious affiliations until the nineteenth century. Nuns in Spanish America wrote treatises, letters, instructional texts, poetry, plays, biography, and autobiography. Notable for their diversity of race and class, the first cohort of writing sisters and subjects in Spanish America hailed from European, indigenous, and, in one known case, subcontinental Indian backgrounds. In particular, geographic diversity characterizes this group. While many came from Mexico City and its environs, others lived in colonial centres in Peru, Chile, and Colombia. Table 2 delineates the religious affiliations, ethnicities, and nationalities of authors who contributed to the first boom in women's writing in the Iberian Atlantic.[36] Given the emerging nature of the field of colonial women's literary and historical studies, it is impossible to include all women in this list. As such, the table shares with its peninsular counterpart an emphasis on women writers who have figured in recent scholarship and about whom we have evidence of textual production either by the women themselves or as transcribed by someone else.

Table 2. Women and textual production in Spanish America (1066–1800)[37]

Name	Description
Agustina de Saint Teresa (Sor) (b. late 1500s)	Conceptionist nun in Puebla; author of biography of María de Jesús de Tomellín del Campo (1630).
Antonia Lucía del Espíritu Santo (Madre) (1646–1709)*	Discalced Carmelite Nazarene nun in Peru whose prophetic vision was recorded by her spiritual daughter, Josefa de la Providencia, in *Account of the Origin and Foundation of the Monastery of the San Joaquín of Nazarene Nuns* (Relación de la fundación del monasterio del Señor San Joaquín de Religiosas Nazareñas, 1793).
Apolonia de la Santísima Trinidad (Sor) (1700s)	Cacique Corpus Christi nun in Mexico City whose life is described in *Notes on Various Lives of Religious Women* (Apuntes de varias vidas de las religiosas).

Table 2.   (*Continued*)

Name	Description
Beatriz de las Vírgenes (Sor) (1583–1645)	Nun in Convento de Santa Catalina in Mexico City who wrote convent chronicle.
Castillo, Francisca Josefa de la Concepción de (Madre) (1671–1742)*	Poor Clare nun in Tunja, New Granada; author of an autobiographical *vida* and spiritual texts such as *Spiritual Affects* (Afectos espirituales) and *The Notebook of Enciso* (El cuaderno de Enciso).
Catarina de San Juan (c. 1607–88)*	Visionary from New Delhi who lived most of her life in Peru; subject of several biographies; known as 'the Asian from Puebla' (la china poblana).
Echegaray, Bárbara de (b. 1700s)	Tried in 1797 for illuminism (*alumbrismo*); purportedly asked confessor to write her *vida*.
Francisca de la Natividad (Sor) (b. 1600s)	Criolla Carmelite nun in the convent of Saint Teresa de Puebla; author of her *vida* in 1630s.
Francisca de los Angeles (Sor) (b. late 1600s)	Visionary *beata* from Querétaro who wrote numerous letters between 1689 and 1736; investigated by Inquisition.
Francisca Josefa de la Concepción (Madre) (1671–1742)	Columbian Conceptionist nun; author of her *vida* (published in 1817) and of lyrical and spiritual poetry included in *Spiritual Affects* (Afectos espirituales).
Gerónima Nava y Saavedra (Madre) (1669–1727)	A.k.a. Gerónima del Espíritu Santo; Poor Clare visionary from Bogotá whose visions were transcribed.
Isabel de la Encarnación (Sor) (c. 1596–1633)	Discalced Carmelite in the Convento de San Joseph de la Puebla de los Angeles; author of letters to her confessor; spiritual teacher to Catarina de San Juan.
Josefa de la Providencia (Madre) (b. 1700s)*	Discalced Carmelite Nazarene nun in Peru; author of *Account of the Origin and Foundation of the Monastery of San Joaquín of Nazarene Nuns* (Relación del origen y fundación del monasterio del señor San Joaquín de Religiosas Nazarenas, 1793).
Juana Inés de la Cruz (Sor) (1648–95)*	Influential Baroque author; Hieronymite nun in Mexico City; author of poems, plays, *La respuesta/The Answer.*
Juana Inés de Maldonado y Paz (Sor) (1598–1666)	Guatemalan Conceptionist nun; author of *Entertainment in Honor of the Flight to Egypt* (Entretenimiento en obsequio de la huida a Epipto).

Table 2. (*Continued*)

Name	Description
María Anna Agueda de San Ignacio (Madre) (1695–1756)*	Criolla Dominican nun in Puebla; author of prayers, mystical theological treatises, and instructional texts, including: *Devotion in Honor of the Purest Milk with which the Child Jesus Was Nourished* (Devoción en honra de la Purísima Leche con que fue alimentado el Niño Jesús) and *Sea of Grace which the Highest Passed on to Most Holy Mary, Mother of the Word Incarnate in the Purest Milk of Her Virginal Breasts* (Mar de gracias que comunicó el Altísimo a María Santísima, Madre del Verbo Humanado en la leche purísima de sus virginales pechos).
María Coleta de San José (Sor) (d. 1776)	Poor Clare nun in Mexico; author of some four hundred pages of letters that tell her life story.
María de Jesús (Sor) (1579–1637)	Carmelite nun in Puebla known as a mystic.
María de Jesús Felipa (Sor) (b. 1700s)	Poor Clare nun in convent of San Juan de la Penitencia, Mexico City; author of spiritual diares.
María de Jesús (Sor) (d. after 1767)	Colombian Discalced Carmelite; author of writings included in *History of the Monastery of the Discalced Carmelites of San José de Bogotá* (Historia del monasterio de Carmelitas Descalzas de San José de Bogotá, 1947).
María de Jesús Tomellín del Campo (Sor) (1574–1637)	Conceptionist nun in Puebla who took vows in 1599; subject of *vida* written by her cellmate, Agustina de Santa Teresa; spiritual teacher to Catarina de San Juan.
María de San José (Madre) (1656–1719)*	Augustinian Criolla nun in Puebla and Oaxaca; author of some two thousand pages that include her 1645 *vida*.
María Felipa de Jesús (Madre) (b. 1700s)*	First Indian prioress of Corpus Christi; descended from Aztec warrior princess; biography in *Notes on Various Lives of Religious Women* (Apuntes de varias vidas de las religiosas).
María Josefa Lina de la Santísima Trinidad (Madre) (b. ~1741)	Founder of Conceptionist Convento de la Purísima Concepción in San Miguel de Allende; a controversy surrounding her leadership led to questionnaires being distributed to nuns.

Table 2.   (*Concluded*)

Name	Description
María Magdalena Lorravaquio Muñoz (Madre) (1576–1636)*	Hieronymite mystic nun in Mexico City who spent forty-three years in bed; wrote her *vida*.
María Magdalena de Jesús (Sor) (b. 1700s)*	Cacique Corpus Christi nun in Mexico City described in *Notes on Various Lives of Religious Women* (Apuntes de varias vidas de las religiosas); earned reputation as a fine nurse.
María Manuela de Santa Ana (Sor) (1700s)	Nun in the Convent of Santa Rosa in Lima, Peru. Author of a *vida* and correspondence.
María Marcela (Madre) (1759–18–)*	Capuchine nun in Querétaro; author of *vida* about contemplative life.
María Rosa (Madre) (Born Josefa de León y Ayala Muñoz) (Spain 1660–Lima 1716)*	Capuchine nun who, with four other sisters, sailed to the Americas to found convent in Peru. Author of *Account of the Journey of Five Capuchine Nuns Who Traveled from their Convents in Madrid to Found the Convent of Jesus, Mary, and Joseph in Lima* (1722).
Mariana de la Encarnación (Sor) (1571–1657)*	Discalced Carmelite nun in Mexico City; author of a partially autobiographical chronicle: *Account of the Foundation of the Ancient Convent of Saint Teresa* (Relación de la fundación del Convento Antiguo de Santa Teresa), which details previous nuns' struggles.
Medinilla, María Estrada de (1600s)	Author of lengthy lyric poems, including *Account of the Happy Entrance in Mexico of Marquis of Villena* (Relación de la feliz entrada en México del marqués de Villena, 1641).
Rosa de Lima (Santa) (1586–1617)*	Mystic Criolla Dominican nun in Lima; canonized in 1671; author of letters, *Angelic Exercise* (Exercicio angélico), and other texts; subject of numerous *vidas* and canonization documents.
Sebastiana de las Vírgenes (Madre) (1671–1737)	Conceptionist nun in Mexico City; author of her *vida* and notes to her confessor.
Sebastiana Josefa de la Santísima Trinidad (Sor) (1709–57)	Born in Mexico City; expelled from Convent of Corpus Christi but allowed to enter Convent of San Juan de la Penitencia; authored spiritual diaries and letters; subject of posthumous biography.
Suárez, Úrsula (Sor) (1666–1749)*	Chilean Franciscan mystic; author of *Autobiographical Account* (Relación autobiográfica).
Teodora de San Agustín (Madre) (1700s)*	Nun in ascetic Corpus Christi Convent of Mexico City; author of letters to archbishop, viceroy, soldiers.

*Available either partially or entirely in English translation

Throughout Spanish America, convents reflected the racial and class politics of the broader society. Non-white women could not become nuns of the black veil; that is, they could not profess in the same way as other women. Families paid dowries for their daughters' entrance into convents, in which, as Stacey Schlau explains, 'servants and slaves came from the same races and ethnic groups as those who served secular patrons: Indians, Africans, mestizas, and mulatas.'[38] While literacy or a prized skill could help a poor woman gain entrance to convents, such institutions primarily housed elite women (usually Criollas) and operated according to internal hierarchies that mirrored the outside world. Many tensions necessarily existed within this structure: governed on a macrocosmic level by the all-male hierarchy of the Catholic Church, women religious nonetheless found opportunities for leadership, economic decision making, and education that gave them privileges unavailable to their 'secular' sisters. By the same token, few, if any, convents in the Catholic world remained completely closed off from secular society: on both sides of the Atlantic, the comings and goings of servants, visitors, donors, and male clerics formed a necessary part of everyday convent life in most instances.

Convents provided important links to the spiritual world for many who lived extramuros. As Kathryn Burns has demonstrated in *Colonial Habits: Convents and the Spiritual Economy of Cuzco, Peru,* nuns engaged in economic, spiritual, and cultural activities that benefited the larger community. In the case studied by Burns, the money-lending nuns offered an important economic service to the colonial city of Cuzco.[39] Sor Juana Inés de la Cruz (1648–95) provides another salient example of a woman who took advantage of the relative intellectual and spiritual independence that convents afforded women. Sor Juana followed in Teresa of Avila's footsteps by positioning herself as a powerful intellectual model for Catholic women in the transatlantic context. Like her foremother, she worked within the church for reform of female monasticism. Similarly, hers was a counter-reform aimed at dismantling post-Tridentine restrictions on women's spirituality and roles within the church.

Whereas Teresa of Avila established a new Catholic order and wrote theological texts in the guise of spiritual treatises and autobiographical texts, Juana Inés de la Cruz wrote literature as well as a complex philosophical defence of religious women's right to pursue intellectual endeavours. This defence, known as *The Answer* (La respuesta), directly attests to the transatlantic links between Spanish and Spanish American women's intellectual history. The controversial text was a response to the bishop of Puebla's attack on her *Crisis of a Sermon* [*Crisis de un ser-*

món], later titled *The Letter Worthy of Athena* (La carta Atenagórica). Upon publishing Sor Juana's original critique, the bishop adopted a female pseudonym (previously used by Saint Frances of Sales) to scold the nun for daring to attack a famous sermon. In response, Sor Juana wrote *The Answer* in 1691. A controversy between the nun and the church leadership ensued, and that same controversy created a sustained interest in the project that eventually led to its publication in Spain in 1700.

While humanism, convent foundations, and Tridentine reforms effected a shift in women's education and writing in late-sixteenth-century Spain, Sor Juana's incursions into writing at the end of the seventeenth century similarly marked the beginning of a writing tradition for women in Spanish America. Indeed, more than any other woman's text besides those of Saint Teresa, *The Answer* bridges women's writing between early modern Spain and colonial Spanish America. Perhaps the most notable link appears in the author's vehement defence of spiritual women's need for education; she mentions Teresa of Avila four times and makes numerous references to other Carmelite authors, including María de San José (Salazar) (1548–1603), María de Agreda (1602–65), and María de la Antigua (1566–1617). Similarly, the rhetoric of humility employed throughout the text was identical to that of other women writers in the Catholic world who spoke of their intellectual abilities in modest terms. Echoing María de Zayas, Mariana de Carvajal, and Teresa of Avila herself, Sor Juana describes her complex theological and philosophical argumentation as but a 'trifle' and a 'simple account.'[40]

As a text grounded in European philosophical, theological, literary, and scientific discourses and written with Spanish and Spanish American nobles, bourgeois, and ecclesiastics in mind, *The Answer* exemplifies the close ties between Spanish America and Europe and the impossibility of separating Iberia from its Atlantic outposts when considering women's history.[41] Only recently have we begun to decipher those links. Although Sor Juana informed readers over three hundred years ago of her awareness of a transatlantic writing community of spiritual women by speaking of Saint Teresa and other Carmelites, we are just beginning to decipher the networks of readership, authorship, and ideology that linked that community.

Deciphering the Gendered Atlantic

The Answer connects the Old and New World traditions and also bridges the two waves in women's writing in the Hispanic diaspora. Linked to her writing sisters through the many mechanisms for communication among convents – including transmission of texts between Europe and the Americas – Sor Juana's writing set the stage for countless other nuns to participate in literary culture. Similar cultural contexts for women's writing throughout the empire substantially informed the literary genres and styles cultivated by women. In terms of genre, spiritual treatises, letters, convent histories, devotional guides, poetry, and autobiographical and biographical writings comprise the bulk of texts. Notably, Spanish American women did not produce prose fiction or secular drama as early or as frequently as their Spanish sisters; indeed, almost all of the writing was produced in convents and centred on religious topics. This difference in writing focus must be understood in the context of extremely low education rates outside convent settings and, crucially, the previously mentioned ban on publication of secular fiction. Convent populations in the Americas were smaller than in Europe because of the simple demographic realities of the colonies, with the result that women in Latin America did not enter the sphere of cultural production in any measurable way until the late seventeenth century. Similarly, since few women writers in seventeenth- and eighteenth-century Spanish America lived outside convents, their work was much more likely to be religious than secular. However, as a point of comparison, few convent writers in Spain produced what we might consider secular fiction, which makes a text like Ana Abarca Francisca de Bolea's pastoral novel, *Vigil and Octavary of Saint John the Baptist* (1679), somewhat of an exception among nuns' cultural production. The Spanish American corollary can be found in Juana Inés de la Cruz's secular play, *Trials of a Household* (Los empeños de una casa).

Sor Juana's playful engagement with the classical dramatic form of the *comedia* raises the possibility that other Spanish American nuns may have written fictional texts that circulated in manuscript form. We also might consider that the absence of extant fictional texts or more non-fiction produced by Spanish American women relates to a lack of a writing community that would have provided a context for an even stronger female writing tradition. Zayas and Caro in Spain praised each other's work in print, which suggests that they and other writers had access to canonical writing from the European tradition and to women's work, yet it is unclear to what extent women in the Americas had similar access to such networks.[42] Sor Juana's mention of her Discalced Carmelite sisters provides a key to begin unlocking this mystery. Such references to European women reinforce the pan-Hispanic points of reference for intellectuals in Spanish America while also emphasizing the importance of a specifically female writing tradition into which someone like Sor Juana might insert her texts.

Sor Juana's awareness of an emerging female intellectual raises the question of the degree to which Catholic rhetoric, dogma, and ideology influenced women's textual and artistic production throughout the Iberian diaspora. The diffusion of Teresa de Jesús' writing in combination with the lives of saints and other reading material common to both continents provided a direct link between women writers in Spanish America and their Spanish predecessors and contemporaries. The rhetoric of humility, which was evident in men's and women's texts alike, and themes related to convent life infused *vidas*, treatises, and letters on both sides of the Atlantic. Women wrote of convent politics and management as well as their community and personal spirituality. Themes, tropes, and rhetorical strategies centre on the tenets of Catholic femininity, which also makes it difficult to penetrate the highly controlled discourse produced by Catholic women in the period. The enactment of Catholic gender expectations in religious women's texts raises the question of what we can actually know about women's lives based on their representation of individual experiences, community histories, and familial and other interpersonal dynamics.

Like Alison Weber's earlier study of Teresa of Avila, Kathryn Joy McKnight's examination of the spiritual autobiography of the Colombian nun Madre Castillo (1671–1742) focuses on the tensions between the nun's abject self-presentation and the important role she played in her convent. As McKnight summarizes, 'Madre Castillo's construction of a spiritual subjectivity that is weak and worthless, and the violent tensions she expresses between devotion and sin, must be read against her rise to power in the convent and in contrast to the language of such documents as those she signed during three terms as abbess.'[43] The gap between the insistent rhetoric of humility and nuns' successes as agents of economic, spiritual, and educational activities appears in numerous women's biographies and autobiographies from Spain and Spanish America. The mystic Gerónima Nava y Saavedra, who had a vision of evangelizing in Asia, engages in what Stacey Schlau terms a 'gendered rhetoric of frailty' that cleverly shifts the blame for her own potential heterodoxy to her confessors.[44] Such manipulation of Catholic codes of femininity – by which women presented themselves as humble, ignorant, and chaste – infuses religious and non-religious women's writing throughout the Iberian and Spanish American Atlantic.[45]

Emblematic use of this self-conscious manipulation of Catholic femininity appears in Nava y Saavedra's self-representation as well as in the corpus of letters and biographies by and about María de Orozco y Luján, a seventeenth-century *beata* from Madrid. As told to us in several biographies written by her confessors, Orozco was a rebellious young woman whose demonic visions and erratic behaviour led to her ouster from a religious girls' school and from a convent. She later refashioned herself – in a seemingly self-conscious way – as a pious, non-sexual, self-sacrificing woman. This specifically religious femininity – crafted with the lives of saints in mind – is reflected in biographical and autobiographical texts about her, including one that mentions what she purportedly told the numerous suitors who, attracted by her piety, wanted to marry her: 'You should know that he who marries me will take with him a good prize – a woman with four marks against her, the worst in the world: [I am] old, ugly, sick, and poor.'[46] Orozco's successful self-fashioning encapsulates the benefits women gleaned from manipulating normative Catholic femininity for their own purposes. By presenting herself in this way, Orozco managed to live as an economically independent single woman with an ever-increasing reputation for piety.

The extent to which women relied on the dominant culture's definitions of femininity is revealed in numerous inquisitional cases involving accusations as diverse as blasphemy, bigamy, sorcery, judaizing, and Illuminism. Depositions in Inquisition cases frequently reveal the impact of gendered models of Catholic piety, as the language used by women of all backgrounds often draws on that used by Fray Luis de León, Luis de Vives, and other humanists to describe 'the perfect wife.'[47] Ana Domenge, a Dominican investigated by the Barcelona Inquisition in 1610, employed this gendered rhetoric in the description of her mystical visions, which were cast almost exclusively in terms of her unique relationship with Christ the husband.[48] The same language was used by men in their efforts to glorify female spirituality, as seen in the case of Catarina de San Juan, who became known as 'la china poblana' (the Asian girl from Puebla), as discussed in Ulrike Strasser and Michelle Molina's chapter in the present volume. Catarina's biographer attempted to elevate her to sainthood by emphasizing her chastity vis-à-vis scurrilous pirates and even a lustful Christ figure who purportedly was frustrated in his attempts to woo the young woman.[49]

Like many texts written by men about women, Inquisition records, literary sources, letters, and diaries by women confirm that the Christian view of femininity dominated the representation of women throughout

the Iberian Atlantic. The examples we can glean from women's texts rei-
fy the idealization of femininity seen in texts written by clerics and male
authors, and they therefore confirm that it is difficult, if not impossible,
to determine the extent to which pressures to comply with normative
Christian femininity also influenced women's experiences. Moments of
textual specificity, which range from defendants' references to friend-
ships to women writers' emphasis on motherhood to Sor Juana's highly
controlled presentation of herself as a victim and also as a person able
to transcend control over her intellectual endeavours, offer the opportunity to explore whether some texts allow us closer access to women's experiences than to their self-conscious manipulation of those experiences
to meet the expectations of readers, inquisitors, or others for whom the
texts were fashioned. In this sense, the history of emotion marks an area
that has not yet been mined fully with regard to such fraught historical documents as Inquisition records, hagiography, and other texts informed by formulaic rhetoric and structural restrictions.

The evidence we can glean so far from women's cultural production
and records of their words, including those in problematic genres such
as inquisitional records or spiritual autobiographies, suggests that codes
of Catholic femininity influenced women's self-representation in consis-
tent and often homogenizing ways. Whether women in similar situations,
geographical locations, and time periods also experienced the culture of
control of the Spanish empire in these ways has yet to be determined.
The commonalities found in sources produced by and about women of
different class, ethnic, and religious backgrounds suggest that the gender ideology of the dominant culture was so powerful that it created
pressure for women to conform to similar norms and thereby influenced
the choices many women made when writing fictional or non-fictional
and secular or religious texts, as well as when speaking in contexts in
which their words were recorded.

The dozens of women writers who have come to the fore confirm that,
as women were positioned as a group unto themselves by shifting definitions of purity of blood, race, and ethnicity, many responded by manipulating dominant beliefs to their own advantage and incorporating
those beliefs into their behaviours and choices. Influenced by rhetoric,
policies, and practices that depicted women as dangerous and unreli-
able, women on both sides of the Atlantic engaged those ideas to their
benefit. Like the nuns' successful incursions into economic activities in
colonial Cuzco, Sor Violante's flaunting of female friendship as superior
to American silver and gold, and Sor Juana's dressing down of male su-

periors' attempts to control her intellectualism, countless other women from early modern Spain and colonial Spanish America manipulated the gender codes imposed on them by both church and state. Acknowledging the extensive evidence for women's self-conscious responses to restrictive gender codes in turn opens up a new vantage point on the Atlantic world.

Women's cultural production clearly demonstrates that Old World views about gender and religion linked New World women to their Iberian sisters in complex and often sophisticated ways. As Spanish American nuns followed their Spanish sisters' examples in writing, reform, and leadership, they simultaneously forged links that informed and reshaped the Atlantic community. On the macro scale, educated women's experiences and writing had, of course, everything to do with the trade routes and imperial enterprises that have been at the centre of Atlantic history. On the micro level, though, women's roles as writers, readers, and economic and cultural actors reveal a very different twist on that history. The network of convents founded in Spanish America established the basis for a pan-Hispanic community of women who were linked by similar religious norms and gender codes. It is now clear that, both inside and outside convents, women formed an important part of the fabric of the Spanish empire. Further analysis of texts produced by and about women throughout the Iberian Atlantic will reveal the roles women played in supporting, challenging, and resisting the imperial enterprise and in defining the blended cultural diaspora that would become the Hispanic world.

Notes

1 Francisca de Miranda's birth and death dates are unknown, but she was under the tutelage of the controversial, often possessed nun Isabel de la Encarnación (c. 1596–1633) when she experienced her miraculous cure. See Doris Bieñko de Peralta, 'Un camino de abrojos y espinas: mística, demonios y melancolía,' in Roger Bartra, ed., *Transgresión y melancolía en el México colonial* (Mexico City: Universidad Nacional Autónoma de México, 2004), 91–114. For more on Teresa of Avila's view of her reform as a transatlantic endeavour, see Carole Slade, *St. Teresa of Avila: Author of a Heroic Life* (Berkeley: University of California Press, 1995), and Gillian T.W. Ahlgren, *Teresa of Avila and the Politics of Sanctity* (Ithaca, N.Y.: Cornell University Press, 1996), particularly 84–114. Another group of nuns who 'crossed' the

Atlantic include those like Madre María de Ágreda and María de San José Palacios Berruecos who bilocated (that is, while physically in one place, they appeared to believers in another).

2 To a friend who lived outside the convent, Sor Violante wrote: 'Belisa, friendship is a treasure / so deserving of eternal esteem / that it is insufficient to measure its worth / against the silver and gold of Arabia and Potosí' (Belisa, el amistad es un tesoro / tan digno de estimarse eternamente, / que a su valor no es paga suficiente / de Arabia, y Potosí la plata y oro). Julián Olivares and Elizabeth Boyce, eds., *Tras el espejo la musa escribe: lírica femenina de los Siglos de Oro* (Madrid: Siglo Veintiuno, 1993), 271. My translation.

3 Stacey Schlau, *Spanish American Women's Use of the Word: Colonial through Contemporary Narratives* (Tucson: University of Arizona Press, 2001), 14.

4 Emerging research on women in the Luso-Brazilian world promises to bring a new corpus of writing into the conversation about Iberian and Latin American women, in particular for the eighteenth century and beyond. See, for example, Vanda Anastácio, 'Cherchez la femme: À propos d'une forme de sociabilité littéraire à Lisbonne à la fin du XVIIeme siècle,' *Arquivos do Centro Cultural Português,* special issue on *Sociabilités intellectuelles XVI–XX siècles, 49* (Paris: Centre Culturel C. Gulbenkian, 2005), 93–101.

5 The 'culture of control' of imperial Spain is explored in Anne J. Cruz and Mary Elizabeth Perry, eds., *Culture and Control in Counter Reformation Spain* (Minneapolis: University of Minnesota Press, 1992).

6 The bibliography on early modern Spain and colonial Spanish America is lengthy. See John Elliott, *Spain and Its World: 1500–1700* (New Haven, Conn., and London: Yale University Press, 1989); Henry Kamen, *Empire: How Spain Became a World Power, 1492–1763* (New York: HarperCollins, 2003) and *Inquisition and Society in Spain in the Sixteenth and Seventeenth Centuries* (Bloomington: Indiana University Press, 1985); and Teófilo Ruiz, *Spanish Society (1400–1600)* (Harlow, U.K., and New York: Longman, 2000).

7 Helen Nader, ed. and intro., *Power and Gender in Renaissance Spain: Eight Women of the Mendoza Family, 1450–1650* (Urbana and Chicago: University of Illinois Press, 2003), 1–26; and James Casey, *Early Modern Spain: A Social History* (New York and London: Routledge, 1999), 27–8, 201–2.

8 Mary Elizabeth Perry, *Gender and Disorder in Early Modern Seville* (Princeton, N.J.: Princeton University Press, 1990), 15–17; and Allyson Poska, *Regulating the People: The Catholic Reformation in Seventeenth-Century Spain* (Boston and Leiden: Brill, 1998) and *Women and Authority in Early Modern Spain: The Peasants of Galicia* (Oxford and New York: Oxford University Press, 2005).

9 See Magdalena Sánchez, *The Empress, the Queen, and the Nun: Women and Power at the Court of Philip III of Spain* (Baltimore and London: Johns Hopkins University Press, 1998); and Nader, *Power and Gender,* 1–26.

10 Research that has significantly added to our knowledge of Jewish and Islamic culture in the late medieval and early modern periods includes L.P. Harvey, *Muslims in Spain, 1500 to 1614* (Chicago and London: University of Chicago Press, 2005); David Nirenberg, 'Conversion, Sex, and Segregation: Jews and Christians in Medieval Spain,' *American Historical Review*, 107, no. 4 (2002): 1065–93; Mary Elizabeth Perry, *The Handless Maiden: Moriscos and the Politics of Religion in Early Modern Spain* (Princeton, N.J.: Princeton University Press, 2005); and Gretchen Starr-LeBeau, *In the Shadow of the Virgin: Inquisitors, Friars, and Conversos in Guadalupe, Spain* (Princeton, N.J.: Princeton University Press, 2003).

11 Kathryn Burns's *Colonial Habits: Convents and the Spiritual Economy of Cuzco, Peru* (Durham, N.C., and London: Duke University Press, 1999) discusses nuns' involvement in 'exchanges that were indissociably economic and spiritual, distinctly colonial, and utterly habitual' (3). Also, see Kimberly Gauderman for more on women's economic and legal activities in Spanish America: *Women's Lives in Colonial Quito: Gender, Law, and Economy in Spanish America* (Austin: University of Texas Press, 2003); and Stephanie Kirk, *Convent Life in Colonial Mexico: A Tale of Two Communities* (Gainesville: University Press of Florida, 2007).

12 Octavio Paz, *Sor Juana, or the Traps of Faith*, trans. Margaret Sayers Peden (Cambridge, Mass.: Belknap Press of Harvard University, 1988), 67.

13 Electa Arenal and Stacey Schlau, *Untold Sisters: Hispanic Nuns in Their Own Works*, trans. Amanda Powell (Albuquerque: University of New Mexico Press, 1989), 339.

14 As noted, current research projects devoted to uncovering women's writing in the Luso-Brazilian world are bringing even more women to light for the Portuguese diaspora. See, for example, Anastácio, '"Mulheres varonis e interesses domésticos": Reflexões acerca do discurso produzido pela História Literária acerca das mulheres escritoras da viragem do século XVIII para o século XIX,' *Cartographies: Mélanges offerts à Maria Alzira Seixo* (Lisboa: Universidade Aberta, 2005), available online at http://www.vanda-anastacio.at/index_files/page0001.htm.

15 For a more detailed explanation of 1580–1700 as the foundational period in Hispanic women's writing, see the Introduction to Lisa Vollendorf, *The Lives of Women: A New History of Inquisitional Spain* (Nashville, Tenn.: Vanderbilt University Press, 2005).

16 See, for instance, the most comprehensive book to date on women's education in the era: Elizabeth Howe, *Education and Women in the Early Modern Hispanic World* (Aldershot, U.K.: Ashgate, 2008).

17 Numerous scholars have suggested the link between Saint Teresa and early modern religious women's negotiations with the written word and questions

of authority. See, for example, Stacey Schlau, 'Following Saint Teresa: Early Modern Women and Religious Authority,' *Modern Language Notes*, 117, no. 2 (2002): 286–309.

18 The difference between sixteenth-century Spain, which saw a dearth of women authors, and the seventeenth century's comparatively large cohort of them bolsters this claim. See, for example, Vollendorf, 'Women Writers of Sixteenth-Century Spain,' in Gregory Kaplan, ed., *Dictionary of Literary Biography: Sixteenth-Century Spain* (Farmington Hills, Mich.: Gale Group, 2005), 334–41.

19 Efraín Kristal, ed. and intro., *The Cambridge Companion to the Latin American Novel* (Cambridge: Cambridge University Press, 2005), 4.

20 Alison Weber and Carole Slade argue persuasively for Saint Teresa's contributions as an intellectual and a reformer. See Weber, *Teresa of Avila and the Rhetoric of Femininity* (Princeton, N.J.: Princeton University Press, 1990); and Slade, 'St. Teresa of Avila as a Social Reformer,' in Janet K. Ruffing, ed., *Mysticism and Social Transformation* (Syracuse, N.Y.: Syracuse University Press, 2001), 91–103.

21 No comprehensive account of women's education exists for the period, although Howe's *Education and Women in the Early Modern Hispanic World* begins to unravel some of the history.

22 For more information on fifteenth- and sixteenth-century precursors to the 1580–1700 cohort of women writers, see Anne J. Cruz, 'Willing Desire: Luisa de Carvajal y Mendoza and Feminine Subjectivity,' in Helen Nader, ed., *The Mendoza Women: Gender and Power in Golden Age Spain* (Champaign-Urbana: University of Illinois Press, 2003), 177–94; Francisca de los Apóstoles, *The Inquisition of Francisca: A Sixteenth-Century Visionary on Trial*, ed. and trans. Gillian T.W. Ahlgren, The Other Voice in Early Modern Europe Series (Chicago: University of Chicago Press, 2005); Ronald E. Surtz, *Writing Women in Late Medieval and Early Modern Spain* (Philadelphia: University of Pennsylvania Press, 1995); Vollendorf, 'Women Writers of Sixteenth-Century Spain'; Barbara Weissberger, 'The Critics and Florencia Pinar: The Problem with Assigning Feminism to a Medieval Court Poet,' in Lisa Vollendorf, ed., *Recovering Spain's Feminist Tradition* (New York: Publications of the Modern Language Association, 2001), 31–47; and idem, *Isabel Rules: Constructing Queenship, Wielding Power* (Minneapolis: University of Minnesota Press, 2003).

23 My research draws extensively on all of the scholars cited in this essay, but in particular I would like to acknowledge my debt to one of the first pioneers in Hispanic women studies, Josefina Muriel, who passed away in 2008. Muriel laid the groundwork for colonial women's studies in *Cultura femenina*

novohispana (Mexico City: Universidad Autónoma de México, 1982), where she convincingly demonstrated colonial women's contributions to literary, intellectual, and political culture. Muriel also included tables of female artists, intellectuals, and politicians (546–9) from Europe and the Américas. Until an anonymous reader of the present volume in manuscript drew my attention to the tables, I was unaware of their existence. Subsequently, I have consulted Muriel's extensive lists, which helped me augment the two tables in this chapter. I include only women whose words are recorded either in their own texts or in texts, such as spiritual biographies, that claim to reproduce the women's words. I do not include painters and sculptors, such as Luisa Roldán (1656–1706) and Josefa de Obidos Ayala (1630–84), for example. In the cases of some of the women on Muriel's list (e.g., Jerónima de Velasco, Sor Juana María de San José, Isabel de la Resurrección, etc.), I could not find enough information to include them. However, in referencing these women, I remind scholars that Muriel's tables continue to be a treasure trove of information.

24 Authors marked with asterisks are available in English translations, but few have seen their entire oeuvre translated. See Teresa of Jesus, *The Complete Works of Saint Teresa of Jesus*, ed. and trans. E. Allison Peers, 3 vols. (London: Sheed, 1946); and Catalina de Erauso, *Memoir of a Basque Lieutenant Nun: Transvestite in the New World*, trans. Michele Stepto and Gabriel Stepto, foreword by Marjorie Garber (Boston: Beacon, 1996). For other translations and modern editions in Spanish, see: Ana de San Bartolomé, *Autobiography and Other Writings*, ed. and trans. Darcy Donahue, The Other Voice in Early Modern Europe Series (Chicago: University of Chicago Press, 2008); Arenal and Schlau, *Untold Sisters*; Isabel Barbeito Carneiro, *Mujeres del Madrid barroco: Voces testimoniales* (Madrid: Ediciones del Orto, 1992); María de San José Salazar, *Book for the Hour of Recreation*, ed. Alison Weber, trans. Amanda Powell, The Other Voice in Early Modern Europe Series (Chicago: University of Chicago Press, 2002); Mary E. Giles, *The Book of Prayer of Sor María of Santo Domingo* (Albany: State University of New York Press, 1990); Amy Katz Kaminsky, *Water Lilies/Flores del agua: An Anthology of Spanish Women Writers from the Fifteenth through the Nineteenth Century* (Minneapolis: University of Minnesota Press, 1996); Bárbara Mujica, *Women Writers of Early Modern Spain: Sophia's Daughters* (New Haven, Conn.: Yale University Press, 2004), 283–91, 321–31; Olivares and Boyce, eds., *Tras el espejo la musa escribe*; Stacey Schlau, *Viva al siglo, muerta al mundo: Selected Works/Obras Escogidas by/de María de San Alberto (1568–1640)* (New Orleans: University Press of the South, 1998); Elizabeth Rhodes, *This Tight Embrace: Luisa de Carvajal y Mendoza (1566–1614)* (Milwaukee, Wis.: Marquette University Press, 2000); Teresa S. Soufas, *Wom-*

en's Acts: Plays by Women Dramatists of Spain's Golden Age (Lexington: University of Kentucky Press, 1997); Zayas y Sotomayor, *The Enchantments of Love*, trans. H. Patsy Boyer (Berkeley: University of California Press, 1990), and *The Disenchantments of Love,* trans. H. Patsy Boyer (Binghamton, N.Y.: SUNY Press, 1997). Most of the writers in the table are discussed in Vollendorf, *The Lives of Women.*

25 Pedro M. Cátedra and Anastasio Rojo, *Bibliotecas y lecturas de mujeres. Siglo XVI* (Salamanca: Instituto de Historia del Libro y de la Lectura, 2004), 39–44. Previous estimates pegged female literacy at 50 per cent of men's, with the highest estimates being 25 per cent for urban women (cf. Sara Nalle, 'Literacy and Culture in Early Modern Castile,' *Past and Present* 125 [November 1989]: 65–96).

26 Cátedra and Rojo, *Bibliotecas y lecturas de mujeres. Siglo XVI,* 289–93.

27 Ibid., 53–67.

28 The Women Writers: Reception of Their Work Database, spearheaded by Suzan van Dijk at the Universit of Utrecht (http://www.databasewomen-writers.nl/), is an empirically driven project that traces women's roles as readers, writers, and transmitters of culture in early·modern Europe. The project represents the kind of research that promises to help scholars map reception and readership as well as authorship for European women.

29 Caro's poems, written for royal occasions and public festivities, are one exception to this focus.

30 See Arenal and Schlau, *Untold Sisters*; Mujica, *Women Writers of Early Modern Spain*; Soufas, *Women's Acts*; and Vollendorf, *Lives of Women.*

31 María de Zayas y Sotomayor, *Desengaños amorosos,* 2nd ed., ed. Alicia Yllera (Madrid: Cátedra, 1993), 511.

32 A translation of two novellas with a critical introduction to Carvajal appears in Noël M. Valis, 'Mariana de Carvajal: The Spanish Storyteller,' in Katharina M. Wilson and Frank J. Warnke, eds., *Women Writers of the Seventeenth Century* (Athens and London: University of Georgia Press, 1989), 251–82.

33 Zayas's term is 'borrones,' whereas Carvajal speaks of 'un aborto de mi corto ingenio.' See Vollendorf, *Lives of Women,* 58–9.

34 Weber coined the phrase in the title to her influential study, *Teresa of Avila and the Rhetoric of Femininity.*

35 For an overview of the church's construction and control of female piety, see Allyson M. Poska and Elizabeth A. Lehfeldt, 'Redefining Expectations: Women and the Church in Early Modern Spain,' in Susan E. Dinan and Debra Meyers, eds., *Women and Religion in Old and New Worlds* (New York: Routledge, 2001), 21–42; and Allan Greer and Jodi Bilinkoff, eds., *Colonial Saints: Discovering the Holy in the Americas, 1500–1800* (New York and London: Routledge, 2003).

36 Sources for studies on cultural production by and about women in Spanish
    America include: Arenal and Schlau, *Untold Sisters*; Jodi Bilinkoff, *Related
    Lives: Confessors and Their Female Penitents, 1450–1750* (Ithaca, N.Y.: Cornell
    University Press, 2005); Margaret Chowning, *Rebellious Nuns: A Troubled
    History of a Mexican Convent (1752–1863)* (New York and Oxford: Oxford
    University Press, 2006); Jacqueline Holler, *Escogidas Plantas: Nuns and Bea-
    tas in Mexico City, 1531–1601* (New York: Columbia University Press, 2002);
    Kristine Ibsen, *Women's Spiritual Autobiography in Colonial Spanish America*
    (Gainesville.: University Press of Florida, 1999); Asunción Lavrin, *Brides
    of Christ: Conventual Life in Colonial Mexico* (Stanford, Calif.: Stanford Uni-
    versity Press, 2008); Asunción Lavrin and Rosalva Loreto López, *Monjas y
    beatas: la escritura femenina en la espiritualidad barroca novohispana: siglos XVII
    y XVIII* (Mexico City: Archivo General de la Nación / Universidad de las
    Américas, 2002); R. Loreto López, 'The Devil, Women, and the Body in Sev-
    enteenth Century Puebla Convents,' *The Americas*, 59, no. 2 (2002): 181–99;
    Stephanie Merrim, *Early Modern Women's Writing and Sor Juana Inés de la
    Cruz* (Nashville, Tenn.: Vanderbilt University Press, 1999); Josefina Muriel,
    Cultura femenina novohispana (Mexico City: Universidad Nacional Autónoma
    de México, 1982); and J. Muriel, ed., *Las Indias caciques de Corpus Christi*
    (Mexico City: Universidad Nacional Autónoma de México, 1963).
37 Kathryn Joy McKnight, *The Mystic of Tunja: The Writings of Madre Castillo,
    1671–1742* (Amherst: University of Massachusetts Press, 1997); Sor Juana
    Inés de la Cruz, *The Answer / La respuesta*, ed. Electa Arenal, trans. Amanda
    Powell (New York: Feminist Press, 1994); María Rosa, *Atlantic Nuns: Journey
    of Five Capuchin Nuns* (1722), ed. and trans. Sarah Owens (forthcoming
    from The Other Voice in Early Modern Europe Series, University of To-
    ronto Press, 2009); Kathleen Myers, *Neither Saints Nor Sinners: Writing the
    Lives of Women in Spanish America* (New York: Oxford University Press, 2003);
    Kathleen Myers and Amanda Powell, *A Wild Country out in the Garden: The
    Spiritual Journals of a Mexican Nun* (Bloomington: Indiana University Press,
    1999); and Grady Wray, *The Devotional Exercises / Los Ejercicios Devotos of Sor
    Juana Inés de la Cruz, Mexico's Prodigious Nun* (1648/51–1695) (Lewiston,
    N.Y.: Edwin Mellen Press, 2005).
38 Schlau, *Spanish American Women's Use of the Word*, 8.
39 Burns, *Colonial Habits*, 101–56.
40 Sor Juana describes *The Answer* as 'drafts and scratches' (unos borrones,
    39), 'a trifle' (un papelillo, 97), and 'a simple account of my inclination to
    letters' (una simple narración de mi inclinación a las letras, 77). References
    are to the bilingual edition of the text: Sor Juana Inés de la Cruz, *La respu-
    esta / The Answer*, Arenal and Powell, eds.
41 The 1968 discovery of a text written by Sor Juana for nuns in a Portuguese

convent exemplifies the evolving nature of modern scholars' understanding of early modern and colonial women's awareness of the role they played in an emerging transatlantic intellectual tradition. See Sor Juana, *Enigmas ofre-cidos a la Casa del Placer*, ed. Antonio Alatorre (Mexico City: Colegio de Mex-ico, 1994). For more on Sor Juana and the transatlantic writing community of Hispanic women, see Lisa Vollendorf, 'Across the Atlantic: Sor Juana, *La respuesta*, and the Hispanic Women's Writing Community,' in Emilie L. Berg-mann and Stacey Schlau, eds., *Approaches to Teaching the Works of Sor Juana Inés de la Cruz* (New York: Modern Language Association, 2007), 95–102.

42 For more on the importance of women's literary tradition for women writ-ers in the early modern and colonial periods, see Amy Katz Kaminsky, 'María de Zayas and the Invention of a Women's Writing Community,' *Re-vista de Estudios Hispánicos*, 35 (2001): 487–509.

43 McKnight, *The Mystic of Tunja*, 5.

44 Schlau, *Spanish American Women's Use of the Word*, 13.

45 The differences between gendered representations of humility have yet to be sufficiently studied, as Alison Weber argues in 'Gender and Mysticism,' in Amy Hollywood and Patricia Beckman, eds., *Cambridge Companion to Chris-tian Mysticism* (Cambridge: Cambridge University Press, forthcoming 2009).

46 Quoted in Isabel Barbeito Carneiro, *María de Orozco y Luján (1635–1709)* (Madrid: Ediciones del Orto, 1997), 33.

47 Emilie Bergmann explores the interface between humanistic rhetoric and social control of women in 'The Exclusion of the Feminine in the Cultural Discourse of the Golden Age: Juan Luis Vives and Fray Luis de León,' in Alain Saint-Saëns, ed., *Religion, Body, and Gender in Early Modern Spain* (San Francisco: Mellen Research University Press, 1991), 124–36.

48 See Elizabeth Rhodes, '"Y yo dije, sí, señor": Ana Domenge and the Barce-lona Inquisition,' in Mary E. Giles, ed., *Women in the Inquisition* (Baltimore: Johns Hopkins University Press, 1999), 134–54.

49 See Kathleen Myers, 'Testimony for Canonization or Proof of Blasphemy?: The New Spanish Inquisition and the Hagiographic Biography of Catarina de San Juan,' in Giles, ed., *Women in the Inquisition*, 270–95. Also, see Mi-chelle Molina and Ulrike Strasser's chapter in the present volume.

PART II

Negotiating Belief and Ethnicity in the Atlantic Basin

Prophets and Helpers: African American Women and the Rise of Black Christianity in the Age of the Slave Trade

JON SENSBACH

'Great Queen!' It was a most unusual salutation to a letter, and surely the queen of Denmark had never read anything quite like what followed.

'At the time when I lived in Papaa, in Africa, I served the Lord Masu,' the letter continued. 'Now I have come into the land of the Whites, and they will not allow me to serve the Lord Jesus. Previously, I did not have any reason to serve Him, but now I do. I am very sad in my heart that the Negro women on St. Thomas are not allowed to serve the Lord Jesus.'

These lines, composed by a former slave named Magdalena in 1739, began one of the most extraordinary and mysterious letters ever to emerge from the African diaspora in the Americas. The correspondence was addressed to Queen Sophia Magdalen of Denmark. Its author, a native of the Slave Coast of West Africa, was an elder in an emerging congregation of black Christians on the Danish Caribbean island of St Thomas (now in the U.S. Virgin Islands); the letter was an appeal from one Christian woman to another for help in her hour of need. The growing popularity of Christianity among the enslaved plantation workers of St Thomas had provoked the anger and fear of white planters worried that religion might inspire a slave revolt. When the planters violently punished the worshipers and imprisoned the missionaries who instructed them, Magdalena and other black leaders organized a vigorous response, almost unthinkable in its boldness: they mobilized hundreds of congregants to sign petitions to the king and queen of Denmark asking for help.

One group of leaders wrote on behalf of more than 'six hundred and fifty black scholars of Jesus Christ,' while Magdalena wrote an additional letter 'in the name of more than two hundred and fifty Negro women.' Adopting a shrewd strategy calculated to arouse the queen's empathy as a woman and a fellow Christian, she emphasized her African identity by referring to herself, in two versions of the letter, with two African names (Damma and Marotta) as well as her Christian name to illustrate spiritual progress. The Dutch-Creole-language version of the letter, beginning with 'Father, the son and the Holy Spirit. Marotta now Madlena [Magdalena] from Poppo in Africa,' made this case to the queen: 'The Whites do not want to obey Him. Let them do as they wish. But when the poor black Brethren and Sisters want to serve the Lord Jesus, they are looked upon as maroons. If the Queen thinks it fitting, please pray to the Lord Jesus for us and let her intercede with the King to allow *Baas Martinus* [a white missionary] to preach the Lord's word, so that we can come to know the Lord and so that he can baptize us in the name of the Father, the son, and the Holy Spirit.' Magdalena's rhetorical strategy allowed her to contrast her own paganism in Africa with the opportunities for Christian redemption now open to her, and to advance the idea of black women as true Christians whose devotion was poised against the planters' unbelief. How could a Christian queen deny such an honest plea?[1]

Africans enslaved in the Americas did not ordinarily write letters to European royalty, and for that reason alone the petitions are an outstanding example of black assertiveness in the face of overwhelming colonial power. But Magdalena's letter to the queen, in particular, is unique in several other ways. First, it was written in an African language of the Ewe-Fon cultural family found in present-day Benin. It was perhaps the earliest written African linguistic representation in the New World. Magdalena might have written the letter herself, since the missionaries taught many congregants to read and write. It is also possible that the missionaries wrote it in her name, following her dictation and transcribing phonetically. Or perhaps the scribe was her son, Domingo Gesu, a literate congregation member and Caribbean-born Creole with his mother's native tongue in his ear. Indeed, perhaps it was he who then translated it into Dutch Creole, the African-Dutch lingua franca of the Danish West Indies, making it readable to European eyes. Whatever the case, the letter represents an unprecedented attempt to render an African language in Western form, and thus remains as an exceptionally rare example of written African cultural transfer to the Americas.

Magdalena's letter also reveals a hidden religious world emerging in the heart of the violent plantation slavery system, an enclave of several hundred black Christian women organizing to preserve their spiritual domain. A century before such famous African American activists as Sojourner Truth and Harriet Tubman invoked the ethical power of Christianity to fight racism in the antebellum United States, an early, mostly unknown generation of black Christian women in the Caribbean helped create and defend a new church as the moral epicentre of their lives under slavery. Christianity gave many of them access to social power and mobility. Remarkably, some, even as slaves, migrated to North America and Europe, enabling them to fashion a transatlantic fellowship triangulated between those continents and the West Indies at the height of the slave trade. Their example proved enormously influential for the germination of Protestant Christianity in the New World, which has been a bedrock of African American culture since the eighteenth century.

Indeed, if we wish to understand the origins of the black church in the modern United States – or at least its evangelical Protestant form, which historically has embraced the great majority of black American Christians – we might view the petition campaign on that Caribbean island as a kind of creation moment, and Magdalena's letter as a foundational text. As historians have long been aware, the transatlantic slave trade to the Americas between the sixteenth and nineteenth centuries fuelled a long-running confrontation between, and often creative fusion of, African religious traditions and various forms of Christianity in New World colonial slave societies.[2] Magdalena's letter derives directly from that momentous series of meetings.

Those religious encounters began when Portuguese and Italian Capuchin monks introduced Catholicism into west-central African kingdoms such as Angola and Kongo in the fifteenth and sixteenth centuries. Catholicism became indigenized in that large region, and hundreds of thousands of Africans taken to the Americas via the slave trade in subsequent centuries brought that religion with them. African Catholics were widely and copiously dispersed among Spanish, Portuguese, French, Dutch, British, and Danish colonies, and in the Catholic Americas the church accepted them and thousands more black converts into the fold.[3]

For the Protestant Americas, scholars have generally identified the period of the Great Awakening in mid-eighteenth-century British North America as the beginning of widespread African American acceptance of evangelical Christianity. 'The conversion of African Americans to Protestant Christianity' that began in that era, write historians Sylvia Frey and Betty Wood, 'was a, perhaps *the*, defining moment in African American history.' The religious revivals so fervently embraced by plantation slaves and urban free blacks gave rise by the early nineteenth century to the Baptist and Methodist churches, many of them independent, that have served as centrepieces for African American education, social life, and political activism ever since. But, as the St Thomas story illustrates, African Protestant worship emerged a generation earlier outside the mainstream British North American religious and cultural circuit, in a remote Caribbean outpost among a group of people normally seen as peripheral – if they are seen at all – to the history of slavery and African American cultural development. The advent and influence of those early black Protestant congregations have yet to be fully explored and accounted for by historians.[4]

Black evangelical women, moreover, have largely been absent from accounts of the rise of black Protestant Christianity in the Americas. Scholars have been disproportionately drawn to a body of African American conversion narratives and spiritual autobiographies written in English by mid- to late-eighteenth-century authors such as Olaudah Equiano, John Jea, George Liele, David George, John Marrant, and others – all men, all considered leaders of various wings of the black evangelical movement that spread throughout the Atlantic from North America to the Caribbean, Canada, Britain, and West Africa. Not until the early nineteenth century did a comparable set of black women's spiritual autobiographies begin to emerge in the United States and the British Caribbean, with the result that historians have not examined thoroughly the role of women in fostering African American Christianity two or three generations earlier. And yet a letter like Magdalena's from the 1730s, seemingly emerging out of nowhere, written in an African language in the name of 250 enslaved women, furnishes startling evidence of women's involvement in that effort from the very beginning. Her petition – a unique early text from an African woman in America – restores women to the very heart of that narrative.[5]

Indeed, Frey and Wood have argued that, as enslaved and free African Americans embraced Protestant Christianity with increasing enthusiasm in the late eighteenth and early nineteenth centuries, women consistently comprised more than half, and often between 60 and 65 per cent, of congregational membership. While scholars have not systematically examined why those proportions should have prevailed, they theorize that evangelical Christianity, with its promise of spiritual equality and eschatological transcendence, proved especially attractive to the most powerless and vulnerable adults in slavery, women. For whatever reason, it appears that black Protestant Christianity was largely feminized from the outset among its lay followers and, to a degree not widely understood, among its leadership corps. Yet the historical literature has not generally either reflected the preponderance of female churchgoers or explored

the formal and informal congregational leadership structures that often gave women a powerful voice in the recruitment, organization, and
management of members. The case of the Caribbean congregation on St
Thomas – the earliest African Protestant church in the Americas – provides a window on the decisive role of women in the formative years of
black evangelical Christianity.[6]

Small and mountainous, St Thomas would seem an unlikely place for
such momentous happenings. Colonized by the Danish in 1672, the island was one of three small Danish colonies in the eastern Caribbean,
along with St John and St Croix. Because the extent of Danish colonization in America was far smaller than that of the other imperial powers
of Britain, Spain, Portugal, France, and the Netherlands, historians have
paid relatively little attention to these three Danish holdings. Like many
other Caribbean colonies, however, their plantation economy based on
cotton and sugar had grown rapidly in the early eighteenth century, pow-
ered by the labour of enslaved Africans imported by Danish traders on
the Gold Coast of West Africa. By 1735, Africans outnumbered European
colonists on St Thomas by 3,741 to 650 – a proportion of about five to
one. Because Dutch landowners were more numerous and influential
than even the Danes on the island, the Africans spoke a Creole mixture
of Dutch and African languages. The tiny white elite ruled a huge enslaved majority with a ferocious machinery of slave codes and violent
punishments. A huge slave rebellion broke out on St John in 1733–4,
when Africans from the Akwamu nation on the Gold Coast seized and
held the island for six months before being repressed, and in the tense
aftermath colonists and slaves lived in heightened fear of each other.[7]

Just as the rebellion was unfolding, German-speaking missionaries arrived in St Thomas in early 1733 intending to preach Christianity to
the slave population. They were members of a religious group called
the Renewed Unity of Brethren, a pietistic offshoot of the Lutheran
Church, more commonly known as Moravians, or Herrnhuters, after
their central congregation town of Hernnhut in eastern Saxony. The
leader of the Brethren, Count Nikolaus Ludwig von Zinzendorf, used
his connections at the Danish court to secure permission for the group
to evangelize among African slaves in the Danish West Indies. Though
not anti-slavery, the Brethren believed in broadcasting their message of
spiritual redemption to all people, regardless of race or worldly status.
The Moravians were not the first Protestants to attempt mission work
in American slave societies, but previous efforts by the Quakers in Bar-
bados in the 1670s and by the Church of England's mission wing, the

Society for the Propagation of the Gospel, in South Carolina during
the early eighteenth century had yielded few converts. Planters often
opposed Christian missions to slaves, fearing that a message of spiritual
equality would promote discontent and rebelliousness among bond-
spersons. The theology and austere formalism of Anglican, Lutheran,
and Reformed worship also repelled many Africans, with the result that
only scattered African Americans joined churches in Protestant British,
Dutch, and Danish colonies.[8]

Likewise, in St Thomas, the Moravian mission made little headway
for the first four years after being met by scepticism from slaves and by
hostility from planters. In the wake of the defeated St John rebellion,
many planters considered the missionaries dangerous incendiaries and
often harassed and attacked them. A few planters, however, gave the
missionaries access to their slaves, believing that Christianity would help
'civilize' and domesticate an African workforce the European colonists
considered barbaric. The missionaries set to work on several plantations
preaching a message that was short on theology and long on emotion,
emphasizing Christ's unconditional love and universal spiritual equality
before God. By no means did they intend to challenge or destabilize the
system of slavery, but they did seek to inculcate a sense that the slaves'
suffering made them an elect group whom Jesus had anointed with his
love precisely because they were damned and outcast. This lesson, per-
sistently driven home in study groups and prayer sessions in the evenings
after plantation work was done, began to bear fruit. By the mid-1730s,
the missionaries had made a few converts, including a handful of Africans and several Caribbean-born Creoles, some of whom had previous
exposure to Christian teachings through the Dutch Reformed Church
and could even read and write. Literacy, in fact, proved a key component of the mission. Despite strong discouragement from planters, the
missionaries conducted lessons in reading and writing that proved enormously popular among the slaves. As numerous scholars have noted, forbidden literacy was highly prized by enslaved populations in America as a
portal to knowledge and a way to demystify the power of the master class.
On St Thomas, one enslaved man held up a Bible and said: 'This book
will make me wise.'[9]

Without a doubt, the most important respondent to the missionaries' teaching in these early sessions was a young free woman of colour
named Rebecca. Born in about 1718 on the British West Indian island of
Antigua, the daughter of a slave mother and a white father, Rebecca had
been kidnapped as a young child and sold as a slave to a Dutch sugar-

planting family, the van Beverhouts, on St Thomas in the mid-1720s. As a domestic house servant, she received some privileges from the van Beverhouts in the form of reading and writing lessons, instruction in Christianity, and eventually freedom by her teen years. Baptized in the early 1730s by a Roman Catholic priest visiting from Puerto Rico, Rebecca had expressed a sense of religious calling by conducting biblical lessons for enslaved women on the household staff even before the Moravian evangelists arrived on St Thomas. When she attended meetings held by the missionaries, they quickly noted her spiritual gifts, realizing that she could be a valuable asset to the mission. One missionary, Friedrich Martin, 'felt that he could discern in her a disposition to become useful as a leader in witnessing for Jesus and in the saving of souls among members of her sex,' whereupon he appointed her as a 'worker' (the German *Arbeiterin*), or special assistant in charge of recruiting and organizing black women. From the very beginning, then, an outreach to women, by women, lay at the heart of this early encounter between Christianity and people of African descent in the Americas.[10]

This dimension proved indispensable in cultivating the enthusiasm with which Christianity was spreading through the slave quarters. The Moravian Brethren took a strongly gendered approach to religion and evangelical work, believing that though men and women were joined in Christ and created in spiritual equality, they led different inner lives that required separate nurturing. The Brethren exalted women's spirituality, feminizing their own congregations in Europe as the 'bride' of Christ and worshiping the Holy Spirit as the 'mother' of the church. They acknowledged and encouraged women's teaching abilities, creating a fleet of female assistants, lay preachers, and 'helpers' – a kind of supervisor-counsellor – to minister to women, just as men did for each other. Though they did not formally preach to the entire congregation, women led prayer groups, nurtured other women, and served in church governance. In these ways, the Brethren technically obeyed biblical injunctions against female preaching while giving women opportunities for self-expression and spiritual leadership.[11]

Realizing the importance of reaching female Africans and Creoles in the West Indian mission, preachers recognized the authority of women of colour to witness and teach Christianity – an extraordinarily radical approach among Protestant groups at a time when many were still debating whether African-descended people were devils or not. Missionary Friedrich Martin described the result this practice achieved by 1738. 'Among the Negro women are at least six who are already beginning to teach on occasion,' he wrote to church leaders in Germany. 'Those who cannot yet read apply themselves diligently and will spell something many times until they can comprehend it. In the evenings they ask me to read to them what they have spelled during their daily work when they have a brief moment to look in their books.'[12]

Martin singled out Rebecca, 'a Mulatto woman whom I have appointed to be a worker among them. If there is ever any problem with one of the Sisters she will write a letter of admonition to her. It is a great joy to me, and a great inclination for this work has been stirred in her. I assure you she can quite properly be called a Sister, and she is quite eager to serve the Saviour.' Rebecca conducted classes in reading, writing, and religious instruction for eager students in the evening hours at a school the missionaries ran in Charlotte Amalie, the capital of St Thomas. 'Rebecca helps teach the Negro women,' Martin wrote in 1737. 'In the evenings when the Negro women come to school, she teaches them. She is true in her understanding and the women love her.' Rebecca also walked long miles as an itinerant missionary at night and on the weekends across the island's rugged terrain, bringing word of the Gospel directly to workers on sugar plantations. Through her recruitment efforts, along with those of several male counterparts, dozens of enslaved Africans and Creoles enlisted in a new congregation and sought baptism. In 1738 the Brethren bought a plantation on the island and built a church there for this burgeoning fellowship.[13]

With the missionaries' encouragement, many neophytes wrote or dictated a short statement providing testimony of their spiritual transformation. Hundreds of these statements, including many by women, were written and collected in the late 1730s and 1740s, and were sent to the Moravian headquarters in Herrnhut, Germany, where they survive today in the church archives. All are written in Dutch or Dutch Creole, some by converts in their own hands, others taken down in dictation by the missionaries. Something short of the common Moravian genre of the *Lebenslauf*, or life story, that most church members wrote, and not quite the anguished conversion narratives later common among the Methodists, these statements provide clues to the way women perceived their engagement with their own spirituality. The letters tend to be fairly formulaic and reveal little personal information. Given their similarity and the consistency of their style, the missionaries unquestionably coached, edited, or influenced the construction of the letters, or perhaps even wrote them in some cases, and so their value as pure statements of Afro-Christian religious expression is undoubtedly compromised. Still, they

do capture something of the inner state of African American spirituality
at a seminal moment of shifting consciousness.

In the style of Pietist self-debasement, the letters tend to emphasize
the writers' insufficient piety along with a hope that Jesus will bestow pity
and grace on them. 'I did not know,' wrote Rebecca, for example, 'that
there was such a thing as spiritual life. Although I had always longed to
find a way to the Lord, I never had the right foundation and have always
longed for a teacher to instruct me. But how good is the Lord! Help me
to praise Him who has pulled me out of darkness. I shall take up His
cross with all my heart and will follow the example given by His poor life.
But how miserable I find myself to be! Remember me in your prayers!'

Writers often compared themselves to worms. Maria, 'Elder of the
black sisters,' wrote: 'This poor and miserable little worm would like to
learn the proper way to love the Savior. Why? He has forgiven my many
sins. I was so lacking faith that I could not imagine that the Savior could
make something out of me. But I feel the greatness of His mercy over
me. I thank Him for the blood He has shed for me and for letting it flow
over my corrupt heart, thus washing it free of its sins.' Similarly, Rosina
testified that 'I still do not love the Savior as much as I would like. I
thank him for having washed out my heart with His dear blood. I am
often saddened that there are still so many among my people who have
not yielded their hearts to the Savior. I lie like a worm at His feet, and I
believe that He will keep me with Him.'[14]

However standard the professions of unworthiness, it is nonetheless
quite possible that the letters also expressed a growing and genuine
sense of trust in Jesus as protector against the debasement of slavery.
Declarations of worthlessness expressed one definition of the self, but
women's actions showed a new self-confidence inspired by that awareness. Short of challenging their bondage directly, enslaved women became emboldened by their direct access to biblical teaching to say and
do things that would have seemed impossible earlier. One woman, repeatedly beaten by a hostile overseer, 'took her Bible in hand and started
to read him several passages from the text. The episode caused him to
relent. Subsequently, he became much more indulgent in his relation
to the Negroes and adopted a friendly attitude toward the Brethren.'
Another woman named Mariana used her knowledge of the Scriptures
to intimidate whites into silence. 'She speaks to some *Blanken* [whites]
with such authority about what she has read in the Bible that they can
not open their mouths against her.' A third enslaved woman, invoking
a prophetic view of the impending apocalypse that would devour the

wicked, told the missionaries that the world would end with the masters
ignorant of the punishment they would face. As these instances indicate,
the notion of prophecy that would become central to African American
Christianity in the antebellum United States – of the Bible as protection
for God's chosen people, as fulfillment of their special destiny and punishment for those who sin against them – was already starting to emerge
in the Caribbean a century earlier.[15]

Some planters, of course, responded vigorously to these perceived
threats to their authority, forbidding slaves from attending Moravian
meetings and punishing those who did. According to a missionary, 'one
Negro woman who lost her resolve, as a result of repeated harsh treatment, abandoned her desire to become converted.' In another case,
however, such beatings had the opposite effect. 'The Negro woman came
to the conclusion – undoubtedly through the grace of God, bestowed
upon her as a blessing for her undeserved suffering – that there had to
be something very important about the lessons. So she resolved to take
advantage of the opportunity, and nothing from then on could dissuade
her from attending the meetings.' While men and women held many
forms of religious experience in common, such as conversion narratives
and a sense of spiritual equality before God, some aspects of Christianity
appear to have been especially attractive to women because of their sexual vulnerability. Evidence suggests, for example, that women wielded
their new faith as a kind of defence against rape by their masters. Missionary Christian Oldendorp wrote that a number of 'Negro women who
no longer wished to allow themselves to be abused for sinful purposes'
invoked the Bible to refuse forced sex, enduring harsh punishment in
return. 'If I had previously been ready to suffer for bad causes,' Oldendorp quoted one woman as saying, 'why should I not now be willing to
suffer a bit for a good cause?' In such ways, the Bible became an active
presence in the lives of enslaved women that gave new order to a violent,
chaotic world. By invoking the authority of Jesus above that of their masters, they claimed the ability to resist some of slavery's worst ravages and
to move and speak in a society deeply hostile not only to female preaching but also to any form of black self-expression.[16]

The missionaries devised new strategies to harness and direct this
spiritual power. Adapting a feature of Moravian worship in Europe,
they created a corps of black 'helpers' to assist in leading the congregation. The first five included four men, Andreas, Johannes, Peter, and
Christoph, and one woman, Anna Maria, all of whom 'had already been
busy among their people [and] were loved and respected by their fellow

slaves.' The helpers exercised 'supervision and guidance of certain small groups who came together once a week to discuss their inner growth in the knowledge of Jesus Christ, to exchange confidences about their individual problems, to encourage one another, and to ask forgiveness for one another.' These knots of five to ten converts were called 'bands,' another standard Moravian practice. Divided by sex, the groups brought together worshipers of similar life circumstance, such as age, African ethnicity, and marital status, who shared bonds of empathy, spiritual discovery, and friendship. 'Through the bands not a single person in the entire congregation is neglected or forgotten,' according to a church official. More helpers were added in subsequent years, and, as a mission assistant, Rebecca supervised black female helpers and the entire female section of the mission.[17]

By felicitous coincidence, this system was probably partly familiar to many African congregants. Men and women throughout West Africa were ritually inducted into adulthood through membership in gender-divided secret societies led by mentors who guided novitiates through the intricacies of the spirit world. African women were therefore accustomed to female spiritual leaders at several strata of social organization: family, clan, secret society, and village. The helper system on St Thomas was a kind of stripped-down but recognizable version of that principle, placing gender at the heart of the evangelical effort by giving helpers and converts a leadership structure and a measure of self-direction in their own spiritual growth. The principle of spiritual kinship embedded in the fictive family of the band helped congregants feel connected to the larger congregational family, giving followers greater guidance, access to spiritual power, and opportunity to voice concerns. For enslaved women, this aspect of the mission was especially appealing, because in a society that militantly devalued their bodies and minds, it was essential that female mentors work with women to encourage their sense of fellowship. The system helped negotiate the complex meeting and fusion of African beliefs with Christianity.[18]

A church membership roster from 1740 illustrates the effectiveness of these practices. The list is neatly separated into bands according to gender. Of 300 congregants, 123 were men, divided into 23 bands supervised by Friedrich Martin and two white assistants. The women's side was larger, with 177 members divided into 28 bands supervised by Rebecca and a white mission assistant. Those figures alone are striking – women, outnumbered by men in the island's slave population, made up 60 per cent of the congregation, exactly the proportion that historians have

identified as a standard feature of later African Christian congregations
in North America. Those numbers might testify to the skill of Rebecca
and others as recruiters, but perhaps they say something as well about
the lure of Jesus' message for enslaved women and about the power of
fellowship to give refuge and comfort to the powerless.[19]

That all of this took place in the face of often massive opposition and
retribution by many Dutch planters on St Thomas offers further testimony to the appeal of evangelical religion in the slave quarters. Historians have sometimes contended that planters forced slaves to convert to
Christianity as a means of social control, an argument that undoubtedly
has merit for some periods of slavery and in some places. In these early
years on St Thomas, however, the reverse was true – the slaves embraced
Christianity in defiance of the masters, for whom the radical spiritual
egalitarianism their bond men and women practised was a source of fear.
The extended circle of fellowship that emerged in the shadow of the
plantation economy was a massive popular movement fuelled by a kind
of African American liberation theology.[20]

This conflict burst into the open in 1738 when Rebecca, the mission
assistant, married a missionary, Matthäus Freundlich. The missionaries
arranged the marriage not out of romantic attachment between the two
but in the belief that Rebecca's 'work among the Negro women, the
majority of whom were married, would be even more effective if she
were married herself.' They also 'thought that any misgivings concerning the propriety of her close association with the Brethren could be
removed if she were married.' The wedding was legal, since there were
no strictures on the Danish colonial books against the marriage of a free
woman of colour to a white man, though such unions were probably
extremely uncommon. Yet, to colonial authorities and planters, the interracial marriage represented one more insolent attempt to breach the
strict racial hierarchy upon which the plantation economy rested. They
arrested and imprisoned the missionaries on trumped-up charges of
theft and, after a trial lasting several months, convicted Rebecca and her
husband of refusing to swear an oath in court. Court testimony strongly
suggests, however, that the real reason for the prosecution was the suspicion that the missionaries were inciting the slaves to rebellion. Rebecca
was sentenced to return to slavery, her husband to lifetime servitude in a
Danish prison. By remarkable coincidence, the Moravian leader, Count
Nikolaus von Zinzendorf, arrived on St Thomas unexpectedly in Janu-
ary 1739 and intervened with the governor, securing the pair's release
from prison.[21]

In the aftermath of this episode, planters hostile to the count un-
leashed a torrent of anger against the mission, putting intense pressure
on the governor to have the Brethren evicted from St Thomas altogether.
They flogged and imprisoned slaves, and on several occasions they raid-
ed the congregants' church to disrupt meetings and disperse worshipers.
As this violence escalated, someone – whether black congregants, missionaries, or Count Zinzendorf – hatched the plan to draft petitions to
the king and queen of Denmark requesting relief. The tactic was unusu-
ally daring in imagination and in risk, and it must have entailed much
discussion among enslaved congregants whether to take that risk. The
missionaries could scarcely have asked the slaves to go over the heads of
the plantation masters to appeal directly to the Danish crown without
their own consent. Thus it was that two letters were written on behalf
of the entire congregation; one by the Creole-born Domingo Gesu, or
Mingo, the other by his African mother, Magdalena, a native 'of the Papaa nation' in West Africa and manumitted former slave. Mingo's petition declared the worshipers' determination to persist 'despite all the
oppression by those who have come to beat and injure us when the *Baas*
[Martin] teaches us about the Savior, by those who burn our books, and
call our baptism the baptism of dogs, and call the Brethren beats, declaring the Negroes must not be saved and that a baptized Negro is no more
than kindling wood for the flames of hell.' Magdalena's letter on behalf
of 250 black women was an extraordinary example of individual and collective African female self-assertion in the face of brutal repression. Condemning white planters for their unbelief, she praised the missionaries
for rescuing her from paganism and declared herself 'very sad in my
heart that the Negro women on St. Thomas are not allowed to serve the
Lord Jesus.' The letter was born of an optimism that, if only the authorities knew how badly the slaves suffered for trying to be better Christians
than their masters, surely they would intervene.[22]

Indeed, the appeals achieved their desired effect. Count Zinzendorf
sailed from the Caribbean to Europe in February 1739 carrying the letters, which he forwarded to the Danish monarchs, who ordered an end
to the persecution. The slaves' daring mobilization had saved their mission. Though planters did not obey at once, they eventually accepted
African Christianization as a component of social control over the slaves.
In a startling transformation from their earlier subversive teachings, beginning in the early 1740s the missionaries responded to the planters'
pressure by vowing to emphasize the slaves' Christian duty to submit to
worldly authority. While the planters remained distrustful for several

years, they eventually came to view the mission as a support, not a challenge, to the plantation system and allowed it to proceed. As church
historian Christian Oldendorp wrote, 'exposure to Christian teachings
tended to convert formerly rebellious, disobedient, and wild slaves into
benevolent, faithful, and genuinely devoted people.' Earlier reviled as
enemies of social order, the Brethren were now welcomed as its loyal
defenders. Indeed, the Brethren themselves even joined the planting
class when they bought plantations and slaves in the Danish islands and
in British Caribbean colonies such as Jamaica and Antigua where their
mission expanded in the 1750s. In this preview of what would happen in
the antebellum southern United States seventy-five to one hundred years
later, the domestication of evangelical Christianity thus became linked to
the defence and survival of slavery.[23]

Still, even though the planters came to view the black church as a but-
tress for the plantation order, enslaved Africans and Creoles on St Thomas and, increasingly, on St Croix and St John continued to flock to its
embrace. By 1768, the missionaries reported having baptized more than
4,500 blacks in those colonies, including 1,985 women, 1,561 men, and
1,014 children. Those figures suggest that, despite ideological changes
rendering the mission more palatable to colonial authorities, congregational life remained highly attractive for the enslaved. Indeed, the black
Protestant population in the Danish West Indies was still easily the largest in the world through the 1780s. Many of the new churches formed to
accommodate this burgeoning membership remained robust during the
slavery period, which ended in the Danish colonies in 1848, and beyond
into the era of freedom; today they survive as thriving congregations in
the modern U.S. Virgin Islands – a durable legacy of African diasporic
achievement in the Americas.[24]

The numbers also suggest that the appeal of the Christian community
was still particularly high for enslaved women, who remained the majority of baptismal recipients. While baptismal and membership statistics
alone are an insufficient index of a people's spirituality, we must at least
speculate that congregational life continued to offer women a refuge
from slavery, however incomplete and circumscribed it might have been.
The church family writ large was vital to women whose husbands and
children might be sold away at any time, or who might find themselves
on the auction block as well. The backbone of the system remained the
elaborate structural lattice of helpers, counsellors, and bands that provided a network of support and spiritual kinship as well as opportunities
for religious leadership and education. The sense that Jesus was a special

friend of the oppressed and downtrodden would remain a staple feature of black Christianity in the Caribbean and North America through slavery and beyond. Literacy lessons continued, though with strict monitoring by the missionaries, and so it is safe to assume that the chance to read biblical texts remained an attraction. It is unknown whether black Moravian women still used the Bible to shame their masters into treating them better, but it is quite possible that they continued to see their suffering as evidence of their own election and of their moral superiority over unchristian masters. Thus, although the church discouraged slave members from overtly resisting slavery, and punished those who did, we should not be surprised that enslaved people still found other reasons to sustain a nurturing environment in its fellowship.

For a handful of women, the Moravian church even provided a rare opportunity to leave the oppressive setting of the West Indies for friendlier places. Beginning in the late 1730s, a few black converts travelled with missionaries to Germany and to the new Moravian congregation-town of Bethlehem, Pennsylvania, founded in 1740. In both of these places, black Christians stayed to live, work, and worship in close quarters with white Moravian counterparts, fully integrated into biracial congregations. Some of these migrants were free, while others were slaves who had been purchased by the church and, in some cases, lived quasi-free in their new homes. By the early 1740s, a kind of spiritual triangle had emerged within the church between three distinctive black religious communities an ocean apart: a large contingent of worshipers in St Thomas and two smaller ones in Bethlehem and Germany. Black Moravians sometimes moved between these communities, enjoying a mobility and breadth of opportunity all too rare among victims of the Atlantic slave trade. For these adherents, religion provided a new and different sense of purpose far from the oppressive slave societies of the Caribbean. Just as black sailors on merchant vessels circulated news and ideas to black communities throughout the Americas, Europe, and Africa, black evangelical Christians were beginning to do the same thing. As the sea and the church became their escape routes from plantation slavery, they began to plant the seeds of the black Protestant international movement. For black Moravian women, this meant the emergence of a transnational black sisterhood.

One of the first women of African descent to help forge this sisterhood was Anna Maria, who had been among the five original mission 'helpers' on St Thomas and had worked to oversee the women's bands there before departing for Germany in 1739. In the Moravian town of Herrnhaag, to the northeast of Frankfurt am Main, she lived in the women's dormitory as a conspicuously dark-skinned sister among a house full of white co-religionists before succumbing to the cold climate and unfamiliar disease environment in 1740. Another such Caribbean refugee was Maria, a congregational eldress on St Thomas who was purchased by the Brethren in 1740 and sent to Bethlehem, where she married Andreas, an enslaved brother and fellow worker from St Thomas. The couple travelled to Germany where they were to receive additional training in mission work before being sent back to the West Indies; instead they ended up staying in Herrnhaag and melding into the congregation. Maria, known as 'the Mooress from St. Thomas' (the German '*die Mohrin von Sanct Thomas*'), became so closely absorbed into the fabric of sacramental life that she was ordained a deaconess, a mid-level church officer who administered the foot-washing ceremony and assisted the pastor in other ways. Though the position did not entitle her to preach, it was nonetheless important enough to require ordination, meaning that Maria might well have been among the first women of African descent known to be ordained in the Western Christian tradition. In a significant reversal of standard eighteenth-century racial and spiritual practices, the title elevated this formerly enslaved woman to a position of spiritual authority and guidance over European women. Inverting the idea of mission, it was Maria, the black Christian, who now schooled her white sisters in the principles of the faith – a remarkable indication of the social and religious fluidity afforded by the Moravian fellowship that regarded closeness to Christ, not outward physical appearance, as the essential marker of salvation. The prestige of her stature was recognized by a portrait painted by church artist Johan Valentin Haidt, whose likenesses of dozens of Moravian leaders and missionaries are now housed in church archives in Germany and Bethlehem. That a mid-eighteenth-century portrait could depict a black woman not as a debased slave or a savage but as a dignified member of Christ's redeemed family indicates both the appeal of that family to women and its potential to challenge the prevailing racial hierarchies of that epoch.[25]

These women were quintessential 'Atlantic Creoles' – products of the slave trade and the black Atlantic, well versed in several languages, representing an amalgamation of cultures and possessing the ability to move easily between them. Perhaps the most remarkable of these international sisters of colour was Rebecca Freundlich, the free woman so instrumental in helping the missionaries reach enslaved women in St Thomas, whose interracial marriage to missionary Matthäus Freundlich had enraged the authorities on St Thomas. Following their trial, conviction, and release from prison, the couple remained on the island until 1742 when, exhausted by their ordeal, they left to gain some rest in Germany. Matthäus died of a fever immediately after arriving in Europe, and Rebecca stayed on to live in the Herrnhaag congregation with her young daughter. Like Maria, her co-worker in St Thomas, she too was ordained as a deaconess and honoured with a portrait in recognition of her service to the mission. In 1745 she remarried; her husband was Christian Protten, son of an African mother of royal descent and a Danish soldier stationed at the Danish fortress of Christiansborg on the Gold Coast of West Africa. Raised in both Africa and Denmark, Protten had joined the Moravian Church in the mid-1730s and returned to Africa as a missionary for several years. After their marriage, he and Rebecca lived in Germany until both left in 1764 for the Gold Coast to serve as schoolteachers in Christiansborg for mixed-race children, who were commonly found in and around the European slave-trading ports in West Africa. As forerunners of the black Christian evangelical movement that would extend from America and Britain to West Africa in the late eighteenth century, both Prottens served in Africa until their deaths, his in 1769 and hers in 1780. Though their work achieved few Christian conversions or other measurable results there, Rebecca's sojourn in Africa nevertheless represented the pinnacle of one woman's extraordinary transatlantic journey from the Caribbean to Europe to Africa in the service of black Christianity and women's education.[26]

St Thomas was but one small place in a galaxy of American slave societies, but the events that took place there in the 1740s had a profound effect on the religious cultures of African America and the Atlantic world. Though the Moravians were a small religious group, they exercised a deep influence on the evangelical Protestant movement germinating in Britain and North America during those years. John Wesley and the Methodists, in particular, were inspired by the emotional 'heart-religion' of the Brethren, and many enslaved Africans and other non-Christians embraced Methodism in the Caribbean. When they began their own missions in earnest in North America and the West Indies in the 1740s and 1750s, the Methodists emulated some of the practices and strategies of their Moravian predecessors. They preached of a new birth and the redeeming power of Christ to transcend racial divides and reach the enslaved outcasts of the plantation world. They relied on itinerant teachers, black and white, cultivated a sense of black brothers and sisters being welcomed into a larger spiritual family, and adopted similar pedagogical

practices such as literacy and small prayer groups. And they empowered
black men *and* women to witness to Christ's saving protection and to
spread that message in the slave quarters. On Antigua, for example, enslaved women reached out to the Methodists with particular vigour. By
the early nineteenth century, most of the colony's 3,516 Methodists were
black women, some of whom were said to have 'good gifts in Prayer and
hold prayer meetings.' Black Christianity spread throughout the Atlantic
world on the strength of such women with 'good gifts in Prayer.'[27]

In the nineteenth-century United States, a new generation of African
American female preachers such as Rebecca Cox Jackson, Jarena Lee,
and Sojourner Truth invoked the Bible to claim not only the right to
preach but also a new moral centre for Christianity in the fight against
slavery. These women were the spiritual descendants of Magdalena, Rebecca, Mariana, and other black women on St Thomas. In the 1850s
Sojourner Truth would shock audiences with her prophetic revelations
about an impending day of judgment, but it was Mariana, after all, who
more than a century earlier had spoken to white planters 'with such authority about what she has read in the Bible that they cannot open their
mouths against her.'

Notes

1 Original manuscript copies of the letters are stored in the Moravian Church
   Archives in Herrnhut, Germany, R15.Ba.1. They were collected and printed
   in a German-language church publication called *Büdingische Sammlung*, 4
   (Büdingen, 1741), in Nikolaus Ludwig von Zinzendorf, *Ergänzungsband*, 7
   (Hildesheim: Olms, 1965), 483–7. On this episode, see also C.G.A. Olden-
   dorp, *History of the Mission of the Evangelical Brethren on the Caribbean Islands of
   St. Thomas, St. Croix, and St. John*, ed. Johann Jakob Bossard, English trans.
   Arnold R. Highfield and Vladimir Barac (Barby, 1777; English ed. Ann
   Arbor, Mich.: Karome Publishers, 1987), 364–5; Angelita Reyes, *Mother-
   ing across Cultures: Postcolonial Representations* (Minneapolis: University of
   Minnesota Press, 2002); and Jon Sensbach, *Rebecca's Revival: Creating Black
   Christianity in the Atlantic World* (Cambridge, Mass.: Harvard University Press,
   2005), 143–8.
2 The literature on African Christianity in the New World is large and growing. For these particular topics, see Sylvia R. Frey and Betty Wood, *Come
   Shouting to Zion: African-American Protestantism in the American South and British Caribbean to 1830* (Chapel Hill: University of North Carolina Press, 1998),

and Albert S. Raboteau, *Slave Religion: The 'Invisible Institution' in the Antebellum South* (New York: Oxford University Press, 1978).

3 On African Catholicism, influential recent treatments include Herman Bennett, *Africans in Colonial Mexico: Absolutism, Christianity, and Afro-Creole Consciousness, 1570–1640* (Bloomington: Indiana University Press, 2003); John Thornton, *Africa and Africans in the Making of the Atlantic World, 1400–1680* (Cambridge: Cambridge University Press, 1998), chapter 9; Thornton, 'On the Trail of Voodoo: African Christianity in Africa and the Americas,' *The Americas*, 44 (1988): 261–78; and James H. Sweet, *Recreating Africa: Culture, Kinship, and Religion in the African-Portuguese World* (Chapel Hill: University of North Carolina Press, 2003).

4 Frey and Wood, in *Come Shouting to Zion* (xi), draw attention to this gap in the scholarship. The pioneering exploration of the rise of black Protestantism is Carter G. Woodson, *The History of the Negro Church*, 2nd ed. (Washington, D.C.: Associated Publishers, 1945; originally published in 1921). More recent examinations include Raboteau, *Slave Religion*; Mechal Sobel, *Trabelin' On: The Slave Journey to an Afro-Baptist Past* (Princeton, N.J.: Princeton University Press, 1988); and Margaret Washington Creel, *"A Peculiar People": Slave Religion and Community-Culture among the Gullahs* (New York: New York University Press, 1988).

5 On African American preaching women in the nineteenth-century United States, see Jean M. Humez, ed., *Gifts of Power: The Writings of Rebecca Cox Jackson, Black Visionary, Shaker Eldress* (Amherst: University of Massachusetts Press, 1981); William L. Andrews, ed., *Sisters of the Spirit: Three Black Women's Autobiographies of the Nineteenth Century* (Bloomington: Indiana University Press, 1986); and Nell Irvin Painter, *Sojourner Truth: A Life, a Symbol* (New York: W.W. Norton, 1996).

6 Frey and Wood, *Come Shouting to Zion*, 163–4.

7 On colonization and slavery in the Danish West Indies, see Waldemar Westergaard, *The Danish West Indies under Company Rule, 1671–1754* (New York: Macmillan, 1917); Neville A.T. Hall, *Slave Society in the Danish West Indies: St. Thomas, St. John, and St. Croix*, ed. B.W. Higman (Mona, Jamaica: University of the West Indies Press, 1992), population figures on 5; Arnold R. Highfield, 'The Danish Atlantic and West Indian Slave Trade,' in George F. Tyson and Arnold R. Highfield, eds., *The Danish West Indian Slave Trade: Virgin Islands Perspectives* (St Croix: Virgin Islands Humanities Council, 1994), 11–32; Karen Fog Olwig, *Cultural Adaptation and Resistance on St. John: Three Centuries of Afro-Caribbean Life* (Gainesville: University Press of Florida, 1985); and idem, 'African Cultural Principles in Caribbean Slave Societies: A View from the Danish West Indies,' in Stephan Palmié, ed., *Slave Cultures*

and the Cultures of Slavery (Knoxville: University of Tennessee Press, 1995),
23–39.

8 A basic text for understanding the origins of the Renewed Unity of Brethren is Kenneth G. Hamilton and J. Taylor Hamilton, *History of the Moravian
Church: The Renewed Unitas Fratrum, 1722–1957* (Bethlehem, Penn.: Interprovincial Board of Christian Education, Moravian Church in America,
1967). On the failure of early mission attempts by the Church of England,
see, among others, Frey and Wood, *Come Shouting to Zion,* chapter 3.

9 Oldendorp, *History of the Mission,* 281. Among many works dealing with slave
literacy, see Henry Louis Gates, *The Signifying Monkey: Towards a Theory of
Afro-American Literary Criticism* (Oxford: Oxford University Press, 1988); and
Janet Duitsman Cornelius, *When I Can Read My Title Clear: Literacy, Slavery
and Religion in the Antebellum South* (Columbia: University of South Carolina
Press, 1992).

10 Details of Rebecca's early life are derived from Oldendorp, *History of the Mission,* 314, and are elaborated in Sensbach, *Rebecca's Revival,* chapters 2–3.

11 Peter Vogt, 'A Voice for Themselves: Women as Participants in Congregational Discourse in the Eighteenth-Century Moravian Movement,' in Beverly
Mayne Kienzle and Pamela J. Walker, eds., *Women Preachers and Prophets
through Two Millennia of Christianity* (Berkeley: University of California Press,
1998), 227–47; Gary Kinkel, *Our Dear Mother the Spirit: An Investigation of
Count Zinzendorf's Theology and Praxis* (Lanham, Md.: University Press of
America, 1990); and Craig Atwood, 'The Mother of God's People: The Adoration of the Holy Spirit in the Eighteenth-Century Brüdergemeine,' *Church
History,* 68 (December 1999): 886–909.

12 Unity Archives, Herrnhut, Germany (hereafter UA), R15, Ba. 10, Friedrich
Martin to Johann Decknatel, 13 Feb. 1737.

13 UA, Martin to Decknatel, 13 Feb. 1737; UA, R15.Ba.10, St Thomas Diary, 14
April 1737.

14 Oldendorp, *History of the Mission,* 330, 412–13.

15 Ibid., 328; St Thomas diary, 30 March and 28 May 1737.

16 Oldendorp, *History of the Mission,* 327, 328.

17 Ibid., 333. In 1760 missionary Georg Weber filed a long report describing
all the helpers in the congregations on St Thomas, St John, and St Croix
– fifty-four men and women, in all – which provides a wealth of information but reveals the African identity of only a few. UA, R15.Ba27.11. The
social and religious organization of the congregation is discussed further
in Arnold R. Highfield, 'Patterns of Accommodation and Resistance: The
Moravian Witness to Slavery in the Danish West Indies,' *Journal of Caribbean
History,* 28 (1994): 138–64.

18 Oldendorp, *History of the Mission,* 333. Helpers are discussed briefly in Frey

and Wood, *Come Shouting to Zion*, 84–5, and Sensbach, *A Separate Canaan: The Making of an Afro-Moravian World in North Carolina, 1763–1840* (Chapel Hill: University of North Carolina Press, 1998), 39. On the role of helpers in the early Moravian church, see Hanns-Joachim Wollstadt, *Geordnetes Dienen in der christlichen Gemeinde* (Goettingen: Vandenhoeck and Ruprecht, 1966), 155–61, 312–15. Bands are discussed in the same volume from 93–9, quote on 96. On African secret societies and their adaptation to an American milieu, see Creel, *'A Peculiar People,'* 288–92. For examples of the comparable organization of Afro-Catholic confraternities in the Americas, see Mary Karasch, *Slave Life in Rio de Janeiro, 1808–1850* (Princeton, N.J.: Princeton University Press, 1987); and Elizabeth W. Kiddy, 'Ethnic and Racial Identity in the Brotherhoods of the Rosary of Minas Gerais, 1700–1830,' *The Americas*, 56 (1999): 221–52.

19 Congregation list included in UA, R15.Ba.1, 'Konferenz-Protokolle von St. Thomas,' 8 Sept. 1740. See also Oldendorp, *History of the Mission*, 388.

20 On the coercive use of Christianity to instill subservience in enslaved workers, see Raboteau, *Slave Religion*, chapter 4, and Janet Duitsman Cornelius, *Slave Missions and the Black Church in the Antebellum South* (Columbia: University of South Carolina Press, 1999).

21 This episode is described in Oldendorp, *History of the Mission*, 337–56.

22 Ibid., 364–5.

23 Ibid., 230, 335. Among a number of works discussing the transformation of Southern planters' outlook towards slave Christianity, see Raboteau, *Slave Religion*, chapter 4, and Sylvia R. Frey, *Water from the Rock: Black Resistance in a Revolutionary Era* (Princeton, N.J.: Princeton University Press, 1991).

24 Oldendorp, *History of the Mission*, 626.

25 UA, R8.33.d, Marienborn Diary, 10 Jan. 1746, and Herrnhaag Diary, R8.33.e, 10 Jan. 1746. For an example of another African woman enslaved in Bethlehem, see Katherine Faull Eze, 'Self-Encounters: Two Eighteenth-Century African Memoirs from Moravian Bethlehem,' in David McBride, Leroy Hopkins, and C. Aisha Blackshire-Belay, eds., *Crosscurrents: African Americans, Africa, and Germany in the Modern World* (Columbia: University of South Carolina Press, 1998), 29–52.

26 Sensbach, *Rebecca's Revival*, chapters 7–8; Ira Berlin, 'From Creoles to African: Atlantic Creoles and the Origins of African-American Society in Mainland North America,' *William and Mary Quarterly*, 3rd ser., 53 (1996): 251–88.

27 Frey and Wood, *Come Shouting to Zion*, 80–8, 104. On the influence of the Moravians on the broader Protestant evangelical movement of the eighteenth century, see also W.R. Ward, *The Protestant Evangelical Awakening* (Cambridge: Cambridge University Press, 1992).

chapter five

'The Most Resplendent Flower of the Indies': Making Saints and Constructing Whiteness in Colonial Peru

RACHEL SARAH O'TOOLE

In 1673 Fray (Brother) Francisco del Risco began secretly to exorcise legions of demonic spirits from his penitent Juana Luisa Benites. Soon, other nuns and residents of the Santa Clara convent on the northern Peruvian coast also were seized by spirits. Alarmed, Lima's Supreme Tribunal of the Inquisition charged its representative in Trujillo to investigate. The resulting trial document contains testimonies from witnesses, correspondence between inquisitorial officials, and a detailed defence penned by Risco at the request of the Holy Office. By November 1675, inquisitors had dismissed rumours that the convent had been bewitched and turned their focus to the mystical aspirations of Juana Luisa Benites. The nun testified that God had willed the demonic appearances as a test of her faith and worthiness.[1] In turn, Fray Risco promoted Benites as a saint who struggled against constant sensations of vaginal penetration that accompanied her visions, the frightful domination of black demons, and the terrifying pursuit of wild beasts. Benites seems to have believed that the physical manifestations were part of a divine purification that would erase her illegitimate birth. As occurred with other spiritual women throughout the Catholic Atlantic world, the Inquisition questioned the veracity of Benites's visions and the depth of her devotions. In 1678 the officials of the Holy Office declared that the young nun was an *ilusa* with 'false and diabolical illusions' and was guilty of heresy, blasphemy, and superstition.[2] Shortly thereafter, Benites, her confessor, and her companion Ana Nuñes were transferred to the secret jails of Lima's Real Audiencia in 1681.[3] In less than a decade, the young *Criolla* (a white woman born in the Americas) had been demoted from her privileged status as a black-veiled nun in Trujillo's sole convent to the disreputable position of a religious criminal.

The spiritual claims of Juana Luisa Benites and her supporters coupled with the Inquisition's punishment were not unusual in the latter half of the seventeenth century. Throughout Europe and the Americas, Catholic religious and laywomen experienced physical manifestations that challenged orthodox parameters of religious devotion. As did others, the Peruvian nun suffered physical torments of the devil that she believed validated the holiness of her prayer, writing, or other required tasks.[4] Some Catholics thought that the sexual nature of the demon provided proof of heroic femininity and defensive piety.[5] Like her European counterparts, Benites proved obedience to her male confessor by conquering the demon that threatened to replace the male authority of clerics or the patriarchal sanctity of God.[6] European religious women such as Teresa of Avila and Catherine of Siena provided pious models for Benites.[7] Likewise, Fray Risco based the assessment of his penitent on a manual for exorcism and other religious texts that commonly circulated between Europe and Spanish America. Benites's spiritual experiences and the inquisitorial investigation provide a point of entry for exploring how church authorities sought to contain women's religiosity throughout the Atlantic world.

In the Americas, Catholic orthodoxy was regularly challenged by the religious and spiritual practices of the indigenous and African peoples who made up the majority of the colonial population. Catholic authorities suspected that Christian 'Indians' regressed to idolatry while Africans and their descendants consorted with the devil even after baptism.[8] When Fray Risco described Benites's tormentor as a 'black demon,' he was reiterating an ideology found on both sides of the Atlantic that linked demons with people of colour.[9] While this practice had deep roots in medieval Europe, the colonial enterprises of the sixteenth and seventeenth centuries gave it new saliency as Spanish Americans increasingly used colonial terms stemming from the caste (*casta*) system to describe the devil. Thus, the devil was known as a 'dirty little Indian,' a 'very ugly *mulato*,' or, in Benites's case, a 'large *negro* [black man].'[10] In using such terms, Fray Risco raised the familiar colonial spectre of racial and gendered danger to prove Benites's mystical suffering.[11] He tapped into anxieties specific to the context where slaveholders' dependency and intimacy with native Americans, Africans, and people of mixed racial descent raised fears of resistance by enslaved and free people alike.[12]

Like his counterparts in Europe, Fray Risco may have exaggerated his descriptions of Benites's sufferings – in this case at the hands of a sexualized black demon – to prove that Benites was a true saint.[13] His exaggerations seem all the more plausible given the ambivalence displayed in the historical records over Benites's reputation among other nuns and among the people of her native city. Part of this ambivalence stemmed from a general assumption among Europeans that the climate, constellations, and the food of the Americas produced indulgent, lazy, and sexually excessive women. [14] For Criollas such as Benites, this fear was amplified since they were native to this dangerous American environment. While these general anxieties about women contributed to the ambivalence towards Benites, the real source of doubt regarding her reputation stemmed from the discovery during her trial that she was the illegitimate child of a priest and elite white woman. For years, she had passed as an ideal Peruvian nun in the sense that she had claimed that she was the legitimate daughter of an elite local family.[15] Once this lie was uncovered, her entire reputation as a pious nun and as an elite white woman was thrown into doubt.

Benites and her confessor expertly articulated Iberian and colonial fears of a black demon as a way to overcome these challenges to her reputation. Her failure to defend her reputation as a virginal and pious nun reveals the interdependence of race, social status, and religion in colonial Spanish America, and also underlines how difficult it was to fulfil and maintain the status of an elite white female in this society.

'She did not consent': Defending Criolla Identity

In 1672 and 1673 Juana Luisa Benites explained to her confessor and to her close companion, Ana Nuñes, that she was experiencing visions and corporeal sensations of angels and devils. Around 1674, her manifestations became more public as the Inquisition's *comisario* reported that over twenty nuns and other servants within the Santa Clara convent were possessed with bad spirits.[16] As the Franciscans (with other clerics) began exorcising members of the convent, Benites distinguished herself by taming the demons of her companion Ana Nuñes.[17] By 1675, the Lima Tribunal had ordered an investigation that focused exclusively on the spiritual claims and devotional practices of Juana Luisa Benites. Catholic authorities in the seventeenth century were growing less tolerant of visionary experiences of God, claims to sainthood, and reports of devil sightings.[18] Like other women studied by Keith Shutt and Jodi Bilinikoff,

Benites presented herself according to a model of sainthood found in circulating printed and manuscript copies of saints' lives.[19] Her claim to spiritual favours also was constructed from and within her reputation as a pious, white nun.

During her only recorded testimony to the inquisitorial representatives in Trujillo, Benites repeatedly emphasized that she had conducted herself with virtue and was experiencing divinely mandated visions. Lima's Tribunal had confiscated her private papers including letters to her confessor which, although now lost, were cited as part of the case. When questioned about her religious practices, she explained that under the guidance of other nuns she learned to 'not falter in her prayers and disciplines and the frequency of the sacraments and other good works.'[20] She reported that she followed her vows as a nun, thereby distancing herself from professed or lay women who claimed to be mystics even though they avoided penance and mortification.[21] She denied having seen or spoken directly to God, both dangerous ventures as the Counter-Reformation church worked to re-establish clerical authority over personal religious expressions.[22] She claimed to follow Saint Teresa of Avila's model, saying that her soul spoke to God and, during these mental prayers, she learned that she was divinely chosen to be his spouse.[23] Like Saint Teresa, she emphasized that God's communication with her had inspired intense humility, the urge to do more good works, to attend morning and afternoon prayers, and to remain in a withdrawn or *recogida* state.[24] In response to the inquisitors' questions, Benites constructed a self-portrait that conformed to a Catholic ideal for female piety shared throughout the Atlantic world.[25]

Benites also described her response to demons in ways that were typical for religious women on both sides of the Atlantic. For instance, she recounted how, once the demons began to possess her, she consulted her confessor, books, and other learned persons in the church for guidance, thus indicating her intense desire to remain in communion with the church.[26] For descriptions of the demons, Benites drew upon traditional imagery of demonic manifestations. For instance, she explained how she suffered from visions of snakes, toads, and other fantastical creatures.[27] She also raised the spectre of a sexual and dominating demon when she told inquisitors that she had seen 'formidable-looking women' and bulls who 'put her ahead and incited her' from behind.[28] Inquisitors pressed her to provide more details. According to her testimony, the demonic figures sexually stimulated her, forcing her into non-reproductive sexual acts.[29] Later, in their deliberations, the Lima Tribunal registered their concern that she felt a constant presence of a 'natural instrument' that issued 'seminal fluid' inside her.[30]

These forms of demonic possession were typical for the early modern Catholic world.[31] For example, the Mexican nun María de San José recounted that a demon 'held [her] so tightly pressed between his infernal arms' and tried to 'force' her 'not with threats and rages but with flattery and caresses.'[32] In such cases, encounters with sexual demons provided mystical women with opportunities to prove their strength and virtue. Like María de San José, Benites described how she defended herself from these assaults and avoided the physical sensations they caused her with cool washings and medical consultations.[33] However, although Benites could combat the physical symptoms of the assaults, she could not exorcise the demon herself, which caused her to suffer further.

While much of Benites's testimony stressed Old World models and tropes to support her case for sanctity, parts of it emphasized her American origins to increase her credibility. Specifically, her narrative of her first demonic encounter benefitted from her Criolla identity since the remote wilds of Americas figured in the Catholic imagination as a location where the devil was particularly active.[34] According to her testimony, her first encounter with the devil took place when she was a child, a period when the devil commonly manifested itself to mystics in Europe and in the Americas.[35] Benites described how, when she was six or seven years old, the demon appeared to her as a hairy, striped snake with horns, ears, and eyes. She was in the corrals in the back of the household during siesta, thus removed from protective family members or servants.[36] By placing this first encounter in a remote area of her family's property, Benites's narrative conformed with accounts given by other Latin American women who had encountered demons. For example, the Oaxacan nun María de San José once described how she was growing up on a rural hacienda when the devil threatened her and tempted her to forsake God.[37] In New Spain's Querétaro, the *beata* Francisca de los Ángeles described how, as a teenager, she succumbed to demonic armies that beat and abused her at night in the household orchard.[38] Thus, Benites's life story showed important similarities with those provided by women recognized as true female mystics in the New World. In these cases, the women's stories fused the Old World belief that the devil lurked in remote places[39] with the more recent assumption that the American wilds were his preferred habitat.

In accordance with saintly biographies, Benites's testimony combined common hagiographical tropes with distinct details from her personal life. These personal details are what ultimately got Benites into trouble. When she described to the inquisitors how the demonic snake first appeared to her, she also told how an unknown man had approached her and gave her some coins to lure her to the back of the house where he then caressed her. As recorded by the attending notary, Benites spoke about this incident in conjunction with her demonic encounter. Away from her father and the rest of the household, the striped snake ('the size and thickness of a knife') appeared between her and the unidentified man. In terms suggesting sexual assault, Juana Luisa Benites recounted that the 'snake ... did a bad thing to her body' as it disappeared between her and the man who had undressed them both.[40] When the inquisitor enquired why she did not scream for help, she explained that she was afraid that the snake would return and kill her, condemning her to hell.

Throughout her interrogations, Benites insisted that all of her experiences with the devil had been coerced and that she had been 'violated by the Demon against her will.' She forcefully defended herself, stating that she 'never consented' to carnal sin or indecent thoughts.[41] In the end, the Lima Tribunal characterized this event as an illicit sexual experience rather than a legitimate struggle against the devil or a coerced sexual assault. Peruvian inquisitors, like their European counterparts, associated sexual impropriety with spiritual heterodoxy and used this association to unravel her reputation as an honourable nun.[42]

From the beginning, Benites's case for sanctity faced challenges given her identity as a Criolla. As Jorge Cañizares-Esguerra has explained, seventeenth-century Europeans believed that the constellations and the climate of the Americas produced emasculation, idleness, and lasciviousness in indigenous populations.[43] The literature of the time commonly portrayed Spanish American men as incompetent governors and Criollas as lacking spiritual capabilities.[44] Religious and secular authorities stereotyped Criolla nuns as indulgent, frivolous, and incapable of keeping their vows.[45] Nonetheless, Benites had reason to hope that her sanctity might be believed. The canonization of Rosa of Lima in 1671 provided a powerful evidence for Criollas such as herself that the Americas could produce saints.

As it turns out, Rosa of Lima's canonization may have been the exception to the rule. In the case of Benites, the local inquisitorial representative and the Lima Tribunal prosecuted her in ways that confirmed the negative stereotypes against Criolla women. Specifically, they attacked her spiritual legitimacy by attacking the legitimacy of her white womanhood. During her testimony, the inquisitor repeatedly asked why she, as a young girl, did not tell her father or the women of the convent about the sexual encounter/demonic attack. To these questions Benites explained that she was afraid that she would be killed by the man, and demon, that had assaulted her.[46] The inquisitors' questions seem to have sprung from a socio-legal understanding that honourable (white) women and girls, by definition, did not consent to assault.[47] According to this logic, if Benites did not resist this assault, then she must have consented to it.

In addition to raising doubts about Benites's honour by scrutinizing her behaviour, the Inquisition achieved the same end by exposing her as the illegitimate daughter of a priest and a local elite woman. She was not, as her name and testimony suggested, the legitimate descendant of two landed Criollo families of colonial Trujillo.[48] The exposure of her identity undermined Benites's claim that she was an honourable Criolla experiencing divinely ordered demonic manifestations. For our purposes, the linking of racial and class identity to the legitimacy of the defendant's claims exposes the interconnectedness of gender, race, and class issues in expressions and validations of religiosity in the Spanish and Spanish American Atlantic diaspora.

Within Orthodoxy: A Bid for Criolla Sainthood

In his construction of Juana Luisa Benites as a Criolla saint, Fray Risco faced formidable obstacles. He and the Franciscans must have been aware that, by the second half of the seventeenth century, Rome had grown increasingly sceptical of visionary practices and sought to curtail the abundance of candidacies for canonization.[49] In the Americas, inquisitorial prosecution of false mystics increased in the mid-seventeenth century.[50] The cleric promoted Benites according to strategies common in Europe and in the Americas. In his description ordered by the Inquisition, Fray Risco emphasized extraordinary diabolical characteristics, seemingly to compensate for Benites's lack of requisite virtues, including her illegitimate birth. According to the cleric, the devil and his minions tortured Benites because she had so 'strongly embraced virtuous things' such as obedience and humility.[51] In describing a ferocious demon, Fray Risco also evoked particular racial anxieties to prove that Benites was a female saint regardless of her origins.

Like Juana Luisa Benites, Fray Risco carefully matched characteristics and visions of the young nun to those shared by female saints throughout the Atlantic world. According to the cleric's account, as he successfully exorcised the demons from Benites, she began to have visionary and corporeal communications with God. The Franciscan claimed that 'Christ our lord spoke through the very same mouth' of Benites during one episode just as God spoke in the voice of Spanish mystic Juan de la Cruz. Benites suffered continual beatings by the demon, but, like other female saints, she suffered in silence, with patience and 'admirable resignation.'[52] Fray Risco claimed to have instructed Benites to pray following 'the rules found in the books' by Saint Teresa of Avila and other spiritual guides.[53] By following what Stacey Schlau calls 'how-to' manuals for orthodox spirituality, he asserted that Benites experienced religious visions.[54] Indeed, Mother Saint Clara (the founder of Benites's order) appeared to the young nun to bestow symbols of chastity and love of God.[55] According to Fray Risco, for more than three weeks Benites experienced bodily pains in her feet, hands, shoulders, and head that directly imitated the passion of Christ.[56]

Fray Risco's attentive references to approved texts was part of a known formula to prove the sanctity of a female mystic, but his assertions also suggest his trepidation in the face of inquisitorial investigation. The direct communication with the divine greatly troubled religious authorities in Europe and in the Americas.[57] The Inquisition had investigated both Saint Teresa of Avila and Saint Rosa of Lima.[58] Both saints had worked closely with religious men, listened attentively to sermons, and carefully read orthodox texts. As Kathleen Myers explains, their successful escape from the Inquisition and their ultimate canonization was in part due to their obedience to Catholic authorities.[59] In contrast, Trujillo's abbess testified that, although Benites was appropriately *recogida* within the convent, she had never demonstrated exceptional devotion, virtue, or discipline since she professed.[60] Even Fray Risco's report to the Inquisition lacked descriptions of any physical mortification, regular acts of penance, or frugal living on her part – all essential qualities for her petition to sainthood. In fact, as revealed by the Lima Tribunal's discussion of the correspondence between confessor and penitent, Fray Risco had repeatedly chastised her for a lacklustre attention to penance and prayer. In subsequent testimonies, the cleric was unable to prove that Benites had the heroic virtues that were increasingly necessary for the candidacy of Counter-Reformation saints.

Perhaps, then, in an attempt to bolster Benites's case through other means, Fray Risco emphasized the formidable nature of the demons she battled in his testimony to the Inquisition. First, he explained that when the devil 'came down' into Benites's body it spoke in Latin and 'the language of Arequipa' (a southern Andean region) while exhibiting unusual strength. After the demon left her body and Benites resumed consciousness, Fray Risco declared that she did not remember what the devil had said or done.[61] Indeed, these were classic indicators of the demon, as Fray Risco carefully pointed out by citing published ecclesiastical authorities. Addressing Lima's Tribunal, Fray Risco asserted that 'some who have been present did not believe and mocked' Benites's rampant demonic possession involving six thousand, six hundred, and sixty-six demons.[62] As if in response to the populace's disbelief, Fray Risco listed pages of terrorizing beasts including a 'hideous snake,' 'the fiercest sow,' and 'a serpent with five wings' that joined with crabs, foxes, tigers, iguanas, and worms in a struggle that could be won only if God favoured Benites.[63] Fray Risco described how the captain of the devils stated that God permitted the devil 'to come into and torment this body as they had done to many martyrs.'[64] As articulated by her confessor, the sheer number of demons exalted Benites' virtues to a doubting Inquisition.

Moreover, Fray Risco constructed a lead demon that could provide a fantastical test of Benites's fortitude and tempt her to forsake her vow of chastity. Other demons were usually mildly seductive, such as the one that appeared nude in Puebla's convents or manifested as handsome men and provoked thoughts of sexual impropriety in Toledan Isabel de Jesús.[65] Yet Fray Risco stressed that Benites experienced extraordinary demonic temptations. In the first page of his description submitted to the Inquisition, he described how the devil made 'men and women constantly touch her dishonestly to provoke her ... making her immobile ... and having the [sex] act with her."[66] Within Fray Risco's narrative, Benites could prove her virtue by not consenting to the lewd acts of a sexual demon.[67] For example, the Toledan abbess Isabel de Jesús regularly combated a 'great army of devils' who, at one point, turned her mind to 'the evil spirit of fornication.'[68] In Peru, Saint Rose of Lima resisted the lustful suggestions of the demon appearing as a male lover.[69] Fitting Benites into narratives of pious and mystical nuns who experienced the test of demonic possession, Fray Risco claimed that the intensity of the devil's sexual overtures tested the young nun's strong virtue.

Bolstering the power of the sexual devil, Fray Risco added that the demon was a black man who resisted white authority. In the list of Benites's demonic manifestations, Fray Risco included a seraphim in a 'black form,' a sambo, a negro, and a 'fierce mulato' who resisted his exorcisms.[70] These forms and figures also appeared in other early modern religious women's accounts of demons in Europe and the Americas. For instance, Sor María de San José saw the devil as a 'very ugly mulato' who declared she belonged to him and not to God.[71] As throughout the Catholic Atlantic, the demon described by Fray Risco threatened both religious and social order by dominating a professed nun and disrupting her vows of chastity.[72]

In this context, the black demon who took Benites 'from behind' upset the racial basis of colonial order. Fray Risco's description of a dominant black demon employed imagery familiar to European as well as American Catholics. His pointed execution of a racial and sexual black demon that plagued a young nun redirected inquisitors away from the young nun's virtues and towards the fears of colonial elites.

At stake was not only the Inquisition's ruling regarding the veracity of Benites's visions but also elite Trujillo's support for their potential saint. In both the Americas and Europe, landholders and merchants had protected mystical women who engaged in decidedly unorthodox practices.[73] Yet Benites had very few supporters. Indeed, the few nuns who defended Benites to the Inquisition did not offer evidence of her exceptional spiritual gifts. In addition, Fray Risco's description to the Inquisition suggests that he was threatened by public opinion. He interpreted one of Benites's visions in which she saw Jesus stepping on thorns as divine anger towards those who expressed doubt that God controlled her demonic forces.[74] Additionally, he claimed that Benites had prophesized that God would 'rain fire from the sky' and would allow the devil to destroy Trujillo if its inhabitants did not believe that she suffered for their benefit. Indeed, Fray Risco converted Benites's struggle against demonic torments into martyrdom. He claimed that the young nun battled the demon because she had been ordered by God to pay penance for the lack of faith in 'all the valleys from here to Lima.'[75] Such predictions may have been received favourably when they came from popular mystics, but Fray Risco's defensive threats in his report to the Inquisition deflected attention from a lack of local support.

Fray Risco was unsuccessful in his claim that Benites was a visionary whose qualities suggested sainthood. His strategy, like many other confessors of religious women throughout the Catholic Atlantic, was to portray her according to common hagiographic tropes. His report suggests the transference of Iberian imagery to the Americas, with terrifying, sexual demons preying on religious women to prove their divinely inspired afflictions.[76] He also invoked a heightened colonial concern with men of African descent in his descriptions of black demons. As explained by Andrew Keitt, by the late seventeenth century, inquisitors were increas-

ingly suspicious of exaggerated accounts of the devil and were more
likely to focus on 'human imposture.'[77] The increased dangers of black
demons did not convince inquisitors that Juana Luisa Benites was, in
Fray Risco's description, 'the most resplendent flower of the Indies' and
a possible saint.[78] Fray Risco's descriptions of dominating, black demons
may have reflected local anxieties but appear to have intensified inquisitorial scrutiny.

A False Criolla, a False Saint

In their final ruling, the inquisitors focused on Benites's social origins
while rejecting her claims to divine visions. Admitted as a child to Trujillo's convent, Benites was said to be the legitimate daughter of two publicly known white parents.[79] Raised by a nun, she had learned to pray,
read, and sew, all respectful skills for a *Criolla doncella*.[80] She described
her family's modest economic status and how she was obliged to solicit
charitable contributions to pay for her dowry and to meet the necessary
expenses during her novitiate.[81] Still, she took her vows after testifying
that she was a legitimate daughter of Old Christians, meaning that her
ancestors had never practised Judaism. After her profession, the abbess
testified that the young nun had been *recogida*, or removed from secular
influences that would taint a spiritually and morally virtuous woman.[82]
According to the abbess, Benites had never pursued those who favoured
her and avoided the *torno* or grille that separated the cloister from the
visiting room.[83] In spite of these positive recommendations, the Inquisition persisted in its investigation of Benites's origins until discovering
that she had violated the entrance requirements to the convent and
posed as a Criolla from a respectable family.

After exposing this lie, the inquisitors denounced Benites's claims to
spiritual visions by using standard European charges against false mystics, which they bolstered with negative Spanish American stereotypes.
For example, in their final report, the Inquisition officials found Benites
to be vain and ignorant, common charges against female spiritual
women throughout the Catholic Atlantic world. True visionary women
demonstrated remarkable humility and a lack of interest in their own
material comfort or the attentions of an adoring public.[84] Instead, the
Holy Office described Benites as vain, preferring linen over wool. She
also allegedly lent her *cilicio* (hair shirt) to another nun.[85] Additionally,
they described her as ambitious, citing witnesses who claimed that she
lobbied to be elected as abbess and even mounted one of her teeth as

a relic for a patron.[86] As further evidence of Benites's pretensions, her companion (Ana Nuñes) drew an *estampa* or representation of her as a crowned saint with sceptre.[87] The inquisitors condemned Ana Nuñes's actions as blasphemous and judged Benites's beliefs in her own spiritual powers to be heretical.[88] The representations were even more egregious because, the inquisitor argued, the two women were too 'cultured' to plead ignorance.[89] Indeed, representatives of the Holy Office suggested that, because Benites was educated, she should have known better.

Yet the Lima Tribunal also honed its accusations to particular characteristics of colonial inhabitants. In Trujillo, the lead investigator asked Juana Luisa Benites a question 'with so much clarity that she would understand even if she was a barbarous Indian.'[90] Clearly couched as an insult, the inquisitor's language implied that she was a false female visionary. In addition, his comparison suggested a slur against Criollas or those born in the Americas and in close proximity to indigenous natives. When she was unable to answer his questions satisfactorily, her failure only supported his suggestion that she was culturally more Indian than Spanish.

To further their condemnation, the inquisitors suggested that Benites exhibited characteristics of Africans and their descendants. Witnesses described how, during her visions, Benites went into a state in which she spoke in the 'little voice' of a child. Her confessor testified that she would remain this way for days while still exhibiting remarkable piety. Throughout the Atlantic world, 'littleness' was a sign of piety.[91] The Dominican inquisitor Fray Martín de Pereira identified her state as similar to a 1637 case of a black woman who, immobile and quiet, spoke 'from the inside' of her body in a 'little voice.'[92] Pereira's findings suggested that the Benites had been attacked by 'dark' demonic forces, a common Iberian and Spanish American manifestation of the devil.[93] Yet it is possible that the inquisitor employed this particular example to condemn Benites by associating her unorthodox visions with those of a black woman. This example was similar to cases of enslaved women prosecuted by the Holy Office in seventeenth-century Mexico who divined and prophesied by speaking 'through their chests.' As Javier Villa-Flores argued, most white Criollas employed possession rather than the practice of sternomancy that the Inquisition associated with the African and demonic.[94] Indeed, by associating Benites with examples of black women, the inquisitor suggested that Benites acted more like a woman of African descent than like other white Criollas accused of false mysticism.

Lima's Supreme Tribunal of the Inquisition accused Benites of false

mysticism because her spiritual experiences did not fit with her honourable position as a Criolla nun. As the Inquisition's investigators picked
apart her religious dedication and unorthodox mystical manifestations,
they also attacked her social origins and race. Her example suggests that
the space available for Criolla women to fashion themselves as white
women was a narrow one, with any misstep on their part threatening to
lower them quickly to the status of 'Indian.'

Conclusion

Juana Luisa Benites and Fray Francisco del Risco constructed the visions
of the young nun with the common Catholic Atlantic language of religious imagery and expected actions of the demon. While Benites apparently sought to use her traumatic childhood experience as a test of
her virtue, the inquisitors could not accept her account, especially given
her revealed status as an illegitimate child. Instead, the Holy Office interpreted her portrayal of the demon as evidence of her own sexually
deviancy and uncontrollable passions. Catholic authorities on both sides
of the Atlantic accused women of unorthodox religious practices and
false promotion of sainthood based on rumours of improper sexuality,
reputations of lower social status, and denigration of female spirituality.[95] Combined with lying about her legitimacy and virginal status, the
inquisitors also exposed Benites as a false Criolla in the process of proving that she was deluded visionary.

Like other religious women in other parts of the Catholic Atlantic,
Benites faced significant barriers to proving the veracity of her mystical
experiences. In spite of the best efforts of her confessor, Fray Risco, to
defend her sanctity, her case was rejected by the inquisitors in Trujillo
and on Lima's Supreme Tribunal. Juana Luisa Benites joined countless
other Spanish American and European women who were unable to convince others of their visionary experiences.

Benites's case also suggests that race was not a fixed identity in the
Spanish Atlantic but was rather something that required careful management and maintenance. The fragility of white identity in Europe was
often threatened by presumptions of Jewish identity or by rumours of
assimilated Muslims.[96] This fragility was even greater in the Americas,
where the demographic majorities of colonized indigenous people and
enslaved Africans and their descendants put a greater burden on white
people to protect their racial identity from doubt. Benites and Fray Risco
appear to have evoked a black demon for her to highlight her white

feminine piety. Their usage suggests that gender and race 'propped each other up' as 'overlapping and related social categories,' as Kirsten Fischer and Kathleen Brown argue for the colonial United States.[97]

Similarly, the inquisitors employed racial stereotypes to dismantle Benites's white gendered identity. The attempts to undermine Benites's spiritual credibility by attacking her race reveal the extent to which the concerns of white colonizers had infiltrated the inquisitorial investigation.[98] While all women in the seventeenth-century Iberian Atlantic had to overcome increasing doubt among Catholic authorities concerning the veracity of their spiritual visions, women in Spanish America had the double burden of overcoming doubts that were rooted in the particular fears and anxieties unique to the colonial context. In turn, this double burden highlights both the continuity and the disjuncture of cultural beliefs regarding race, religion, and gender on both sides of the Atlantic. To the extent that cultural beliefs about these fundamental aspects of human identity were shared in the Atlantic world, they were also fragile and under constant negotiation.

Notes

I thank Sharon Block, Ann Kakaliouras, Daniella Kostroun, Lisa Vollendorf, and two anonymous reviewers for their suggestions and corrections on numerous versions of this chapter. Research was funded by an Albert J. Beveridge Grant for Research in the History of the Western Hemisphere from the American Historical Association (2003) and a Short-Term Research Fellowship from the International Seminar on the History of the Atlantic World at Harvard University (2003).

1 Archivo Histórico de la Nación (AHN), Inquisición (Inq.), Legajo (Leg.) 1648, Expediente (Exp.) 6, 'Copia de diferentes dichas y hechas de la causa que en este Santo Oficio se sigue sobre las Religiosas que se hallan obsesas en el Convento de Santa Clara de la Ciudad de Trujillo de este reyno del Perú' (1697, f.97v).
2 AHN, Inq. Leg. 1648, Exp. 6 (1677), ff.283.
3 Lourdes Blanco has emphasized the agency of Ana Nuñes and Juana Luisa Benites by exploring how the young nuns attempted to create an alternative spirituality. See Lourdes Blanco, 'Poder y pasión: espíritus entretejidos,' in Manuel Ramos Medina, ed., *El Monacato Femenino en el Imperio Español: Monasterios, Beaterios, Recogimientos y Colegios* (Mexico City: Centro de Estudios

de Historia de México CONDUMEX, 1995), 369–80; and idem, 'Las monjas de Santa Clara: el erotismo de la fe y la subversión de la autoridad sacerdotal,' in Luis Millones and Moisés Lemlij, eds., *En el nombre del Señor: shamanes, demonios y curanderos del norte del Perú* (Lima: Biblioteca de Psicoanálisis. Seminario Interdisciplinario de Estudios Andinos, 1994), 184–98.

4 Sherry Velasco, *Demons, Nausea, and Resistance in the Autobiography of Isabel de Jesús, 1611–1682* (Albuquerque: University of New Mexico Press, 1996), 4, 10, 14, 103; Sonya Lipsett-Rivera, '"Mira lo que hace el Diablo": The Devil in Mexican Popular Culture, 1750–1856,' *The Americas*, 59, no. 2 (2002): 201–20, 208.

5 Ellen Gunnarsdóttir, *Mexican Karismata: The Baroque Vocation of Francisca de los Ángeles 1674–1744* (Lincoln: University of Nebraska Press, 2004), 39, 47; Stacey Schlau, '"Yo no tengo necesidad que me lleven a la inquisición": Las Ilusas María Rita Vargas y María Lucía Celis,' in Mabel Moraña, ed., *Mujer y Cultura en la Colonia Hispanoamericana* (Pittsburgh: Instituto Internacional de Literatura Iberoamericana, University of Pittsburgh, 1996), 183–93, 188–9.

6 Moshe Sluhovsky, *Believe Not Every Spirit: Possession, Mysticism, & Discernment in Early Modern Catholicism* (Chicago: University of Chicago Press, 2007), 251–2; Gunnarsdóttir, *Mexican Karismata*, 122–3.

7 Jodi Bilinkoff, *Related Lives: Confessors and Their Female Penitents, 1450–1750* (Ithaca, N.Y.: Cornell University Press, 2005), 104,106; Kathleen Ann Myers, *Neither Saints Nor Sinners: Writing the Lives of Women in Spanish America* (New York and Oxford: Oxford University Press, 2003), 25, 37.

8 Kenneth Mills, *Idolatry and Its Enemies: Colonial Andean Religion and Extirpation, 1640–1750* (Princeton, N.J.: Princeton University Press, 1997); Laura de Mello e Souza, *The Devil and the Land of the Holy Cross: Witchcraft, Slavery, and Popular Religion in Colonial Brazil* (Austin: University of Texas Press / Teresa Lozano Long Institute of Latin American Studies [1986] 2003), 126–7.

9 Velasco, *Demons*, 40; Ruth Behar, 'Sexual Witchcraft, Colonialism, and Women's Powers: Views from the Mexican Inquisition,' in Asunción Lavrin, ed., *Sexuality and Marriage in Colonial Latin America* (Lincoln: University of Nebraska Press, 1989), 178–206, 191.

10 Kristine Ibsen, *Women's Spiritual Autobiography in Colonial Spanish America* (Gainesville: University Press of Florida, 1999), 13; Stacey Schlau, *Spanish American Women's Use of the Word: Colonial through Contemporary Narratives* (Tucson: University of Arizona Press, 2001), 40.

11 Laura A. Lewis, *Hall of Mirrors: Power, Witchcraft, and Caste in Colonial Mexico* (Durham, N.C.: Duke University Press, 2003), 30–1; Mello e Souza, *The Devil and the Land of the Holy Cross*, 164.

12 Vincent Brown, 'Spiritual Terror and Sacred Authority in Jamaican Slave Society,' *Slavery & Abolition*, 24, no. 1 (2003): 24–53; Walter Johnson, *Soul by Soul: Life inside the Antebellum Slave Market* (Cambridge. Mass.: Harvard University Press, 1999), 125; María Elena Martínez, 'The Black Blood of New Spain: *Limpieza de Sangre*, Racial Violence, and Gendered Power in Early Colonial Mexico,' *William and Mary Quarterly*, 61, no. 3 (2004): 479–520, 494–5.

13 Sluhovsky, *Believe Not Every Spirit*, 50–1, 253–4.

14 According to Elsa Sampson Vera Tudela, saintly nuns 'were always in danger of going native, of sliding into pagan prehistory.' *Colonial Angels: Narratives of Gender and Spirituality in Mexico, 1580–1750* (Austin: University of Texas Press, 2000), 51, 62, 64.

15 Ronald Morgan, *Spanish American Saints and the Rhetoric of Identity 1600–1810* (Tucson: University of Arizona Press, 2002), 6, 66; Karen Vieira Powers, *Women in the Crucible of Conquest: The Gendered Genesis of Latin American Society, 1500–1600* (Albuquerque: University of New Mexico Press, 2005), 113; Susan Migden Socolow, *The Women of Colonial Latin America* (Cambridge: Cambridge University Press, 2000), 15, 78.

16 AHN, Inq. Leg. 1648, Exp. 6 (1677), f.55.

17 AHN, Inq. Leg. 1648, Exp. 6 (1677), ff.15v, 33.

18 Myers, *Neither Saints Nor Sinners*, 32; Sluhovsky, *Believe Not Every Spirit*, 172.

19 Bilinkoff, *Related Lives*, 98–9; Andrew Keitt, *Inventing the Sacred: Imposture, Inquisition, and the Boundaries of the Supernatural in Golden Age Spain* (Leiden: Brill, 2005), 115.

20 AHN, Inq. Leg. 1648, Exp. 6 (1677), f.98.

21 Alison Weber, 'Between Ecstasy and Exorcism: Religious Negotiation in Sixteenth-Century Spain,' *Journal of Medieval and Renaissance Studies*, 23, no. 2 (1993): 221–34, 227.

22 AHN, Inq. Leg. 1648, Exp. 6 (1677), f.99v.

23 AHN, Inq. Leg. 1648, Exp. 6 (1677), ff.101, 103.

24 AHN, Inq. Leg. 1648, Exp. 6 (1677), ff.101, 102. A discussion of Teresa of Avila's use of humility tropes can be found in Alison Weber, *Teresa of Avila and the Rhetoric of Femininity* (Princeton, N.J.: Princeton University Press, 1990).

25 Kathryn Joy McKnight, *The Mystic of Tunja: The Writings of Madre Castillo, 1671–1742* (Amherst: University of Massachusetts Press, 1997), 51.

26 AHN, Inq. Leg. 1648, Exp. 6 (1677), f.98; Kathleen Ann Myers, 'The Mystic Triad in Colonial Mexican Nuns' Discourse: Divine Author, Visionary Scribe, and Clerical Mediator,' *Colonial Latin American Historical Review*, 6, no. 4 (1997): 479–524, 486.

27 Gunnarsdóttir, *Mexican Karismata*, 122; Velasco, *Demons*, 83, 87.

28 AHN, Inq. Leg. 1648, Exp. 6 (1677), f.97v.

29 Luiz Mott, 'Crypto-Sodomites in Colonial Brazil,' in Pete Sigal, ed., *Infamous Desire: Male Homosexuality in Colonial Latin America* (Chicago: University of Chicago Press, 2003), 168–96, 172, 188–9.

30 AHN. Inq. Leg. 1648. Exp. 6 (1677), f.97v.

31 Anne Jacobson Schutte, *Aspiring Saints: Pretense of Holiness, Inquisition, and Gender in the Republic of Venice, 1618–1750* (Baltimore: Johns Hopkins University Press, 2001), 216; Sluhovsky, *Believe Not Every Spirit*, 250–1.

32 Madre María de San José, *A Wild Country out in the Garden: The Spiritual Journals of a Colonial Mexican Nun*, Kathleen Myers and Amanda Powell, eds. (Bloomington: Indiana University Press, 1999), 212, 214.

33 AHN, Inq. Leg. 1648, Exp. 6 (1677), f.98.

34 Fernando Cervantes, *The Devil in the New World: The Impact of Diabolism in New Spain* (New Haven, Conn.: Yale University Press, 1994), 91–2, 94.

35 For example, Castilian Ana de San Bartolomé explained that the devil had 'displayed all his wiles' when she, as a young girl, was engaged in traumatic forms of penance. Electa Arenal and Stacey Schlau, eds., *Untold Sisters: Hispanic Nuns in Their Own Works* (Albuquerque: University of New Mexico Press, 1989), 56.

36 AHN, Inq. Leg. 1648, Exp. 6 (1677), ff.98v, 99.

37 AHN, Inq. Leg. 1648, Exp. 6 (1677), ff.95, 133.

38 Gunnarsdottir, *Mexican Karismata*, 119–20.

39 Michael Goodich, 'Introduction,' *Other Middle Ages: Witnesses at the Margins of Medieval Society* (Philadelphia: University of Pennsylvania Press, 1998), 12.

40 AHN, Inq. Leg. 1648, Exp. 6 (1677), f.98v.

41 AHN, Inq. Leg. 1648, Exp. 6 (1677), ff.98, 99v.

42 Bilinkoff, *Related Lives*, 23; Keitt, *Inventing the Sacred*, 180; Schutte, *Aspiring Saints*, 216.

43 Jorge Cañizares-Esguerra, 'New World, New Stars: Patriotic Astrology and the Invention of Indian and Creole Bodies in Colonial Spanish America, 1600–1650,' *American Historical Review*, 104, no. 1 (1999): 33–68, 37, 45.

44 Morgan, *Spanish American Saints*, 6, 8, 66; Myers, *Neither Saints nor Sinners*, 45, 161.

45 Ibsen, *Women's Spiritual Auotbioography*, 7, 12; Tudela, *Colonial Angels*, xiv, xv, 24, 51.

46 AHN, Inq. Leg. 1648, Exp. 6 (1677), f.99.

47 Steve Stern, *The Secret History of Gender: Women, Men, and Power in Late Colonial Mexico* (Chapel Hill: University of North Carolina Press, 1995), 76, 95.

48 Rachel Sarah O'Toole, 'Danger in the Convent: Colonial Demons, Idola-
    trous *Indias*, and Bewitching *Negras* in Santa Clara (Trujillo del Perú),' *Jour-
    nal of Colonialism and Colonial History*, 7, no. 1 (2006), http://muse.jhu.edu/
    journals/journal_of_colonialism_and_colonial_history/v007/7.1otoole.
    html, para. 19.
49 Myers, *Niether Saints Nor Sinners*, 32.
50 Nora Jaffary, *False Mystics: Deviant Orthodoxy in Colonial* Mexico (Lincoln:
    University of Nebraska Press, 2004), 88–9, 97.
51 AHN, Inq. Leg. 1648, Exp. 6 (1677), ff.5, 5v.
52 AHN, Inq. Leg. 1648, Exp. 6 (1677), ff.27, 28v.
53 AHN, Inq. Leg. 1648, Exp. 6 (1677), f.13.
54 Kathleen Myers, 'Introduction,' in María de San José, ed., *Word from New
    Spain: The Spiritual Autobiography of Madre Maria de San José (1656–1719)*
    (Liverpool: Liverpool University Press, 1993), 1–76, 14, 24; Schlau, *Spanish
    American Women's Use of the Word*, 4.
55 AHN, Inq. Leg. 1648, Exp. 6 (1677), f.18.
56 AHN, Inq. Leg. 1648, Exp. 6 (1677), ff.15v, 20v, 21.
57 Jaffary, *False Mystics*, 111; Ronald Surtz, *The Guitar of God: Gender, Power, and
    Authority in the Visionary World of Mother Juana de la Cruz (1481–1534)* (Phila-
    delphia: University of Pennsylvania Press, 1990), 74.
58 Frank Graziano, *Wounds of Love: The Mystical Marriage of Saint Rose of Lima*
    (Oxford: Oxford University Press, 2004), 44, 61–63; Myers, *Neither Saints Nor
    Sinners*, 25.
59 Myers, *Neither Saints Nor Sinners*, 37.
60 AHN, Inq. Leg. 1648, Exp. 6 (1677), f.34.
61 AHN, Inq. Leg. 1648, Exp. 6 (1677), f.3v.
62 AHN, Inq. Leg. 1648, Exp. 6 (1677), f.7.
63 AHN, Inq. Leg. 1648, Exp. 6 (1677), ff.5v, 6, 7, 97v.
64 AHN, Inq. Leg. 1648, Exp. 6 (1677), f.7v.
65 Velasco, *Demons*, 55.
66 AHN, Inq. Leg. 1648, Exp. 6 (1677), f.1.
67 Manuel Ramos Medina, *Místicas y descalzas: Fundaciones femeninas carmelitas
    en la Nueva España* (Mexico City: CONDUMEX, 1997), 239.
68 Electa Arenal, 'The Convent as Catalyst for Autonomy: Two Hispanic Nuns
    of the Seventeenth Century,' in Beth Miller, ed., *Women in Hispanic Litera-
    ture: Icons and Fallen Idols* (Berkeley: University of California Press, 1983),
    147–83, 157, 159.
69 Graziano, *Wounds of Love*, 195.
70 AHN, Inq. Leg. 1648, Exp. 6 (1677), ff.41v, 42v, 44, 44v.
71 Madre María de San José, *Word from New Spain: The Spiritual Autobiography of*

154 Rachel Sarah O'Toole

Madre María de San José (1656–1719), Kathleen Myers, ed. (Liverpool: Liverpool University Press, 1993), 133, 135.

72 Kathryn Burns, *Colonial Habits: Convents and the Spiritual Economy of Cuzco, Peru* (Durham, N.C.: Duke University Press, 1999), 130–1; Sluhovsky, *Believe Not Every Spirit*, 6–7, 244–5.

73 Bilinokoff, *Related Lives*, 26; Gunnarsdóttir, *Mexican Karismata*, 201.

74 AHN, Inq. Leg. 1648, Exp. 6 (1677), ff.18–18v.

75 AHN, Inq. Leg. 1648, Exp. 6 (1677), f.5, 8v.

76 Cervantes, *The Devil in the New World*, 102.

77 Keitt, *Inventing the Sacred*, 178–9.

78 AHN, Inq. Leg. 1648, Exp. 6 (1677), f.24v.

79 AHN, Inq. Leg. 1648, Exp. 6 (1677), f.97.

80 AHN, Inq. Leg. 1648, Exp. 6 (1677), f.144v.

81 AHN, Inq. Leg. 1648, Exp. 6 (1677), ff.140v, 145.

82 Nancy E. van Deusen, *Between the Sacred and the Worldly: The Institutional and Cultural Practice of Recogimiento in Colonial Lima* (Stanford, Calif.: Stanford University Press, 2001), 18.

83 Other studies of Latin American convents have revealed that the visiting room was often a sociable space. Burns, *Colonial Habits*, 112–13.

84 'An Account of the Origin and Foundation of the Monastery of San Joaquin, of Discalced Carmelite Nazarene Nuns, in the City of Lima,' in Arenal and Schlau, eds., *Untold Sisters*, 325; Luis Corteguera, 'The Making of a Visionary Woman: The Life of Beatriz Ana Ruiz, 1666–1735,' in Marta Vicente and Luis Corteguera, eds., *Women, Texts, and Authority in the Early Modern Spanish World* (Aldershot, U.K.: Ashgate, 2003), 165–82, 173; Michelle Marshman, 'Exorcism as Empowerment: A New Idiom,' *Journal of Religious History*, 23, no. 3 (1999): 265–81, 277.

85 AHN, Inq. Leg. 1648, Exp. 6 (1677), ff.242v, 281v.

86 AHN, Inq. Leg. 1648, Exp. 6 (1677), f.244v.

87 AHN, Inq. Leg. 1648, Exp. 6 (1677), ff.47, 54. For an example of nuns creating sacred images, see Arenal and Schlau, eds., *Untold Sisters*, 198.

88 AHN, Inq. Leg. 1648, Exp. 6 (1677), ff.263, 263v, 267, 270v, 276v.

89 AHN, Inq. Leg. 1648, Exp. 6 (1677), f 277v.

90 AHN, Inq. Leg. 1648, Exp. 6 (1677), f.240v.

91 McKnight, *The Mystic of Tunja*, 51, 163; Weber, *Teresa of Avila*, 77–8.

92 AHN, Inq. Leg. 1648, Exp. 6 (1677), ff.250v–251.

93 Cervantes, *The Devil in the New World*, 37; Mello e Souza, *Devil and the Land of the Holy Cross*, 161.

94 Javier Villa-Flores, 'Talking through the Chest: Divination and Ventriloquism among African Slave Women in Seventeenth-Century Mexico,' *Colonial Latin American Review*, 14, no. 2 (2005): 299–321, 302, 304.

95 Keitt, *Inventing the Sacred*, 110, 180; Schutte, *Aspiring Saints*, 91, 203, 216; Bilinkoff, *Related Lives*, 23.

96 Jonathan Schorsch, 'Blacks, Jews and the Racial Imagination in the Writings of Sephardim in the Long Seventeenth Century,' *Jewish History*, 19, no. 109 (2005): 109–35, 115, 124; Mary Elizabeth Perry, *The Handless Maiden: Moriscos and the Politics of Religion in Early Modern Spain* (Princeton, N.J.: Princeton University Press, 2005), 140–1.

97 Kirsten Fischer, *Suspect Relations: Sex, Race, and Resistance in Colonial North Carolina* (Ithaca, N.Y.: Cornell University Press, 2002), 5; Kathleen Brown, *Good Wives, Nasty Wenches, & Anxious Patriarchs: Gender, Race, and Power in Colonial Virginia* (Chapel Hill: Omohundro Institute of Early American History and Culture by the University of North Carolina Press, 1996), 4.

98 Allan Greer, 'Iroquois Virgin: The Story of Catherine Tekakwitha in New France and New Spain,' in Allan Greer and Jodi Bilinkoff, eds., *Colonial Saints: Discovering the Holy in the Americas* (New York: Routledge, 2003), 235–51, 242; Mello e Souza, *The Devil and the Land of the Holy Cross*, 126.

chapter six

Missionary Men and the Global Currency of Female Sanctity

J. MICHELLE MOLINA AND ULRIKE STRASSER

In an important study Jodi Bilinkoff has made a convincing case that the intense relationships between female penitents and male confessors, as well as the hundreds of written hagiographies spawned by these relationships, were key to the emergence, consolidation, and perpetuation of a transatlantic Catholic culture in the early modern period. As clerics offered written documentation of the lives of holy women from the traditional centres of Christianity in Europe to the most contested colonial frontiers in the Americas, they supplied audiences separated by vast geographical and cultural differences with a shared set of Christian values and exemplary lives to be emulated by Christians everywhere. Much more engaging than dry doctrinal treatises, the widely read *vitae* (lives) of holy women helped to forge a Catholic Atlantic community that in turn fuelled the twin enterprises of overseas conversion and colonization.[1] Bilinkoff aptly terms these hagiographies of holy women by male clerics a form of 'life-writing' and points out that they were usually the textual product of a collaborative relationship of sorts between the supposed subject and the alleged author of the story.

This felicitous characterization recognizes the unique value of all auto/biographical sources for scholars of the pre-modern. More crucially still, it opens up hagiographical texts so often dismissed for their formulaic quality to the systematic study of individual lives and subjectivities, female as well as male. Bilinkoff indeed argues that these texts have much to reveal not only about religious women but also about the religious men who wrote their stories. 'Suddenly, as it were, men so often lumped together as "the clergy" or, even less accurately, "the Church" emerge as fully drawn individuals.'[2] Bilinkoff's work is an inspiration to put flesh and bones on a frequently typecast social group, Catholic priests.

This chapter expands on Bilinkoff's insights into hagiography's role in the formation of transatlantic Catholicism and its usefulness for the study of female as well as male religious identities. Adopting Bilinkoff's definition of hagiography as a form of 'life-writing,' we contend that this genre, in spite of its obvious interpretive difficulties, can be mined for the reconstruction of life histories – as long as it is used with caution and, ideally, paired with other, non-hagiographic source materials. Moreover, the life histories at the heart of our essay are those of the male authors rather than those of their female subjects, since we seek to expand this volume's analytical framework beyond women's religious experience to the gendered religious experiences of men. Thus, we centre our analysis on the authors of two life-histories of Catarina de San Juan, renowned mystic from colonial Mexico and subject of a number of hagiographies. The two hagiographic texts that concern us were written in the seventeenth century when the publication and circulation of female *Lives* by male clerics reached its peak. The first text under consideration is a voluminous *vita* written by her long-time spiritual director, the Spanish Jesuit Alonso Ramos. The second text is by a Jesuit from the German empire, Adam Kaller, who composed a much briefer account of Catarina's life during a stopover in New Spain on his way to Asia.

The authors of our texts both belonged to the religious order most active in the production of this genre, the Jesuits. Yet they also represent very diverse backgrounds, having lived most of their lives in different parts of the world and under different circumstances. Not surprisingly, their reasons for promoting Catarina's life story reflect both their shared institutional training as Jesuits and their individual differences. While their commonalities can be traced back to the Jesuit order's global orientation and its efforts to forge a world Christianity through a unified devotional literature, the differences in the narratives point to the ways in which the global is fractured by local and individual factors.

Beyond the hagiographic myth making, the bare outlines of Catarina de San Juan's life appear as follows. She was born in India, captured by half-caste Portuguese pirates, sold as a slave in Manila, and sent to New Spain on a Manila galleon. She arrived in Puebla de los Angeles in 1624 as a slave. Following her master's death, she was freed and worked as a servant for a priest, who arranged for her to marry his slave, a man named Diego who was also from Asia. Catarina agreed to this marriage, which took place in 1626, on the condition that she could remain a vir-

gin. In the struggle to maintain her vow of chastity within the vows of
marriage, she began to perform miracles to keep her husband out of her
bedroom. This brought her to the attention of local priests, who determined that she was a holy woman.[3] In 1688 she died a locally renowned
and beloved holy woman, drawing crowds from the citizens of Puebla to
her funeral.

Death transformed Catarina de San Juan into a figure of projection,
from a revered holy woman in the seventeenth century to an icon of
feminine nationalism in the nineteenth and twentieth centuries. In this
chapter, we explore the stakes that Ramos and Kaller had in telling Catarina's complex life story. By analysing how these two Jesuits used the
saintly woman to promote their own goals, we peel away some of the
layers of myth making that surround her figure. Yet we leave the very
different question of whether her story can be discerned amidst the layers of myth to other scholars, with the caveat that our efforts to present
the multiple motivations of these two seventeenth-century biographers
lay critical groundwork for those who might wish to study her history
proper.

For our part, we are keen to shed light on a frequently typecast group:
Europeans. Scholars have grappled with the difficulties of understanding colonial 'others' as historical actors with complex identities, particularly given that most extant sources were produced by colonists and not
by the native peoples of Africa and the Americas. As Luke Clossey contends, 'the most alarming disadvantage to this approach is the resulting
tendency to see the "other's" counterpart, that is, the European, in terms
of sameness.'[4] Our approach seeks to complicate the notion of the 'European' to arrive at a better understanding of the relationship between
'European' and 'other,' Catholic missionaries and New World converts.[5]
Specifically, we seek to understand and deconstruct the individual lenses
of Catarina de San Juan's two biographers in order to make visible heretofore unexplored networks of connection in the Atlantic world. Uti-
lizing 'religion' as a tool for conceptualizing the Atlantic (rather than
the more expected tools of politics and economy) allows us to focus on
previously overlooked historical actors like Kaller, who hailed not from a
traditional 'Atlantic world' region but from Central Europe. The story of
Catarina de San Juan, which allows us to contrast a German with a Spanish actor, explodes customary understandings of 'colonialism' as linked
to overseas empires. We suggest that, theoretically, the term 'colonial'
has, like the wide blue Atlantic Ocean itself, operated as a barrier that
limits our ability to discern the connectedness of a wider Europe with

the New World more generally, and with Latin America in particular, via global Catholicism. Thinking about how hagiography was adapted to meet the needs of a geographically diverse community of Catholic believers contributes to recent scholarship that has made critical moves to see Latin America enmeshed in the connective tissues of transatlantic as well as global intellectual and cultural trends.[6] Our efforts to see the life of a Mexican mystic with lenses that are simultaneously European, Atlantic, *and* global highlight how the European contribution to the 'Spanish American' world was not solely reliant upon Spanish intellectual, social, and cultural trends.

'Whom the Mughal gave to the world and Puebla de Los Angeles gave to Heaven': Alonso Ramos's Catarina de San Juan

When Alonso Ramos took up his pen to write the life story of Catarina de San Juan, he engaged in a complex struggle to meet the multiple needs of an Atlantic audience: he sought to address his local Mexican would-be readers as well as to meet transatlantic Catholic Reformation demands for a credible saint's life story, all the while including evidence from the newly emerging field of natural history. This was a tall task and in what follows we will meet a man who struggled and failed to stay on top of all the 'facts' in his efforts to write a credible life narrative.

Ramos was a Spanish Jesuit who arrived in New Spain in 1658. He first taught at the Jesuit College in Guatemala and later was assigned to teach grammar and philosophy at the Jesuit Colegio Ildefonso in Puebla de Los Angeles. High intellectual aspirations and an acute understanding of the religious, ethnic, and social-economic norms of the Spanish empire would come to play an important role in Ramos's rendition of Catarina de San Juan's life history. By the time he met Catarina, she was an elderly woman. According to Ramos, however, she had experienced a vision in 1658 in which God revealed to her that a new confessor had recently arrived in New Spain.[7] She had to wait fifteen years to meet him, since Ramos did not become her confessor until 1673. By this time, an almost-blind Catarina passed most of her days in solitude in the Jesuit church, praying for the souls of sinners around the world and heaping scorn upon those revellers who took part in festivals in town.[8] It is unclear when Catarina began to gain notoriety among the general population of Puebla. Yet we know that, upon her death in 1688, when Ramos took up his pen to convince the church hierarchy that a local holy woman and his own spiritual daughter was worthy of sainthood, he demonstrated great enthusiasm and perhaps had grand visions of his career. He invested considerable emotional and intellectual resources, as well as over one thousand sheets of expensive paper, in writing the most voluminous life story of a religious woman ever to be published in the Americas.[9] The first volume was published in 1689, with two more volumes appearing in 1690 and 1693. He promised a fourth volume but such hopes were cut short, as we shall see, by an edict from the Holy Office in Madrid.

Alonso Ramos characterized Catarina de San Juan as his 'spiritual daughter' who had led a life worthy of sainthood. His voluminous work served the added purpose of locating the Society of Jesus as the vanguard of the drive for a universal Christian empire, and, to this end, he capitalized on language that emphasized how her life's history encompassed a world history. Moreover, Ramos elevated New Spain, and particularly Puebla de Los Angeles, within that empire. Thus, the telling of Catarina's life was informed not only by the universal Christian mission of the Jesuits but also by Creole identity formation in New Spain.[10]

Ramos emphasized Catarina's South Asian ancestry because it served to highlight the world mission of the Jesuits. Further, references to her ancestry allowed Ramos to discuss the most cutting-edge geographical information coming from Jesuit missionaries in Asia, thereby facilitating a vicarious participation in the exciting and burgeoning field of natural history. Indeed, in bolstering his knowledge of Asia by quoting the Jesuit polymath Athanasius Kircher's *China illustrata,* Ramos passed current information about Asia to the reader.[11] Yet taking Catarina's Asian roots seriously provided him with a very local stumbling block. She had been brought to the New World a slave. She died a *casta* servant. One of the scholars studying Catarina's life, Kathleen Myers, was confounded as to why the Jesuits and the city of Puebla itself 'would fervently promote a nonwhite, lay holy woman when she deviated so vividly from the model of female saint promoted by the Counter Reformation church.'[12] If we step back to encompass the global dimensions of her life story, we find at least one answer to the question: her story highlighted the history of evangelization of the Society of Jesus in Asia and its promotion of a universal Christian empire.

The letter Ramos wrote prefacing the biography offers clear indication that he felt it necessary to contend with her low status directly. When Ramos wrote to the Pueblan bishop, Fernández de Santa Cruz, to request his approval for publication, he used a technique common to hagiography, manipulating the 'voice' of the now deceased Catarina de

San Juan.[13] He wrote as if she were pleading her own case: 'I am a poor coarse foreigner marked with infirmities.' Ramos then moved in to compensate for this, remarking upon the fact that she was nonetheless well connected in Pueblan society. He reminded the bishop of Puebla that his predecessor, Diego Osorio Escobar, had called Catarina to his bedside in order to 'alleviate the anguish of that critical moment ... [and] to benefit from her prayers and tears.' Ramos took on the voice of Catarina a second time, but now she 'spoke' as she entered into the current bishop's palace in the form of the biography and made a 'personal' request for his holy patronage: 'I am but a vile worm ... before I was afraid to enter [the palace], before they had to drag me, like a vile worm ... but now reduced, by virtue and grace of our good God, from worm to phoenix (not that happy Arabia, in which I was born, but the more joyful West, in which I was reborn) I fly to the heaven of your Illustrious protection in this book.'

Ramos continued to play with a notion of mapping the world, promising that readers would be provided accounts of the two worlds from which Catarina, this luminous star from the Orient, came to the Occident. Her travels gave him the opportunity to tell of ports in both worlds and of land and sea, and, of course, to put Puebla de Los Angeles on the map. He wrote that the narration of the life and death of 'this prodigious flower who tread the earth in the Orient until she arrived at the pinnacle of perfection in this Occident, has, resulting from her journeys, bestowed upon us a Map imbued with virtue, providing a sure path with which to guide our way.'[14] Here Ramos played with a dual notion of Catarina's life experiences, providing a map both of the physical world and of a moral or spiritual route. This was not only Ramos's opinion. Catarina de San Juan was interred in the Jesuit church in Puebla, her tombstone reading, 'Guard this sepulchre, the venerable virgin in Christ, Catarina de San Juan, whom the Mughal (*el Mogor*) gave to the world and Puebla de Los Angeles gave to heaven.'[15]

Yet Ramos could not evade questions about the facts of her birth. His descriptions of her mysterious land of birth served not merely to provide rare information about India but facilitated the critical function of verifying Catarina's lineage. Catarina's status as a slave and servant would have been an issue in a society highly concerned with ethno-social status. Indeed, one might assume that her status would have had a negative effect on the very possibility that she be considered a holy woman. In fact, the eight celebrated mystics in colonial Puebla were almost entirely of the elite classes. Catarina de San Juan provided the only exception. The other seven had taken vows, an indication of economic as well as religious standing since joining a convent required a dowry.[16] Furthermore, Catarina did not live in a convent, and uncloistered women were considered a threat. In Inquisition trials, independent *beatas* (lay religious women) in the Americas were twice more likely to be convicted than women who lived communally.[17]

Ultimately, the bishop of Puebla approved publication of the book, yet his blessing alone would not suffice to account for the unknown circumstances of Catarina's birth. Ramos would further compensate for Catarina's status as a *casta* servant by claiming nobility for her. He informed his readers that her mother came from a line of Arab emperors and her father was of the even more illustrious and prominent Mughal kingdom. 'Comparing all of the historical information which we have about Catarina,' Ramos wrote, 'including the chronicle and philosophical evidence which I discuss, I intend to show that the subject of this history was the niece or joined very closely with the unvanquished Mughal emperor, Mahameth Zeladin Ecchabar, or Akbar, who died in the year 1605.' Ramos added that he would give 'a brief notice of the grandeur of his person and his empire.' Anyone who wanted to read in greater detail, he advised, should consult Kircher's *China Illustrata* as well as Danielo Bartoli's biography of the martyr Rudolfo Aquaviva.[18] Ramos claimed that he offered details about Akbar in honour of the loving affection Catarina de San Juan had received from the Mughal, but, given the dearth of information about India in the *China Illustrata*, he could tell of little other than the grandeur of Akbar.

There were at least three reasons that Ramos called upon the legacy of Akbar. First, in Ramos's struggle to account for Catarina's social background in a status-conscious society, it helped if he could trace her to royalty. Secondly, this move to document her status was, in part, circumscribed by the kind of information available to him. Since, as mentioned, Akbar took centre stage in Kircher's work on India, this worked in his favour because, thirdly, it reinforced the image of the Jesuits, special friends of Akbar, as key players in the struggle for a universal Christian empire.

Furthermore, the narrative structure of hagiography demands a story that includes the birth of the saint, his or her life of progress along a path of virtue, and an edifying death.[19] Ramos had the life and death, but he required information about the birth of Catarina de San Juan and the signs of grace that accompanied her entry into the world. Reference to Kircher's work, again, showcased his familiarity with the most recent knowledge of Asia. Yet information contained therein also proved useful in providing Ramos the necessary facts to narrate Catarina's signs of grace at birth and during her childhood. Thus, this seemingly outlandish story actually furnished the typical components of a saint's life story.[20] For example, Mary appeared to her mother before and after her birth; she was miraculously saved from drowning in a nearby river; while lost in the forest, she remained unscathed even though she fell into a pit of vipers. Her mother had a vision that foretold Catarina's sanctity as well as the fact that she would travel to many foreign lands.

But in naming Akbar or a close relative as her father, Ramos put himself into yet another bind. Now he had a problem greater than simply providing a complete life history for Catarina de San Juan. Her given name was Myrrah. This was a Muslim name. She was not a Hindu – a people described by Kircher as 'modern barbarians' – but fell into the much more maligned category of 'Moor.' The *China Illustrata,* with Kircher's map of the spread of Christianity, provided Ramos with a graceful exit. Ramos claimed that Catarina's parents 'had heard and knew of the Apostle St. Thomas whose preaching in the Orient reached the Mughal Emire, as is expressly affirmed by Padre Athanansio Kircherio.'[21] These 'glimmers of the true Faith' were evident in their lives. He claimed that her father, although not Christian, was sympathetic to Christianity. And not only did her mother have visions of Mary but, Ramos assured the reader, the entire family was forced to throw their riches into a deep lake and flee when their homeland was invaded by the Turks. Ramos writes that the piety of Catarina's father had infuriated the devil, who feared the ruin of his infernal dominion in those lands. Thus, the devil provoked the Turks to take up arms against 'this enemy of Idolatry.' Although Ramos drew many of his speculations about the Mughal empire and its relation to Catarina de San Juan from Kircher's *China Illustrata,* he concocted many others, including this invasion. What could be a greater sign of a region's Christian status than an invasion by the infidel?[22] Ramos was also careful to note that the infant Catarina was always either in the crib or in her mother's arms. She was not cared for by the idolatrous servants, whose false gods her mother despised. In fact, Catarina took only the sweet milk of her mother and refused the breasts of other women.[23] Here Ramos marked both the religious and the bio-cultural segregation of Catarina from the Muslim majority.

Ramos still had to deal with the issue of credibility. One of the introductory letters to his biography, written by the Jesuit Antonio Núñez de Miranda, suggested as much. Miranda titled his letter 'Some Difficulties

That May Result upon the First Reading of This History.' He argued:
'The mere telling does not assure its truth, if it is lacking in prudent
opinions. Is one gullible, does one take things lightly, to believe such
praiseworthy things about a poor Chinese slave, only because she imagined it and recounted it? It is divine prudence and canonical opinion to
believe that matters of the Soul do not have the possibility of witnesses.
Nor is there an informant other than her confessor, the sole arbitrator,
supreme and truly divine conscience in the Sacrosanct law and venerated
court of the Confession.'[24] Núñez de Miranda was interested in the theological correctness of the biography and rightly so, for, as we shall see,
the Inquisition ultimately suppressed the book because the descriptions
of Catarina's visions were considered blasphemous. Yet something analo-
gous was true of Catarina de San Juan's early life in India. Just as 'matters
of the Soul' could not be witnessed, matters pertaining to India were
difficult for most people in New Spain to verify. This dynamic points to
tensions raised when defining 'truth' in the seventeenth century. On the
one hand, ultimate authority rested with God. But, on the other, scholars
increasingly established legitimacy with documentary evidence and eyewitness accounts, the latter requiring a careful examination of authority
and truthfulness. [25] Jorge Cañizares-Esguerra has argued that this 'art of
reading,' particular to the Renaissance, gave way in the eighteenth century to a manner of reading that valued the internal consistency of an
account, relying less on the 'eyewitness.'[26] Ramos, however, was keen to
establish the nobility and social standing of the witness because, in New
Spain, status, ethnicity, and gender mattered.[27] As Ramos's opening lines
indicate, Catarina de San Juan was a 'poor Chinese slave,' 'a vile worm'
who lacked an authoritative voice. Thus, Kircher may have given Ramos
precious little to go on, but he was a credible 'informant' and his book
spoke volumes in terms of authority.

Although discussion of Catarina's spiritual visions are beyond the
scope of this chapter, the edict of the Madrid Holy Office clearly criticized the unorthodoxy of her visions:

Written by Padre Alonso Ramos, a professed member of the Society of
Jesus, printed in Puebla in the printing plant of Diego Fernández de León,
1689; for containing revelations, visions, and apparitions that are useless,
untrue, full of contradictions and comparisons that are improper, indecent
and fearful, and that are almost blasphemies ... abusive of the highest and
ineffable ministry of the Incarnation of the Son of God, and of other parts
of the holy scripture, and containing doctrines that are fearful, danger-

ous and contrary to the sense of the doctors and practice of the Universal Church, without more basis than the vain credulity of the author.[28]

Here we see that the inquisitor's 'art of reading' was most similar to that of eighteenth- century intellectuals.[29] As Cañizares-Esguerra argues: 'Philosophical compilations of travel accounts thus began to emphasize the internal over the external; that is, to apportion credit to reports based on the merits of the story itself and not on an evaluation of the character of the reporter.'[30] Ramos was still operating under older assumptions. In the preface to the book, Ramos guaranteed the reader that the biography was built upon 'qualified testimony,' and added what he must have hoped would be reassuring: the information was obtained from her 'actual Confessor.' Yet the inquisitors who read Ramos's *Prodigios de . . . Catharina de S. Joan* placed a high value on internal consistency and rational judgment in hagiographic narratives. They deemed Ramos an unfit scholar. His account was 'useless, untrue and full of contradictions.' The factors that had so concerned Ramos (with his literate public in mind) passed without comment: neither the facts of Catarina's birth, nor her condition of servitude in New Spain, nor her Muslim heritage raised eyebrows. As the above quote illustrates, the Inquisition placed the blame for the suppression of the hagiography squarely at the feet of its 'vain' author, Ramos. Fortunately, the world did not have to rely upon Ramos alone to disseminate the fascinating story of Catarina de San Juan's life.

Mapping the Unknown, Finding the Familiar: Adam Kaller's Catarina de San Juan

In March 1688, a few months after Catarina's death, the Bohemian Jesuit Adam Kaller decided that he too should commit a version of her story to writing. Less ambitious and more pressed for time than Ramos, Kaller chose the prototypical Jesuit genre of the missionary letter to accomplish this goal. His *vita* of Catarina appeared in an epistle to Johannes Ulke, a Jesuit priest back home in Prague.[31] Arguably on account of this more personal genre, Adam Kaller's *vita*, more sharply than Ramos's high-profile publication, bears the imprint of Kaller's own life history, in particular his outsider status in the Spanish empire and his missionary journey towards potential martyrdom in Asia.

The German-speaking Kaller hailed from the lands of the Austrian Habsburg monarchy. Born in Eger in 1657, he attended the local Jesuit school before he resolved to join the Society. In 1674 and 1675 he completed his novitiate in Brünn and then went on to study philosophy in Olmütz for three years. After a brief teaching stint in Glatz, Kaller moved to Prague in 1684 and studied theology there until he was sent to 'the Indies' in the spring of 1687. He headed for Cadiz and, together with other missionaries from German lands, boarded a ship for the long and perilous journey to Vera Cruz. From there the group travelled by mule into the Mexican highlands towards Mexico City. A part of the group, Kaller included, was to go on to the Philippines and the Mariana Islands but had to await the annual departure of the fleet from Acapulco.[32]

At the time of his travels, Kaller was one among very few German Jesuits abroad even as their numbers were growing. German involvement in the Jesuit missions had come very slowly, not for lack of interest among Germans but rather on account of formidable inner and outer obstacles to their participation in evangelization abroad. Within Germany, the religious conflicts and confessional divisions following the Reformation tied down the energies of the German Society of Jesus until the Peace of Westphalia in 1648. Some German Jesuits themselves wondered about the wisdom of leaving their country behind for the overseas missions. When the first four Germans departed for 'the Indies' from Ingolstadt in 1616, their rector, Jakob Rem, objected: 'Why do they to go to faraway lands? The time is nearing when we in Germany will have our own India for which the number of workers that are now in our province will not suffice.'[33]

On the colonial stage, the Spanish and Portuguese crown put the brakes on the admission of foreign missionaries in the territories over which they claimed political control, or where they hoped to extend their influence through evangelization.[34] Between 1600 and 1620, a mere eleven Germans were admitted to the missions in 'the Indies.' Another twenty followed between 1620 and 1670, bringing the total for the period from 1600 to 1670 to thirty-one.[35]

By the time Kaller embarked upon his journey, the Spanish crown had opened the door to greater involvement of Germans in colonial evangelization, and northern Mexico slowly turned into a base for German Jesuits.[36] Kaller's mission, then, coincided with a moment of possibility when Germans began to claim their place in the global evangelization drive but were also just beginning to write their participation into the narratives of the conversion of 'the Indies' that were circulating in seventeenth-century Europe in growing numbers.[37]

In all likelihood, Kaller knew of Ramos's more ambitious hagiographic undertaking. The two men moved in the same clerical circles, and they could easily have met in 1688 when both spent time at the Jesuit colleges in Puebla and Mexico City. Indeed, Kaller's short account parallels Ramos's verbose tale in very broad outlines. It is possible that Kaller had seen the Spaniard's text or had spoken to him about Catarina, or that both men based their narratives on the hagiographic sermon that the Jesuit Francisco de Aguilera had delivered at Catarina's funeral.[38]

But, even if Kaller drew on Ramos as a source and inspiration, he rendered Catarina's life story in a distinct idiom reflective of his own situation and cultural background. At the time of writing, Kaller, unlike Ramos, negotiated a doubly unknown world: the culture of the Americas under another European power's system of colonial rule. The culture of the colonizers, and not just the colonized, represented a terra incognita he had to master. One of the first observations in his letter concerned the way Spaniards made life difficult for foreign missionaries, something he was not alone in noticing.[39] In this instance, his group of German-speaking missionaries initially suffered communication problems since the Spaniards refused to speak Latin with them. Only after the German speakers improved their Spanish to the point of being able to hear confessions were they treated well, virtually like peers. Aware of the imperial usages of language, Kaller commented how 'the Spanish in the two Indies, like the ancient Romans, insist that their language together with their authority be perpetuated throughout the world.'[40] He understood that he was dealing with an imperial power that in some ways was as far removed from his home as ancient Rome.

Kaller also struggled with questions of cultural classification. A recurring theme in his *vita* of Catarina is that of appearance and recognition, which Kaller uses to map his struggles with perceiving and classifying an unknown world onto her and her story. The account is sprinkled with the vocabulary of seeing and perceiving. The act of seeing occurs in dreams, apparitions, and visions. It happens on the level of human interaction where Catarina's sanctity at times remains hidden and invisible but at others becomes revealed and obvious. More crucially still, what had Kaller's mind turning was the question of Catarina's descent, skin colour, and place in the colonial empire he had just entered. This stands in sharp contrast to Ramos, who was attuned to colonial hierarchies to the point where he anticipated and tried to fend off any questions that his readership might have had about Catarina's ethno-social status in his writing of her story. Not so Kaller. He seems to have written to understand rather than explain.

How does an enslaved woman from pagan Asia become a Christian saint? To answer this (implicit) question satisfactorily, Kaller's account of Catarina's early life in the East and her travels to New Spain has her go through several sets of quasi-parental figures who moved her further and further into the orbit of the European Christianity he knew: first, noble-yet-impoverished birth parents in Cochinchina; second, pirates who kidnap her on account of her noble looks and bring her to the Philippines; third, Jesuit fathers who baptize her in the Philippines and bring her into the Christian fold; and finally, a Portuguese man who purchases her on the local slave market to take her to New Spain 'so that she be raised there not as a slave but like a daughter of his own flesh.' The fictional re-birthing thus culminates in an acquisition of European descent as Kaller reinterprets her enslavement by a European into upward ethno-social mobility. The real nature of the relationship between the European man and the Asian woman, however, shines through the interstices of Kaller's text. The following sentence relates the fate of Catarina's fictive adoptive father upon arriving in New Spain and gives away her true status: 'The unfathomable foresight of God soon called her *master* and his wife from this world ... [and] she found herself forced to be a *servant to another woman*.'[41]

Catarina's dark appearance presented another puzzle for Kaller. It marked her as someone of low status and so an object of colonial domination in New Spain but equally made her an opaque person for the Central European, who had little knowledge of colonial hierarchies. How to explain the dark face of the holy woman? 'When she noticed in her youth that her beautiful appearance endangered her chastity, she received through prayers an ugly, wrinkled, and brown visage from God.'[42] Kaller thus interpreted Catarina's appearance as God's ultimate safeguard against sexual impurity – a second hymen that sealed her body from the desires of others. This metaphysical explanation turned upside down the social logic of ethno-social colonial hierarchies in which dark-skinned women as slaves and servants were most vulnerable to sexual assault and exploitation. Perhaps the browning-miracle resonated with Kaller because of the famous European precedent of Catherine of Siena, whose pockmarked face allegedly spared her from unwanted courtship. Did God extend the salutary disfigurement to the non-white Catarina by adding colour to the scars? Certainly, this could be one way of translating the culturally opaque into familiar categories of recognition.[43]

A similar epistemological transposition into a Central European register occurred with respect to Catarina's ethnic classification in New

Spain. The text continues: 'On account of this she was thereafter known
as *mulata*.' Kaller explained that this was the local nomenclature given to
those who, just like mules, had a dual pedigree, white as well as black.[44]
So here we have Kaller trying to make sense of Spanish colonial society
with his knowledge of Latin. Perhaps as a non-white outsider, the Asian
Catarina was indeed misread as partially black in colonial Puebla. (Kaller
apparently associated the term *mulatto* with *mula,* the Latin word for the
female mule, a term that resonated with European assumptions of the
animal nature of indigenous people.) Simultaneously, Kaller's interpretation of 'mulatto' again enabled him to claim some European ancestry
for his Catarina. It is noteworthy that Ramos never referred to Catarina
as 'mulata.' African ancestry would have made it all the more difficult for
Ramos to make an argument for Catarina's noble ancestry. Did Kaller's
use of the term reflect the 'street' view of Catarina, or does it reflect
his own confusion about colonial *casta* categories, which were confused
to begin with? Kaller's narrative arc of Europeanizing the dark-skinned
heroine fittingly culminates in the description of her death. Rather than
saintly odour, Catarina's dead body emitted a luminous whiteness. Kaller
recounts how 'the brown color of her entire body turned to white while
simultaneously her beautiful appearance was restored.'[45]

Arguably one glimpses a fantasy here of the 'whitening' powers of
Jesuit missionary work that bespeaks not only Kaller's personal attempt
to absorb the alien into the known but, more broadly, the Society of Jesus' adamant insistence on the capacity of 'savages' to become true Christians. It seems no coincidence that the *vita* of another holy woman from
the Americas and contemporary of Catarina de San Juan, namely the
life history of Catherine Tekakwitha written by the French Jesuit Pierre
Cholenec, also reports that the face of the famous Mohawk convert from
New France was graced with white colour at the time of death.[46] 'Natives'
and 'women,' spiritually disadvantaged and prone to fall into sexual sin,
the two Catarinas from the Americas were trophy converts, so to speak.
Their life histories reflected most favourably on the Society and its global
missionary work because they demonstrated the potential of non-Europeans to turn into exemplary Christians, as well as the Jesuits' stellar
ability of actualizing this potential.[47]

A second leitmotif distinguishes Kaller's narrative. While the Spaniard
Ramos had come to New Spain in order to stay, the German Kaller used
the Americas only as a springboard to his final destination: the Mariana
Islands, known as the most perilous site of Jesuit missionary work. Just
three years before Kaller left on his own journey, a group of Central Eu-

ropean Jesuits, including a man named Augustinus Strobach, had been
brutally murdered on the islands during an uprising.

Kaller's letter about Catarina alluded to the fate of these men repeat--
edly, starting with the very first paragraph in which he remarked that
there were only five Jesuits on the Marianas after the killings.[48] The martyrdom of their colleagues could not help but bring to mind the possibility of Kaller's own death for the faith, especially since Strobach could
have been a powerful figure of identification for him. Eight years older
than Kaller, Strobach came from the same Jesuit province of Bohemia
and, like Kaller, had been a student in Olmütz. In 1682 Strobach travelled to the Philippines and the Marianas on essentially the same route
that Kaller would take via New Spain to Manila.[49]

To be sure, the prospect of martyrdom drew men like Strobach and
Kaller into the overseas missions in the first place, and the Society of
Jesus, more than other religious orders, commemorated and celebrated its martyrs.[50] Facing the reality of martyrdom was a different matter,
though. The overseas journeys themselves were perilous and frighten-
ing, not least because they threatened to cut short any hopes for a more
glorified death. Between 1686 and 1727, at least 113 Jesuits died in ship-
wrecks, and Jesuit letters contain many a tale of hardship and danger
on the ocean journey.[51] Those who survived tumultuous seas, pirate attacks, and hunger and disease on board faced an uncertain future that
was bound to raise ambivalent feelings. Martyrdom was what they wished
for but it often also spelled the end of a missionary presence in a given
locale; it represented a setback on another level and conflicted with a
contradictory impulse – the pronounced sense of responsibility for pre-
serving one's life for the missions that also characterized the order.[52]
Moreover, even some of the most devout Jesuits were no strangers to fear
when faced with the prospect of martyrdom and might find themselves
longing for a quick death.[53]

Kaller's stay in New Spain marked a liminal time in his life when conflicting feelings could easily arise. He had survived the first half of his
dangerous journey but was now waiting to travel to an even more dangerous place. Writing Catarina's story helped him grapple with his potential
fate in the Pacific, from whence she had come and where others from
his homeland had lost their lives. Kaller's Catarina is cast as a protective patroness of travelling missionaries and a visionary witness to acts
of redemption. Tellingly, her missions are connected to places Kaller
either came from or was about to travel to. Since he was on his way from
New Spain to the Mariana Islands via the Philippines, Kaller was actu-

ally retracing a good part of Catarina's journey in reverse. In Kaller's version, unlike Ramos's, Catarina reaches Central European regions, at least in her visions. In 1664, before the news could reach Puebla, she 'announced and described in all its circumstances the battle at St. Gotthard during which the Turks were defeated by the [Austrian] Imperial [forces].' While Kaller, the Jesuit, was confronting the prospect of dying at the hands of infidels in the pagan Indies, Kaller, the author, narrated how an infidel-turned-convert watched a major Christian victory of his imperial overlords in the heart of Europe.[54] The narrative reversal of Kaller's situation in time and space registers the psychological difficulties of his situation.

Kaller's Catarina also journeyed with his fleet across the perilous ocean. 'Before they knew anything in Puebla of the arrival of our fleet on which we came she told that she was present to the same [fleet] from Puerto Rico to Vera Cruz.' Kaller was convinced that Catarina's protective presence thwarted the efforts of 'devilish spirits that would otherwise have drowned them in the sea.' But the lay woman was in illustrious company on this rescue mission, for 'Saints Ignatius and Franciscus Xavier ... accompanied the same [fleet].'[55] This unusual troika of European male saints and a non-white holy lay woman offers an ideal representation of the kind of universal patchwork family that Jesuits strove to establish through their global missionary work. On this imaginary level, differences of race, class, and gender are resolved in the congenial collaboration to save Kaller's fleet and secure the generational continuity of the global Christian family, as well as the safety of those working for this family.

Not surprisingly, Catarina's visionary powers extend to the Mariana Islands as well. Once she reportedly saw the Virgin of Guadalupe, herself a powerful female symbol of the sanctity of the Americas, 'fly across [the islands] and shield [them] against imminent demise.' More poignantly still, Kaller's Catarina has an encounter with the Mariana martyrs. It occurs in Puebla, through which Augustinus Strobach and his companions, like Kaller himself, had travelled on their journey to the Pacific. An otherwise virtually blind Catarina discovers the group during a celebration of the Eucharist in the local cathedral. She 'saw nothing else except Christ present in the holy sacrament among various groups of people but nonetheless she recognized the face of each one of our missionaries and described them.'[56] The vision thus blends the successful Christianization of the foreign woman who is completely focused on Christ – blind to everything else – with her appreciative recognition of the European men who sacrificed their lives to bring people like her to

Christ. With the Bohemian Strobach as his proxy, Kaller was virtually foreseeing his own potential martyrdom through Catarina's eyes and envisioning its redemptive meaning.

The holy woman's vision also served to authenticate Strobach's stature as a martyr, allowing Kaller to advance Catarina de San Juan's case for sanctity together with that of Augustinus Strobach in one piece of hagiographic writing. The 'global' holy woman's story here functions as a means of constructing a memory of Strobach as one of the Society's holy martyrs, a type of memory-work that was key to the order's spiritual life and global community building. Bilinkoff detects the same strategy in other Jesuit hagiographies.[57]

Kaller, when all is said and done, indeed spent some time evangelizing on the Mariana Islands but did not lose his life there. In 1702 he died peacefully in the Philippines, where, according to his own account, the Jesuits baptized Catarina.[58] Kaller had committed Catarina's story to memory during a transitional moment in his life when he first entered the alien world of the Spanish overseas empire but had not yet arrived at his final destination. His investment in her story seems rooted in this fact. For the German Jesuit, Catarina de San Juan was a fantastic – in both senses of the word – figure for integrating the known and the unknown and moving the missionary along his journey to the East. She helped normalize unfamiliar places and offered much-needed consolation. Exotic-slave-cum-comforting-Christian, she was as much a part of the 'marvels' of the New World as she was a part of the miracles of God that made the evangelization of unknown worlds a cognitive and psychological possibility in the first place. She was also a global traveller who had traced Kaller's future footsteps in reverse; the world of the Pacific, her saintly life proved, was not a dreaded destination but already a home to Christians and Christians-in-the-making.

A Much-Travelled Female Saint

Even in the notoriously formulaic genre of hagiography, local colour and individual lives leave their unalterable traces. Our two authors of the life history of Catarina de San Juan, although they wrote in the same genre and Ramos influenced Kaller, ended up telling distinct tales of the holy woman, reflective of their specific cultural and rhetorical contexts. Catarina's ability to prepare excellent chocolate mole, for instance, inspired Ramos to wax lyrically about her ability as a cook for his audience of New Spaniards. Kaller, who has nothing to say about Catarina's culinary skills, in turn extended her travel itinerary to Austrian Habsburg battle sites in Central Europe.

On a deeper level, Kaller and Ramos, as members of two different empires that positioned them differently on the colonial grid, diverged in their appropriation of Catarina's story. Kaller's portrayal resonates with his own discomfort in the Spanish empire. To adapt Natalie Davis's phrase, one might say that he was 'a man on the margins.' Kaller accordingly drew on Catarina's life history to negotiate his more precarious place in an alien world of colonized as well as colonizers. Likewise, he deployed her story to grapple with his own potential fate in the even more unfamiliar world of the Pacific from which she had come and where others from his homeland had lost their lives. Ramos, in comparison, appeared to have proudly claimed New Spain (or at least Puebla de los Angeles) as a home. He was clearly attuned to his local readership, anticipating the potential questions that it might have about Catarina's ethno-social status. He was, unfortunately, not as attuned to inquisitorial demands for a more 'rational' and coherent hagiography.

Membership in a global organization dedicated to the successful conversion of 'slaves' and 'pagans' drew the men together. This shared membership accounts for their shared passion for telling the story of the exceptional holy woman. In spite of the great differences in the texts they wrote, what shines through is a fascination with the global reach of Catarina's life history, and hence both Kaller's brief account and Ramos's verbose *vita* express a discernable absorption in Catarina's 'Oriental' origins. Such intense interest was missing in another contemporary hagiography written by a secular cleric, José Castillo de Graxeda. His *Compendio de la vida y virtudes de la venerable Catarina de San Juan* appeared in 1692 and only briefly touched on the subject.[59] Catarina's early life in the East would have found greater resonance among the Jesuits. As members of the international Society of Jesus, they were dedicated to missionary work in the 'Indies' and aspired to a truly global spread of Christianity.

Although Alonso Ramos and Adam Kaller were members of the same global organization and participated in the shaping of transatlantic Catholicism at the same historical moment, their stories have hitherto not been told together. Rather, the two men appear within separate historiographies that still largely view the early modern period through the prism of nationalistic histories. Subjects from the German-speaking lands in particular do not commonly feature in discussions of transatlantic culture or colonial expansion since the highly decentralized German empire did not have colonial possessions in the early modern period.[60] Colonial (read 'national') geographies continue to inform the production of knowledge about Europeans in the 'Indies.' As such, the fact that this period of Latin American history is called 'colonial' means that, when historians move to tell a trans-regional version of Latin America's history, they often look first to Spain, less often to Asia, and never to the German states.

Given this rigidity, it is worthwhile to pause and gather up the multiple meanings of 'colonial' in current historical literature: The term is a complex and contested term for the early modern period. We find it useful as a gloss for a number of phenomena that mark European expansion: from trading-post empires to settler colonies, from mastery of a geographic space to a set of imaginary claims, such as the will to know, classify, and also the will to convert. Dealing with the Society of Jesus necessarily means that one enters all these domains and hence alerts us to the profound linkages between them. In bringing the stories of these two Jesuit priests together, we have attempted to decipher 'the colonial' in early modern German history and the 'early modern' in colonial Latin America. An early modern culture of Catholicism connected the German Kaller to the Spaniard Ramos. This Catholic culture overlapped but was not coterminous with the colonial.

The analysis of Catarina de San Juan's appropriation by different Jesuits also suggests that we need to pay attention to the role of the Pacific in the 'Atlantic world.' Our approach redirects scholarly attention to flows of people and information *from* the Pacific, through the New World, and, finally, back across the Atlantic. Catarina, the slave-turned-Christian in colonial Mexico, was very much the product of the history of human commerce we often associate only with the Atlantic world. Yet her life story extends to places that do not border on the Atlantic or belong to a different ocean-world altogether. The fact that this story became a rallying point for men from different parts of Europe pushes our conceptions of the reach of the trans-Pacific/Atlantic worlds and the religious women in it. In the dense thicket of narratives, Catarina as a living woman is lost to us, yet her life story travelled all the way from the Pacific to the Atlantic world and Central Europe, which is no small accomplishment. It throws into stark relief the fact that the Atlantic was not a static space hosting a bounded community but rather a mobile and transitory zone with shifting configurations of people. Her much-travelled story illustrates the importance of colonial Mexico as a significant nodal point for those who moved along Jesuit missionary networks, a movement of peoples and ideas that did much to further the globalization of Catholicism.

Notes

1 Jodi Bilinkoff, *Related Lives: Confessors and Their Female Penitents, 1450–1750* (Ithaca, N.Y.: Cornell University Press, 2005).

2 Ibid., 117.

3 For accounts that discuss Catarina de San Juan's life history, see Ronald J. Morgan, 'Saints, Biographers, and Creole Identity Formation in Colonial Spanish America,' PhD thesis, University of California at Santa Barbara, 1998; Kathleen Myers, 'Testimony for Canonization or Proof of Blasphemy? The New Spanish Inquisition and the Hagiographic Biography of Catarina De San Juan,' in Mary E. Giles, ed., *Women in the Inquisition: Spain and the New World* (Baltimore: Johns Hopkins University Press, 1999), 270–95; Francisco de la Maza, *Catarina de San Juan: Princesa de la India y visionaria de Puebla* (Mexico City: Cien de México, 1990); and José del Castillo Graxeda, *Compendio de la vida y virtudes de la venerable Catarina de San Juan* (Puebla: Gobierno del Estado de Puebla, 1987 [1692]).

4 Luke Clossey, 'Distant Souls: Global Religion and the Jesuit Missions of Germany, Mexico and China, 1595–1705,' PhD thesis, University of California, Berkeley, 2004, 8.

5 On Catholic missionaries in New World contexts, see also various essays in Allan Greer and Jodi Bilinkoff, eds., *Colonial Saints: Discovering the Holy in the Americas* (New York: Routledge, 2003). On religious women in New World contexts and their activities, see Susan E. Dinan and Debra Meyers, eds., *Women and Religion in Old and New Worlds* (New York: Routledge, 2001).

6 Jorge Cañizares-Esguerra, *How to Write the History of the New World: Histories, Epistemologies, Identities in the Eighteenth-Century Atlantic World* (Stanford, Calif.: Stanford University Press, 2001).

7 In a chapter titled 'Soul Mates,' Bilinkoff recounts that many anguished holy women searched for a good confessor, and she detects a discourse of 'destiny' in many descriptions of how confessors-penitents 'found' each other (*Related Lives*, 76–95).

8 Alonso Ramos, *Primera parte de los prodigios de la omnipotencia, y milagros de la gracia en la vida de la venerable sierva de dios Catharina De S. Joan; natural del gran Mogor, difunta en esta imperial ciudad de la Puebla de los Angeles en la Nueva Espana* (Puebla: Imprenta de Diego Fernández de León, 1689).

9 Myers, 'Testimony for Canonization,' 277.

176   J. Michelle Molina and Ulrike Strasser

10 For more on Creole consciousness in the New World, see Antonio Rubial García, *La santidad controvertida: Hagiografía y conciencia criolla alrededor de los venerables no canonizados de Nueva España* (Mexico City: UNAM/FCE, 1999).

11 J. Michelle Molina, 'True Lies: Athanasius Kircher's *China Illustrata* and the Life Story of a Mexican Mystic,' in Paula Findlen, ed., *Athanasius Kircher: The Last Man Who Knew Everything* (New York: Routledge, 2004).

12 Myers, 'Testimony for Canonization,' 294.

13 Bilinkoff discusses occasions when biographers utilized the voices of their penitents within the body of their hagiographies. Sometimes the confessors took direct quotes from the women's letters or journals. In this case, however, it seems clear that Ramos was acting as ventriloquist (Bilinkoff, *Related Lives*, 65ff.).

14 Ramos, *Primera parte.*

15 Nicolás León, *Catarina de San Juan y la china poblana. Estudio etnográfico crítico* (Mexico City: Biblioteca Aportación Histórica, 1946).

16 Michael Thomas Destefano, 'Miracles and Monasticism in Mid-Colonial Puebla, 1600–1750: Charismatic Religion in a Conservative Society,' PhD thesis, University of Florida, 1977, 28.

17 See Nora Jaffary, 'Virtue and Transgression: The Certification of Authentic Mysticism in the Mexican Inquisition,' *Catholic Southwest,* 10 (1999): 9–28. For Spain, see Mary Elizabeth Perry, 'Beatas and the Inquisition in Early Modern Seville,' in Stephen Haliczer, trans. and ed., *Inquisition and Society in Early Modern Europe* (Totowa, N.J.: Barnes and Noble, 1987), 147–68. This article subsequently appeared as a chapter in Perry's *Gender and Disorder in Early Modern Seville* (Princeton, N.J.: Princeton University Press, 1990).

18 Daniello Bartoli, *Missione al gran Mogol del Ridolfo Aquaviva della compagnia di Giesu, sua vita e morte* (Roma: Varese, 1663).

19 Rubial García, *La santidad controvertida,* 42.

20 José Luis Sánchez Lora, *Mujeres, conventos y formas de la religiosidad barroca* (Madrid: Fundación Universitaria Española, 1988).

21 Ramos, *Primera parte,* 7.

22 Gauvin Alexander Bailey, 'A Mughal Princess in Baroque New Spain: Catarina De San Juan (1606–1688), the *China Poblana,' Anales del Instituto de Investigaciones Estéticas,* 71 (1997): 37–73, 47.

23 Ramos, *Primera parte,* 14.

24 Antonio Núñez de Miranda, S.J., 'Carta y discuros preocupativo, de algunas dificultades, que pueden resaltar luego a la primera vista de esta historia,' in Ramos, *Primera parte* (n.p.).

25 For issues of truth and credibility in sixteenth-century New World histories, see Anthony Pagden, *European Encounters with the New World: From Renais-*

sance to Romanticism (New Haven, Conn.: Yale University Press, 1993), 51–88.

26 Cañizares-Esguerra, *How to Write the History of the New World,* 12.
27 According to King Phillip II, in a court of law 'two Indians or three women presented as witnesses are worth one Spanish man.' See Anthony Pagden, *The Fall of Natural Man: The American Indian and the Origins of Comparative Ethnology* (Cambridge and New York: Cambridge University Press, 1986), 44.
28 As quoted in Destefano, 'Miracles and Monasticism,' 68.
29 See chapter 1, 'Toward a New Art of Reading and New Historical Interpretations,' in Cañizares-Esguerra, *How to Write the History of the New World.*
30 Cañizares-Esguerra, *How to Write the History of the New World,* 26.
31 Printed in Joseph Stöcklein, *Allerhand so lehr- als geistreiche Brief, Schrifften und Reis-beschreibungen, welchen von denen Missionariis der Gesellschaft Jesu aus beyden Indien, und andern über Meer gelegenen Ländern seit An. 1642 biss auf das Jahr 1726 in Europa angelangt seynd. Erster Bund oder die 8. Erste Teil* (Augsburg und Grätz: Verlag Philip, Martins und Joh. Veith seel. Erben, 1726), 72–5. A copy of the original Latin letter can be found in Státni Ústrêdní Archiv v Praze (henceforth SUA), Jesuitica, Kall 6, ff.113–14.
32 Rudolf Grulich, *Der Beitrag der böhmischen Länder yur Weltmission des 17. und 18. Jahrhunderts* (Königstein: Institut für Kirchengeschichte von Böhmen, Mähren, Schlesien, 1981), 95; Bernd Hausberger, *Jesuiten aus Mitteleuropa im kolonialen Mexiko. Eine Bio-Bibliographie* (Munich: Oldenbourg, 1995), 192.
33 Anton Huonder, *Deutsche Jesuitenmissionäre des 17. und 18. Jahrhunderts* (Freiburg im Breisgau: Herder'sche Verlagsbuchhandlung, 1899), 11–14; quote 14.
34 Bernard Duhr, *Deutsche Auslandssehnsucht im 18. Jahrhundert: Aus der überseeischen Missionsarbeit deutscher Jesuiten* (Stuttgart: Ausland und Heimatverlags-Aktiengesellschaft, 1928); Hausberger, *Jesuiten aus Mitteleuropa,* 34–6.
35 Huonder, *Deutsche Jesuitenmissionäre,* 14; Hausberger, *Jesuiten aus Mitteleuropa,* 37–8.
36 Charles G. Herbermann, 'Der Neue Welt-Bott: Introduction,' *Historical Records and Studies,* 8 (1915): 157–67, 161.
37 Printed in Stöcklein, *Allerhand so lehr- als geistreiche Brief,* ff.72–5. The original Latin letter can be found in SUA, Jesuitica, Kall 6, ff.113–114.
38 On the funerary sermon as source for Ramos, see Myers, 'Testimony for Canonization,' 276.
39 Hausberger, *Jesuiten aus Mitteleuropa,* 87–92.
40 Stöcklein, *Allerhand so lehr- als geistreiche Brief,* f.73; SUA, Jesuitica, Kall 6, f.114.
41 Stöcklein, *Allerhand so lehr- als geistreiche Brief,* f.74; SUA, Jesuitica, Kall 6, f.114. Emphasis added.

42 Ibid.
43 On the issue of cultural opaqueness and the inevitability of mistranslating into the familiar, see Pagden, *European Encounters*.
44 Stöcklein translated the original *nigro* as 'brown.' Stöcklein, *Allerhand so lehr-als geistreiche Brief,* f.74; SUA, Jesuitica, Kall 6, f.114.
45 Ibid.
46 Pierre Cholenec, *Catherine Tekakwitha: Her Life,* William Lonc, S.J., trans. (Hamilton, Ont.: William Lonc, 2002), 70.
47 Allan Greer, *Mohawk Saint: Catherine Tekakwitha and the Jesuits* (Oxford: Oxford University Press, 2005), especially 187, where he discusses the polemical uses of Catherine Tekakwitha's biography in contemporary debates among Jesuits, deists, and Augustinians. See also Allan Greer, 'Iroquois Virgin: The Story of Catherine Tekakwitha in New France and New Spain,' in Allan Greer and Jodi Bilinkoff, eds., *Colonial Saints: Discovering the Holy in the Americas* (New York: Routledge, 2003), 235–51.
48 Stöcklein, *Allerhand so lehr- als geistreiche Brief,* f.73; SUA, Jesuitica, Kall 6, f.114.
49 Huonder, *Deutsche Jesuitenmissionäre,* 33–41.
50 Peter Burschel, *Sterben und Unsterblichkeit. Zur Kultur des Martyriums in der frühen Neuzeit* (Munich: Oldenbourg, 2004), especially 229–45, 263–88.
51 Huonder, *Deutsche Jesuitenmissionäre,* 38–9.
52 Ines G. Zupanov, *Missionary Tropics: The Catholic Frontier in India (16th–17th Centuries)* (Ann Arbor: University of Michigan Press, 2005), chapter 4, 'The Art of Dying in the Tropics,' 147–71.
53 For example, Antonio Ruiz de Montoya's famous account of the early history of the Paraguay missions relates how Father Cristobal de Mendoza, whom he calls a 'dauntless martyr,' expressed his desire 'for a short, quick martyrdom so that he would not have to stare death in the face for long.' *The Spiritual Conquest: Accomplished by the Religious of the Society of Jesus in the Provinces of Paraguay, Paraná, Uruguay, and Tape Written by Father Antonio Ruiz de Montoya (1639),* C.J. McNaspy, S.J., trans. (St Louis: Institute of Jesuit Sources, 1993), 173.
54 Stöcklein, *Allerhand so lehr- als geistreiche Brief,* f.74; SUA, Jesuitica, Kall 6, f.114.
55 Ibid.
56 Ibid.
57 A case in point is the *vita* of Catherine de Saint Augustin by the French Jesuit Paul Ragueneau. Ragueneau made a point of including lengthy quotations by Catherine in which she sang the praises of the famed Jesuit martyr Jean de Brebeuf (Bilinkoff, *Related Lives,* 70–5).

58 Hausberger, *Jesuiten aus Mitteleuropa*, 192–3.
59 Myers, 'Testimony for Canonization,' 282.
60 The absence of colonies drove a vivid colonial fantasy life unimpeded by the messy realities of colonialism. Susanne Zantop, *Colonial Fantasies: Conquest, Family, and Nation in Precolonial Germany, 1770–1870* (Durham, N.C.: Duke University Press, 1997).

chapter seven

Patriarchs, Petitions, and Prayers: Intersections of Gender and *Calidad* in Colonial Mexico

JOAN CAMERON BRISTOL

In 1606, in colonial Mexico, a West African woman named Esperanza appeared of her own volition before the Inquisition to denounce herself for blaspheming.[1] Esperanza testified that more than a year earlier her mistress had been hitting her 'cruelly,' causing her to renounce God 'with the pain of the lashes.' According to her, her outburst only made her mistress intensify the beating.[2] Esperanza told the inquisitors that she repented her renunciation, explaining that her sin was involuntary. Her words, she claimed, were provoked by the severe beating her mistress had given her. In response to standard inquisitorial questioning, Esperanza declared that 'she is Christian and knows the Our Father, María, Creed, and Salve Regina and the commandments,'[3] the standard prayers Christians were expected to know. She also claimed that she participated regularly in the sacrament of confession. Further establishing herself as a good Christian, Esperanza explained that she had tarried in denouncing herself only because she had been ill.

This case was not particularly unusual. Violence was normal in relationships between owners and slaves in colonial Mexico, and, as in this case, mistresses were as likely to mete out punishment as masters were. Slaves like Esperanza regularly responded with blasphemies. Over one hundred and fifty Afro-Mexicans were accused of renouncing God, the Virgin Mary, or the saints over the course of the seventeenth century. Such blasphemies were, in fact, specifically associated with Afro-Mexicans, especially slaves but also free servants and others serving sentences of bound labour. These cases reveal the extent of Afro-Mexicans' abilities to draw on ideas about Christian morality and their understandings of the colonial religious and social structures. Esperanza was not the only enslaved individual who depicted herself as a responsible Christian, nor was she the only one who seemed to make an implicit comparison between her own practice of Christianity and that of her owner. Not only did she blame her mistress for inspiring her blasphemy, Esperanza may have been implying that her owner was negligent in not bringing the matter to the court's attention earlier.

In part because of the competing versions of events that blasphemy cases offer, historians have found them fertile ground for discussions of master-slave relations and Afro-Mexican resistance to the conditions of slavery.[4] This chapter uses gender to analyse blasphemy cases involving workers and masters and pairs them with three other cases: two in which women denounced their husbands for blasphemy and one in which a slave accused her owner of mistreatment.[5] Looking at these cases through the lens of gender and not merely race, as others have done, allows us to see Afro-Mexican men and women within an Atlantic context. Afro-Mexicans were not just members of the African diaspora but members of a broad Atlantic underclass whose experience of subjugation, and their responses to it, were shaped by gender and class as well as race and ethnicity. As part of this underclass, Afro-Mexican men as well as women shared certain experiences and survival tactics with others, particularly women, from other Atlantic regions and social groups. For example, we will see below that Afro-Mexican slaves and servants drew on ideas about femininity and masculinity to defend themselves before inquisitors. Natalie Zemon Davis has shown how a similar tactic was used in sixteenth-century France, when wives and female servants accused of crimes modulated their testimonies before the king in order to defend their actions and present themselves as humble and modest in accordance with the prevailing model of femininity.[6]

As we saw above in the case of Esperanza, Afro-Mexicans testifying at the Inquisition also portrayed themselves as good Christians struggling to maintain their moral standing in the face of attacks by others. We see a similar tactic in a 1635 Spanish example described by Mary Elizabeth Perry, in which a Christian woman originally from Berbery suspected her husband of plotting to take her back to the Muslim region. Presenting herself as a good Christian, "'moved by zeal for the same faith and for her salvation,'" she went to the Inquisition to accuse her husband of practising Islam.[7] Looking at these cases through the lens of gender reveals the Mexican Inquisition as one of several Atlantic institutions that underrepresented people used as a forum within which to present themselves and their actions in a favourable light. We also see how Afro-

Mexicans adopted tactics often associated with women in other contexts, raising questions about whether men in other regions who were marginalized by class rather than race may have adopted similar tactics.

Within the Mexican context, placing the blasphemy cases alongside those involving husbands and wives and a slave and her master suggests ways to examine the intersection of Spanish colonial ideologies of gender, race, and class. Inquisition cases show that these ideologies were not always linked in predictable ways; those with more authority by reason of gender, class, or race did not automatically prevail over those with less institutional power. Non-Spaniards had some recourse against the elite Spaniards who wielded power over them, although such opposition was often unsuccessful in terms of changing relationships with superiors. Afro-Mexicans, like other denizens of the Atlantic world, found ways of negotiating their relationships with immediate authorities – masters and mistresses, in the case of slaves and servants, and husbands, in the case of wives – by appealing to other authorities. In the process they confronted and even manipulated the gendered assumptions upon which colonial forms of authority rested.

The Inquisition as Patriarch

New Spain was a patriarchal society, in which authority was vested in men. In Gerda Lerner's classic formulation, patriarchy is 'the manifestation and institutionalization of male dominance over women and children in the family and the extension of male dominance over women in society in general.' This dominance creates a situation in which women are deprived of access to the power embodied in 'all the important institutions of society.'[8] Maleness was not the only prerequisite for power, of course, just as gender is not the only component of patriarchal authority: the colonial social hierarchy also organized itself around *calidad* (literally translated as quality or status). The concept of *calidad* was used to differentiate 'pure' Spaniards from the majority of the colonial population by classifying and defining individuals according to their skin colour, clothing, occupation, personal relationships, cultural practices, status as slave or free, and *limpieza de sangre,* or purity of blood.[9] Only Old Christians who could prove the purity of their lineage from any Jewish, Muslim, or other non-Christian influence could claim the *calidad* of a Spaniard. Thus *calidad,* and especially the constituent factors that we would now call class and race, played a role in notions of patriarchal hierarchy along with gender.

The relationship between *calidad* and gender in the colonial hierarchy of authority is thrown into sharp relief when we consider the place of Spanish women (primarily Creole but also Spanish-born) in colonial society. Along with Africans and their descendants of both sexes, and most indigenous people as well, Spanish women could not hold public office outside the convent or attend university. However, Spanish women, particularly elite ones, had more status and authority than non-Spaniards of either sex, and this was expressed in part through gender identity. Elite Spanish women claimed a superior form of femininity relative to lower-class women and women of colour, and elite Spanish men a superior masculinity relative to lower-class men and men of colour.[10] Thus, although most Spanish women were not active in the higher echelons of civil or religious life, they did have officially sanctioned authority in the form of honour, just as Spanish men did. Honour had two related meanings in the colonial world: honour-status (*honor*), which was based on birth, and the more flexible *honra,* or honour-virtue, which was based on character. Non-Spaniards, who by definition lacked the *limpieza de sangre* necessary for *honor,* could gain *honra* by exhibiting courage, skill, generosity, and other traits.[11] There was a strong link between early modern Spanish gender ideologies and honour. Elite Spanish women's sexuality was supposed to be strictly controlled through either marriage or the convent because of concerns that they might produce illegitimate children who would threaten the *limpieza de sangre* of their families. Thus, both *honor* and *honra* were gendered; men and women expressed them differently. For example, Patricia Seed has looked at the case of marriage to show that, particularly before the eighteenth century, Spanish men's honour-virtue was predicated on keeping their promise to marry, while women's was predicated on limiting their sexual activities to marriage.[12] Both of these behaviours would ensure the honour-status of their families.

The Inquisition, established to uphold orthodoxy, provides a powerful example of the gendered nature of colonial authority. Presided over by Spanish men, the tribunal represented the combined patriarchal power of the Catholic Church and the crown in the colonies. It had a great degree of autonomy from these institutions, however, since it owed allegiance to the king but received its power from the pope.[13] As an authority in its own right, the Inquisition was authorized to peer into colonial residents' private lives if blasphemy, heresy, or other religious infractions were suspected.[14] Colonial residents would have witnessed the expression of the court's authority at public sentencings (*autos de fe*), when convicts were paraded through the streets and their punishments read out loud.[15] After sentencing (often the following day), convicts were corporally punished. Although burnings, reserved for the gravest crimes, were unusual in New Spain, punishments were harsh.

The Inquisition's punitive power and surveillance functions suggest that it represented not just patriarchal power in general but rather a particular form. The inquisitors' roles and mission brings to mind the Old Testament God, the exacting and vengeful father figure who tested Abraham by asking him to kill his own son and sent the Israelites to wander in the desert for forty years as punishment for worshipping the Golden Calf. This may have been the kind of authority figure that colonial residents had in mind when they appealed to inquisitors to curb slave owners' behaviour.

Yet the Inquisition, terrifying in its public acts, also presented colonial residents with the possibility of relief from daily oppression. Cases such as Esperanza's, in which slaves and servants renounced God, represented attempts by Afro-Mexicans to use the same religious practices and forms of knowledge that upheld the official system of authority to try to negotiate that system of authority. Elsewhere I have argued that slaves and servants deliberately blasphemed so that they would be brought to the Inquisition, where they then complained to ecclesiastical authorities about the mistreatment they suffered at the hands of their masters.[16] Perhaps, then, the New Testament patriarch – the benevolent, protective, help-giving father – was also in their minds when they approached the Inquisition.

Gender ideology played a powerful role in such challenges to the power of the masters. Borrowing a concept from Steve J. Stern, we might argue that slaves and servants were 'pluralizing the patriarchs' in their appearances at the Inquisition. According to Stern, this was a 'strategy [that] set up male-male rivalries and hierarchies as a check on the power of the patriarch with the most immediate claim of authority.'[17] In essence, blasphemers were going over the head of the immediate household patriarch (the master) to appeal to another (the inquisitor). The dynamic is even more apparent in cases involving wives who directly accused husbands of blasphemy. This was a tactic used by others in the Atlantic world: Stern discusses poor eighteenth- and nineteenth-century Mexican women of different social groups who appealed to criminal courts to combat husbands' ill treatment. Poor Mexican women were not the only people to use such a tactic. Seed describes how elite couples hoping to marry in sixteenth-century Mexico successfully appealed to the church to support their choices in the face of parental objections, although ecclesiastical willingness to fly in the face of parental wishes changed in succeeding centuries.[18] In another work, Stern shows six-teenth-century indigenous Andean leaders appealing to Spanish courts to override the labour obligations owed to the state.[19] Perry's example, discussed above, of a woman accusing her husband before the Spanish Inquisition in order to prevent him from taking her back to Berbery against her will, also represents an attempt to pluralize the patriarchs.

In the case of Mexico, the tactic of appealing to inquisitors did not always end well for those who employed it. In many cases, the accusations were not pursued. Thus, if wives hoped to see their husbands convicted of blasphemy, or if slaves and servants hoped to involve their masters. in a protracted hearing at the court, many were not successful. In fact, the actions of wives and workers likely earned them more abuse once their experience at the court was over.[20] Whatever our judgment about the motives and success of accusers and accused, however, the cases dis-cussed below give us a sense of the gaps in the armour of patriarchal authority. They reveal colonial residents developing tactics to negotiate and manipulate these gaps, and give us an appreciation for the role of gender in power relations at the levels of both household and society.

Household Affairs and the Inquisition: Wives and Husbands

In 1599 Augustina Delgadillo, described as a *natural,* or native of Mexico City (perhaps a native American), went to the Inquisition to denounce her husband, Juan Bedor, a mulatto fruit seller.[21] She was accompanied by her *comadre* (a term indicating filial ties created through godparent-age), Magdalena de la Cruz, who also testified. Magdalena's caste was not specified. According to Augustina and Magdalena, two weeks earlier the two women had returned from attending a sermon to see an enraged Juan smashing the deadbolt on the front door of the house. Magdale-na reported that Juan said to his wife, 'Proven whore[,] where are you coming from?'[22] When he heard her answer, Magdalena claimed, Juan became even angrier and said that Augustina should have been attend-ing to his needs instead of going to the sermon. As he spoke he hit her. The Inquisition did not care about marital quarrels, however; personal relations per se were not its jurisdiction. For the purposes of the testimo-nies, Juan's violent language and behaviour were mere context for the blasphemous words he uttered next. According to both women, Juan then said that Augustina should obey him because his words were more valuable than God's.[23] This was the focus of the women's testimonies, and the detail that was bound to catch the attention of the inquisitors. In claiming authority above that of God, Juan committed the sin of blasphemy. In making his transgression a matter for the Inquisition instead of an event that remained in the privacy of the home, and by appealing to men whose authority was greater than Juan's by reason of *calidad* and *honor*, Augustina and Magdalena challenged Juan's role as head of the household. Magdalena concluded that she judged Juan to be a bad Christian, adding that he was often drunk. She was, however, careful to say that Juan was not drunk at the time of the event, since drunkenness might excuse him from responsibility for the crime, making it spontaneous and not deliberate.

Making her case even more strongly than Magdalena, Augustina described other instances in which Juan had blasphemed. She claimed that a month earlier she and Juan were at home, where they had a painting of Christ descending from the cross (*el descendimiento de la cruz que estaba pintado en un papel*). Augustina claimed that Juan had grabbed the image and threatened to rip it up and use it to wipe his 'hidden parts' (*partes ocultas*). [24] By repeating this scandalous and blasphemous statement, Augustina likely hoped to grab the inquisitors' attention. Augustina ended her testimony by recounting an incident in which Juan had commented on a statue or small figurine of a baby Jesus on which Augustina had taken a vow. He said that the image was nothing more than a dressed-up little stick. [25] Perhaps Juan felt that his own authority was undermined by his wife's reliance on religious activities and religious articles. Whatever Juan's motivations for blaspheming, it seems that Augustina hoped to use the Inquisition as a way to control her husband, not only by curbing his blasphemies but also by curbing his mistreatment of her. Although she and Magdalena described only one event in which he beat her, this was likely not the first or only time this occurred.

The women's descriptions of Juan's behaviour failed to alarm the inquisitors, however. The inquisitorial consultant did agree that Juan's first reported infraction, when he said that his words valued more than God's, could be defined as blasphemy. Yet, given the specific events, he ruled that Juan's words were not blasphemous because they were provoked by his wife's behaviour. [26] According to the consultant, Juan's words were aimed at chastising Augustina for going to the sermon rather than obeying him, and thus did not have true blasphemous intent. Even though, as a mulatto man, Juan did not have officially defined honour, the inquisitors acknowledged Juan's power over his family; in effect, they recognized his position as patriarch. The consultant did claim that

Juan's other statements were suspicious because they showed a lack of the proper respect owed to religious images. Nevertheless, Juan was not punished.

We see a similar attempt to weaken the authority of a husband, and to seek protection from him, in the testimony of Isabel Chávez, a free black woman. In 1606 Isabel went to the Inquisition to denounce her husband, Antonio Veneciano. He was described as a 'foreigner,' probably, as his name implies, from Venice.[27] Isabel claimed that eight months earlier, after she had requested something of her husband, Antonio said, 'I renounce God and all his saints, [since] a black woman asks something from me.' Antonio then beat her, only stopping when a friar who heard the commotion arrived to separate them and scold Antonio. Thus, even before the case got to the court, the patriarchs were pluralized when a cleric intervened in household affairs. Isabel also recounted another more recent event in which she asked her husband why he had taken the rent money, and he had responded with a curse. According to Isabel, Antonio said that even if all the saints of heaven came to his house and asked for the money he would refuse them.

After delivering the testimony about Antonio's blasphemous words at the court, Isabel tried to incriminate her husband further by saying that in the decade that they had been married she had never seen him take communion and knew of only two occasions when he confessed. These sacraments were required of all Christians on a regular basis. Isabel reported that when Antonio attended Mass it was with reluctance and that he missed some holidays. Moreover, she said, during Mass Antonio often fussed over his mustache rather than paying attention to the service, and even when he seemed to be kneeling during services he was only supporting himself on one knee. Isabel concluded from this evidence that Antonio was a bad Christian, and ended her statement by reminding the court that her husband was a foreigner. With this testimony Isabel showed that she understood ideas about morality and *calidad*. In fact, she may have been manipulating such ideas to give her words the extra weight she needed as a black woman, doubly marginalized, to convince the inquisitors of the truth of her statements. Like Augustina, Isabel seems to have hoped to control her husband's mistreatment of her by using his blasphemies as a way to invite official intervention into her unhappy domestic situation. If inquisitors found Antonio guilty of blaspheming he would be punished. This would remove him temporarily from the home. She may also have hoped that he would think twice before mistreating her in the future.

Augustina and Isabel may have had additional reasons to hope that the inquisitors would find their husbands worthy of punishment. Juan Bedor, as a mulatto, did not have the *calidad* that allowed him to claim honour, and even Antonio Veneciano was on somewhat shaky ground. As a European he had status, but as a foreigner, as Isabel implied, he may not have been seen as having the honour of a Spaniard. Both Isabel and Augustina may have hoped that their husbands' backgrounds would sway the inquisitors' sympathies in their favour. If this was the case, however, their hopes were dashed. As with Augustina, Isabel's attempt to pluralize the patriarchs did not meet with success. The inquisitors did not pursue the accusation.

Approaching the Inquisition with a denunciation was a significant act and entailed major risks. These women must not have done so lightly. First, Augustina and Isabel put their husbands at risk of punishment. Although only a fraction of denunciations ended in conviction, the possibility of a guilty verdict certainly existed. Even if alleged blasphemers were not convicted, they might be subject to a long, drawn-out trial and a lengthy stay in the inquisitorial prison. If convicted, they might be exiled and suffer physical punishment. The fact that Augustina and Isabel put their husbands in this position attests to more than mere willingness to rid themselves of these men; it likely demonstrates their hatred of them as well. Secondly, the women incurred significant risks themselves: denouncers might end up being investigated alongside those they denounced. Or, if the men were not convicted (as happened in both cases) and they learned who had denounced them, the women risked their husbands' abuse. Augustina and Isabel may have been genuinely disturbed by their husbands' blasphemies and felt obligated to report them. Their actions, taken in the face of such potential danger, signal their desperation. Similarly, their willingness to take risks also reveals their attitude towards the Inquisition; Augustina and Isabel placed hope and trust in the Inquisition's patriarchal role, in both its punishing and its protective guises.

A 1643 case from Mexico City represents a more direct attempt to overcome a household patriarch's power by appealing to inquisitors. Magdalena de la Cruz, an enslaved woman identified as originally being from Angola, went to the Inquisition to complain about her owner, Martin de Ortega, a *familiar* (lay official) of the Inquisition.[28] Although she was not accusing him of a religious crime, her owner's position as an inquisitorial officer made her complaint the court's purview. This was the third time that Magdalena had appeared in the court for this purpose. Although the inquisitors had admonished Don Martin on the previous occasions, telling him to moderate his punishments of his slaves, Magdalena charged that he had not changed his behaviour. Moreover, she complained, her owner had retaliated against her for appealing to the Inquisition by denying her the weekly visits with her husband that he allowed other slaves. Finally, Magdalena said that Don Martin had told her that he would sell her, but that when she brought him prospective buyers he asked for unreasonably large sums of money.[29] According to Magdalena, this indicated that he planned to make her life a miserable and inescapable cycle of punishment. Magdalena asked that the inquisitors intervene on her behalf to force her owner to sell her to a buyer whom she had found. Her testimony was accompanied by testimonies by a Spanish acquaintance of her owner and a Flemish merchant, both of whom corroborated her story.[30]

In her actions outside the court, and through her testimony at the court, Magdalena attacked her owner's authority as a patriarch on several levels. First, on her previous visits she had persuaded the inquisitors, already his superiors at the Inquisition, to chide Don Martin and interfere in matters pertaining to his home, where he was supposed to be in charge. His refusal to allow Magdalena to visit her husband reminds us that he had power over not just his own family but over other families too. Secondly, Magdalena appealed to other men to buy her and remove her from her owner's home, again challenging Martin de Ortega's identity as the ultimate authority in his own household. Finally, rather than relying on the support of witnesses with status equal to her own, Magdalena enlisted European men to confirm her claims, individuals who may have had relatively equal class status to her owner. Unlike Augustina and Isabel, Magdalena played authorities against each other with some degree of success, albeit posthumously: by the time a case was brought against Martin de Ortega in 1647,[31] Magdalena had died.[32]

Although these cases involved diverse relationships and accusations, together they represent women's attempts to get colonial authorities to intervene in household affairs. Such women were marginalized by *calidad* as well as gender and, in the case of the second Magdalena, slave status. These cases clearly document the practice of pluralizing the patriarchs, since all three women went over the head of the household patriarch to appeal to a higher colonial power. Yet they were not attacking the patriarchal structure as such. Rather, by appealing to one patriarch to check the power of another, they were forging a tactical alliance with patriarchy. This tactic may be less clear in the two renunciation cases discussed below in which slaves and servants were accused of crimes themselves. Because of their defensive postures, it may be less easy to see these slaves and servants as agents than it is to see Augustina, Isabel, and Magdalena in that role. Yet the renunciation cases also represent attempts to limit the power of a household patriarch by appealing to the power of an institutional patriarch. Again we see the dual character of the patriarchal power represented by inquisitors: Afro-Mexican slaves and servants may have hoped to call down the wrath of the strict father on their oppressors, while at the same time placing themselves under the protective wing of the benevolent father.

Renunciation cases, like those involving married couples, also add to our understanding of colonial ideologies of gender and *calidad* by giving us examples of the way that different parties might manipulate ideas about gender roles. In the cases below we see accusers and accused employing ideas about gender to claim the moral high ground. In the process we see the links between *calidad,* gender, and honour (both *honor* and *honra*) being stretched in ways not intended by the Spaniards whose status rested on a particular interpretation of these concepts.

Renouncing God, Renouncing Authority: Slaves and Servants

Renunciation cases show that the boundaries of colonial power and authority could shift as the power of masters confronted that of inquisitors. This plurality of power gave slaves and servants room to grasp some autonomy for themselves. Ideas about gender were central to the expression of authority and to the challenges it faced. We see this in a 1610 case in which Juan, a sixteen-year-old Creole black slave, was denounced to the Inquisition for renouncing God.[33] The case began when Juan's owner had his son, Don Juan Zapata de Sandoval, beat Juan as punishment for running away while another son, Don Francisco de Sandoval, looked on. Both sons were identified in the Inquisition's records as Spanish with relatively high social status (as indicated by the use of the honorific term 'don'). Juan's owner may have charged his sons with meting out Juan's punishment as a way to reinforce his own masculinity and position as the head of the household. When masters prevailed upon those with less prestige and power to do their dirty work, they reinforced an authority based not only in *calidad* but also in gender and age. The sons, in turn, shared in his authority by punishing a subordinate.

According to the sons' testimonies, even before the whipping began Juan threatened to renounce God if he were hit. Don Juan remembered that after Don Francisco asked Juan for what he blamed God, Juan responded that God 'had much blame because he had made the world.'[34] Such an outrageous statement earned Juan even harsher punishment. Don Francisco described the way that Juan was gagged and then whipped thirty to forty times, at which point he threatened to blaspheme. Then, he claimed, after a few more lashes Juan did renounce God.[35]

Don Juan, Juan's assailant, claimed that the whipping had not been harsh and that his only motive was to reform the slave and correct his behaviour. He claimed that he had heard Juan blaspheme before, and stated that he did not consider the slave a good Christian 'since [Juan] is very *ladino* [and] knows and understands that it is a misdeed to renounce and blaspheme God.'[36] As a *ladino*, or a Hispanized non-Spaniard, Juan was expected to know all about Christian practice.

This characterization of Juan as a *ladino* who deliberately blasphemed, rather than as a misguided or ignorant neophyte, may tell us more about the Sandoval brothers than it does about Juan. Don Juan and Don Francisco may have hoped that, by painting Juan's renunciation as premeditated, they would protect themselves from the accusation that their brutality had led to Juan's renunciation of God. In describing how they had defended God's name by asking Juan why he blamed Him, and by beating him when he did renounce, Don Juan and Don Francisco characterized themselves as honourable, pious men and protectors of the Christian faith. While Juan's identity as a black slave precluded him from claiming honour by birth, Don Juan and Don Francisco's testimony also worked to deny him any *honra*, based on virtue. These Spaniards were claiming authority that was theirs by reason of the hierarchy of *calidad*, and they were employing ideas about gender and religion to consolidate this authority.

The slave Juan's testimony differed from that of his owner's sons in notable ways and showed a profound understanding of the workings of the Inquisition. In his earlier testimony, Juan said that the exchange about whether God was at fault or not had happened before he was gagged, but that after he was gagged he had not been able to talk and therefore had not renounced.[37] This was, in fact, supported by testimony from the Sandoval brothers, who testified that they had gagged him after his first outburst. However, when Juan was called before the Inquisition for the final time, his story changed. He admitted to the crime of renouncing God. Yet, even while admitting guilt, Juan continued to lay the blame for his action squarely at the feet of the masters' sons, blaming them for the harsh treatment that led him to renounce. He said: 'Don Juan and Don Francisco [had] whipped him very cruelly, and having asked them many times for God and all the saints to leave him, seeing that they didn't, with [the] great pain of the lashes and affliction that he had [suffered], thinking that they would leave him more quickly, he said that he renounced God once, not with intention to offend him but rather to liberate himself from the punishment and later he repented.'[38] This allegation, that the brothers had ignored appeals made in God's name, had the effect of contrasting Juan's piety to the brothers' lack of Christian mercy. Yet Juan's attempt to excuse his words by passing blame onto the owners' sons failed, and may only have increased his punishment. Juan was condemned to more lashes and was paraded through the streets on a donkey, naked from the waist up, gagged once again, with a crier announcing his offence.[39]

Juan's testimony represents an attempt to play authorities against each other similar to that seen in the cases above. Renouncing God was the ultimate way of acknowledging the layers of power that undergirded novohispano society. He appealed to the Inquisition to take the masters' sons' behaviour into account in trying his case, and he explained their actions in the worst light possible. Don Juan and Don Francisco, in turn, tried to paint themselves as models of the patriarchal system – they were sons following orders from their father and their church, honourably preventing a slave from blaspheming. In these testimonies we do not only see competing ideas about a series of events. We also see competing gender claims, as each witness made reference to characteristics associated with honourable masculinity, particularly piety, and moral rectitude to justify his own behaviour and denigrate that of the other party. Although neither Juan's renunciation nor his testimony worked to stop the initial beating or subsequent punishment by the Inquisition, he forced his owner's sons to explain their actions before the court, and thus to acknowledge the superior authority of the Inquisition and its extension into their private realm. This symbolic victory must have been little comfort in the face of the very real physical punishment meted out by inquisitors. We can only imagine what happened when Juan was returned to his owner. It is likely that further punishment awaited him there.

In some ways the outlines of patriarchal authority are easy to see in a case involving men, because patriarchy is often viewed as a system based on masculine authority that benefits males. In this view, women are part of the patriarchal equation as subordinated beings, but they do not appear as authority figures. According to Lerner, however, patriarchal rule does not mean that women have no rights or influence, even though they do not have access to civic power.[40] This assertion raises the question of whether we can see patriarchal power at work in a situation in which women were the actors. A case from 1659, in which a nun named Juana de la Cruz denounced a teenage mulatto servant named Gertrudis de Escobar for renouncing God, provides such an example.[41] The nun testified that Gertrudis committed an unnamed offence. As punishment, Juana lashed her with a scourge (a whip with multiple extensions used by nuns for penitential self-beatings).[42] According to the nun, when the punishment began Gertrudis became 'rebellious' and threatened to renounce God if the beating continued.[43] Ignoring this threat, Juana continued to beat her. Gertrudis then 'said that she renounced God and his saints and that she did not believe in God and this she said two or three times.' Juana seems to have felt that her own decision, to continue the punishment even in the face of Gertrudis's threat to blaspheme, required some explanation. She excused her actions by saying that she thought that Gertrudis was merely making an idle threat in order to force her to relent.[44] Juana was especially distraught because she had been so angered by Gertrudis's threat that she had responded, in effect, that she did not care if Gertrudis did renounce. After Gertrudis renounced three or four more times, Juana finally stopped beating her.

Juana may have worried that the inquisitors would question her claim that initially she did not believe that Gertrudis had really blasphemed. She bolstered this statement by saying that Gertrudis later admitted that she had not renounced God wholeheartedly, implying that even if she had really renounced, it had no significance. According to another nun who was present, Gertrudis said that she knew of a mulatto named Scorpion who had also renounced during a beating.[45] This lent credence to Juana's claim that Gertrudis had renounced deliberately, for the practical purpose of ending the punishment. Juana further illustrated Gertrudis's lack of respect for her authority by reporting that when Gertrudis was threatened with a trip to the Inquisition, she replied recklessly that she would repeat what she had said even if it were outside the convent.

This case, like Juan's above, gives us a vivid glimpse into the often violent relationship between subordinates and their overseers. Looking at the case through the lens of gender brings to the fore other aspects of colonial power relations. Like the testimonies of the Sandoval brothers, Juana's testimony did not only depict Gertrudis as disrespectful and profane, but also served to portray herself as Gertrudis's moral superior. Juana contrasted Gertrudis's lack of respect for Christian practice with her own identity as a devout Christian. Her behaviour had not been exemplary; Juana admitted that, instead of bringing the servant directly to the Inquisition, she had continued the beating even after Gertrudis had renounced. The nun justified her action, however, by claiming, first, that initially she had not realized that Gertrudis had actually renounced, and, secondly, that Gertrudis had renounced intentionally to stop the beating. In effect, Juana argued that she was so attuned to moral behaviour that she could distinguish between tactical renunciations and blasphemies of a more significant nature.

Gender was central to this definition of Christian morality. In her testimony Juana implied that she was superior to Gertrudis because her behaviour better matched Spanish ideals of feminine comportment. Femininity was closely linked to ideas about Christian character and conduct – women, particularly Spaniards, were supposed to be pious, retiring, chaste, and modest. Ideally, women would be enclosed in order to preserve their modesty, either in the convent or at home caring for children. According to Asunción Lavrin, although motherhood was necessary for the practical goal of reproduction, chastity and enclosure was considered the ideal feminine state for women.[46] *Calidad* was also an important part of this feminine ideal, since only Spanish women could hope to fulfil these expectations. Non-Spanish women were generally poor and had to work in order to support themselves and their families. Thus, they had active lives outside the home. Not only was Juana a Spanish woman, she was a nun, a state that represented the very embodiment of feminine piety and virtue. It also reflected an elite background, since, with few exceptions, cloistered nuns were Spaniards, and many were wealthy, since most convents required dowries. Inquisitors would have been reminded of Juana's status continually throughout the process since her testimony had to be taken in the convent. Her denunciation then had to be sent from there to the court, because she could not leave the convent's protective walls.

Juana built on her favourable image as a nun by reminding the inquisitors of her gender. She emphasized her physical weakness: an attribute associated with women, and particularly sheltered elite women. Her claim that she used her 'scant strength' to whip Gertrudis may have invited the inquisitors' protective impulses, as might her claim that she was frightened by Gertrudis's actions.[47] In describing her horror at Gertrudis's behaviour, Juana implicitly contrasted the servant's actions with her own, supposedly more civilized, behaviour. In Juana's testimony, her vicious beating of Gertrudis paled in comparison with the depiction of Gertrudis as 'rebellious,' lacking respect, wilful, and reckless with the name of God. This depiction contrasted sharply with the ideal qualities of reserve, piety, and humility that elite women were supposed to live up to. By portraying Gertrudis as transgressing not only religious ideals but also gender ideals, the nun sought credibility by reinforcing the patriarchal system of authority that formed the basis for relations between Spaniards (particularly elite ones) and Afro-Mexicans.

Gertrudis's testimony made use of the ideals of modesty, reserve, and piety that were closely associated with Catholic women's piety. She testified on the same day that the court received Juana's initial declaration, and, like Juana, she tried to discredit the other woman and further her own cause by emphasizing her Christian character. The contrast between Gertrudis's and Juana's testimonies highlight the ways that each woman used rhetorical strategies drawn from her knowledge of the *calidad*/gender hierarchy and her position within it. In this case, both women presented themselves as honourable and agreed on the actual events but their interpretations of those events differed.

In Gertrudis's testimony, she stated that her mistress had sent her to the Inquisition because of 'some nonsense,' explaining that two weeks before an indigenous maid had informed the nun that Gertrudis wanted to run away.[48] She described how, when Juana questioned her about the rumour, she denied it, thus making Juana very angry. Gertrudis detailed the severe beating that ensued, stating that Juana whipped her on the back while the maid hit Gertrudis in the head with a bunch of keys. Gertrudis asked that they 'for the love of God leave her alone,' and said twice that she would have to renounce although she was a Christian.[49] To this Juana said, 'Well renounce, mulata, you have to renounce.'[50] This testimony coincided with Juana's claim that she did not initially take Gertrudis's threats seriously. While Juana painted Gertrudis as threatening to blaspheme in a calculating manner, Gertrudis portrayed herself as being tortured to the point of renunciation, thus inverting the supposed superiority claimed by Juana.

In her telling of events, Gertrudis was the pious, prudent, Christian woman while Juana was passionately enraged, uncontrolled, and reckless with her words and actions, inviting Gertrudis's blasphemy. By claiming to embody the feminine ideals of piety and meekness, Gertrudis tried to use characterizations associated with Spanish women, placing herself within a set of roles that she was not meant to occupy because of her *calidad*. Yet her testimony shows that Gertrudis was well aware of these gender roles and the larger system of authority with which they were linked. In essence, both Juana and Gertrudis were claiming that the other woman was dishonourable. While Gertrudis's *calidad* as a mulatto precluded her from claiming honour, she was using ideas about Christian piety to claim *honra*.

According to Gertrudis's testimony, it was her threat of blasphemy, and its dismissal, that brought events to the breaking point. She also emphasized that, contrary to claims that she had renounced two or three times, she had done so only once. This was an important detail since the severity of the crime increased with the number of renunciations.[51] Gertrudis claimed that the beating continued after the renunciation, and described how the scourge was put around her throat as if to choke her.[52] When another nun who was present questioned Gertrudis about her alleged sin, Gertrudis admitted that she had blasphemed but said that she had not said it wholeheartedly. She had, she claimed, renounced only to make the beating stop.[53] Thus, her explanation was the same as Juana's: both claimed that the blasphemy was not sincere. However, in Gertrudis's case, this information was used to undermine Juana's honour by portraying her as a woman ruled by uncontrollable passion, rather than Christian concern.

Gertrudis did not say that she had learned of the effect of a blasphemous renunciation from another mulatto, as Juana claimed, since this would have made her outburst seem premeditated. She also testified that the claim of Juana and the other nun that she had renounced more than once was false. She added that Juana had brought her to her confessor a few days after the incident but prevented Gertrudis from confessing her blasphemy. Instead, after Juana had confessed, she brought the servant back to her cell and again beat her until 'she bathed her in blood,' according to Gertrudis.[54] With this statement Gertrudis once more presented herself as a good Christian woman, eager to confess. Her self-portrayal contrasts sharply with her rendering of Juana as a violent harridan who forced her to renounce and denied her the opportunity to participate in the important sacrament of confession. Gertrudis said that she repented for having said such 'nonsense' because she was Christian and she asked for mercy from the Inquisition.[55] In asking inquisitors to believe her rather than Juana, Gertrudis was using her knowledge of the multilayered system of power in New Spain to pluralize the patriarchs, playing off the inquisitors against her mistress.

The idea that Gertrudis was pluralizing the patriarchs by appealing to inquisitors to help her against her mistress may seem curious upon first consideration. Clearly, as powerful men and representatives of the combined power of church and crown, the inquisitors were patriarchs.

Juana, as a woman, does not fit the traditional idea of a patriarch. Yet it was Juana's social position within the patriarchal system of New Spain – stemming from her *calidad* as an elite Spanish woman – that gave her authority over Gertrudis. Thus, although Juana may not have been a patriarch in the most literal sense, she was a representative of the patriarchal order and she benefited from it.

After hearing the testimonies of Juana, Gertrudis, and the other nun who witnessed the beating, the inquisitors formally accused and convicted Gertrudis of blasphemy. They decided that her blasphemies were not provoked by the whipping, as she had claimed, because neither 'the instrument, nor the oppression, nor the rigour of the punishment could explain an outburst so terrible and reckless but rather it was only her bad and perverse nature and wicked inclination' which caused her to blaspheme in such a way.[56] According to the court, the fact that Gertrudis had threatened to renounce before the beating, and then did so when she received the first blow, showed that the blasphemy was premeditated, and not a desperate response to extreme pain as Gertrudis claimed. Although she had been admonished by the inquisitors to confess the truth, Gertrudis did not do it with the 'sincerity and necessary repentance but rather [she was] looking for false pretexts to excuse herself.'[57] Thus, the initial blasphemy was made worse because Gertrudis had employed it as a tactic to affect the behaviour of the nuns and later to manipulate the Inquisition.

Ultimately it was her audacity and lack of sincerity, as defined through the nuns' testimony and the inquisitors' opinions, which got Gertrudis into trouble and earned her the Inquisition's wrath. As a result, she was sentenced to public punishment and paraded through the streets. Although Gertrudis was formally accused of blasphemy, it seems that she was also guilty of daring to challenge the religious and moral structure upheld by the Inquisition. Gender roles were central to this structure, and Gertrudis had transgressed the boundaries of proper behaviour for women, for mulattos, and for servants. Looked at from one perspective, Gertrudis's tactics of appealing to one authority to help her against another, blaming her blasphemy on Juana's harsh treatment, and asking the inquisitors for mercy were ineffective; they spared her neither punishment nor public humiliation. Yet, from another perspective, Gertrudis's renunciation did cause small ripples in her mistress's life. Gertrudis forced Juana to explain her actions to representatives of the court and, in so doing, exposed Juana's cruelty. She made Juana work hard to fit the model of feminine behaviour.

Through their blasphemies and their explanations, Gertrudis and Juan indirectly critiqued the gendered and racialized nature of authority in New Spain. Neither Juan nor Gertrudis attacked the basis upon which that authority rested; rather, they exposed their superiors' failure to live up to the duties associated with that authority. Europeans justified slavery in large part through religion: enslavement would bring Africans into the Christian fold, thereby saving their souls. Although slaveowners often ignored their duties to Christianize their slaves, in theory they were expected to ensure that their dependants practised Christianity. Yet Juana prevented Gertrudis from fulfilling a Christian duty by denying her the opportunity to confess her sins. As if this were not bad enough, Juan and Gertrudis charged that their superiors drove them to sin by beating them mercilessly, leaving them no choice but to blaspheme. By using the patriarchal structure of the Inquisition to attack the patriarchs of their households, Juan and Gertrudis made use of the system of checks and balances that was, as Kimberly Gauderman has argued, an essential part of the colonial system.[58] Through this process they were upholding and enforcing the power of the Inquisition in colonial society. By inviting the inquisitors to examine their intimate relationships with owners, blaspheming slaves helped expand the power of the Inquisition over individual members of the colonial population.

Conclusion

The blasphemy cases discussed here, involving husbands and wives and servants and masters, show that people with little *honor* or power based on *calidad* used ideas about gender both to confront and to appeal to representatives of patriarchal authority. They also show that the very ideologies of *calidad* and gender that underlay definitions of colonial authority did not always fit together seamlessly. We see cleavages among ideas about *calidad,* gender, *honor,* and *honra* when a woman such as Augustina tried to use inquisitorial power to rein in her husband's behaviour in the home and when a black woman such as Isabel Chávez dared to accuse her European husband of blasphemy. We see these cleavages, too, when an African slave such as Magdalena de la Cruz not only held her owner accountable for his treatment of her but enlisted the aid of other European men, and when Afro-Mexican slaves such as Juan and Gertrudis used the Inquisition as a forum in which to challenge their superiors by implying that they were not living up to Christian ideals or to the gender ideals associated with their social positions. Essentially, these wives and workers were claiming that they had certain moral authority that allowed them to accuse their supposed superiors of bad behaviour, even though they were in a structurally inferior position to the husbands and supervisors whose actions they challenged. This moral authority could be based on ideas about honourable femininity and masculinity, and thus these cases show us that gender was an important component of *calidad*. Yet the cases also suggest that ideas about gender and *calidad* could operate independently of each other in colonial Mexico. The cleavages that we see here between ideas about *calidad* and gender indicate that these ideas could be disentangled, manipulated, and linked in tactical ways by people at different levels of the colonial power structure. While Spanish ideologies constructed the links between gender and *calidad,* Spanish women were supposed to uphold the hierarchy of *calidad* through their pious chastity and Spanish men through their pious strength. The cases examined in this chapter demonstrate not only that non-Spaniards understood and used these ideas but that they rearticulated them in new and surprising ways in the colonial context. They also reveal some of the complex ways in which the Spanish ideas regarding *calidad* and gender that were used to support the imperial enterprise in the Atlantic basin were simultaneously reinforced and transformed at the local levels.

Notes

I would like to thank Nicole Eustace, Daniella Kostroun, Lisa Vollendorf, and the anonymous readers for the University of Toronto Press for their generous help with this chapter.

1 Archivo General de la Nación (hereafter AGN), Inquisición 471.52, 171–2.
2 AGN, Inquisición 471.52, 171.
3 Ibid.
4 For other discussions of renunciations associated with people of African descent in Mexico, see Colin Palmer, *Slaves of the White God: Blacks in Mexico, 1570–1650* (Cambridge, Mass.: Harvard University Press, 1976), 148–53; Solange Alberro, *Inquisición y Sociedad, 1571–1700* (Mexico City: Fondo de Cultura Económica, 1988; repr., Mexico City: Fondo de Cultura Económica, 1993), 455–79; Fernando Cervantes, *The Devil in the New World* (New Haven, Conn.: Yale University Press, 1994), 78–80; Kathryn Joy McKnight, 'Blasphemy as Resistance: An African Slave Woman before the Mexican Inquisition,' in Mary E. Giles, ed., *Women in the Inquisition: Spain and the New World* (Bal-

timore: Johns Hopkins University Press, 1999), 229–53; Javier Villa-Flores, '"To Lose One's Soul": Blasphemy and Slavery in New Spain, 1596–1669,' *Hispanic American Historical Review*, 82, no. 3 (2002): 435–68; Frank T. Proctor, 'Slavery, Identity, and Culture: An Afro-Mexican Counterpoint, 1640–1763,' PhD thesis, Emory University, 2003, 235–80; and Joan Cameron Bristol, *Christians, Blasphemers, and Witches* (Albuquerque: University of New Mexico Press, 2007), 113–48.

5 These cases use the term 'husband' (*marido*) to describe the men's relationship to their wives, although it is likely that the people in question were not legally married since intercaste marriage was still relatively rare in the seventeenth century.

6 Natalie Zemon Davis, *Fiction in the Archives: Pardon Tales and Their Tellers in Sixteenth-Century France* (Stanford, Calif.: Stanford University Press, 1987), 104. Although Davis discusses how both men and women humbled themselves before the king in an effort to win his pardon for their crimes, she places women's supplications within a larger context of women's actions: 'Wives were used to assuming the language and posture of humility and subjection, even when they played a central role in running the household and family.'

7 Mary Elizabeth Perry, *The Handless Maiden: Moriscos and the Politics of Religion in Early Modern Spain* (Princeton, N.J.: Princeton University Press, 2005), 177.

8 Gerda Lerner, *The Creation of Patriarchy* (New York: Oxford University Press, 1986), 239.

9 Robert McCaa, 'Calidad, Class, and Marriage in Colonial Mexico: The Case of Parral, 1788–1790,' *Hispanic American Historical Review*, 64, no. 3 (1984): 477–8; Magali M. Carrera, *Imagining Identity in New Spain: Race, Lineage, and the Colonial Body in Portraiture and Casta Painting* (Austin: University of Texas Press, 2003), 6–21.

10 Steve J. Stern, *The Secret History of Gender: Men, Women and Power in Late Colonial Mexico* (Chapel Hill: University of North Carolina Press, 1995), 21.

11 Lyman L. Johnson and Sonya Lipsett-Rivera, 'Introduction' in *Faces of Honor: Sex, Shame, and Violence in Colonial Latin America* (Albuquerque: University of New Mexico Press, 1998), 1–17, 3–4, 10–11.

12 Patricia Seed, *To Love, Honor and Obey in Colonial Mexico: Conflicts over Marriage Choice* (Stanford, Calif.: Stanford University Press, 1988), 62–5. Seed sees a transformation in ideas about honour over time, arguing that the elite definition of honour as honour-virtue in the sixteenth century was transformed by the eighteenth century to a definition of honour as honor-status. Ramón Gutiérrez suggests that women did not have honour at all;

that instead *vergüenza* (shame) was associated with women and honour with men. The most that women could hope for was to escape shaming themselves and their families. Ramón A. Gutiérrez, *When Jesus Came, the Corn Mothers Went Away: Marriage, Sexuality, and Power in New Mexico, 1500–1846* (Stanford, Calif.: Stanford University Press, 1991), 209.

13 For a discussion of the independent nature of the Inquisition, see Alejandro Cañeque, *The King's Living Image: The Culture and Politics of Viceregal Power in Colonial Mexico* (New York: Routledge, 2004), 107–17.

14 Admittedly, there were limits to the tribunal's power. The vast area it was meant to control – stretching from modern-day New Mexico to Nicaragua and including the Philippines, Cuba, and Santo Domingo – was impossible to regulate with only a handful of officials in major cities. Moreover, the court needed dense populations to function, since it relied on individuals keeping tabs on each other and reporting suspicious behaviour. Alberro, *Inquisición y Sociedad*, 23–9, 589–93.

15 Alejandro Cañeque characterizes the ceremony as a 'ritual of imperial legitimation' which articulated the Spanish king's role as the defender of Catholicism. Alejandro Cañeque, 'Theater of Power: Writing and Representing the Auto de Fe in Colonial Mexico,' *Americas*, 52, no. 3 (1996): 321–44, 325.

16 Bristol, *Christians, Blasphemers, amd Witches*, 113–48.

17 Stern, *The Secret History of Gender*, 99–103.

18 Seed, *To Love, Honor and Obey*, passim.

19 Steve J. Stern, *Peru's Indian Peoples and the Challenge of Spanish Conquest: Huamanga to 1640*, 2nd ed. (Madison: University of Wisconsin Press, 1993), 113–47.

20 See AGN, Inquisición 353.6, 22–32, for rare information about a slaves' experience after returning from the court. Juan de Leyba was punished, and eventually killed, by his owner's major-domo after he used a self-denunciation to complain about the conditions in his master's house. The inquisitors had sent his owner a message telling him to improve his treatment of his slave.

21 AGN, Inquisición, 249.3, 54–60.

22 AGN, Inquisición, 249.3, 59.

23 AGN, Inquisición, 249.3, 56.

24 Ibid.

25 AGN, Inquisición, 249.3, 57v.

26 AGN, Inquisición, 249.3, 56.

27 AGN, Inquisición 471.53, 173.

28 AGN, Inquisición 418.4, 320–36v.

29 AGN, Inquisición 418.4, 320–1.

202 Joan Cameron Bristol

30 AGN, Inquisición 418.4, 333–6.
31 AGN, Inquisición, 418.5, 337–63v.
32 AGN, Inquisición, 418.5, 336.
33 AGN, Inquisición 288.4, 224–47r.
34 AGN, Inquisición 288.4, 227.
35 Ibid.
36 AGN, Inquisición 288.4, 228.
37 AGN, Inquisición 288.4, 233.
38 AGN, Inquisición 288.4, 241.
39 Ibid.
40 Lerner, *The Creation of Patriarchy*, 239.
41 AGN, Inquisición 446.6, 161–219. Juana de la Cruz claimed that Gertrudis was sixteen; Gertrudis herself claimed that she was fourteen.
42 AGN, Inquisición 446.6, 162.
43 Ibid.
44 AGN, Inquisición 446.6, 165v.
45 AGN, Inquisición 446.6, 165v–166 (quotation), 167, 180. Juan de los Santos, alias Alacrán, was convicted of blasphemy in an *auto de fe* of 1656. AGN Inquisición 599.19, 1654, Amilpas.
46 Asunción Lavrin, 'In Search of the Colonial Woman in Mexico: The Seventeenth and Eighteenth Centuries,' in Ascunción Lavrin, ed., *Latin American Women: Historical Perspectives* (Westport, Conn.: Greenwood Press, 1978), 25–6.
47 AGN, Inquisición 446.6, 162.
48 AGN, Inquisición 446.6, 162v.
49 AGN, Inquisición 446.6, 163.
50 Ibid.
51 AGN, Inquisición 446.6, 163v.
52 AGN, Inquisición 446.6, 163.
53 AGN, Inquisición 446.6, 163v.
54 AGN, Inquisición 446.6, 164.
55 AGN, Inquisición 446.6, 163.
56 AGN, Inquisición 446.6, 180.
57 Ibid.
58 Kimberly Gauderman, *Women's Lives in Colonial Quito: Gender, Law, and Economy in Spanish America* (Austin: University of Texas Press, 2003), 6–7.

PART III

Authority and Identity in the Catholic Atlantic

Atlantic World Monsters: Monstrous Births and the Politics of Pregnancy in Colonial Guatemala

MARTHA FEW

Historical accounts of strange pregnancies and monstrous births can be found throughout the early modern world, including in Spanish colonial Guatemala, an area that stretched from what is today Chiapas in southern Mexico through much of contemporary Central America. Debates surrounding the interpretation of monstrous births formed a key part of the larger history of reproduction and women's health in colonial medicine and local healing cultures in Spanish colonial Guatemala. These debates also reflected the increasing political, religious, and medical attention paid to pregnancy, childbirth, and early infant heath by the colonial state. Other issues linked to monstrous births included laws mandating the practice of post-mortem cesarean operations as part of colonial religious and legal policy, the creation of new medical instruments and therapeutics for women's health care, and the development of obstetrics in the colony's formal medical cultures and at the medical school of the University of San Carlos, located in Santiago de Guatemala, the capital city of colonial Central America.[1]

This chapter explores how monstrous birth accounts found in colonial Guatemala from the sixteenth to the early eighteenth centuries acted as flashpoints for cross-cultural conflicts and community tensions surrounding pregnancy. The accounts also shed light on debates in the early modern era about the meanings and representations of wonders that preoccupied European intellectual and popular cultures in this period.[2] Both European colonizers and indigenous Guatemalans had a particular interest in signs and portents, and conflicts over the meanings of monstrous births were at the heart of struggles to control pregnancy. As the age of exploration passed into the era of conquest and colonization of the New World, monstrous birth accounts describing such things as conjoined twins, 'half-human, half-toad' babies, and other types of deformities were informed by both European and Mesoamerican conceptions of wonder. Representations and interpretive frameworks of monstrosity related to pregnancy reflected the similarities and differences among the ways in which European and Mesoamerican cultures interpreted human deformity, as well as the surrounding context.[3]

This chapter contends that interpretations of monstrous births found in colonial Guatemala not only drew on European cultures of wonder but also were connected to, and influenced by, Mesoamerican ideas about physical exceptionalism in humans and its association with omens, prophecy, and special access to supernatural power. European and Mesoamerican cultures of wonder and interpretations of strange pregnancies and monstrous births interacted with each other and circulated through the Atlantic world. In the process, interpretations of monsters and their representation came to represent new ideas that were linked to both European and Mesoamerican traditions of wonder and yet, at the same time, were specifically tailored to New World historical and cultural contexts.

The context for colonial Guatemala and the rest of New Spain included the ongoing campaigns of religious conversion of native peoples and the establishment and maintenance of racial and gender hierarchies that worked to structure Spanish colonialism. Descriptions of pregnancies resulting in monstrous births provide evidence regarding colonial strategies used to delegitimize male and female indigenous and mixed-race ritual specialists, especially healers and midwives, described in colonial-era documents as 'witches' (*brujo/as*), 'sorcerers' (*hechicero/as*), and 'necromancers' (*nigromántico/as*). Colonial institutions such as the Catholic Church made attempts to mediate exceptional signs when they occurred, seeking to put its own ideological spin on monstrous births.

Monstrous birth accounts, then, provide evidence about how the Catholic Church, through its secular and missionary clergy, sought to establish itself as the legitimate interpreter of colonial monsters and other types of wondrous exceptionalism in the New World. The case studies examined here point to the broad circulation in the Atlantic world of interpretations linked to Mesoamerican and European traditions that were recreated in the context of community-level conflicts over pregnancy and childbirth.

Monstrous Births in the Early Modern World

Many scholars working on the history of Renaissance and early modern Europe have noted the explosion in the appearance of wondrous objects, both monstrous and marvellous, in the era.[4] Accounts describing monstrous births and other wonders circulated in oral and written cultures and in popular, elite, intellectual, and religious circles.[5] For Renaissance Italy, Ottavia Niccoli has tied the preoccupations with monstrous births there to the rise in prophetic cultures during the Counter-Reformation, a time when the 'unity of prophetic knowledge was destroyed and divinatory science was degraded into a negative body of knowledge possessed by the negative – the female – part of society.'[6] This led to what Niccoli has called a 'frenzy' of deformed births and their interpretation as portents in Italian urban cultures. News of the births, their interpretations, and their images circulated through society via printed sources, songs, and sermons.[7] Niccoli has asserted that monstrous births should not be seen as simply anomalous events but instead should be considered a key aspect of Italian Renaissance urban culture.[8]

While concern with monsters as signs was a Europe-wide phenomenon, local contexts shaped how they were viewed and interpreted as wondrous occurrences. For sixteenth-century England, for example, Kathryn Brammwall argues that monsters as signs became more flexible as their interpretations were increasingly contextualized by political, social, and religious debates of the day. She outlines the emergence by the 1570s of what she calls a 'new rhetoric of monstrosity,' which placed less emphasis on physical monstrosities and more on what were considered moral and behavioural 'deformities,' pride, greed, and tyranny.[9] The rhetoric of monstrosity surrounding behaviour was directly linked to Reformation debates about exposing and identifying heresy.

European preoccupations with monsters and their links to debates over heresy continued into the seventeenth century, and these preoccupations spread to the New World. For example, Anne Jacobson Schutte has described seventeenth-century England as 'an intellectual terrain swarming with monsters.' Schutte analyses written accounts that described two monstrous births during the antinomian controversy (1636–8), the first major religious conflict in colonial New England, for evidence of European ideas of monstrosity in colonial America.[10] Anne Hutchinson, the key opposition figure in the controversy, presided over the childbirth of a female supporter and the resulting 'stillborn monster.' Two days later, she herself gave birth to a deformed infant. Interestingly, Schutte argues that the interpretations of the events were not influenced by the cultural contexts of colonial and frontier America. Instead, she maintains that all the authors were familiar with European, and specifically English, popular monstrous birth accounts. Moreover, their interpretations of the events reflected European cultures of wonder. In contrast, evidence for colonial Guatemala suggests that the circulation in the Atlantic world of ideas and representations of monsters as signs reveals New World conceptions of wonder that were not simply informed by European cultures but also were shaped by indigenous cultures within distinct colonial contexts. Conceptions of monsters in the Atlantic world emerged from this dynamic process.

Mesoamerican Perspectives on Deformity

There is a growing consensus among pre-colonial Mesoamerican scholars that certain physical deformities were considered important signs which attributed additional supernatural power to an individual within that culture. This can be seen in recent research on the Olmec,[11] the Maya, and the Nahuas. For example, Carolyn Tate and Gordon Bendersky have tentatively identified a group of Olmec portable stone sculptures as fetus effigies dating from 900–600 BCE that depict individuals with marked physical deformities, such as dwarfism and polydactylism.[12] Their analysis focuses on sculptural representations of the human fetus that contain specific naturalistic details of fetal anatomy of gestational age. They note specific abnormalities observed in actual fetal development, including *agnathia,* congenital absence of the lower jaw, and *macrocephalie,* congenital enlargement of the head that often results in some degree of mental retardation.

The fetal effigies also show shared cultural attributes associated with Olmec shamanic rulers, and therefore, according to Tate and Bendersky, provide the deformed fetal figures with political-religious status. These include specific helmet-like headgear associated with Olmec rulers; or characteristics of the Olmec Dragon, a supernatural creature associated with ritual specialists (or *shamans*). The figures are often depicted carrying maize sacks, the maize sprout being the principal symbol of Olmec leaders. Mesoamerican culture more broadly depicts humans created from maize, as in the *Popol Vuh.*[13] This evidence leads the authors to suggest that the depiction of the fetus, both normal and anomalous, played a variety of key roles in Olmec culture.

Maya sculptures and paintings dating from the classic period emphasize the significance of physical deformity in their repeated portrayal of dwarves and hunchbacks as important members of the courts of Maya rulers. Dwarves and hunchbacks were thought to be especially wise and they occupied high-status positions across Mesoamerica, with special roles as intimates of Maya kings and queens.[14] Moreover, the Mexica emperor Motecuhzoma (1509–19), who ruled Tenochtitlan at the time of the Spanish arrival in the Americas, reportedly kept 'an entourage of dwarves around him, whose political counsel he sought during the Spanish invasion of his empire.'[15]

In addition, certain kinds of physical deformities in Mesoamerican cultures could be seen as omens of major events to come. A series of omens – comets, a deformed crane with a mirror in its head, and an unexplained fire in an important Aztec temple – presaged the arrival of Cortés and the ensuing destruction of the capital of Tenochtitlan. This included the eighth omen: 'thistle-men having two heads [but] only one body,' an image similar to that of conjoined twins.[16] Serge Gruzinski has characterized these and other omens as specifically Nahua signs, evidence of the operation of indigenous notions of power and its representation into the colonial period. In both pre- and post-conquest Mesoamerican societies, appropriate ritual specialists interpreted these types of signs, a fact that reveals the important role they played as interpreters of exceptional events.[17] In post-conquest Mesoamerica, the Catholic Church sought to counteract and delegitimize indigenous ritual specialists, including healers and midwives.

Gruzinski, along with the art historian Ceclia Klein, has analysed cultural change and its effects on Nahua representations of power within the process of European colonization.[18] Their work highlights the complex transformations of indigenous cultures of power and its representation in post-conquest Mesoamerica. As Klein argues: 'We can only identify and fully understand the nature and the range of colonial-period representational processes if we can locate those points at which Renaissance representations both resembled and differed from indigenous modes of conceptualization.'[19] Here, monstrous birth accounts describing physical deformity and corrupted childbirth processes can be used as a point of entry from which to view and analyse the range of representational and interpretive issues surrounding the appearance of monsters in colonial society. And, I suggest, they also reveal emerging and complex Atlantic world cultures of wonder recreated in this colonial context.

A Monstrous Birth of Snakes

In the second half of the seventeenth century, Antonio Fuentes y
Guzmán wrote his monumental history of colonial Guatemala, *Recordación Flórida*, which included a discussion of the difficulties faced by
members of the Franciscan order in their early efforts to convert native
peoples to Catholicism.[20] Describing conflicts during the early stages
of conversion there, Fuentes y Guzmán relied on accusations of cannibalism, a common trope of European imperial expansion to the New
World.[21] He complained that the Maya peoples whom the Franciscans
wished to convert, especially indigenous mothers, insisted on cooking
and eating their children. Franciscan efforts to halt this reputed practice continued to be ignored until one priest threatened the people
with a terrible illness during a sermon: 'But one day the priest continued his ardent preaching [against these acts], and lit with the zeal of
God, threatened those who would eat their children with the punishment of heaven, telling them that those who ate [their children] from
then on would surely be turned into snakes [*culebras*], who would break
their entrails into pieces.'[22]

In this sermon denouncing cannibalism, as recounted by Fuentes y
Guzmán, the Franciscan drew on his special connection to the Catholic
supernatural world, a strategy that meshed with the connections in Mesoamerican cultures between ritual specialists and access to supernatural
power.[23] By injecting the use of snakes, with its clear reference to the
Book of Genesis, into the framework of the debate, Fuentes y Guzmán
appears to have been influenced by European anti-heresy rhetoric. In
seventeenth-century religious conflicts, Protestants and Catholics often
insulted each other with references to snakes and other similar kinds of
monsters that had biblical significance.[24]

Following the story of the sermon, Fuentes y Guzmán singled out one
unnamed indigenous mother as someone who refused to convert to Catholicism. This set the context for the ensuing monstrous birth of snakes:
'But one of the Indian women who heard the threat began mocking the
priest [and his warning] and she dared to roast and eat her infant son
who was still breast-feeding. But later, before the end of the night, she
began to feel extremely harsh pains in her womb,[25] which moved, coiled,
and uncoiled as a snake did. These sensations passed from her womb to
her muscles, and from there returned to her womb, [then] to the stom-
ach and arms. And remaining tormented in that way, with pains as if [she
were] in labour, she began to give birth to (*echar por las vías*) deformed

snakes, and with the fear and torments she suffered, she died still expelling the vermin from her body.'[26]

Here Fuentes y Guzmán blamed the indigenous mother for the monstrous birth of snakes, the result of her supposed actions of infanticide and cannibalism. In early modern Europe, the mother could be blamed for monstrous births through what Valeria Finucci has called the fear of 'uncontrolled maternal fantasy': the influence of a mother's imagination on her developing fetus.[27] In the case recounted by Fuentes y Guzmán, however, it was not the mother's imagination that caused the birth of snakes, but instead her refusal to convert to Catholicism. The monstrous birth also acted as a warning to the larger community about what would happen if they followed this woman's lead.

Fuentes y Guzmán identified the illness as *cumatz*, the K'iche' Maya word for snake. The tie made between the illness cumatz and the refusal of native peoples to convert to Catholicism also meshed with Mesoamerican and European ideas about the division of illness into natural and supernatural causes. The ability to cast and cure illness in Maya culture was in the hands of ritual specialists, and healers and midwives were thought to have the dual ability both to cause and to cure illness. Within the Spanish interpretive framework, disease, especially epidemic disease, was often seen as divine punishment delivered to an individual or community. The communities then utilized various strategies to deflect the epidemic: public religious processions, *novenas,* and other prayers, along with individual and communal acts of penance and expressions of piety.

Cumatz, with its 'snake-like' convulsive movements, appears to have referred to a type of illness that the Spanish probably had not seen before, or one that displayed physical symptoms that Spanish priests on the ground were not familiar with. Otherwise, presumably, Fuentes y Guzmán would have called the illness by its Spanish or Latin name. It also appears that cumatz might have been an epidemic disease, given its extreme symptoms, the rapidity with which it killed afflicted individuals, and its quick spread among the community.[28] Moreover, the word 'cumatz' is similar to an epidemic disease known in K'iche' Maya as *k'ukumatz* and sometimes as *gucumatz*. This also suggests that Fuentes y Guzmán's 'cumatz' may have been part of the epidemic, or at least related to it.

Cumatz was known in Central Mexico and Nahua-speaking areas as *cocolitzli*. A series of cocolitzli epidemics swept through New Spain during the sixteenth and seventeenth centuries, which overlaps with the time period and geographic area covered in Fuentes y Guzmán's history.[29] Indigenous accounts of the illness focused on its symptoms, especially the hemorrhagic bleeding (*flujo de sangre* – literally 'bloody flux') from the eyes ears, nose, mouth, and other orifices.[30] In Fuentes y Guzmán's account, cumatz has a similar expulsive trajectory, with the afflicted person expelling 'deformed snakes' from all orifices. Fuentes y Guzmán used a rhetoric of blame to describe the origins of cumatz. He linked the illness and ensuing monstrous birth of snakes on the Indian mother, which then spread to the rest of the community. The rhetoric tying indigenous peoples' illnesses to their refusal to convert reveals the outlines of the discursive and ideological work used to link colonial medicine and Catholicism.[31] This account of the monstrous snakes born to a reluctant female indigenous convert also reflects discourses of early modern European monstrosity that sought to control various forms of deviancy. Yet the discourses here move past European notions of deviancy and instead explicitly reflect power relations within European colonialism in the Atlantic world, and the ethnic, gender, and religious conflicts faced there.

The Natural Monster

Fuentes y Guzmán, so outraged in the previous depiction of a monstrous birth of snakes, also noted another exceptional childbirth in his history of Guatemala: conjoined twins. In this instance, he had a markedly different reaction. He wrote: 'On the 12th of August 1675, a natural monster was born from an Indian woman from the pueblo of Santo Domingo Sinacoa … monstrous and admirable in the formation of its body, of a beautiful shape and perfectly human in its perfection and physionomical symmetry.'[32] Even though Fuentes y Guzmán noted that the mother in this case was indigenous, he provided no accusations of cannibalism, nor did he attribute the deformity to punishment from God. In fact, he barely mentioned the mother, and labelled the twins a 'natural' monster, an object of keen interest and wonder rather than one of repugnance and disgust.

Fuentes y Guzmán attributed the twins' deformity to the outcome of nature and natural causes, rather than as the outcome of sinful behaviour as in the previous example. This was a key way that early modern Europeans explained the occurrence of monstrous births, and the ascription of natural origins for infant deformity acted as a competing explanation to divine origins.[33] Fuentes y Guzmán's characterization of the conjoined twins as a natural monster suggests that he was aware of multiple explanations for monsters circulating in an Atlantic world context, and applied one or the other based on the specific circumstances for the monstrous births he wrote about and sometimes even witnessed.

His account, however, lacks even a hint of the association with infanticide/cannibalism that framed his previous analysis. Instead, the priest involved focuses his descriptive gaze on the monster itself: 'From one single womb were born two distinctly perfect bodies, separate and apart for most of the trunks of their bodies, each one of them with two perfectly formed arms and hands, with pleasing and beautiful faces, with the same similarity and appearance overall, two well-proportioned legs, and at the waist another very short little leg (*pernezuela*), also accompanied like the other two by its corresponding foot and toes. They [the twins] did not show members[34] that indicated the true class and nature of their sex, because from that part of the body there has sprouted and born one of the three legs, that of the small one.'[35]

In the context of this monstrous birth, Fuentes y Guzmán uses words such as 'beautiful' and 'admirable' to characterize the twins' body. Inexplicably, he categorizes them as male despite the apparent lack of a penis. He also insists on their humanity, labelling them 'perfectly human,' even though they appeared, according to his description, to have three legs and no genitalia. The parish priest of Santo Domingo baptized the twins after they died in childbirth, an action that would not have occurred if the priest had harboured any suspicion of unnatural or diabolical origins for the monstrous birth. In fact, the twins' body and their mother's were eventually all buried in consecrated ground in the parish church of Santo Domingo.

Fuentes y Guzmán's account of the 'natural monster' indicates not only that he was aware of early modern European conceptions of monstrous births but also that he was familiar with Mesoamerican ideas regarding deformity and monstrous births that continued to circulate in post-conquest Guatemala. For example, he ended his detailed description of the twins' physical body with the following comparison of the language associated with conjoined twins and monsters in the Mesoamerican and European cultural traditions: 'This has to be what the Indians call *chachaguates* and what we call *gemelos*. And they were born united as I have described, that which they [the Indians] call *nannosos* and what we [the Spanish] call *monstruos*.'[36]

Gemelos is the Spanish word for twin without any special connotation. *Chachaguates,* a word commonly used by local indigenous peoples, is a Hispanicized version of the Nahuatl word *chachahuatl,* meaning bind-

ing or stuck together and indicating conjoined twins.[37] Thus, the indigenous word for the birth was even more specific ('stuck together' and
'binding') than the Spanish *gemelos* (which has no connotation of being physically bound together). *Monstruo* in Spanish means 'monster,'
defined in the seventeenth century as 'a newborn infant or production
against the regular order of nature.' Possibly the word *nannoso* is related
to the Spanish word *enano*, which means 'dwarf.'[38] Fuentes y Guzman's
use of both words to refer to the conjoined twins in his narrative suggests that, rather than hybridized understandings of monstrous births,
separate Mesoamerican and European discourses continued to operate
in colonial Guatemala into the seventeenth century.

After the birth, Santo Domingo's parish priest took control of the
twins' corpse and acted as the interpreter of the 'monster' to the larger
Spanish population of the capital city of Santiago de Guatemala. In an
action that would be shocking today but was perfectly normal within the
prevailing cultures of wonder of the time, the priest carried the dead
body to the capital and displayed it in the homes Santiago's elite citizens,
all the while, supposedly, expounding on its meaning. Here, the conjoined twins' body functioned as an object of curiosity carefully mediated by the priest. He also showed the twins' body to medical surgeons.
According to Fuentes y Guzmán, 'there was not a distinguished or admirable citizen that [the priest] did not visit.' One of those citizens was
Fuentes y Guzmán himself, who, after carefully examining the body, had
a portrait painting made of it.[39]

Members of Guatemala's religious and political elite were fascinated
by the so-called natural monster. Fuentes y Guzmán explained that the
intention 'with this singular and rare dead body [was] to treat it in the
same style as the bodies of distinguished men and great heroes that were
preserved with the aromatic [and] expensive balsam of extreme unction,
whose cost would be borne by the President [of the Audiencia of Gua-
temala] ... with the mind to send the body to Spain. But the surgeons
discovered that there was not time to do so, because of some corruption
introduced into the admirable and wondrous cadaver.'[40]

This case indicates that not only did monstrous births act as significant
cultural signs that circulated through the Atlantic world, but that the
monsters themselves circulated as well, as they did in Europe. The conjoined twins' corpse travelled from their birthplace to different social
spaces of colonial Guatemalan life, including elite households and local
surgeons' offices. The corpse would have travelled to Spain as well if it
had not already deteriorated too much to make the journey.[41]

Doña María Cecilia and the Half-Toad Baby

As we have seen, monstrous births acted as a sign of religious conversion and community conflicts surrounding it, and also as a sign to be interpreted, a contested process in colonial Guatemala as elsewhere.[42] The following account of a half-human, half-toad baby born to an elite Spanish woman shows that pregnancy and childbirth, especially in the case of the monstrous birth of a deformed infant, became an important point for competing interpretations by various social groups in colonial society: the Guatemalan Inquisition, male members of the missionary orders active there, and community members themselves.

In 1729 Doña María Cecilia de Paniagua, a twenty-nine-year-old elite Spanish woman married to a public scribe, denounced two mixed-race women to the Inquisition for practising sorcery.[43] In her Inquisition testimony, Doña María Cecilia related an account of her recent pregnancy and childbirth in which she gave birth to a stillborn, deformed infant that she described as a half-human, half-toad baby. When she was five months' pregnant, she came into an unspecified conflict with the sorcerer María Savina, a single *mestiza* who lived in a nearby neighborhood in the capital. After the conflict ended, Savina brought a peace offering to Doña María Cecilia in the form of a pot of beef stew. Doña María Cecilia reported that she had suspicions about the stew and did not want to taste it, but she relented after Savina insisted and finally ate one mouthful. From then on through the last four months of her pregnancy, Doña María Cecilia said that every night from dusk until dawn she heard a toad croaking, and the sound followed her even when she changed rooms. Nor was she the only one who heard the sounds; other family members and her servants heard them as well.

After a nine-month pregnancy, Doña María Cecilia described giving birth to a *monstruo muerto* (a dead monster) whose top half was shaped like a toad, with a toad-like head and long arms that reached almost to the infant's feet.[44] The bottom half appeared human, and the entire body was covered with very rough skin like a toad's. María Cecilia Paniagua also reported that the blood and afterbirth 'were not like natural blood but muddy like mud from a lake,' the kind of natural environment in which toads live.[45] When the Dominican priest Tomás Serrano viewed the 'monster,' he declared it to be the result of an *hechizo* or spell. Doña María Cecilia asserted that the toad's croaking that she heard every night for the last four months of her pregnancy ceased as soon as she gave birth.

Doña María Cecilia's Inquisition testimony reveals classic elements of sorcery accusations in colonial Guatemala: recent conflict with a well-known female sorcerer; the strange behaviour of an animal, insect, or bird; and the use of food or drink (in this case stew) as a method of casting spells, and in which there later appeared worms (*gusanos*).[46] The language Doña María Cecilia used in the testimony joined the language of infection and witchcraft: *infección de maleficio*. The priest seemed to agree, judging the birth 'unnatural' and refusing to baptize the infant.

Religious handbooks in Guatemala and elsewhere in New Spain contained guidelines on whether and in what way to baptize in the case of miscarriages, monstrous births, and other difficult births. Francisco Sunzin de Herrera's 'Practical-moral handbook in which it is asked if miscarried fetuses can be baptized,' published in Guatemala in 1756, counselled that monstrous infants should, in fact, be baptized: 'It is not against the custom of the Church nor against [its practices] to baptize fetuses (*fetos*) if they live; if it is alive, baptize. Nor is it [against the custom of the church] to baptize monstrous births whose nature (*naturaleza*) is in doubt.'[47] Official church policy on the issue called for priests to baptize miscarried and monstrous births if the infant was judged to be alive, whether or not the attending priests believed the birth to be natural or unnatural. In the previous example of conjoined twins, the priest baptized them even though they were born dead. In this case, the Dominican priest Tomás Serrano was most likely present at the birth of Doña María Cecilia's child in order to baptize it. Given Doña María Cecilia's position as an elite Spanish woman in Guatemalan society, this would be an expected practice. However, Serrano reportedly based his ultimate refusal to perform the baptism on the fact that the deformity had been caused by a sorcery spell cast by a mixed-race female.

As much as the Catholic Church, through its priests and the Inquisition, would have liked to be the sole interpreter of wondrous signs and their causes, and to present a unified interpretation of them, that did not always work in practice. The example of Doña María Cecilia's half-toad baby, a 'monster' that the priest Serrano believed was the result of an interpersonal conflict between a mixed-race female sorcerer and one of her clients, shows competing explanations for monstrous births between formal religious cultures and local populations, and within religious populations themselves. Doña María Cecilia provided an even more elaborate framework to explain the monstrous birth, citing the sorcerer's use of bewitched food to cause the 'infection spell.' She carefully noted all the details that pointed to supernatural intervention.

Both she and Serrano, therefore, attributed the monstrous birth to the power of a ritual specialist, called by the Inquisition an *hechicera* or 'sorcerer,' who allegedly had the power to intervene magically in pregnancies and subvert them. Neither attributed the deformity to the power of God or nature; instead, the blame was placed solely on a mixed-race female sorcerer.

Conclusion

Evidence from colonial Guatemala suggests that monsters acted as a significant sign with varied meanings in the New World, just as they had in Europe. Yet some key issues related to the historical and cultural context of colonial Guatemala shaped the preoccupation with monsters as signs. These issues, which also can be detected in post-conquest sources such as Inquisition records and chronicles, provide proof that Mesoamerican conceptions of deformity continued to operate through the seventeenth century. Evidence for these co-existing belief systems can be found, for example, in the language used by Spanish priests and native peoples to describe monstrous births. These different terms endured into the late seventeenth century, and were well enough known to be noted by a historical chronicler.

While some aspects of Mesoamerican cultures of wonder continued to operate into the colonial period, they interacted with European cultures of wonder and thus were reshaped over time. The dialogue about monsters that occurred on the edges of the Spanish empire in colonial Guatemala and elsewhere in New Spain built on Mesoamerican and European cultures of wonder. The interplay between the two cultures worked to provide new meanings for monstrous births in different times and places.

New World monsters reflected colonial anxieties over strange or difficult pregnancies and physical deformity in fetuses and infants, which were interpreted as significant signs with links to cannibalism, unruly indigenous women, the role of native and mixed-race ritual specialists, and the problems associated with religious conversion. It is not a coincidence that monstrous birth accounts appeared in both secular and religiously generated sources. For colonial Guatemala, the existence of large indigenous populations and the colonial project of their religious conversion helped shape explanations for the appearance of monsters and their interpretations, drawing on array of European, Mesoamerican, and local knowledge.

Atlantic world discourses of monstrosity can be seen as intimately linked to the colonization process, and so do not simply reflect hybridized understandings of monstrous births. The accounts worked to outline new contexts for deviancy along ethnic, gender, and religious lines, using language and imagery that reflected explicitly colonial fractures: an Indian woman who refused to convert to Christianity, a Spanish woman who consulted a mixed-race female sorcerer. Monstrous birth accounts, then, could function as emblematic reflections of disorder and deviancy in colonial social relations. At the same time, the accounts could also describe and critique continued Mesoamerican associations of physical deformity with politico-religious power, the resonance of indigenous and mixed-race ritual specialists, and their importance in post-conquest colonial Atlantic world societies.

Notes

I am grateful to Traci Ardren for her helpful discussion of pre-colonial Mesoamerican perspectives on the meaning of deformity and the growing literature on the topic, and to Daniella Kostroun, Lisa Vollendorf, and the anonymous reviewers for their helpful suggestions for revising the manuscript. Previous versions of this chapter were presented at the Gender, Religion and Atlantic World Seminar held at the William Andrews Clark Memorial Library, UCLA, in April 2005, and at the John Carter Brown Library at Brown University, Providence, R.I., in October 2005.

1 All of this issues surrounding the politics of pregnancy will be explored further in my book manuscript (in process), tentatively titled 'Colonial Medicine and Local Healing Cultures in Guatemala, 17th to the 19th Centuries.' For an examination of female curing and midwifery as it related to contemporary understandings of sorcery practices, supernatural illnesses, and community conflict, see Martha Few, *Women Who Live Evil Lives: Gender, Religion and the Politics of Power in Colonial Guatemala* (Austin: University of Texas Press, 2002).

2 Lorraine Daston and Katharine Park define European cultures of wonder as both process and object, a way to interpret the natural world and to mark boundaries within it: 'As theorized by medieval and early modern intellectuals, wonder was a cognitive passion, as much about knowing as about feeling. To register wonder was to register a breached boundary, a classification subverted.' *Wonders and the Order of Nature* (New York: Zone Books, 1998), 14.

3 The same was probably true of African culture as well, but this issue is much harder to trace in colonial-era sources and so I am leaving it aside for the moment. However, it is worth noting that Guatemala had significant African, black, and mulatto populations that counted female midwives among their numbers.

4 Daston and Park, *Wonders*, especially 173–6.

5 Ottavia Niccoli, *Prophecy and People in Renaissance Italy*, trans. Lydia G. Cochrane (Princeton, N.J.: Princeton University Press, 1990).

6 Ibid., xvi.

7 Ibid., xiii–xvi.

8 Ibid., 31.

9 Kathryn N. Brammwall, 'Monstrous Metamorphosis: Nature, Morality and the Rhetoric of Monstrosity in Tudor England,' *Sixteenth Century Journal*, 27, no.1 (1996): 3–21, 5–6.

10 Anne Jacobson Schutte, '"Such Monstrous Births": A Neglected Aspect of the Antinomian Controversy,' *Renaissance Quarterly*, 38, no. 1 (1985): 85–106.

11 Carolyn Tate and Gordon Bendersky write that the term Olmec 'refers to various peoples in Mexico and Central America who, between 1200–400 BCE, did not all speak the same language but communicated certain ideas by means of visual representation of humans and other subjects in portable stone carvings.' This interaction was especially intense between 900 and 600 BCE. See their article 'Olmec Sculptures of the Human Fetus,' *Perspectives in Biology and Medicine*, 42, no. 3 (1999): 303–32.

12 Ibid.

13 *Popol Vuh: The Definitive Edition of the Mayan Book of the Dawn of Life and the Glories of Gods and Kings*, trans. Dennis Tedlock (New York: Touchstone, 1996).

14 The discussion of the significance of dwarves and hunchbacks in Mesoamerican culture in this paragraph draws on Mary Miller and Simon Martin, *Courtly Art of the Ancient Maya* (New York: Thames on Hudson, 2004), especially 24–5.

15 Ibid., 25.

16 Bernardino de Sahagún, *General History of the Things of New Spain: Florentine Codex*, Book 12, 'The Conquest of Mexico,' trans. Arthur J.O. Anderson and Charles E. Dribble (Santa Fe, N.M.: School of American Research, 1975), 3.

17 Serge Gruzinski, *Man-Gods in the Mexican Highlands: Indian Power and Colonial Society, 1520–1800*, trans. Eileen Corrigan (Stanford, Calif.: Stanford University Press, 1989).

18 Ibid. and Cecilia F. Klein, 'Wild Woman in Colonial Mexico: An Encounter

of European and Aztec Concepts of Other,' in Claire Farrago, ed., *Reframing the Renaissance* (New Haven, Conn.: Yale University Press, 1995), 244–64.

19 Klein, 'Wild Woman,' 246.

20 Antonio de Fuentes y Guzmán, *Recordación Flórida: Discurso Historial y Demostración Natural, Material, Militar, y Política del Reyno de Guatemala*, 2 vols. (Guatemala: Tipografia Nacional, 1932–3), vol. 1, book 5, chapter 11, 156–8: 'Que trata del principio que tuvo entre los indios deste reyno de Goathemala, la enfermedad cumatz, y fué de sus abominaciones.' Francisco Antonio de Fuentes y Guzmán was born in 1643 in Santiago de Guatemala, capital city of colonial Central America. He served as *alcalde* of Santiago de Guatemala and *alcalde mayor* of Totonicapán (1661) and Sosonate (1699). His history of Guatemala relied on his own experience and on documents written by religious and secular authorities and indigenous elites. For more on Fuentes y Guzmán, see Robert M. Carmack, *Quichean Civilization: The Ethnohistoric, Ethnographic, and Archaeological Sources* (Berkeley and Los Angeles: University of California Press, 1973), 183–7.

21 The literature on cannibals and their meanings within the process of European colonialism is extensive. See especially Francis Barker, Peter Hulme, and Margaret Iverson, eds., *Cannibalism and the Colonial World* (New York: Cambridge University Press, 1998), including Hulme's 'Introduction: The Cannibal Scene,' 1–38.

22 Fuentes y Guzmán, *Recordación Flórida*, 157.

23 For a more in-depth discussion of casting illness in community conflicts in seventeenth-century Guatemala, see Few, *Women Who Live Evil Lives*.

24 I thank Danna Kostroun for pointing out this link. For more on the subject, see Bernard Dompnier, *Le venin de l'hérésie: Image du protestantisme et combat catholique au XVIIe siécle* (Paris: Editions du Centurion, 1985).

25 The term *vientre* can refer to womb or belly. Here I interpret *vientre* as womb, since it is used in reference to a woman's body and the actions described as childbirth. Later, when the illness is described in men, they are depicted as having similar physical symptoms of snake-like movements without the expulsions of deformed snakes, presumably because they have no womb.

26 Fuentes y Guzmán, *Recordación Flórida*, 157.

27 Valeria Finucci, 'Genealogical Pleasures, Genealogical Disruptions,' in Valeria Finucci and Kevin Brownlee, eds., *Generation and Degeneration: Tropes of Reproduction in Literature and History from Antiquity to Early Modern Europe*. (Durham, N.C.: Duke University Press, 2001), 1–14, 6. In the same volume, see Finucci's essay 'Maternal Imagination and Monstrous Birth: Tasso's *Gerusalemme liberate*,' 41–80.

28 The illness *cumatz* is described elsewhere in Fuentes y Guzmán's history but not in relation to monstrous births.

29 Hanns J. Prem, 'Disease Outbreaks in Central Mexico during the Sixteenth Century,' in Noble David Cook and W. George Lovell, eds., *Secret Judgments of God: Old World Disease in New World Contexts* (Norman: University of Oklahoma Press, 1991), 20–48, 8. For more on cocolitzli, see Martha Few, 'Indian Autopsy and Epidemic Disease in Early Colonial Mexico,' in Rebecca Brienen and Margaret Jackson, eds., *Invasion and Transformation: Interdisciplinary Perspectives on the Conquest of Mexico,* Mesoamerica Worlds Series (Boulder: University of Colorado Press, 2007), 153–65.

30 Prem, 'Disease Outbreaks,' 38; Elsa Malvido and Carlos Viesca, 'La epidemia de cocolitzli de 1576,' *Historias,* 11 (1985): 28.

31 I plan to explore this issue further in my larger book project, 'Colonial Medicine and Local Healing Cultures.'

32 Santo Domingo Sinacoa is located near the present-day Guatemalan town of Sumpango. Francisco Antonio de Fuentes y Guzmán, *Historia de Guatemala ó Recordación Flórida* (Madrid: L. Navarro, 1882–3), vol. 2, book 13, chapter 6, 978: 'De un singular y admirable monstruo que nació de una india, natural y vecina del pueblo de Santo Domingo Sinacao.'

33 Daston and Park, *Wonders and the Order of Nature,* 176.

34 The word *miembro* here literally translates into 'member,' a colonial-era term that in this context signifies the phallus.

35 Fuentes y Guzmán, *Historia de Guatemala,* vol. 2 , 978.

36 Ibid. The original Spanish reads: 'Estos habían de ser lo que llaman los indios chachaguates y nosotros gemelos, y nacieron por haberse unido como refiero, lo que ellos llaman nannosos y nosotros monstruos.'

37 *Diccionario de Mejicanismos.*

38 I am continuing to investigate this issue.

39 I have not yet been able to locate this painting.

40 Fuentes y Guzmán, *Historia de Guatemala,* vol. 2, 978.

41 Niccoli in *Prophecy and People* discusses the societal spaces where the monstrous birth also physically circulated in Italy, including the marketplace, the church, and the Vatican. This circulation is noted as well in Daston and Park, *Wonders and the Order of Nature,* 180.

42 Helaine Razovsky, 'Early Popular Hermeneutics: Monstrous Children in English Renaissance Broadside Ballads,' *Early Modern Literary Studies,* 2, no. 3 (1996): 1–34.

43 Archivo General de la Nación (Mexico City), Ramo de la Inquisición, vol. 830, exp. 7, ff.100–28. The documentation that specifically refers to the monstrous birth comes primarily from f.108f-v. and f.124f-v.

44 It is described as a toad (*sapo*) and not a frog (*rana*). One of the Inquisi-
    tion officials noted in correspondence surrounding the case that the toad
    is common to Santiago de Guatemala, often gets caught in peoples houses,
    and can, according to this official, live for months there without dying.
45 The excerpt, found on f.108v, reads: 'y la sangre que del parto echó no hera
    sangre natural sino lodo o como lodo de laguna.'
46 For more on this, see Few, *Women Who Live Evil Lives*.
47 John Carter Brown Library, Francisco Sunzin de Herrera, *Consulta práctico-
    moral en que se pregunta si los fetos abortivos se podrán bautizar a lo menos debaxo
    de condición, a los primeros días de concebidos* (Guatemala: Imprenta nueva de
    Sebastián de Arébalo, 1756), n.p. See section 'Argumento sexto' for the
    following excerpt: 'No es contra la costumbre de la Iglesia ni fuera de ella
    bautizar a los fetos si viven, *si vixerit baptizar*. Ni el bautizar a los partos mon-
    struosos de cuya naturaleza se duda.'

A Judaizing 'Old Christian' Woman and the Mexican Inquisition: The 'Unusual' Case of María de Zárate

STACEY SCHLAU

The inquisitional trial record of María de Zárate, born and raised Christian and arrested in Mexico City in 1656 for being a judaizer, illuminates not exceptional occurrences but rather the lives of average people who, because of their socio-religious standing and the operations of ecclesiastical machinery, became extraordinary. Zárate's unflagging dedication to her Crypto-Jewish husband and to members of her family in the face of enormous social pressure to distance herself from them seems remarkable. Even under torture, she revealed nothing to incriminate herself or anyone else in her community. Although filtered through the hegemonic, gendered, racialized discourses and methodologies of inquisitional proceedings, María de Zárate's expressed woes, desires, words, and actions speak to the larger social picture of the Iberian Atlantic.

This woman's story is at once uncommon and ordinary for mid-seventeenth-century judaizers in the Hispanic world. Of 'Old Christian' lineage, and therefore considered to be free of any taint of Jewish or Muslim heritage, she was said to have converted to Judaism as an adult, which makes her case 'unusual'; her conversion merits attention.[1] Boleslao Lewin, who edited and published in 1971 the documents pertaining to her trial, finds the case distinctive for a number of primarily juridical reasons.[2] In addition to its legal interest, this case, in which an Old Christian is accused of judaizing, challenges a common practice among scholars to equate 'judaizers' with 'New Christians.' The tendency to equate these groups dates back from the time when popular antipathy towards Jews was transfered to New Christians in early modern Spain. After 31 July 1492 Jews had been prohibited, on penalty of death, from entering into or being in any Spanish territories.[3] Lingering anxiety over Jews thereafter became particularly focused on the New Christian community. Here, the Holy Office sought out those whom they surmised were judaizers, that is, false converts to Christianity who secretly practised Judaism while pretending to be Catholic. Given the prohibition of all displays of Judaism and the high level of scrutiny surrounding the policing of such displays, private acts gained importance. This shift was particularly pertinent for women accused of judaizing, since they were held accountable for passing on clandestine religious instruction to their children within the confines of the home.

In addition to challenging the traditional correlation between 'judaizers' and 'New Christians,' Zárate's case also sheds insight on family life in the early modern Atlantic. Specifically, it reveals how family configurations were flexible and porous in Spain and in the New World. After all, in Spain the racial and ethnic mixing on all levels of society commonly known as *convivencia* (living together) had, despite eruptions of anti-Semitic violence, characterized the development of Spanish cultural norms and national consciousness. Family and culture were even more complex in the colonies vis-à-vis the diversity of religious, racial, and economic reality of the Americas. Thus, while the Crypto-Jewish community in the Americas depended on family and other connections for survival, the definition of 'family' by no means reflected a unified or coherent unit.

Zárate was first accused of judaizing by her adoptive mestizo son, José Sánchez. Both accuser and accused were socially marginalized, by virtue of race, religion, and/or class. The evolution of an apparently affectionate maternal-filial relationship into one of fierce antagonism can be explained only in the context of extended and multi-generational family dynamics within the Crypto-Jewish community. Those dynamics, in turn, must be understood in terms of the dominant racist and anti-Semitic attitudes and behaviours of church and state. All these factors came into play in a climate of ethnic/racial hybridity, intolerance, and violence in mid-seventeenth-century New Spain.

Race, Class, and Sexual Politics within an Extended Family

In her study of the difficulties faced by sixteenth- and seventeenth-century Spanish judaizing communities, Pilar Huerga Criado notes that 'the family was extraordinarily important, because in it a network of solidarity of multiple dimensions was woven ... But also that same structure transformed the family into a framework in which tensions and conflicts

of a distinct type that continuously threatened solidarity were generated.'[4] For Huerga Criado, the intensity and interdependence of family economic and social relations among Crypto-Jews, largely shaped by
the realities of external pressures from the Inquisition and its related
regulating bodies and documents, was constantly undermined. Thus,
although rich Crypto-Jews gave alms to the poor in exchange for performing Jewish observances such as fasting, religious diversity weakened
unity within the community.[5] Indeed, Huerga Criado asserts, the vast
majority of denunciations for judaizing originated from New, not Old,
Christians.[6] The scenario she describes seems to have arisen across the
Atlantic, as revealed in the case of María de Zárate and her family.

Born in Mexico of Spanish parents, the Creole María de Zárate was
an Old Christian of illustrious lineage and the great-niece of Martínez
Silíceo, archbishop of Toledo and tutor to Philip II.[7] Silíceo, who had
stated publicly that the rise of Protestantism and the revolt of the *co-
muneros* (supporters of the old communities in Castile) were due to the
influence of the New Christians,[8] also had helped shape the ideology
that framed inquisitional procedures. His peasant ancestry is significant.
Since Spain's Jews had never been peasants and generally did not inter-
marry with the agricultural poor, their claims to purity of blood were
therefore readily believed and easily proven.[9] Ironically, Martínez Silíceo's great-niece married a Crypto-Jew in 1636, when she was thirty years
old.[10] Excluded from the voluminous inquisitional proceedings against
her is the story of how she met Francisco Botello, a man who, by the time
of her (and his) arrest, had already been found guilty once of judaizing.
The record states that she did not actually convert to Judaism until the
years of Botello's first imprisonment by the Inquisition (1642–9). Whether Zárate was a practising judaizer remains ambiguous, as we shall see.

A few biographical details about Botello emerge from his wife's trial proceedings. He was born in Andalucía in about 1593 and married
María de Zárate in 1636, when he was forty-two years old. His case is
framed by the trajectory of the 'gran complicidad' (great conspiracy)
– the term that mid-seventeenth-century colonial inquisitional officials
used to refer to what they perceived as a resurgence of judaizing. He was
imprisoned the first time in 1642 and the proceedings were concluded
when he was reconciled in the 1649 *auto de fe*, a public ceremony of
penitence and punishment. Botello was arrested a second time in 1656
after his foster son Sánchez denounced him. Sánchez accused Botello of
many specific heresies, asserting that he had criticized the Holy Office
for mistreating prisoners, for assuming that all people of Portuguese an-

cestry were Jewish, and for arresting some individuals only to confiscate
their wealth.[11] Declared a relapsed heretic, he was turned over to the
secular authorities to be burned at the stake on 8 October 1659. Such
a procedure, known as being 'relaxed' to the secular arm of the law, allowed inquisitiors to condemn individuals to death and, since they were
church officials, avoid carrying out the penalty themselves.

The official chronicler of the event maintained that Botello was 'the
firmest Jew of any who had been punished by the Holy Office in many
centuries; without it being possible to get him to name Jesus or the Most
Holy Virgin, His mother, he allowed himself to be burned alive.'[12] Certainly there could be no greater condemnation, not only of the prisoner, but also of the Inquisition itself, since in this instance the Holy
Office had failed to offer to the public the spectacle of the repentant
sinner. Statements such as this must be understood as flowing from the
ideological intent of the narrative: chronicles of *autos* not only described
events but also narrated them in a way that supported an image of the
Inquisition as defending orthodoxy over heresy and of the vice-royalty as
a consolidating power. The public *autos* had eschatological meaning as
dramatizations of the last judgment. They also functioned as legitimizing
rituals of imperial authority, intertwining religion and politics in order to
create what Alejandro Cañeque has designated as a 'theater of power.'[13]

Botello seems to have made a religiously motivated decision to reject
Catholicism during his trial. First, it was common knowledge that a second arrest by the Inquisition would result in his conviction as a *relapso*
(relapsed sinner), which would then lead to his execution. Since he did
not confess to any crime, he appears to have chosen a painful death over
giving up his faith. While it is possible that he had simply hoped that he
would not get caught again, his rejection of conversion during the *auto de
fe* – which would have saved him from being burned alive and led to his
being garroted instead – points to a religious motivation. The strength
of his faith may have been reflected in his wife's choices and decisions.

In terms of her defence, another familial source of legal problems for
María de Zárate was Baltasar de Burgos, her nephew by marriage, whose
mother had been found guilty by the Inquisition years earlier. One part
of the denunciation and subsequently the accusation against Zárate asserted that Burgos had translated Psalms from Latin into Spanish, so
that she might read them.[14] He had lived with his aunt from the time
he was ten years old until he was nineteen (1639–48), as well as during
his university studies. After obtaining his diploma, having been denied
a licence by the medical board because of his status as a New Christian,

he lied and said that Ana Gómez was not really his biological mother but had found him. Zárate testified on his behalf, confirming the lie, which she was later, during her inquisitional trial, forced to admit as a falsehood. Despite these efforts, however, he was not granted permission to practise medicine in Mexico City. He moved to Toluca, where he died and thereby avoided the fate of his relatives.[15]

The other foster son authored the original denunciation against Zárate and Botello. Offspring of a migrant Spanish soldier of 'pure' blood and a woman of inferior social status, presumably of indigenous ancestry, the mestizo José Sánchez (also known as José Zárate and José del Castillo) was abandoned by his mother when he was less than a year old. (She had been previously abandoned by his father.) Zárate's mother, María de la Paz, raised the child until she died in 1643, when he was nine years old; her daughter then took over his care. Indeed, in her defence statement, Zárate asserted that even before her mother died, 'she always took care of him, teaching him Christian doctrine, to read, write, and count, and paying for a tutor for him and giving him clothes, as though he were her own son.'[16] Typically for that time and place in terms of the race relations between those of European and those of indigenous descent, Sánchez's social status was 'juridically indefinite,' as Lewin notes. He remained a member of the household, 'half servant and half a part of the family.'[17] Complex emotions and a web of complicated social, economic, and affective interactions influenced the relationship between María Zárate and her mestizo foster son.

When María Zárate became Sánchez's guardian, her husband, Francisco Botello, was still a prisoner in the inquisitional jail. After his release, they raised him together. Sánchez and Zárate's niece, Ana de la Serna, fell in love because, according to Zárate, they had grown up together. When Ana de la Serna became pregnant by Sánchez, they wanted to marry. Both Zárate, an Old Christian by birth, and Botello, a Crypto-Jew, vigorously opposed the match. This conflict, which also laid the groundwork for subsequent disputes, contributed to José Sánchez's appearance before the inquisitor on 2 May 1656 to denounce Zárate and Botello. His denunciation evinces the truism that, despite officials' requirement that witnesses swear that their testimony did not spring from personal animosity, the Inquisition was 'an institution that could be manipulated for widely differing personal ends.'[18]

Framed in her response to Sánchez's declaration, Zárate's overt racism, enunciated before inquisitorial officials, reflected the dominant ideologies of her time and place. A prime example of this phenomenon occurred when her sister came to her with the dilemma about her daughter Ana's pregnancy and proposed marriage. According to the 'Answer to the Accusation' and the 'Defence,' Zárate insisted that her sister forbid the marriage because 'she knew that said José was a mestizo and she had known his mother and knew who she was, so the best thing would be to throw the child that her daughter bore out the door and whip the said daughter to death for her doings, and give the said José a beating and give notice of this to a judge or a magistrate so they would deport him to China, so that a mestizo dog like him wouldn't marry her daughter and besmirch her lineage.'[19] In this statement, race, class, and sexual politics mix: there were 'valid' objections to Sánchez because he was illegitimate, mestizo, and poor. Zárate's solution was a common punishment for common criminals: to have him deported.[20] Calling Sánchez a 'mestizo dog,' Zárate named his desire to marry her niece an insult to their family. By lashing out at him and her niece, Zárate revealed that, in her case, deeply rooted, culturally reinforced feelings outweighed affective bonds.

Zárate claimed that she chose not to tell her husband about Ana de la Serna and José Sánchez's relationship because she wanted to spare him. When he found out about their marriage after the fact, he was predictably furious and even accused his putative son of robbery.[21] The young couple escaped his wrath by returning to Mexico City. The contempt that Zárate and Botello displayed towards her ward, framed as primarily because of his race, triggered (or at least contributed to) a series of events that resulted in his turning the tables on them. Ironically, they found themselves caught by those with access to far greater structural power than they or he, and paid for it with their lives.

The battles had increasingly high stakes. Undoubtedly they were fuelled by the fact that the entire extended family lived together in the same house. Months later, when another niece married, Botello offered to host the wedding feast. Ana de la Serna and José Sánchez were invited, but they were not permitted to eat at the same table as the hosts.[22] The situation continued to deteriorate rapidly. When Botello asked Sánchez to bring a mule to a client in Mexico City, Sánchez refused, whereupon Botello called him a 'pícaro desvergonzado' (shameless rogue).[23] Then, upon Zárate's scolding him for not respecting her husband, he replied that she and he had dishonoured him by calling him a mestizo and a thief. They had further dishonoured him, he claimed, not only by calling him a 'mestizo dog' but also by hosting a celebration for the wedding of another niece, María de la Serna, to Antonio Pinto, but not for his and Ana's wedding.[24] Zárate reported that Sánchez learned what she and

Botello had said about him through Ana's side of the family, making it evident that a large part of the extended family had become involved in the dispute. She harped on his lack of gratitude for their having raised him. He replied that the fact that he had grown up in their house should have meant that they would not dishonour him. He then declared himself their mortal enemy and all communication ceased.[25] Sánchez did not even invite them to his child's baptism.

Despite this animosity between Sánchez and his foster parents, Botello (surprisingly) asked Sánchez, via his sister-in-law, to collect fifteen pesos from Mexico City for him. A short while later, Ana de la Serna reported to Botello that Sánchez had collected the money but had then been robbed on the trip home. A week later, yet another niece told Zárate that Sánchez had brought home material for shirts and shoes for his wife and himself, as well as soap. From this information Zárate surmised that Sánchez had kept the money for himself and, being facile of tongue ('very talkative and presumptuous'), made up the story about being robbed.[26]

The power struggles within this family appear to have centred around generational as well as a racial conflicts. The drama played out with a degree of ferocity and underlying violence that is obvious in spite of the formulaic language of the trial transcript. Zárate's rendition of the history of Botello's and her relationship with Sánchez was meant to discredit him. This was, of course, essential to her case, since she proceeded on the (correct) assumption that his testimony constituted the primary evidence against them.[27] Indeed, the charges outlined in the prosecutor's 'Accusation' exactly mirror the record of Sánchez's denunciations. In her 'Responses to the Accusation,' Zárate requested that Sánchez's testimony and his wife's be excluded.[28] Ultimately, despite being a mestizo, Sánchez emerged victorious from the battle with his erstwhile foster parents. As a result of his accusations, both were arrested, tried, and convicted of judaizing, the crime for which he accused them.

While Francisco Botello was found guilty of being a relapsed heretic, the inquisitorial judges decided that neither the prosecution nor the defence had proved their case for María de Zárate (which did not mean, however, that they did not suspect judaizing). Consequently, they expressed their ambivalence in the verdict. Because she had not relapsed, the sentence was far milder than her husband's. The courts demanded from her an abjuration *de levi* (a solemn oath of denial for a slight suspicion of heresy) and sentenced her with reclusion and service in a hospital, a common punishment for women convicted by the Holy Office.[29] The prosecutor appealed the judgment for a lighter sentence, but noth-

ing came of his petition. In 1665 Zárate's last petition to the Tribunal was
tendered. No further record of her fate has appeared.

From Old Christian to Judaizer

Although María de Zárate was not arrested by the Holy Office until 1656,
several years after the second period of intense persecution of *judaizantes*,
her life was nevertheless shaped by the so-called 'great conspiracy.' Zárate
denied being a Crypto-Jew, or a 'Jewish judaizer,' as the transcription of
the proceedings named her.[30] While it is true that most of the evidence
against her sprang from José Sánchez's testimony, the Inquisition always
undertook its own investigation, following the juridical standards of the
period. Her arrest in and of itself, even if only for guilt by association
(being married to a Crypto-Jew), meant that the Tribunal was convinced
that she was a judaizer. Naturally, her decision to deny the charge was
one of only a few options available to the accused; even more, I suggest
that she had no choice except to protest her innocence. A confession
in the social climate of the decade after the 'great conspiracy' would
most likely have not been treated with much mercy. Zárate's assertion of
innocence was supported by her sister's testimony. But others testified
against her. Certainly, the prosecutor's statement asserting her guilt was
filled with many examples of highly stereotypical 'crimes' of judaizing,
some of which undoubtedly sprang from his imagination (see below).
Yet her loyalty to her husband and the particular configuration of wifely
duties during that period suggest that she did indeed participate, at least
nominally, in his judaizing practices. In any event, Zárate's protestations
of innocence and the prosecutor's avowal of her guilt conform to the
standard rhetorical strategies evident in countless trial records from the
Tribunal archives.

The highly ritualized and codified language and structures of interrogation would make any other format impossible. In the final analysis,
what seems most authentic today is not whether Zárate judaized or not
but the love and loyalty she displayed especially for her husband and
a racialized hatred of her enemy, as well as the strength and courage
she drew upon even under torture. While judaizers on both sides of the
Atlantic had often attempted to thread their way through inquisitional
processes by seeking to confess to 'lesser' crimes and claiming innocence
regarding others,[31] María de Zárate's defence consisted of a combination of attacks on the veracity of José Sánchez's words, counter-asser-
tions, expressions of confusion, and denials of wrongdoing.

In her 'Defences,' 'Responses to the Accusation,' and 'Responses to the Publication of Witnesses,' as well as in the torture chamber, Zárate continuously and consistently blamed Sánchez for the situation in which she found herself. Calling him a 'pícaro' (rogue), she repeatedly denied the charges against her, asserting that Sánchez had fabricated them to get back at her and her husband because of their dispute.[32] Naturally, she recounted her version of the conflict as background, openly stating for the record that his mestizo status should have precluded him from marrying her niece; she continued to insist that she did not want to 'dirty her lineage.'[33]

Statements about Sánchez's perfidy abound. For instance, responding to chapter 28 of the 'Accusation,' she declared that 'none of the things referred to in said chapter seem credible, because they are chimeras and pretenses of some condemned soul who has only tried and tries to take his life with so many testimonies as he gives.'[34] In the 'Answer to the Publication of Witnesses,' she maintained that there was only one witness against her: his testimony was false and she presumed it was her enemy's, José Sánchez, 'the mestizo.'[35] Therefore, as noted above, she requested that his testimony and his wife's be excluded.[36] On numerous occasions in her defence statements, she stressed that he had lied, reiterating various tenses of the verb 'to lie' (e.g., 'he lied' several times, 'he lies,' and 'he lies in everything and about everything') or using the noun ('he continues his lies').[37] As a legal strategy, the primacy she accorded to impugning Sánchez's reliability as a witness originated in dire necessity, since the 'Accusation' was almost entirely based on his 'Denunciation.' Had it worked, she would have been set free.[38]

An example of his dubious assertions also challenged one of the charges, that she had no Christian images in her home: 'If I, as the witness says, were a Jew, I would not give as I gave him an image of Christ Our Lord nor would there be a reason to pretend to.'[39] Moreover, Zárate used the issues of what is 'natural' and 'verisimilar' to further her case: 'If the author of these bad things is the mestizo José, he lies in everything and for everything, and I know that about him, because of his bad inclinations and natural malevolence.'[40] She also engaged in philosophical meditation: 'Just as the verisimile imitates and appears to be natural, what is not verisimile destroys it.'[41] She then noted the 'not verisimile things' in Sánchez's testimony, which correspond to chapters 8, 24, 30, and 37 of the formal 'Accusation.'

As is true of most inquisitional documents, except the few written in the speaker's own hand, the question of 'voice' here is complicated.

Generally the accused person did not actually write official documents, although s/he may have written a draft. In Zárate's case, the defence documents are presented in her (first-person) voice, but her lawyer, Doctor Rodrigo Ruiz de Cepeda Martínez, probably formulated them; he certainly signed them. Using a kind of ventriloquism, he speaks (writes) as Zárate. Also, all actors on this stage were ensnared in the imbalance of social power created by the institution in which they articulated their position, which necessarily affected communication. The resultant hybridity of language and voice increases the difficulty of sorting out which ideas and/or turns of phrase were originally Zárate's. Nevertheless, legal and ordinary discourses reflect fairly distinct and unmistakable registers. Relying on the strong probability that the words indeed reflect the defendant's stance, even when they are not verbatim transcriptions, I continue to speak of them as hers.

Inquisitional scribes applied similar accuracy to their recording of torture sessions, even if we take into account that they conformed to the areas of concern and listed methodologies of interrogation prescribed in the manuals of the Holy Office. As Gretchen Starr-LeBeau has noted about the Spanish tribunals, 'like inquisitorial procedures generally, elaborate ritual was used to control, structure, and make meaningful both the torture and its results – to convince the inquisitors that they would be gaining a glimpse of a hidden reality.'[42]

On 4 September 1659 the prisoner was informed of the decision to submit her to torture.[43] As the session began, she affirmed, preparing the groundwork ahead of time, that if she said anything, it would be because of fear.[44] She did manage to insist that the entire case rested on Sánchez's false accusations, insulting him with race- and class-based slurs in the process: 'It is testimony that that coyote gave against me' and 'it is that rogue who has given testimony against me.'[45] Nevertheless, perhaps inspired by her husband's example, she admitted to nothing, but only repeated, 'I don't owe it, I don't owe it'[46] – an ambiguous phrase loaded with multiple possible meanings. Certainly, one allusion must be to the *débito* (marital debt), the juridical and religious concept that a wife was required to fulfil her marriage contract with sexual and other forms of service to her husband.[47] The notion was widely accepted both in secular courts and in the church, where priests, for instance, admonished their confessants 'to pay the debt.' Another possible interpretation of the phrase might be to consider that, with those words, Zárate articulated a stance in which she saw herself as free of guilt: she was arguing that she did not need to be tortured or punished, because she was not judaizing.

Denial constituted an important line of defence. While being tortured, Zárate declared that 'if she knew that her husband were a Jew she would not have made a life with him for anything in the world.'[48] She stated categorically from the outset of her 'Answer' that she was a good Catholic, who believed that the Holy Office helped to rid the world of evil and who practised all the daily rituals that a good Catholic should.[49] She had no idea who Moses was, so she could not have followed his laws, nor did she know if there were Jews in Rome, so she could not have said that they lived freely there.[50] She did not abstain from any foods that would mark her as a Jew, except blood sausage, 'because many years ago, after eating a little, she became deathly ill and since then has hated it.'[51] This last admission constituted a significant obstacle, since, while many judaizers ate pork, they all abstained from blood sausage, probably because it combined two Jewish dietary prohibitions: blood and pork.[52]

She categorically denied another piece of damning evidence: the prosecutor claimed that, because men cannot be circumcised for fear of being found out as Jewish, some *judaizantes* cut out a piece of flesh from a woman's shoulder, as a sign of reverence and community. He requested that Zárate be examined to see if she had a scar on her shoulder.[53] The same day, the doctors who examined her found three marks, one high up on the right shoulder, 'from a scar made with a cutting instrument.'[54] The prosecutor interpreted the find as proof of her judaizing, and, as corroborating evidence, he requested that copies of testimony from another trial, against one Duarte de León, be appended to the documents for the proceeding against Zárate. According to his three daughters' testimony, the judaizing Duarte de León, who also circumcised his son, had cut off a piece of skin from each of their shoulders, subsequently roasting the flesh over live coals and eating it, together with those in attendance.[55] Was Duarte de León alone in this practice? How much of the testimony was actually true? Whether or not Zárate had indeed participated in some similar ritual, the issue could not have helped her case: How does one prove a negative?

Suppositions about what it meant to be Jewish, and the notion of cannibalism derived from the descriptions, tell us a great deal about the ideological underpinnings with which the inquisitors operated. Like Indians, Jews were perceived as barbaric and bloodthirsty, altogether 'primitive' and possibly not even human, worthy of the disdain of 'good' Christians. Unlike indigenous people, however, there was no assumption of a priori innocence in the legal-religious treatment of presumed Jews and judaizers, since they had deliberately turned their backs on the 'true' religion, Catholicism.

Another strategy – obfuscation – also served the defendant poorly.
Zárate's testimony regarding her husband, as reproduced in the court
documents, implied a complex set of contradictory expectations and impulses. On the one hand, she clearly loved him very much. More than
one witness quoted her as saying that she would never divorce her husband, 'that even if they burned Botello, she would gather the ashes and
make a life with them.'[56] Having been accused of returning to her relationship with her husband when he was released from jail in 1649, she
said that she did so because she had never heard him say or seen him
do anything that violated Catholic precepts, although with a caveat: 'Her
husband crossed himself and fasted correctly, except because of old age
and illness.'[57] Also, she claimed, his family had insulted and abandoned
him. Finally, she wanted him back 'to avenge herself of them and destroy
their eyes, as is said, and seeing herself sick, alone, poor and already ag-
ing, she wanted to get support from her husband.'[58] This statement is
remarkable for its admission of her requirements for survival: she could
turn to her husband only in times of need. Indeed, she maintained that
she had been ill and had kept to her bed almost the entire time that
Botello was in prison.[59] That Zárate contradicted herself is apparent: as
we have seen above, elsewhere she denied that she would have stayed
with him had she known he was a judaizer.

Torn between, on the one hand, her loyalty to and economic dependence on her husband and, on the other, her Old Christian heritage
as well as the Catholic precepts of marriage that required her to follow
her husband's lead, Zárate attempted to thread her way through a maze
of conflicting values and social expectations that blurred the boundaries between the categories of judaizer and practising Catholic. She may
not have even seen any contradiction in her behaviours, actions, and
words: in a set of circumstances in which she needed and wanted to be a
good 'Christian' wife, how might she remain true to her husband and at
the same time convince the inquisitors of her innocence? An impossible
task, but one that she endeavoured to carry out with great determination
and, at times, even courage.

At issue, too, were those of Zárate's actions that seemed to prove
that she saw herself as a member of the Crypto-Jewish community: she
washed clothes and cooked for several prisoners who appeared in the
1646 *auto de fe*; in general, 'she interacted with people who had been
found guilty'; and she helped other prisoners.[60] But, according to the
transcripts, she was not charitable towards Old Christians.[61] In addition,
after Botello's release in 1649, when another former prisoner with whom

he had become friends fell ill, he brought him home and they took care of him.[62] This kind of community-based cooperation and mutual support smacked of judaizing to inquisitorial officials.

A large number of other minor infractions included in the chapters of the 'Accusation' were intended to signal to inquisitional judges that she was a judaizer: she was accused, for instance, of rejecting the Holy Spirit; avoiding crossing herself upon rising in the morning; reciting a psalm in Spanish; saying, 'Blessed be the most holy Lord God of Abraham, Isaac, and Jacob'; 'never praising the Holy Sacrament [of the Eucharist] or Jesus'; not having any holy images or going to Mass; eating meat during Lent; eating only certain meats and fish (only those whom Noah had taken into the ark); taking communion without having been absolved; and neglecting to pray the rosary.[63] A recounting of these and other misdoings aimed to build the case for her guilt through cumulative effect. The actions, which reflected the questionable behaviours listed in the Edicts of Faith, were by the mid-seventeenth century automatically accepted as judaizing practices.

Zárate was accused of considerable animosity towards Catholics, Catholic doctrine, and Catholic institutions, especially the Holy Office. The prosecutor noted that, 'as though contaminated by the foul wickedness of Judaism,'[64] she had alleged, as had her husband, that the inquisitional prisons were unjust, the Holy Office detained prisoners in order to confiscate their money, and inquisitional officials stole goods sequestered from prisoners.[65] In an inventive stretch of the imagination, he even asserted that Zárate had stated that the Inquisition was founded because Isabel was jealous of Ferdinand's Jewish lover![66] And finally, she was reported as having remarked that wearing the *sambenito* – the penitential robe worn by those who had been sentenced and reconciled to Catholicism, and which marked them as ex-heretics – was an honour.[67]

Zárate was also accused of rejecting the authority of priests and the pope.[68] The prosecutor attacked her as 'this perverse riffraff, unbelieving of the incarnation of the divine word and of the mysteries of his passion and death and the founding of his church.'[69] With respect to her alleged practice of eating meat during Lent and fasting only on certain days, she was said to have insisted that 'sin did not enter by the mouth nor did it harm the body, that what came out harmed the soul.'[70] In general, she detested Christians, and especially priests, monks, and nuns. She blasphemed and spoke ill of saints and 'beatified persons.'[71] She did not recite the prayer of the Virgin Mary because she was a Jew.[72]

Another important aspect of the 'Accusation' relied on the contention that María de Zárate had spoken well of and believed in Judaism. According to the prosecutor, she believed in the durability of 'the invalid and dead Law of Moses' – a cliché of Spanish ecclesiastic discourse of the period – so much that she asserted that if she had children she would teach them Jewish law, 'although she might lose a thousand lives because of it.'[73] She avowed that learning the law of Moses had saved her[74] and that God had promised the Jews beauty and wealth, which was proven by the fact that there were so few rich Old Christians.[75] Another statement that the prosecutor attributed to Zárate regarded proselytizing: converting others to Judaism gained merit for God.[76] Further, she prayed the Psalms 'in the Jewish manner' (that is, without Christian additions).[77] Indeed, the prosecutor suggested that she and Botello used to pray looking west into the sky just after the first star appeared, which was 'undoubtedly a Jewish ritual and ceremony.'[78] Other actions that he put forth as confirming her Judaism included her burning her nails[79] and fasting as Jews do.[80] He quoted her as having maintained that being Jewish was not for fools or simpleminded people.[81] In sum, he stated that he felt (rhetorically) certain of having proved her to be highly observant of the law of Moses.[82]

All these accusations – and many others I have not listed – reveal a number of commonalities that María de Zárate's case shares with those of other Crypto-Jews, especially women, in Mexico, other Spanish colonies, and Spain. Set against the historic, religious, and social background that defined the early modern period in Hispanic lands, the particulars of her story reveal not only cultural hybridity and racial divisions but also gender norms. The account of this woman's travails with inquisitorial apparatuses and personnel also reflects the climate of constant fear of upheaval and loss – economic disasters, Indian rebellions, and religious heresies, for example – prevalent among ecclesiastic and state officials in colonial Mexico, especially in the vice-royalty's administrative centre, Mexico City, where she (mostly) lived.

The Social Context

While relatively few Jews and judaizers were prosecuted by the Spanish Inquisition proportionate to the volume of cases processed, the Spanish persecution of those persons suspected of Judaic practices has come to symbolize the most devastating aspects of the machinery employed by that institution. In our contemporary popular imagination, the Inquisition did almost nothing except kill Jews. There is a grain of truth in that belief; inquisitorial officials did seek to eradicate judaizers, but the fact is that their zeal depended on the historical period and location. Undoubtedly, the ideologies, behaviours, and institutional structures that the Holy Office brought to bear against judaizers reflected prevailing socio-religious norms, and therefore reveal the cultural underpinnings of Hispanic societies. Of most of the cases pursued by the various tribunals, however, accusations of judaizing made up only a small percentage. The severity of institutional oppression of judaizers varied. Certainly, many Jews and judaizers were condemned, hundreds were burned at the stake, and, by the mid-seventeenth century, the *judaizante* communities of Spain, Mexico, and Peru were, for all practical purposes, annihilated.[83]

After the signing on 31 March 1492 of the Edict of Expulsion, which required all Jews to leave Spain by 31 July of that year or convert, half of those exiled (about 100,000 people) went to Portugal. Those who remained became New Christians and could not exhibit any external sign – including circumcision – of being Jews, nor own any symbolic object that connected them with Judaism.[84] Indeed, the requirement of 'purity of blood,' proof that one had no Moorish or Jewish ancestry, loomed so large that it was not removed as a precondition for holding public office in Spain until 1865.[85]

The periods of worst persecution generally reflected the wider historical moment in which they occurred. The first phase of the Inquisition in Spain (1481–1550) was basically devoted to judaizers.[86] During the second half of the sixteenth century, the tribunals of Andalucía, Extremadura, La Mancha, and Murcia all conducted trials; in Granada, for instance, in two *autos de fe* in 1593 and 1595, 146 people participated as judaizers, over 80 per cent of the total number of those found guilty of crimes.[87] Then, most famously, following the reunification of the Iberian peninsula in 1580, a heavy influx of Portuguese Jews into Spain and, to a lesser extent, its colonies, led to a period of 'wholesale arrests and trials' that left some of the wealthiest men in Spain ruined.[88] The first trial of a Portuguese *converso* in Spain occurred in 1632,[89] but the number and proportion of cases against judaizers varied by tribunal. Thus, although possibly only 3 per cent of the cases dealt with by the Toledo Inquisition from 1531 to 1560 concerned judaizers,[90] in the last decades of the seventeenth century they made up nearly half of that tribunal's proceedings.[91] Another famous example: in the 1662 *auto* in Llerena, out of 110 penitents, 101 participated as judaizers.[92]

Although a Crypto-Jewish community existed and contributed to the

economy in Castile throughout the second half of the seventeenth century,[93] within a generation after the Edict of Expulsion most Spanish
New Christians had become more Christian than Jewish. The religion
of those who judaized was to a large extent shaped by external – inquisitorial – pressures, although internal tensions also played a role: 'Religious, personal, political, and social differences divided conversos [sic]
as much as they helped distinguish New from Old Christian.'[94] Regarding the influence of inquisitional pressure on judaizing, Gitlitz has pointedly remarked that the 'Inquisition impelled Crypto-Judaism to develop
strategies of secrecy. It influenced the choice of which Judaic customs
would survive and which would quickly atrophy': '[Judaizers who] clung
to whatever remnants of practice and belief they could muster were at
the same time practicing (if not always believing) Catholics. The crypto-
Jews had no Jewish books, no one to instruct their children in Hebrew,
no Talmudic scholars to refine the understanding of adults, and no Sab-
bath afternoon study sessions in which to debate the finer points of the
Law.'[95] They were Jews in the sense that they identified as Jews; believed
that being Jewish would lead to their salvation; and were sustained by
five core beliefs: God is one; the Messiah is coming; belief in the Law
of Moses is a prerequisite for individual salvation; observance, as well as
belief, is required; and Judaism is the preferred religion. Mostly, though,
they did not conform to, because they had little knowledge of, the traditions of Jewish practice, as written in the Talmud and other rabbinical
documents. For instance, they did not (could not) pray together, except
in some family gatherings. They did try, however, to rest and wear clean
clothing on Saturdays; fast on certain days, especially Purim; avoid eating
pork; and recite the Psalms without Christian additions.[96]

Although during the years of the reunification of Spain and Portugal
(1580–1640) many Jews and New Christians returned to Spain, some,
seeking greater freedom to practise the religion they still held to secretly,
came to America.[97] The vast majority of those immigrants were of Portuguese descent, people whose ancestors had fled Spain when the Catholic
monarchs expelled them at the end of the fifteenth century. The number of New Christians who came to the colonies was fairly low, but they
nevertheless suffered disproportionately from inquisitional persecution,
especially during two periods: in Mexico, 1589–1601 and 1642–9.

During its entire history (1521–1823), the Holy Office in New Spain
left a total record of prosecutions consisting of 1,553 volumes, each containing 800–1,000 folios.[98] In contrast to the large number of defendants
who were of African descent – nearly 50 per cent of the cases[99]– only a

small percentage of the cases (under 500) were for judaizing.[100] Of the
cases against judaizers, a roughly equal number of women and men were
arrested and received approximately the same punishment.[101] There
were many fewer New Christians in Peru than in Mexico, but from 1635
to 1639, culminating in the great *auto de fe* that year, eighty-four people
were tried for judaizing; eighty-one were men.[102] Of these, sixty-four
were of Portuguese extraction. The unquestioned association of Portuguese and New Christian affected judaizers no less in Peru and Mexico
than in Spain. In both of the major colonial centres, the transpeninsular
and transatlantic dimensions of the demographics and the institution
are easily discerned.

     During the sixteenth century, the first New Christian immigrants to ar-
rive in New Spain were mostly Spaniards who arrived seeking economic
opportunity. The men were artisans and small-time merchants. Trials
beginning in the late 1570s reveal a well-established, well-networked, observant judaizing community centred in Mexico City. The first round
of persecutions featured the arrest of the governor of the province of
Nuevo León, Luis de Carvajal el Viejo, and members of his family, in
1589. A few years later, Luis de Carvajal the Younger and his family, the
most famous of the condemned *judaizantes* of the late sixteenth century,
were arrested. They had helped to maintain Jewish customs by making
their home into a place where judaizers could meet and exercise their
religion. In the library of the school where he was employed as a tutor,
Carvajal had discovered a treatise by Moses Maimonides that outlined
thirteen fundamental precepts of Judaism.[103] Horrified by how Chris-
tianized his family had become, Carvajal, who was also a mystic and a
poet, attempted to convert as many as possible to (what he knew of) Jewish beliefs and rituals. His zeal may be summed up in a much-repeated
rhyme attributed to him: 'Mas quiero ser pregonero / de la Casa del Señor / que no Emperador / de este Mundo entero' (I much prefer to be
the crier of the Lord's house than the emperor of this whole world).[104]
Carvajal was arrested in 1590, then reconciled in October 1594. Upon
his second arrest in February 1595, he declared his intention of dying a
Jew.[105] While in prison, he converted his cellmate, a monk placed there
to spy on him, which provided further evidence of the subversive threat
of a possible 'great conspiracy' of judaizers.[106] Until February 1596, he
had testified only against himself, his mother, and his sisters, but in the
torture chamber he began to testify against his whole family, his friends,
and his acquaintances. He was executed in December 1596.[107] This complicated story has its origins in struggles for political power, but, as a

result of the inquisitional proceedings of 1590, 1596, and 1601, the vast majority of judaizers were imprisoned, executed, or deported. The community as a whole was ruined financially and ceased to have political influence.[108]

Substantial New Christian immigration to Mexico during the second half of the sixteenth century and again in the first half of the seventeenth century replenished the population. In general, Crypto-Jews belonged to the middle class; the men worked in the mining industry, internal and international commerce, medicine, and the skilled trades.[109] The second wave of Crypto-Jews was made up largely of Portuguese or Spanish-born children of Portuguese who had migrated after the reunification of Spain and Portugal. The majority of men in this group engaged in commercial trades, although a wide variety of other professions was represented. A royal decree and a papal pardon, both published in 1604, allowed for the reconciliation of all Jews of Portuguese origin but American inquisitors chose not to respect either document, even though they knew that both had been promulgated.[110] Ecclesiastic officials behaved in a typical manner in Mexico: they published the order that Jews were allowed to leave the territory on 25 May 1605, while also stipulating that they were required to depart immediately. But, since they delayed announcing the order until only a few days before the flotilla embarked from Veracruz, it was too late for anybody to get away.

As had happened in Spain, within the Mexican judaizing community the essence of Jewish identity, the religion, gradually eroded.[111] That is, Crypto-Jews were trapped in a situation in which, having lost touch with the fundamentals of Jewish community and intellectual life, they nevertheless fervently desired to continue being Jews. For reasons of survival and in order to hide their 'true' identity, Crypto-Jews had to seem as Christian as anyone else. They practised Catholicism and taught it to their children: 'In truth, all Crypto-Jews, before teaching their children their religion, made them good Christians.'[112] The mechanisms, rules, and behaviours of inquisitional officials and their subordinates determined to a large extent the extremely limited ways in which *judaizantes* might retain knowledge of their traditions. In the end, these oppressive practices proved effective in eradicating judaizing practices.

Numerous examples reinforce the picture of increasing assimilation over time, despite the fact that New Spanish New Christians mostly married within their community – they were 96 per cent endogamous[113] – and judaizers insisted that any prospective family member swear an oath to judaize within the marriage.[114] Eva Alexandra Uchmany's observation with respect to many Spanish Crypto-Jews – 'although Christianity as a religion had never convinced them, they were assimilated into the life style of peninsular society'[115] – also holds true for colonial Mexico and Peru. The concept of communal salvation had eroded into a belief in personal salvation.[116] Ironically, Crypto-Jews' sources of Jewish law and custom were mostly Christian: the Edicts of Faith and the works of such theologians and devotional writers as Fray Luis de Granada (1504–88), Fray Pedro de Rivadeneira (1527–1611), and Fray Alejo Villegas (1534–1604).[117] Nevertheless, immigrants from some European communities where Judaism was openly practised, such as Ferrara (Italy), arrived in Mexico despite prohibitions, during the first decades of the seventeenth century, and brought first-hand knowledge of Jewish law with them.[118]

By the mid-seventeenth century, when María Zárate lived in Mexico City, after two and a half centuries of oppression and censorship, the Crypto-Jewish religion had been reduced to a distorted form of messianism adapted from Christianity whose followers firmly believed that the Messiah would be born from among them.[119] Their interest in messianism was natural; as Uchmany puts it, 'because the Crypto-Jews lacked an active present, their historical interest was limited to texts that pointed to a future for them.'[120]

Unlike male Catholics, who needed only to hear Mass to fulfil their religious obligations, and whose literacy rates were low, Jewish men, led by rabbis and other learned men, had to be able to read and discuss the Torah, Talmud, and other texts, and so were almost 100 per cent literate.[121] In Crypto-Jewish life, in contrast, religious practice occurred primarily in the domestic sphere. Women formed the centre of continued Jewish involvement. In general, however, women had little or no access to Jewish liturgy or sacred texts; their information about and enactment of ritual were limited to those areas and roles that had traditionally been female. As Solange Alberrro writes: 'They did not know Hebrew, were deprived of books, of texts and were incapable of sustaining speculation and commentary. Their fierce efforts revolved around the observance of ritual: fasts, ritual baths, precepts relative to foods and sex, death rituals; they transmitted at most some fragments of religious discourse bathed in legend and undermined by uncertainty.'[122] Although Alberro is undoubtedly right in the largest sense, the picture she paints allows for no deviance at all from the rule of female ignorance and passivity: we cannot exclude the possibility that there were at least a few women, especially in the first generations after the establishment of the Inquisition, who questioned or even debated sacred rules.[123] And women's nurturing and homemaking tasks meant that children of both genders were exposed early on to domestic judaizing practices, although of course this did not mean that they understood Judaism as a religion.

Food constitutes one telling example of the continuing tension between assimilation and autonomy for Crypto-Jews. In the Mexican provinces they substituted tortillas for matzohs; when wine was not available for the Kiddush, they substituted chocolate.[124] Alberro expands on the subject of food and its significance for understanding the situation in which judaizers lived: 'Together with products and foods traditionally consumed in the Iberian peninsula, they integrated meats and foods whose American origin could not be doubted, in order to facilitate the observance of the judaizer in New Spain: tortillas, sweet potatoes, squash and pumpkins, chiles, tropical fruits, wild greens, tamales, corn flour drinks, broths and various fried foods, and above all, chocolate, which is at once a drink, food, a sweet, and medication.'[125] Alberro sees the process of adapting to local food as something that accompanied the gradual attenuation of adherence to Jewish dietary and other laws because of the absence of rabbis and scholars, but I would argue that the use of indigenous food products paradoxically allowed Crypto-Jews to continue to identify as Jewish. The substitution of tortillas for matzoh, or of chocolate – itself heavily loaded with religious and cultural symbolism of Christian colonization, proselytizing, and syncretism with indigenous culture in New Spain,[126] and, as Alberro notes, a food, drink, treat, and medicine – for Kiddush wine, and the consumption of vegetables, fruits, and other flora and fauna indigenous to the New World could easily fit into dietary laws because they had not been available on the other side of the Atlantic. This meant that judaizers 'felt' Jewish even when they had little concept of what keeping kosher meant, literally or conceptually.

Mexican Crypto-Jews maintained a strong sense of community. They formed networks to help each other; women, as keepers of the home, were essential to that assistance. Of course, in some periods, they had more need for mutual support than in others, since severity of institutional oppression of judaizers varied. The story of Esperanza Rodríguez, a *mulata* judaizer born in Seville (Spain) in 1574 to a black Guinean slave and New Christian dressmaker, Francisco Rodríguez, amply demonstrates the interlocking connections in the judaizing community. It also illustrates the ease with which even those people forbidden by law – such as New Christians – crossed the Atlantic, as well as the ways in which such transactions of the Atlantic world as slavery affected individual lives. Esperanza Rodríguez married the German sculptor Juan Baptista del

Bosque, who brought her to Guadalajara (Mexico). When he died she became a slave to Catalina Rodríguez, a principal judaizer in that city. Esperanza's two daughters, Juana del Bosque (who married a fugitive Portuguese judaizer) and María del Bosque, were, like their mother, also sentenced as judaizers.[127]

Colonial tribunals varied a great deal. In Cartagena, New Granada (modern Colombia), Beatriz López was one of a small number of people, of whom a very few were women, charged with being a Crypto-Jew. A Spaniard, she was arrested in 1634, accused of whipping a statue of Jesus. Her parents were Portuguese and had been arrested in Lima, along with her husband and brother. In prison for six months, she was released as a result of being judged insane.[128] In Mexico, the numbers were greater and punishment tended to be more severe, although, of a total of about 1,500 cases concerning Crypto-Jews, fewer than one hundred resulted in executions.[129] Because of the 'great conspiracy,' as noted above, harassment of judaizers had increased in the mid-seventeenth century, especially 1634–9 in Peru and 1642–9 in Mexico, to such an extent that afterwards their respective Jewish populations no longer existed as communities.

As mentioned earlier, in New Spain the first wave of persecutions began in 1589, with the arrest of the governor of Nuevo León, Luis de Carvajal the Elder, and members of his family. After ten years of politically motivated trials resulting in the ruin of the Carvajal family, the New Christian community lost its prominence. Then, after decades of quiescence, again for complicated, primarily political reasons, the Inquisition undertook another massive campaign against judaizers in the 1640s, especially during the years 1642–9, by the end of which the Jewish community had been effectively destroyed in Mexico. Of the 380 *judaizantes* about whom inquisitional proceedings were at least begun, 34–7 were burned at the stake, 96–107 were burned as effigies, and an undetermined but high number died of illness, old age, desperation, suicide, or madness while imprisoned.[130]

In sum, by the early seventeenth century in Mexico, the Crypto-Jewish community had very few sources of learning with which to sustain their beliefs and customs. Rabbis and other religious leaders, the Torah and other holy books, and external manifestations such as circumcision, diet, and days of rest were all denied to these people. Paradoxically, the Edicts of Faith, although intended to alert 'good' Christians of possible transgressions, which they had an obligation to report, provided a wealth of information for Crypto-Jews in their description of Jewish customs. Yet it was not enough. Combined with waves of inquisitional persecution and an environment in which one's family, friends, neighbours, business associates, servants, and slaves could report one's transgressions, the practices of *judaizantes* metamorphosed into a distorted facsimile of traditional Judaism. The religion of judaizers became home-based, practised and passed on primarily by women who, because of their confinement to the domestic sphere, could exercise their rituals and credos with relative impunity compared to men. Although María de Zárate was not born into Judaism, she nevertheless followed this pattern to a large extent, especially since her husband had spent seven years of their marriage imprisoned as a judaizer.

Conclusion

Since she was relatively new to the faith, sustained by her relationships with Baltasar de Burgos, her husband, and other (male) members of the Crypto-Jewish community, what we 'hear' of Zárate's domestic life is based primarily on José Sánchez's testimony. The principal women in her life whom we 'meet' are her sister and nieces, all Old Christians. While the relationship with her niece Ana (Sánchez's wife) deteriorates, her sister (Ana's mother) testifies on Zárate's behalf. Still, although she denies her Crypto-Judaism, and continues to protest her innocence throughout the years of her trial, even during torture, and although the final verdict of abjuration *de levi* and reclusion suggest that the inquisitors were not totally convinced by the prosecutor's allegations of her guilt, her close connection to her husband, and possibly the need for financial and social survival, indicate that, after all, there must have been some basis to the accusations.

Useful for illuminating the complexities of life for a particular subset of ordinary people in seventeenth-century Mexico, Zárate's case provides one means of understanding the multicultural, political, and socio-religious currents of colonial society. The Crypto-Jewish community of her time and place has been studied in depth by several scholars. Nevertheless, the ways in which her life collided with the expectations, fears, and hegemonic strategies of both the state and the church demonstrate with unusual clarity the intersections and tensions between individual and society, between (crypto) Jewish and Christian ideologies, and between those with the most access to structural power and those who seized opportunities available to them in ordinary life to achieve personal goals. The struggles among members of the erstwhile Botello-Zárate-Sánchez family enact on a micro-level all these tendencies.

María de Zárate was imbued with the dominant racist ideologies of her time, but she was also caught up in circumstances that stigmatized her in terrifying ways. Her case must be seen as both normal and unusual: while the accusations and the trajectory of the proceedings matched those of many other judaizing cases and mirrored the cultural, historical, religious, and social conflicts built into this particular colonial situation, Zárate's testimony and circumstances provide an uncommon story that arose out of the circumstances of her individual life trajectory.

Notes

I thank Emilie Bergmann, Daniella Koustron, Lisa Vollendorf, and the anonymous readers of the University of Toronto Press for their cogent readings of drafts of this chapter.

1 A 'New Christian' had Muslim or Jewish ancestors. A converse either was a convert or had ancestors who converted to Christianity. In practice, the terms were interchangeable.
2 Lewin entitles his edition of the trial documents *La Inquisición en México. Racismo inquisitorial: El Singular Caso de María de Zárate* (Puebla: J.M. Caijca, Jr, 1971). Hereafter, all page numbers referring to inquisitional records about and from Zárate's case come from this edition. Lewin asserts that Zárate's was the first inquisitional trial in Latin America to benefit from the involvement of an inspector from the Supreme Council: she was allowed the services of a defence attorney and witnesses who testified on her behalf were heard (52). Another first: when the sentence was pronounced, the prosecuting attorney, not believing it to be severe enough, appealed (53).
3 Because, juridically, unconverted Jews no longer lived in Spain, there were no special legal apparatuses to deal with them.
4 Pilar Huerga Criado, 'El problema de la comunidad judeoconversa,' *Historia de la Inquisición en España y América*, vol. 3, Temas y problemas, 2nd ed., Joaquín Pérez Villanueva and Bartolomé Escandell Bonet, eds. (Madrid: Biblioteca de Autores Cristianos, Centro de Estudios Inquisitoriales, 2000), 441–97, 482. All translations from the Spanish are mine, unless otherwise indicated. Spanish versions of quotes from the trial appear in the endnotes.
5 Ibid., 473.
6 Ibid., 495.
7 Juan Martínez Silíceo, of peasant stock and an Old Christian, became archbishop of Toledo in 1546. Basing his position on the claim that *limpieza de*

sangre (purity of blood) was already being practised in Spain by military orders, university colleges, and religious orders, he pushed through a statute of *limpieza* in July 1547 which prohibited New Christians from holding office in the cathedral. The prince (Philip) suspended the statute, and it was not allowed to be enforced for nine years. Henry Kamen, *The Spanish Inquisition: A Historical Revision* (New Haven, Conn.: Yale University Press, 1997), 236–7.

8 Boleslao Lewin, *Los criptojudíos: Un fenómeno religioso y social* (Buenos Aires: Editorial Milá, 1987), 21.

9 Gitlitz, *Secrecy and Deceit*, 14.

10 Lewin, *La inquisición en México*, 21.

11 Ibid., 74–5.

12 Ibid., 33.

13 Alejandro Cañeque, 'Theater of Power: Writing and Representing the *Auto de fe* in Colonial Mexico,' *The Americas*, 52, no. 3 (1996): 321–44, 334, 323, 321.

14 In Lewin's edition, the text of one Psalm is offered (*La inquisición en México*, 51).

15 Ibid., 52.

16 Ibid., 517. Another version of this statement appears on page 284.

17 Ibid., 22.

18 Gretchen Starr-LeBeau, 'Mari Sánchez and Inés González: Conflict and Cooperation among Crypto-Jews,' in Mary E. Giles, ed., *Women in the Inquisition: Spain and the New World* (Baltimore: Johns Hopkins University Press, 1999), 19–41.

19 'Sabía que dicho José era mestizo y había conocido a su madre y sabía quién era, que lo mejor sería echar la muchacha que había parido su hija a una puerta y a la dicha su hija matarla a azotes por aquella bellaquería y al dicho José hacerle dar muchos palos y dar noticia de ello a un oidor o alcalde de corte para que lo echasen a China, para que un perro mestizo como aquél no se casase con su hija y afrentase su linaje' (Lewin, *La inquisición en México*, 259, 518).

20 Being sent to 'China' was a popular lexical means of referring to official punishment at the time, associated with being sent to the Philippines and having to serve in the galleys.

21 Lewin, *La inquisición en México*, 520.

22 Ibid., 521.

23 Ibid., 522.

24 Ibid., 523.

25 Ibid., 524.

26 Ibid., 525.

27 According to standard inquisitional procedures, defendants were required to submit their response to the charges without being told the names of the witnesses who had testified against them.

28 Lewin, *La inquisición en México*, 273.

29 The punishment of seclusion cannot escape a gender analysis. As Lisa Vollendorf pointed out to me in a personal communication, bigamists also received a sentence of seclusion. Nevertheless, given the gender norms of colonial society, the sentence must have carried particular resonance for women. In most of the inquisitional cases of female defendants that I have examined in Mexico and Peru, part of the sentence always included ten years of involuntary service, working in and confined to a hospital. See, for instance, my 'Gendered Crime and Punishment in New Spain: Inquisitional Cases against *ilusas*,' in Félix Alvaro Bolaños and Gustavo Verdesio, eds., *Colonialism Past and Present* (Albany: State University of New York Press, 2001), 151–73.

30 Lewin, *La inquisición en México*, 420.

31 See, for instance, Gretchen Starr-LeBeau, *In the Shadow of the Virgin: Inquisitors, Friars, and Conversos in Guadalupe, Spain* (Princeton, N.J., and Oxford: Princeton University Press, 2003), 181, 184.

32 Lewin, *La inquisición en México*, 244.

33 Ibid., 249–50.

34 Ibid., 250.

35 Ibid., 272.

36 Ibid., 273.

37 Ibid., 278, 280–1, 283.

38 Since the accused were not arrested until the Holy Office had conducted an investigation of the charges and already decided that they were guilty, verdicts of innocence were extremely rare.

39 Lewin, *La inquisición en México*, 285.

40 Ibid., 283.

41 Ibid., 288.

42 Starr-LeBeau, *In the Shadow of the Virgin*, 164.

43 Lewin, *La inquisición en México*, 422. Generally, the accused were put to torture when the judges thought that they were lying, or omitting something, or prevaricating in some other way.

44 Ibid., 426.

45 Ibid., 427, 429. Significantly, the first witness –undoubtedly José Sánchez – testified to another kind of racial slur that he claimed Zárate uttered while criticizing many Catholic saints: 'Decía de San Benito de Palermo que ¿cómo podía ser santo un negro?' (498) (She used to say about Benedict of Palermo that, how could a black man be a saint?).

46 'No lo debo, no lo debo.'

47 Asunción Lavrin, 'Sexuality in Colonial Mexico: A Church Dilemma," in
    Asunción Lavrin, ed., *Sexuality and Marriage in Colonial Latin America* (Lin-
    coln and London: University of Nebraska Press, 1989), 47–95, 5–6.

48 Lewin, *La inquisición en México*, 424.

49 Ibid., 238–9, 242.

50 Ibid., 276, 256.

51 Ibid., 248.

52 Solange Alberro, *Inquisición y sociedad en México, 1571–1700*, 3rd ed. (Mexico
    City: Fondo de Cultura Económica, 1998), 430.

53 Lewin, *La inquisición en México*, 152.

54 Ibid., 154.

55 Ibid., 159.

56 Ibid., 232.

57 Ibid., 283.

58 Ibid., 254.

59 Ibid., 278.

60 Ibid., 226–7.

61 Ibid., 228.

62 Ibid., 252.

63 Ibid., 212, 216, 217, 219, 223.

64 Ibid., 210. As some critics have noted, inquisitional documents frequently
    employed the metaphor of disease to refer to whichever crime is under dis-
    cussion.

65 Ibid., 210–11.

66 Ibid., 211.

67 Ibid., 236.

68 The accusations appear in ibid., 215–17; Zárate's response, 221.

69 Ibid., 217.

70 Ibid., 219.

71 Ibid., 219–21.

72 Ibid., 222–3.

73 Ibid., 213, 230–1.

74 Ibid., 232.

75 Ibid., 214.

76 Ibid., 215.

77 Ibid., 233.

78 Ibid.

79 Ibid., 234.

80 Ibid., 224.

81 Ibid., 234.

82 Ibid., 236.

83 The tribunal in Cartagena, New Granada (now Colombia), was considered more lenient with the few Jews who lived or were brought up on charges there. Also, some scholars have argued that judaizing practices have survived to this day; if that is so, they are remnants of customs, not full-blown cosmologies.

84 Lewin, *Los criptojudíos*, 99.

85 Stephen Haliczer, 'The First Holocaust: The Inquisition and the Converted Jews of Spain and Portugal,' in Stephen Haliczer, ed., *Inquisition and Society in Early Modern Europe* (London and Sydney: Croom Helm, 1987), 7–18, 6. To prove 'purity of blood,' the testimony of twelve witnesses confirmed as Old Christians, preferably employees of the Inquisition, was required. If men were not available, women could testify instead. See Lewin, *Los criptojudíos*, 76.

86 Renée Levine Melammed, *Heretics or Daughters of Israel?: The Crypto-Jewish Women of Castile* (New York: Oxford University Press, 1999), 9.

87 Huerga Criado, 'El problema de la comunidad judeoconversa,' 489.

88 Kamen, *The Spanish Inquisition*, 291, 293.

89 Melammed, *Heretics or Daughters of Israel?* 9.

90 Kamen, *The Spanish Inquisition*, 283.

91 Ibid., 296; Haliczer, 'The First Holocaust,' 14.

92 Huerga Criado, 'El problema de la comunidad judeoconversa,' 495.

93 Markus Schreiber, 'Cristianos nuevos de Madrid ante la Inquisición de Cuenca (1650–1670),' *Historia de la Inquisición en España y América*, vol. 3: Temas y problemas, 2nd ed., Joaquín Pérez Villanueva and Bartolomé Escandell Bonet, eds. (Madrid: Biblioteca de Autores Cristianos, Centro de Estudios Inquisitoriales, 2000), 531–56, 545.

94 Starr-LeBeau, 'Mari Sánchez,' 41.

95 Gitlitz, *Secrecy and Deceit*, 18–19, 99.

96 Lewin, *Los criptojudíos*, 100. Gitlitz points out that many of the affirming aspects of Jewish festival observance were replaced with avoidance: Purim carnival became the Fast of Esther, and Rosh Hashanah and Hanukkah were dropped from the liturgical calendar (*Secrecy and Deceit*, 137).

97 Other favoured destinations were the Low Countries and Turkey.

98 Alberro, *Inquisición y sociedad*, 8–9.

99 Herman Bennett, *Africans in Colonial Mexico: Absolutism, Christianity, and Afro-Creole Consciousness, 1570–1640* (Bloomington and Indianapolis: Indiana University Press, 2003), 53.

100 Alberro, *Inquisición y sociedad*, 172.

101 Solange Alberro, 'Herejes, brujas y beatas: Mujeres ante el tribunal del Santo Oficio de la Inquisición en la Nueva España,' in Carmen Ramos Escandón ed., *Presencia y transparencia: La mujer en la historia de México* (Mexico City: Colegio de México, 1987), 79–94, 85; Alberro, *Inquisición y sociedad*, 185.

102 Gitlitz, *Secrecy and Deceit*, 59.

103 See, for instance, Eva Alexandra Uchmany, *La vida entre el judaísmo y el cristianismo en la Nueva España, 1580–1606* (Mexico City: Archivo General de la Nación, Fondo de Cultura Económica, 1992), 66.

104 Ibid., 70.

105 See, for instance, ibid., 75.

106 Most contemporary scholars concur on this point, but Arnold Wiznitzer, 'Crypto-Jews in Mexico during the Seventeenth Century,' *American Jewish Historical Quarterly*, 51 (1961): 222–68, on the contrary, presents this person as one of the damaging witnesses against Carvajal, a man who colluded with the authorities in getting his cellmate to incriminate himself (200–2). He even calls the monk, Dias, an 'agent-provocateur' (201).

107 Carvajal chose last-minute repentance and conversion to avoid death by fire; he was garroted before being burned at the stake.

108 Uchmany, *La vida entre el judaísmo y el cristianismo*, 55.

109 Lewin, *Los criptojudíos*, 110.

110 Uchmany, *La vida entre el judaísmo y el cristianismo*, 174.

111 Alberro, *Inquisición y sociedad*, 427.

112 Uchmany, *La vida entre el judaísmo y el cristianismo*, 1992), 93.

113 Alberro, *Inquisición y sociedad*, 434.

114 Gitlitz, *Secrecy and Deceit*, 248.

115 Uchmany, *La vida entre el judaísmo y el cristianismo*, 62.

116 Gitlitz, *Secrecy and Deceit*, 100.

117 Lewin, *Los criptojudíos*, 100.

118 Gitlitz, *Secrecy and Deceit*, 54. See, for instance, the case of Ruy Díaz Nieto, studied in detail in Uchmany, *La vida entre el judaísmo y el cristianismo*.

119 In fact, Gitlitz argues that messianism was strongest in Mexico (*Secrecy and Deceit*, 108).

120 Uchmany, *La vida entre el judaísmo y el cristianismo*, 70.

121 Gitlitz, *Secrecy and Deceit*, 14.

122 Alberro, *Inquisición y sociedad*, 429.

123 While no written evidence has thus far been found to support the assertion that early modern women in the Hispanic world secretly studied the Talmud, we should not discard the possibility that some women had access to sacred writings. In medieval France, for instance, the famous Rabbi

Rashi (Rabbi Shlomo ben Yitzchak, 1040–1105) had no sons and three daughters, all of whom married rabbinical scholars. Women in families such as his may have learned the language and texts that their father and husbands studied and discussed daily.

124 Gitlitz, *Secrecy and Deceit*, 57.
125 Alberro, *Inquisición y sociedad*, 429.
126 See, for instance, Electa Arenal, 'Monjas chocolateras: Contextualizaciones agridulces,' in Mabel Moraña and Yolanda Martínez-San Miguel, eds., *Nictímene ... sacrílega: Estudios coloniales en homenaje a Georgina Sabat-Rivers* (Mexico City: Universidad del Claustro de Sor Juana, Instituto Internacional de Literatura Iberoamericana, 2003), 135–55.
127 Gitlitz, *Secrecy and Deceit*, 262. Gitlitz cites as his source Genaro García, *Autos de fe de la Inquisición de México con extractos de sus causas, 1646–48, Documentos inéditos o muy raros para la historia de México 28* (Mexico City: Viuda de Charles Bouret, 1910), 47, 56, 77.
128 Anna María Splendiani, José Sánchez Bohórquez, and Emma Cecilia Luque de Salazar, *Cincuenta años de inquisición en el Tribunal de Cartagena de Indias. 1610–1660*, 4 vols. (Bogotá: Centro Editorial Javieriano CEJA, Instituto Colombiano de Cultura Hispánica, 1997), 171.
129 Gitlitz, *Secrecy and Deceit*, 55.
130 Alberro, *Inquisición y sociedad*, 172. For one perspective on the reasons for the 1642–9 persecutions, as well as a lucid account of relations between Mexican Crypto-Jews and their servants and slaves, see Robert Ferry, 'Don't Drink the Chocolate: Domestic Slavery and the Exigencies of Fasting for Crypto-Jews in Seventeenth-Century Mexico,' *Nuevo Mundo Mundos Nuevos*, 5 (2005), http://nuevomundo.revues.org/documento934.html.

chapter ten

A World of Women and a World of Men? Pueblo Witchcraft in Eighteenth-Century New Mexico

TRACY BROWN

In 1713 Don Lorenzo Coimagea, principal Indian elder of Picuris Pueblo, accused Jerónimo Dirucaca, the native governor of the pueblo, of a number of egregious acts.[1] Coimagea alleged that Dirucaca spoke against the missionary of the pueblo, telling people one day after church that he did not believe anything the priest said but only what his ancestors taught. Dirucaca bragged that he lived in concubinage and no friar or Spanish official had been able to stop him. Finally, he either bewitched or killed a number of people with witchcraft.[2] Both Coimagea and the other elders of the pueblo felt that they were 'unable to speak' while Dirucaca was governor of the pueblo.[3] In fact, Dirucaca made it clear that he had a great deal of power: more than the governor of New Mexico and at least as much as the Spanish king.[4] Based on those allegations, Coimagea insisted that Spanish authorities remove Dirucaca from office.[5]

Two years later, another witchcraft investigation unfolded in dramatic fashion in Santa Fe. In 1715 Spaniard Antonia Luján accused her neighbour, a San Juan Indian woman named Francisca Caza, of bewitching her and making her ill three years earlier.[6] Luján had gone to Caza numerous times for cures, but after she did so in search of a cure to her poverty she suddenly became ill.[7] Luján told investigators that she believed her husband and Caza were having an affair, thus implying that Caza bewitched her out of sexual jealousy.

This chapter explores the gendered use of witchcraft by the Pueblo men and women by comparing 'male-dominated' and 'female-dominated' investigations such as the ones involving Dirucaca and Caza. An analysis of the extant colonial-period Pueblo witchcraft investigations reveals that Pueblo men and women used the power of witchcraft for different reasons and with differing results.

As can be seen in Table 1, six of seven extant cases related to Pueblo witchcraft show that accusations remained within gendered boundaries: men accused men whereas women accused women.[8] In the investigations involving women, the accusers were always Spanish women living in Spanish towns such as Santa Fe and Santa Cruz while the accused parties were Pueblo women. In the men's investigations, the accuser could be either a Spanish or Pueblo male and they lived not in Spanish towns but near the communities in which the accused men resided.

The investigations involving women and witchcraft illustrate that multiracial networks were formed between Spanish and Pueblo women in colonial New Mexico and that such ties frequently broke down because of class and race prejudice. They also give us a glimpse into the intimate lives of women since Spanish women tended to solicit Pueblo witches for help with personal problems such as illness or sexual jealousy. Pueblo women were also known for practising 'economic' witchcraft and, as in the Caza investigation, were sought by Spanish women to locate wealth.[9] Women's practice of witchcraft in colonial New Mexico, therefore, can be described as individualized and interpersonal.

While some cases of male accusers and witches also centred on individual and interpersonal problems, other cases differed from the female experience by taking on a political dimension insofar as Pueblo men used witchcraft to influence political processes in Pueblo communities or to resist Spanish domination.[10] Dirucaca, his accusers complained, not only practised sexual immorality but also used his power to govern Picuris Pueblo in a dictator-like fashion.

Thus, the Caza and Dirucaca investigations reveal that, while both Pueblo men and women were accused of witchcraft in eighteenth-century New Mexico, their cases differed in terms of the physical spaces in which they operated, the targets of their witchcraft, and their prescribed motivations. In exploring the reasons for the gendering of witchcraft in this context, the following ethnohistorical analysis opens up larger questions about Pueblo power dynamics, gender, and community in eighteenth-century New Mexico. When we compare men's and women's practice of witchcraft, it becomes evident that Pueblo men and women sometimes operated in different social spheres in their communities and wielded differing levels of power in those communities.

This analysis fills a gap in our current understanding of colonial New Mexico since analyses of gender issues and witchcraft cases are rare in both the current historiography and the anthropology of Pueblo peoples.[11] Indeed, gender roles in colonial-period Pueblo communities are particularly absent from the literature, probably because the documents

Table 1. Summary of extant Pueblo witchcraft investigations

Name, ethnicity, gender, and residence of accuser and accused	Location of alleged witchcraft	Name, ethnicity, gender, and residence of the bewitched	Date of investigation	Archival designation
Juana de Apodaca of Santa Fe (SF) / Felipa de la Cruz of Tesuque (PF)	Santa Fe (S)	Numerous Spanish women of Santa Fe	1704	Bandelier Papers, reel 2, group 4, #1
Leonore Domínguez of Santa Fe (SF) / 3 San Juan Indias (PF): Catherina Rosa, Angelina Pumazho, Catarina Luján	Santa Cruz de la Cañada (S)	Doña Leonore Domínguez of Santa Fe (SF)	1708	SANM 4: 74–109
Lorenzo Coimagea (PM) / Jerónimo Dirucaca (PM), both of Picuris	Picuris (P)	Numerous Picuris individuals (PM&PF)	1713	SANM 4: 841–84
Antonia Luján (SF) / Francisca Caza (PF), both of Santa Fe	Santa Fe (S)	Antonia Luján and other Spanish women of Santa Fe	1715	SANM 5: 165–83
Francisco Tafoya (PM) / Pedro Munpa (PM), both of San Ildefonso	San Ildefonso (P)	Francisco Tafoya, church 'fiscal' (assistant) (PM); numerous women (PF)	1725	SANM 6: 336–55
Ramón García Jurado of Bernalillo (SM) / Francisco and Lucas Morones of Santa Ana (PM)	Santa Ana (P)	Ramón García Jurado, alcalde mayor (SM)	1732	SANM 6: 977–96
Alonzo Rael (SM) / 4 Isleta Indios (PM&PF): Melchor Trujillo, Juan the *cacique*, and 2 women under Juan's control	Isleta (P)	Numerous Spanish and Pueblo women and men (including a governor and the church cantor) from Isleta and surrounding area	1733	SANM 7: 35–46

S = Spanish; P = Pueblo; F = female; M = male

themselves are largely silent on this issue.[12] Furthermore, the historiography and anthropology of New Mexico seldom contains insight into the daily lives of Pueblo peoples or the functioning of Pueblo communities in the eighteenth century.

The cases examined here contain depositions from Pueblo individuals with an immediacy regarding their experiences and community life that is largely missing from other colonial period sources. On a broader level, the chapter contributes to a growing scholarship on colonial Latin American witchcraft because it illustrates sharp distinctions in the ways that men and women used witchcraft. Such a comparison is lacking in the scholarly literature, in which historians and anthropologists have typically focused upon women's witchcraft as one of the few documented examples of their resistance to state and church power.[13] The value in comparing Pueblo men's and women's witchcraft cases lies not in disproving or critiquing these earlier studies, but in using witchcraft investigations to study the gendered micropolitical functioning of power in indigenous communities.

In a direct sense, then, this chapter contributes to the study of the Atlantic world system. A central premise of the Atlantic Studies paradigm is that 1492 ushered in an era of cultural, political, and economic interchange between European and American peoples. A 'hemispheric community' was the result: one in which 'everyone ... had values which if they were not shared around the Atlantic were certainly reshaped in some way by others living in different parts of the Atlantic basins.'[14] By the time the witchcraft investigations took place in New Mexico, the first chaotic stages of colonization had long since passed, and many indigenous communities were integrated to some degree into Spanish economic, political, and cultural systems. Like many other locales in the Atlantic world, New Mexico sat on one border of this hemispheric community; it was a place in which Spanish and Indian women formed a community. Seen from this perspective, the circulation of ideas concerning healing and sorcery between Spanish and Pueblo peoples in New Mexico was part of the larger circulation of ideas between Old and New Worlds that took place in the Atlantic basin.

A World of Women: Pueblo Witches, Interpersonal Witchcraft, and the Spanish Women of Santa Fe

Antonia Luján and Francisca Caza's case reveals a community network of several women who relied on each other for economic, social, and

emotional support. Luján had approached her neighbour Caza for assistance with various problems in Santa Fe numerous times.[15] According
to Caza, Luján complained to her that she 'was very poor' and that 'she
did not even have a shirt' to wear. Caza therefore offered to make her a
drink of powdered shell mixed in water that, if ingested, would induce
God to 'give her clothes'[16] or help her to find deerskin with which to
purchase clothing.[17] The use of economic witchcraft to find lost objects
or objects of value was common across colonial Latin America.[18] Caza
apparently specialized in this type of witchcraft and profited from her
skills, for, despite her Indian origins, she appeared to be better off mate-
rially than Luján. In offering her assistance in locating wealth, she told
Luján that 'she would be equal to her,' implying that she was wealthier
than Luján.[19] Caza's mother also declared in her testimony to Spanish
officials that she and her daughter were 'rich.'[20]

Luján testified that she refused the powdered drink offered by Caza,
saying to her, 'Look, we Spaniards follow the law of God.'[21] Soon after this refusal, Luján began to experience 'grave pains' over her entire
body. She then concluded she had been bewitched. In Caza's version
of events, Luján never rejected the offer of a cure for poverty. Nor did
Luján insist to Caza that, as a Spaniard, she was a strict follower of the
laws of God and was therefore not interested in using witchcraft to end
her poverty. This, of course, does not mean that Luján did not make
the comment to Caza: since Luján was speaking to Spanish authorities
about unlawful and immoral behaviour, it was in her best interest to try
to distance herself as much as possible from that activity. She did so by
insisting that she had rebuffed Caza and also by emphasizing her strict
adherence to the Catholic faith.[22]

The comment appeared to have served its purpose well, for Spanish authorities did not consider prosecuting Luján even though she admitted
in the same declaration that she had returned to Caza for assistance after
she got sick.[23] In other words, Luján's elite status as a Spanish Catholic
may have protected her from prosecution, while Caza's Indianness made
her vulnerable to it.[24] That Luján was not prosecuted may also have been
because civil authorities were then more interested in pursuing Indian
religious transgressions than the transgressions of the Spanish population. As noted previously, all of the Pueblo witchcraft investigations occurred within the first thirty years or so following the reconquest of New
Mexico.[25] Punishing such transgressions might therefore have been a
matter of 'national security' in the minds of Spanish civil authorities. Fi-

nally, civil authorities may have believed that prosecuting such activities among the Spanish population was the responsibility of the Inquisition, which had restarted its operations in the province in 1706.[26]

Pueblo women's witchcraft was concerned with resolving interpersonal problems between individuals, as this case attests. In Luján's only declaration in the investigation, she simply stated that she became ill after she rebuffed Caza's offer to cure her of her poverty, and thus returned to her some months later for a cure to her sickness. She never explained why she thought she became ill. However, when asked by Spanish officials at the end of her interview if she had anything else to add to the narrative, Luján commented offhandedly that she suspected that Caza was having an affair with her husband.[27] This statement implied that Luján believed Caza made her ill out of sexual jealousy. Caza knew of Luján's suspicions. When Luján asked her to cure her illness, Caza offered to do so by acquiring a special 'herb' from Galisteo. Then, when Caza was unable to procure the 'herb,' Luján got very angry and yelled at her, saying that Caza had cured her in the past but because Caza was now sleeping with Luján's husband, the illness had returned.[28]

Luján's behaviour raises a perplexing question: Why ask the person you suspected had bewitched you to cure you of the resulting illness? Luján could have asked another Pueblo healer for assistance. But, as Laura Lewis asserts in *Hall of Mirrors: Power, Witchcraft, and Caste in Colonial Mexico*, in cases such as this, Spaniards 'continued to have faith … in the Indian healers who were ultimately the very source of their bedevilment.'[29] Luján may have believed, as was common in Latin America as well as Europe, that the bewitcher's permission – if not the bewitcher's actual participation – was required for the cure to be effective. If so, one might argue that Caza had the upper hand in this situation because Luján could not free herself from the harmful spell without Caza's permission.

However, a strong case can be made that it was Luján who had the upper hand. She, unlike Caza, had access to the Spanish justice system, which could investigate her claims and punish her wrongdoer if the investigation resulted in a conviction. That Luján turned Caza over to Spanish civil authorities indicates that she remained unhappy, despite Caza's efforts to cure her of her various ailments. She ultimately resorted to the Spanish system of justice to resolve that unhappiness. Luján thus used state power to 'cure' her dissatisfaction with Caza. In this sense, judicial authority trumped witchcraft in Luján's life as a power that she could employ to manage and resolve her problems.

Caza, on the other hand, lacked such resources; she could not go to Spanish authorities to 'cure' her difficulties with Luján, a woman who may have been her sexual rival[30] or, at the very least, a difficult client and neighbour.[31] Spanish authorities would probably not have been very sympathetic to an Indian sorceress's complaints, especially in the wake of the 1680 revolt and the 1692 reconquest of the province. Thus, Caza had to attempt to resolve her difficulties with Luján outside the realm of Spanish judicial authority by attempting to placate her with offers of cures for her poverty and her illnesses. If this was her strategy, then Caza's attempts to placate Luján via her cures were successful for a time. Luján did not complain to Spanish authorities until three or four years after the poverty cure, which suggests that the two women attempted to work out their differences extrajudicially.[32]

Even if the investigation does not provide a perfect explanation as to why Caza and Luján behaved the way they did, it does reveal that their relationship was strained by fears and accusations of adultery. Class and racial prejudice also made their relationship potentially volatile. Luján's response to Caza's offer to cure her poverty points to these prejudices. Recall that, in rejecting Caza's poverty cure, Luján insisted that 'we the Spanish follow the law of God.' While this comment distanced Luján from the practice of witchcraft, it also had a secondary – and more subtle – meaning and effect. Her insistence that it was *we the Spanish* who followed the law of God implied that Spaniards were a class of people to whom Caza did not belong – no matter how wealthy Caza was, or how Hispanicized. The implied meaning of the comment was that Luján's racial and class superiority would always trump Caza's material wealth as an index of status in Santa Fe.

A strict racial and class hierarchy operated in colonial New Mexican society as it did elsewhere in Latin America.[33] Indian peoples occupied the lowest rung in the racial hierarchy, following mixed-bloods or mestizos. Spaniards – those with pure blood – occupied the top rung.[34] Furthermore, race, religion, and class superiority were tightly wound together. In the ideal colonial order, those people with racial purity (Spaniards) were supposed to be the wealthiest part of the population, living in fine houses with Indian servants. Indians were supposed to be in lowly, subservient occupations. They were not supposed to lift a Spaniard out of poverty or have more wealth than Spaniards. Thus, the situation in which Luján found herself was anomalous. The comment 'we the Spanish follow the law of God' perhaps implies that she had an awareness of this reversal of fortune.

Thus, while the two women appeared to have been on friendly terms, at least on the surface, there were tensions, prejudices, and power inequalities that underwrote their relationship, making it a fragile one. The investigation of their conflict illustrates the ways in which the two women attempted to manage, if not resolve, the tensions inherent in their relationship via the use of witchcraft or the witchcraft accusation. In the end, despite their efforts, the relationship disintegrated in the wake of Luján's witchcraft accusation. The record does not indicate if Caza ever was punished. Her mother, however, was arrested in connection with the case and she died in prison. It is difficult to imagine that Caza and Luján remained on friendly terms after her death. Thus, the investigation reveals the delicate play of power that shaped Spanish and Pueblo women's interpersonal relations. It also reveals the political implications of both the practice of witchcraft and the witchcraft accusation itself: whether intentional or not, this activity appears to have aggravated interracial fault lines that shaped the relationships between Spanish and Pueblo women in colonial New Mexico.[35]

Interracial fault lines were similarly evident in a second female-dominated witchcraft investigation in colonial New Mexico, this time in the Spanish town of Santa Cruz.[36] In 1708 Doña Leonore Domínguez, whose relatively high rank is suggested by the 'doña' attached to her name, accused three San Juan women of bewitching her and making her sick. She explained that one of the San Juan women had chased her in the church of Santa Cruz. When she fell down, her attacker placed a hand on her back 'beside her heart.' Almost immediately she began to experience itching over her entire body, and the sickness had not left her since that day. Domínguez testified that, at the time of the incident, she had assumed that her assailant was trying to steal the buttons off of the cape that she was wearing.[37] The papers from the investigation make it clear that the four women had known each other for quite some time and had an established relationship: one of the San Juan accused, for example, was the goddaughter of Domínguez's brother-in-law, and Domínguez described visiting the San Juan women in their homes prior to the incident.[38] Yet Domínguez was not above believing that the women might attempt to steal from her, revealing, again, the class and race prejudice that circumscribed Pueblo/Spanish relationships in New Mexico.

Later in the investigation, Domínguez decided that the woman had touched her because her daughter was having an affair with Domínguez's husband and wanted to bewitch her for that reason. However, the San Juan woman who touched Domínguez in the Santa Cruz church

explained to Spanish officials that she merely wanted to understand
Domínguez's illness so she could cure it. Moreover, she wanted to prevent Domínguez from making a witchcraft accusation against her daughter since, as she explained, 'Spanish women say that witchcraft is the
cause of whatever sickness they have.'[39] Thus, the behaviour of the accused was similar in both the Caza and Domínguez investigations: both
Caza and the San Juan women sought to cure their accusers to prevent
them from denouncing them (or their loved ones) to Spanish authorities. The behaviour of the accusers in both investigations was also similar:
Domínguez, like Luján, used the Spanish system of justice to investigate
her concerns. Finally, the Domínguez investigation is similar to the Lu-
ján/Caza investigation in that the problem that triggered it was sexual
jealousy. These findings suggest that witchcraft accusations were a way
for women to punish their sexual rivals.

Class and racial prejudice clearly shaped the interpersonal relations
between accused and accuser in the third and final extant female-dominated witchcraft investigation. In 1704 the Spaniard Juana de Apodaca
accused Felipa de la Cruz of Tesuque of saying that she was a witch. Apodaca complained that, since the accusation hurt her reputation as an
upstanding citizen ('vecina') of Santa Fe, she wished to have the matter
investigated to clear her good name. Apodaca also wanted de la Cruz
to be punished, to make her an example to other 'insolent, coarse people.'[40] The investigation revealed that de la Cruz had attempted to cure
a woman who had been bewitched by Apodaca.[41] The accused told the
sick woman that Apodaca was her bewitcher.[42] The news apparently got
back to Apodaca, for de la Cruz claimed that after each subsequent attempt to cure the sick woman, Apodaca 'hurt' her.[43] The news also, apparently, caused Apodaca to go to the Spanish authorities to turn de la
Cruz in.

The interpersonal problem between the accused and accuser in this
investigation was not, as in the other cases, sexual jealousy but fear of
being labelled a witch because of the taint of Indianness that close proximity to witchcraft implied. Apodaca's desire to clear her name and her
belief that the Tesuque woman was 'coarse' point to a concern over race
and class purity as being one – if not the main – reason that motivated
Apodaca to make the initial complaint. Therefore, this investigation –
like those involving Caza and Domínguez – provides evidence of the racial tensions that existed between Pueblo and Spaniard in Spanish towns
like Santa Fe. It also reveals that Apodaca, like the other Spanish female

accusers profiled here, used the Spanish system of justice to resolve her difficulties with the accused. However, de la Cruz, like the other accused, did not complain to Spanish authorities about her difficulties with her accuser. It does not even appear that she attempted to placate her accuser, as did the other Pueblo accused.

In the three witchcraft cases involving women exclusively, the accuser was Spanish, the accused Pueblo. These investigations are not, then, about Pueblo community politics, or even interpersonal relations between Pueblo women in their home communities; they are instead about the types of relations that Pueblo and Spanish women formed in Spanish towns, and the role that witchcraft and the Spanish justice system played in shaping, managing, and resolving problems in those relationships. The investigations reveal an interracial 'female network' built upon the exchange of ideas and practices concerning curing and sorcery. Such networks were common in the Atlantic world, as scholars of gender and religion in this region have demonstrated. What makes this particular network interesting is that the transmission of ideas and practices highlighted by the investigations did not flow from Spanish to Pueblo, but rather from Pueblo to Spanish: Spanish women turned to, and paid, Pueblo women for their knowledge of curing, healing, and sorcery. These ideas and practices survived, even with Spanish church and state efforts to wipe them out. Perhaps one reason for their survival was that Spanish women, like the ones discussed above, found them so useful. This surely encouraged Pueblo women to maintain such practices.

The investigations also highlight the variety of problems that developed in the relationships between Spanish and Pueblo women (sexual jealousy, anger at being labelled a witch, discomfort over a lack of material wealth). However, the resolutions to these various tensions were strikingly similar in the cases: the three Spanish accusers eventually turned to Spanish authorities to resolve difficulties they were having with Pueblo sorceresses, curers, and healers. In turn, the Pueblo women attempted to manage their difficulties with their accusers outside the official realm of justice through the use of more witchcraft. While the accused were not punished formally, they suffered because of the accusations. In Caza's case, her house was searched and her mother was put into prison, where she died. The other accused also faced interrogations and imprisonments. Thus, the costs of practising an interpersonal form of witchcraft could greatly outweigh the benefits for Pueblo women if this practice led to accusations and a trial.

A World of Men: Pueblo Sorcerers and 'Politicized' Witchcraft

As noted at the beginning of this chapter, in 1713 Don Lorenzo Co-imagea, principal Indian of Picuris Pueblo, accused Jerónimo Dirucaca, governor of the pueblo, of egregious acts. In levelling his accusations, Coimagea made it clear that Dirucaca saw himself as all-powerful and was ruling the pueblo without taking the leaders' opinions into consideration.[44] According to witnesses, Dirucaca had stated that 'only the king [of Spain] was equal to him.'[45] According to another witness, he told people that 'the law of the Spanish was one and what he told them was another.'[46] The leadership of the pueblo had been unable to do anything about Dirucaca's behaviour 'for he was like God.'[47] Thus, Dirucaca disregarded the ruling elite of his own pueblo and also the power of the Spanish state. He allegedly ignored the teachings of the church, too, and insisted that others do the same, saying that it was not necessary for the Picuris people to obey the law of God or avoid committing idolatry, concubinage, or witchcraft.

That Dirucaca could live in concubinage without punishment and could kill with sorcery was evidence of his power. In declaration after declaration, Picuris Pueblo residents stressed Dirucaca's deviant morals and tyranny. They charged him with sleeping with a mother and at least one of her daughters (who was his 'intended' and with whom he lived outside the state of matrimony).[48] They also claimed that he used witchcraft to bend women to his will, or to kill them if they refused his advances.[49] Because Dirucaca had done these things, Coimagea insisted that he be removed from his post as governor while the Spanish authorities investigated the matter.[50] In his initial accusation, Coimagea explained that he had been called to speak out in the name of all the elders.[51] The fact that Pueblo elders turned to Spanish authorities to help them in ousting Dirucaca from power is an indication of just how much a problem he was for the community. The elders had made previous attempts to remove Dirucaca from his office, which, according to the testimony given, he had held since the time of the governorship of Diego de Vargas (1691–7 and 1703–4). He could not be removed by traditional means so Pueblo elders had to turn to an outside authority.

Although little is known about the inner workings of pueblo politics, parallels between the charges levelled against Dirucaca and those directed at the 'killer shamans' of lowland South America suggest that Dirucaca's alleged witchcraft was grounded in a political process of native origin. According to anthropologist Frank Salomon, shamanism was a 'stateless form of political process' that flourished in peripheral regions of empire in the colonial period because Spanish authority remained ineffective there.[52] By this, Salomon means that 'intragroup conflicts were commonly expressed and political preeminence established through a complex of magical aggression and cure [in] numerous South American lowland societies lacking states or hereditary chieftaincies.'[53] In other words, in small-scale, non-state societies, witchcraft could become politicized in the sense that a person might use it to establish political power, to influence and control a local community, and both to stoke and to resolve community-wide conflict. Spanish authorities sought to prosecute such activity, not only because they perceived it to be immoral, but also because they understood that it might be transformed into a form of politics that could escape their control. Yet, in Salomon's view, the witchcraft investigations legitimized shamanistic power by making plain that the Spanish 'fully believed in the accused man's magical efficacy.'[54]

One killer shaman profiled by Salomon was accused of committing twenty-four acts of magical aggression against immigrant cattle ranchers and community members for not paying him enough respect.[55] This killer shaman had formerly been an officer of the local government, but he claimed that people hostile to him – including those friendly with the immigrant cattle ranchers – had arranged his removal from office.[56] There was, in other words, a community divide between the immigrants, or newcomers, versus the old guard, represented by this killer shaman. While in office, the shaman used sorcery to prevent outsiders from settling in his community or from influencing its political and social life. According to witnesses, eighteen of the twenty-four bewitched individuals eventually died. On account of these deaths, he was removed from office.

Certainly there are similarities between this case and Dirucaca's activities at Picuris Pueblo. Dirucaca, too, saw himself as all-powerful – to the point that other leaders were silenced in their efforts to participate in the political processes of their community. While the investigation does not contain evidence of Dirucaca threatening political rivals with sorcery, it is possible to imagine that those who were 'silenced' by him experienced the threat of this particular form of retaliation. Both the lowland region of South America and New Mexico were peripheral regions of empire, where Spanish power was weak. This resulted in traditional

political processes, which were dominated by men who used witchcraft
to bolster their political power, existing long after colonization.

In the case of the killer shaman described by Salomon, the community
members attributed their survival to the efforts of a 'curing shaman' who
worked diligently to detect the accused man's sorcery. This curing shaman equated the troubled social order under the accused to an '"illness"
that could be "cured."'[57] In New Mexico, Picuris Pueblo, too, could be
said to have been 'diseased' under Dirucaca – a community elder who
used his office as governor for both sanctioned and unsanctioned ends,
even killing those who did not bend to his will. Getting rid of Dirucaca
could thus be equated to ridding Picuris Pueblo of a disease, of 'curing'
the community of its social ills.

Dirucaca was not the only Pueblo man to practise politicized sorcery
– sorcery used to influence local political processes or to resist Spanish
domination. Several other extant, male-dominated witchcraft investigations reveal Pueblo sorcerers behaving in similar ways. Two investigations revealed sorcerers who used their power to encourage resistance
to Spanish domination. Pedro Munpa bewitched the fiscal[58] of the San
Ildefonso mission in 1725. After the fiscal had whipped Munpa for conducting witchcraft, he reported that Munpa bewitched him in revenge.
When the fiscal asked Munpa for a 'pardon,' Munpa told him that he
must deny 'the law of the Spanish' and acknowledge that 'only he [Mun-
pa] was God' and that it was only through Munpa that 'the creatures
lived, the plants grew, and rain fell.'[59] Munpa himself told the authorities
that he had bewitched or killed numerous other people.[60]

In another investigation, Pueblo Francisco Morones made Ramón
García Jurado, the Spanish *alcalde* of Santa Ana, sick with witchcraft in
1732.[61] The reason for the bewitching is never provided in the documentation. However, García Jurado's status as the local representative
of the Spanish judicial system meant that, even if Morones's motives for
the attack were personal, his aggression nonetheless entailed an affront
to the authority of the state. A third extant investigation featured two
Pueblo sorcerers who used their power to influence political processes
in their home communities. In 1733 a Pueblo sorcerer, Melchor Trujillo,
bewitched the governor of Isleta Pueblo, the lead singer of the mission,
and numerous other Spanish and Pueblo individuals living in or near
the pueblo. The lead singer subsequently died. That the targets of Trujillo's sorcery were officials of Isleta's government and the local mission
suggests that he was attempting to influence the political life of his home

pueblo. The same investigation revealed that Juan, the *cacique* (the head of Pueblo governement as known to Spaniards) of Isleta, controlled a coterie of witches (some of them women) who bewitched people at his command.[62] Several declarants explained that, if they had bewitched anybody, 'it was by order of Juan the cacique ... and it was he who governed them.'[63] The implication is that Juan, like Dirucaca, used his office for unsanctioned ends, forcing those who followed him to commit sorcery against anyone who challenged his power at Isleta.

Thus, male-dominated witchcraft cases provide evidence of the types of politico-religious disputes that occurred within Pueblo towns in the colonial period because the accused was always a resident of a Pueblo community. If the accuser – the target of the Pueblo sorcerer – was not Pueblo, he either worked in a Pueblo town (as in the case of García Jurado) or lived near one (Melchor Trujillo was denounced by several Spanish men living near Isleta). The purpose of their sorcery was, again, often political: to influence political processes in home communities (as in the cases of Dirucaca, Trujillo, and Juan the cacique) or to undermine state or church power (Dirucaca, Morones, and Munpa). Many of the investigations revealed that the actions of the accused had caused community-wide discord: a number of the sorcerers had bewitched whole groups of people and/or used sorcery to influence governmental functioning in their home pueblos. Finally, the investigations suggest that the affected communities were so desperate to rid themselves of these Pueblo sorcerers that they turned to the Spanish system of justice – an outside, colonizing, authority – to accomplish this task.

Conclusion

The witchcraft investigations profiled in this chapter reveal gender-related patterns in alleged Pueblo witchcraft. The first pattern relates to the location of witchcraft: Pueblo women operated in Spanish communities while Pueblo men operated in Pueblo communities. Second, women denounced women, while men denounced men. Finally, the purpose of witchcraft usage varied across gender lines: Pueblo women practised interpersonal witchcraft whereas Pueblo men practised both interpersonal and politicized forms of witchcraft.

These three patterns point to several aspects of Pueblo social life in the colonial context. The location and target of Pueblo women's activity – outside Pueblo communities and among non-Pueblo women – suggests that women's power was circumscribed *within* Pueblo communities in ways that male power was not. In other words, Pueblo women operated in a narrower political sphere in their home communities than did Pueblo men. This caused some Pueblo women to seek out other arenas to exercise power and to gain prestige. They learned to move between Spanish and Pueblo society, sometimes even choosing to live in Santa Fe (as in the case of Caza). That some of the Pueblo women accused of witchcraft were fluent in Spanish also provides evidence of this social fluidity.[64]

In contrast, the patterns suggest that the accused Pueblo men were more firmly rooted in their home communities. Many of the accused did not speak Spanish. They required interpreters when interrogated[65] and they targeted Spaniards who either lived near or worked in their home communities. Pueblo sorcerers bewitched those Spanish men who happened to enter Pueblo home communities, which represented the Pueblo men's primary realm of power. Pueblo men did not move with ease between Spanish and Pueblo communities because they had no need to do so. The men's lack of social fluidity is evidenced in their lack of ability to speak Spanish. Unlike Pueblo women, they already had a social arena in their home communities in which to exercise power, and so they did not need to seek that power elsewhere.

Ethnohistorical reconstruction of how power functioned historically in Pueblo communities helps to explain the existence of the patterns concerning the location, targets, and purpose of Pueblo men's and women's witchcraft. Peter Whiteley's assertions about the Hopi are applicable here: the 'politico-ritual arena' was 'articulated almost entirely by … men.'[66] Women did not hold formal office and were not prominent in this sphere of Pueblo society, although they could and did informally make their opinions known concerning the governance of their communities. An early observer of Pueblo life in the post-contact period noted that, even though they did not hold formal office, Pueblo women were always consulted about political issues before a decision was made.[67] They thus retained an informal voice in the political affairs of each pueblo.

Lack of access to formal offices does not mean that Pueblo women were not prominent in other arenas of life, such as in the household or in the economy. The household, in fact, was the centre of economic life in Pueblo communities and for this reason cannot be designated as a private realm (as opposed to a public realm of politics). Women had

jurisdiction over the home and, especially within the matrilineal communities in the western pueblos, exercised authority and ownership over
that space. 'The female household head was custodian of its rights and
possessions: the agricultural plots their husbands and sons worked, all
the food and seed reserves, and the sacred fetishes and ritual objects of
the clan.'[68] Given Pueblo women's prominence in this important arena
of Pueblo life, it is incorrect to conclude that women completely lacked
power or influence in Pueblo communities, or that they were relegated
to a private, hidden realm of society. However, it still is true that they
held only informal roles in the politico-ritual arena.

Regarding the politico-ritual arena, which men dominated, Whiteley
argues that 'the primary source of power lies in esoteric ritual knowledge.'[69] The Pueblo men who knew the 'essential core of rites' were the
most politically powerful in Pueblo society. Pueblo peoples thus used
access to secret knowledge rather than property ownership as their index of social and political status.[70] Given the nature of power in Pueblo
society, it makes sense that one would find Pueblo men – but not Pueblo
women – using politicized witchcraft in Pueblo communities in the extant colonial documentation. Because they did not hold formal office,
Pueblo women had no platform from which to wield community-wide
power in order to influence political processes or to lead broad-scale
resistance against state and church authorities in Pueblo communities.
Even if they gained access to secret knowledge, their possession of this
knowledge was unauthorized and therefore could not be manipulated
or used in a public forum. It is clear that some esoteric knowledge concerning Pueblo ritual and healing practices was passed down within families and thus leaked to Pueblo women: Caza, for example, explained
in her declaration to Spanish authorities that she had learned her skills
from her father.[71] Nonetheless, men ultimately were the keepers of sacred knowledge in Pueblo communities; they were the ones who held
political power publicly. This dynamic motivated woman to find realms
in which they could be more fully empowered, such as with Spanish
women and in Spanish towns like Santa Fe.

As J. Andrew Darling has explained with regard to witchcraft in the
American southwest, 'accusations of witchcraft ... tended to be directed
toward males of higher social standing or reputation.'[72] This is different
from witchcraft prosecution in Europe, where the accused were typically
poor women because they were believed to be spiritually weak and possessed of a voracious sexual appetite, which, in combination with their

alleged inferior moral status, motivated them to seek power by making pacts with the devil.[73] However, among the Pueblo, those most often accused of witchcraft were powerful men who were thought to possess a large cache of secret knowledge which they used for evil purposes.[74]

In light of the small amount of documentation that exists, it is difficult to generalize about the implications of sorcery, curing, and healing for Pueblo social life. It might be that Pueblo men practised interpersonal forms of sorcery in Spanish towns, for Spanish clients of both genders, but evidence supporting this is not extant in the New Mexico documentary record. Moreover, Pueblo women may have practised interpersonal forms of sorcery, curing, or healing in Pueblo communities for clients of both genders. Yet, given the distribution of political power and the gendered nature of access to that power within Pueblo communities, it would be difficult to locate examples of women practising politicized – in the sense of influencing governmental processes – forms of witchcraft. In other words, the patterns found in the witchcraft cases would likely hold true even if more Pueblo witchcraft investigations could be located. The point, then, is not to argue that no female witches existed in Pueblo communities, only that they were typically witches of a different sort than Pueblo men because of their social standing in their communities. They lived, to a degree, in separate worlds.

A comparison of female and male witchcraft highlights the ways in which power and religion were gendered in the indigenous worlds of the Atlantic world. How can we know the degree to which native women were empowered by the use of witchcraft – a common argument in the colonial Latin American witchcraft historiography – if we do not also look at the ways in which other groups (in this case, native men) used witchcraft? We can, of course, see that women were witches, and sometimes powerful ones, but to produce a nuanced, more complex, understanding of the nature of their power, it is necessary to take into consideration other individuals who also used witchcraft in their daily lives.

Notes

I dedicate this essay to Kiyomi Kutsuzawa, who taught me a great deal about gender analysis.

 1 The case is located at Spanish Archives of New Mexico, 4: 841–84; all subsequent citations to this collection are cited as SANM, followed by reel and

frame number. Throughout the chapter, the capitalized word 'Pueblo' refers to the Pueblo people; the lower-case 'pueblo' is a Spanish term for village or town. Picuris Pueblo refers both to a people and a place.

2 The terms 'witch' and 'witchcraft' ('hechicera/o' and 'hechicería' in the New Mexican documentation) are of obvious Spanish extraction. In colonial Latin America, they were used to 'described state-censured sets of moral violations ranging from unorthodox religious behavior, including trysts and pacts with the devil, to popular forms of sorcery or "black magic"': Laura Lewis, *Hall of Mirrors: Power, Witchcraft, and Caste in Colonial Mexico* (Durham, N.C.: Duke University Press, 2003), 6. The terms were applied to a range of Pueblo practices involving curing, healing, illness, and other acts perceived to be 'idolatrous' or immoral. Once labelled in such a way, these practices were criminalized and prosecuted by Spanish authorities. This history makes it difficult to write about Pueblo healing, curing, and ritual practices today, since any terminology one might choose to describe these activities has pejorative connotations to greater or lesser degrees. Accordingly, I have employed terms that have less of a pejorative connotation. I use 'sorcerer' to mean someone who exercised their powers for evil or to bewitch or kill, 'curer' to designate someone who used their powers to cure illnesses or other difficulties, and 'witchcraft' to refer to the group of activities embodied in sorcery and curing.

3 SANM, 4: 841–2.

4 Ibid., 860.

5 Ibid., 842.

6 SANM, 5: 165–83.

7 Ibid., 176.

8 There are seven extant Pueblo witchcraft investigations from the northern Rio Grande (the Albuquerque and Santa Fe region). These investigations all occurred between 1704 and 1733. Why all of the investigations occurred within the first thirty years or so of the eighteenth century is a difficult question to answer. Part of it has to do with the governors of New Mexico during that period: several of them were intent upon prosecuting Pueblo witchcraft and idolatry. For example, three out of the seven investigations occurred during the tenure of Governor Chacón (1707–12). Feeling that Franciscan friars had become lax in their duties to extirpate idolatry and sacrilege in the colony, he took matters into his own hands, prosecuting witchcraft and other forms of idolatry: Jim Norris, *After "The Year Eighty": The Demise of Franciscan Power in Spanish New Mexico* (Albuquerque: University of New Mexico Press, 2000), 56–7. Other reasons for the dating of the investigations might include document loss and destruction as well as poor record keeping dur-

ing times of intense nomadic raiding (which occurred during various periods throughout the century).

9· The term 'economic' witchcraft comes from Martha Few, *Women Who Live
Evil Lives: Gender, Religion and the Politics of Power in Colonial Guatemala* (Austin: University of Texas Press, 2002), 104.

10 My use of the terms 'interpersonal' and 'politicized' witchcraft should not
be read to mean that Pueblo women exclusively inhabited a private realm
that had little political impact in, or implications for, their communities,
while men inhabited a public realm of power and politics. I do argue that
Pueblo men and women sometimes (but not always) inhabited different
social arenas; however, what I do *not* argue is that these social arenas can be
correlated with a public/private split. Interpersonal relationships had political implications, and Pueblo women's activities did not occur in a private,
hidden sphere.

11 The only other publication to deal extensively with colonial-period witchcraft in New Mexico is Malcolm Ebright and Rick Hendricks, *The Witches of
Abiquiu: The Governor, the Priest, the Genízaro Indians, and the Devil* (Albuquerque: University of New Mexico Press, 2006). This book analyses a mid-cen-
tury witchcraft investigation at Abiquiu, a *genízaro* (detribalized, non-Pueblo
Indian) town located northwest of Santa Fe.

12 For sources that provide insight into Pueblo gender roles and interrelations
in the contemporary period, see Alice Schlegel, 'Sexual Antagonism among
the Sexually Egalitarian Hopi,' *Ethos*, 7 (1979): 124–41, and M. Jane Young,
'Women, Reproduction and Religion in Western Puebloan Society,' *Journal
of American Folklore*, 100 (1987): 436–45. For a broad summary of Pueblo
women's roles in the early colonial period that relies solely on published
English translations of documents, see Cheryl Foote and Sandra Schackel,
'Indian Women of New Mexico 1535–1680,' in J. Jensen and D. Miller, eds.,
New Mexico Women: Intercultural Perspectives (Albuquerque: University of
New Mexico Press, 1986), 17–40. There are quite a few articles that analyse
colonial New Mexican women's wills. Pueblo women's wills are studied in
Angelina F. Veyna, '"It Is My Last Wish That …": A Look at Colonial Nuevo
Mexicanas through Their Testaments,' in Adela de la Torre and Beatriz
Pesquera, eds., *Building with Our Hands: New Directions in Chicana Studies*
(Berkeley: University of California Press, 1993), 91–109. Also see Deena
J. González, 'Juanotilla of Cochiti, Vecina and Coyota Nuevomexicanas in
the Eighteenth Century,' in Richard Etulain, ed., *New Mexican Lives: Profiles
and Historical Stories* (Albuquerque: University of New Mexico Press, 2002),
78–105.

13 For case studies that argue that women did use witchcraft to thwart state

or church power in colonial Latin America, see Ruth Behar, 'Sex and Sin, Witchcraft and the Devil in Late-Colonial Mexico,' *American Ethnologist*, 14 (1987): 35–55; Ruth Behar, 'The Visions of a Guachichil Witch in 1599: A Window on the Subjugation of Mexico's Hunter-Gatherers,' *Ethnohistory*, 34, no. 2 (1987): 115–38; Ruth Behar, 'Sexual Witchcraft, Colonialism, and Women's Powers: Views from the Mexican Inquisition,' in Asunción Lavrin, ed., *Sexuality and Marriage in Colonial Latin America* (Lincoln: University of Nebraska Press, 1989), 178–206; and Irene Silverblatt, *Moon, Sun, and Witches: Gender Ideologies and Class in Inca and Colonial Peru* (Princeton, N.J.: Princeton University Press, 1987), especially chapters 9 and 10. I am unaware of research from colonial Latin America that attempts to compare women's and men's witchcraft. However, the criticism that studies of European witchcraft have been too heavily focused upon women alone has been made. See, for example, William Monter, 'Toads and Eucharists: The Male Witches of Normandy, 1564–1660,' *French Historical Studies*, 20, no. 4 (1997): 563–95.

14 Bernard Bailyn, *Atlantic History: Concept and Contours* (Cambridge, Mass.: Harvard University Press, 2005), 59.
15 SANM, 5: 176.
16 Ibid., 170.
17 Ibid., 175.
18 Few argues that 'economic sorcery' – or the location of wealth for clients – was a big business in colonial Guatemala (*Women Who Live Evil Lives*, 104).
19 SANM, 5: 166.
20 Ibid., 173. Few points out that female sorcerers were not necessarily poor and therefore the Inquisition did not necessarily always target poor women, as has been generally argued (*Women Who Live Evil Lives*, 103).
21 SANM, 5: 166.
22 As Lewis correctly argues, 'proximity to Spanishness and Spaniards indicated conformity to proper colonial values. Conversely, proximity to Indians and Indianness marked a potent and nonconforming supernaturalism' (*Hall of Mirrors*, 4).
23 SANM, 5: 166–7.
24 Elite status protected women from prosecution in other areas of Latin America as well (Few, *Women Who Live Evil Lives*, 114).
25 The Pueblo Revolt occurred in 1680, driving all Spaniards from the province. They returned to re-establish the Spanish colony in New Mexico in 1692.
26 In eighteenth-century New Mexico, witchcraft cases involving Indian peoples were handled by civil authorities – not the Inquisition. Indian peoples

were formally removed from the jurisdiction of the Inquisition throughout
Latin America in 1571; after that time, control over the prosecution of Indian sacrilege fell to the bishop's or archbishop's office: Richard Greenleaf,
'The Inquisition and the Indians of New Spain: A Study in Jurisdictional
Confusion,' *The Americas*, 22, no. 2 (1965): 138–66, 141. With no vicar-
general to oversee such cases in New Mexico, and little interest on the part
of Franciscan missionaries in pursuing them, civil power began to assume
jurisdiction over witchcraft as early as 1708: Richard Greenleaf, 'The Inquisition in Eighteenth-Century New Mexico,' *New Mexico Historical Review*, 60,
no. 1 (1985): 29–60, 34. Governors' assistants, such as the *alcaldes mayores*,
handled the investigative work themselves; governors then read the resulting papers and made decisions regarding the guilt, innocence, and/or
punishment of the accused. These investigations did not mimic inquisitorial procedure, as they might in other areas of Latin America; nor did they
focus on the same sorts of issues as the New Mexican Inquisition. The latter
institution typically prosecuted cases of bigamy, sexual morality, and heresy
among the Spanish and mixed-blood population of New Mexico. Pueblo
peoples were typically prosecuted by civil authorities for sorcery and curing:
ibid., 34.

27 SANM, 5: 167.

28 Ibid., 176.

29 Lewis, *Hall of Mirrors*, 160.

30 Caza denied having an affair with Luján's husband: SANM, 5: 172.

31 According to Caza, Luján called her a 'perra hechicera' (lousy witch) when
   she told her she could not procure the herb from Galisteo to cure her. She
   also threw a shoe through Caza's mother's window because she advised Caza
   to stay away from her. SANM, 5: 176.

32 Gaps between the time of the witchcraft and the accusation are common,
   indicating that many accused and accusers attempted to work things out in
   this manner. See Few, *Women Who Live Evil Lives*, 110.

33 Ramón Gutiérrez, *When Jesus Came, the Corn Mothers Went Away: Marriage,
   Sexuality, and Power in New Mexico, 1500–1846* (Stanford, Calif.: Stanford
   University Press, 1991), 194. Douglas Cope argues that, in Mexico City, only
   black slaves were below Indians in status: *The Limits of Racial Domination:
   Plebeian Society in Colonial Mexico City, 1660–1720* (Madison: University of
   Wisconsin Press, 1994), 24. There were few people of African descent in
   New Mexico during the colonial period, leaving Indian peoples to occupy
   the lowest rung in the racial hierarchy. Lewis, in *Hall of Mirrors*, discusses
   times in which the racial order in Mexico was upended (199n.120).

34 Gutiérrez, *When Jesus Came*, 194.

35 The use of the term 'fault lines' in this context comes from Few, *Women Who Live Evil Lives*, 110.
36 SANM, 4: 74–109. Ralph Twitchell includes an English translation of this document – one that is faithful to the original – in *The Spanish Archives of New Mexico* (Cedar Rapids, Iowa: Torch Press, 1914), 142–63.
37 Ibid., 79.
38 Ibid., 85, 91–2.
39 Ibid., 106.
40 'Claim made by Juana de Apodaca against Miguel Garatuza and Felipa de la Cruz,' Bandelier Collection of Copies of Documents Relative to the History of New Mexico and Arizona, microfilm edition on deposit at Perkins Library, Duke University, reel 2, group 4, no. 1, 1 .
41 Ibid., 5.
42 Ibid., 5.
43 Ibid., 6.
44 Ibid., 841–2.
45 Ibid., 860.
46 Ibid., 856.
47 Ibid.
48 Ibid., 843.
49 Ibid., 855.
50 Ibid., 842.
51 Ibid., 855.
52 Salomon, 'Shamanism and Politics in Late-Colonial Ecuador,' *American Ethnologist*, 10, no. 3 (1983): 413–28, 414.
53 Ibid., 413.
54 Ibid., 422.
55 Ibid., 418.
56 Ibid.
57 Ibid., 419.
58 Pueblo assistant to the resident missionary.
59 The case is located at SANM, 6: 336–55. Quote is from frame 337.
60 Ibid., 347.
61 The case is located at SANM, 6: 977–96. This is not an actual witchcraft investigation but consists of documents concerning Ramón García Jurado's attempts to get his son and several other men out of jail. These men had helped to whip and then arrest Francisco Morones in an attempt to get him to confess to bewitching García Jurado – which he did do, as a result of the physical punishment.
62 The case is located at SANM, 7: 35–46.

63 Ibid., 46.

64 Caza is described in the documentation as an 'India Ladina,' which meant
    an Indian person who was very Hispanicized in appearance and could speak
    the Spanish language (SANM, 5: 166). This is not surprising, given that she
    lived in Santa Fe. Spanish authorities describe two of the three San Juan
    Indias accused by Doña Leonore Domínguez (Catarina Rosa and Catarina
    Luján) as being ladinas who were fluent in Spanish (SANM, 4: 84–5). Felipa
    de la Cruz, the accused in Apodaca's investigation, is described by authori-
    ties as speaking Spanish very well (Bandelier Papers, reel 2, group 4, no.1,
    19).

65 Jerónimo Dirucaca used an interpreter for his declaration (SANM, 4: 858),
    as did Pedro Munpa (SANM, 6: 346) and Juan the cacique (SANM, 7: 39).
    There is no indication that Francisco Morones used an interpreter, and
    Melchor Trujillo's declaration is not extant. None of these is described as
    ladino; and Juan the cacique had to reassure Spanish authorities that he was
    capable of being sworn properly, which leads me to believe that authorities
    were unsure of his ability to understand the judicial proceeding that was to
    follow.

66 Peter Whiteley, 'The Interpretation of Politics: A Hopi Conundrum,' *Man*,
    22 (1987): 696–714, 699. What Whiteley writes concerning power in Hopi
    society is true for Pueblo society in general. See, for example, Elizabeth
    Brandt, 'The Role of Secrecy in a Pueblo Society,' in T.C. Blackburn, ed.,
    *Flowers in the Wind: Papers on Ritual, Myth and Symbolism in California and the
    Southwest* (Socorro, N.M.: Ballena Press, 1977), 11–28.

67 Foote and Schackel, 'Indian Women of New Mexico 1535–1680,' 30.

68 Gutiérrez, *When Jesus Came*, 15.

69 Whiteley, 'Hopi Conundrum,' 703.

70 Ibid., 703.

71 SANM, 5: 181. According to Darling, 'witch power' was acquired via inheri-
    tance or parental teachings. It might also be acquired by 'an exchange of
    goods or contractual obligations' between a sorcerer and trainee. 'Mass In-
    humation and the Execution of Witches in the American Southwest,' *Ameri-
    can Anthropologist*, 100, no. 3 (1999): 732–52, 734.

72 Ibid., 743. According to Darling, this pattern continued well into the nine-
    teenth century. Ibid., 746.

73 Richard Golden, 'Satan in Europe: The Geography of the Witch Hunts,'
    in Brian P. Levack, ed., *New Perspectives on Witchcraft, Magic, and Demonology:
    Witchcraft in Continental Europe* (New York: Routledge, 2001), 2–33, 5.

74 Whitely, 'Hopi Conundrum,' 705.

chapter eleven

The Maidens, the Monks, and Their Mothers: Patriarchal Authority and Holy Vows in Colonial Lima, 1650–1715

BIANCA PREMO

In late March 1681, the summer in Lima was ending and so too were the adolescent dreams of fourteen-year-old María Teresa Saénz. She stood in the candle-lit cathedral, in front of her relieved parents, and longed to run away. What she really wanted for her life was to enter a convent and become a nun, but instead she was exchanging marriage vows with a young man of her mother's choosing.[1] Two decades before and ten blocks north of the church where María Teresa took her long walk down the aisle, Juan de Chavarre stood in the doorway to the Convento de Magdalena and dreamed of escape. His life, too, had changed dramatically at the age of fourteen. Like María Teresa, Juan wanted to escape – not from marriage, but from a monastery. Juan hated being a Dominican friar, but his mother repeatedly sent word that if he tried to leave the order, she would poison him or send him off as a soldier to a *presidio* in Chile.[2]

Throughout the Catholic regions of the Atlantic world, taking a sacramental vow could be a moment of intense intergenerational struggle. Upper-class families in France or Italy might erupt in loud, even violent, contests over whether a maiden daughter would be married off or would enter a convent, whether a younger brother would don a monastic robe or would run the family's estate. Historians of Europe, most writing within the vein of national history, have shown that contests between adults and children over vocations often dramatized larger political histories of power struggles between the aristocracy, the Catholic Church, and absolutist states.[3] Thus, these were more than mere personal squabbles. Just as Joan Scott has shown that political history is often enacted on the field of gender, these studies reveal how it was also enacted within families and between generations.[4]

In the capital city of Spanish colonial South America, things were hardly different. In many ways, Lima's ecclesiastical courts, and the contests over generational rights and vocations staged within them, provide one more theatre in the larger drama of early modern church and state relations. But the colonial character of Lima mattered. Although Lima's population was not proportionally representative of the vice-royalty in terms of caste, the capital city was a showcase for the region's ethnic diversity. From its founding in 1542, the capital city became a destination for a small (by Andean standards) population of rural indigenous migrants, Spanish immigrants, and African slaves, as well as the birthplace of the descendants of earlier arrivals and an ever-growing population of mixed-race peoples. While Spanish colonial laws and social practices imposed rigid juridical and social distinctions between individuals based on wealth, occupation, lineage, and colour, the ways in which Lima's inhabitants interacted in their daily lives – even the way they reared their children, an issue critical for this chapter – drew these diverse castes and classes together into intimate bonds.[5] By the end of the seventeenth century, elite inhabitants of the capital city had begun to fret over this proximity among castes, and initiated concerted efforts to insulate their families and institutions from a growing population of non-whites.[6]

If Lima was a colonial crucible in terms of race, it was also, in many ways, a city of women. By 1700, women had come statistically to dominate the population, comprising 58 per cent of Lima's inhabitants.[7] A staggering 20 per cent of these women lived in all-female religious institutions headed by mother superiors, abbesses, and headmistresses, where they enjoyed a certain degree of autonomy from everyday domination by men.[8] Even in private residences, women headed and ran their own households, often presiding over large numbers of occupants of all ages and castes. According to my sample of a 1700 city census, women headed one-quarter of the city's households, a figure consonant with Latin America women's historical tendency to live independently of men.[9]

The city in which María and Juan lived, then, was in many ways a typically 'European' city, in which Catholic Church officials adjudicating intergenerational conflict balanced classical theological ideas about marriage and profession with concerns about Rome and the throne. It was also an intensely colonial place, where elites struggled to preserve caste and where a large proportion of women lived independently of men. Intergenerational conflicts over sacramental vows in Lima both shaped and were shaped by this mix of European and colonial influences that were a hallmark of the Atlantic world.

This chapter examines over 150 annulment suits from the period 1650–1715 filed by litigants who claimed that elders had forced them into unwanted vocations and marriages. Given the number of Lima's women who lived independently of men, and given the proximity between castes in everyday life, ecclesiastical lawsuits based on intergenerational conflict took on a unique character: many of the elder litigants blamed for forcing children into unwanted vows were not their fathers. Therefore, rather than focus mainly on the reasons that elders forced children into vocations, I instead seek to show how colonial inhabitants embroiled in these annulment suits confronted the contradictions between legal norms concerning male right established in Europe and the exigencies of living in a colonial society where diverse adults, and a great number of single women, held authority over children. When they aired their conflicts over holy vows in the church tribunals of the city, children, elders, lawyers, and judges openly debated the meaning of patriarchal authority over children, providing for us important theoretical lessons about the interaction between the lived colonial experience and metropolitan religious and secular discourses on gender.

The overlap between male right and elder right appeared seamless in written Spanish law, and in the royal courts of Lima during the period there was little dispute that men held ultimate rights over children. Secular law codes directly related *patria potestad*, or the civil legal authority fathers possessed over their minor children, to the authority of the Spanish king over his subjects.[10] As a result, secular judges saw it as their responsibility to protect fathers' economic and political power over their offspring – and over minors of age in general – in all but the rarest of circumstances. Royal judges in colonial Lima appointed only male guardians to children whose fathers had died, even when the children's mothers were living. It was nearly unheard of for judges in royal courts to admit cases over child custody or guardianship in which women were the principal litigants.[11]

Thus, gender right and elder authority served as complementary fields of political power in the secular courts. In general, legal authority over children had a male face. But in the city's households – and in its ecclesiastical courts – authority was a more flexible concept. There, in fact, existed a disjuncture between the ideal functioning of patriarchal authority codified in Spanish civil law and the city's reliance on women to produce offspring to maintain its population. Many of the adults who raised children in the capital of vice-regal Peru were not ideal-typical patriarchs. Instead, they were mothers, non-white servants, slave women, and other adults unrelated to children by kinship –in other words, individuals whose own rights and authority were bridled by the colonial legal system. According to my sample of the 1700 census of the city, only 2 per cent of all of the city's households contained children but no women, whereas 54 per cent of households claimed children but no men.[12] What is more, even the most stereotypical of colonial households – homes where a strong, white patriarch resided – were intensely diverse, serving as both familial hearths and sites of labour for slaves, servants, artisans, apprentices, and wet nurses. In practice, multiple strata of adult authority coexisted and sometimes overlapped inside the city's homes.

As a result, the lived generational order could complicate colonial ideologies of rule founded on patriarchal principles. When intergenerational conflict over holy vows brought the inhabitants of Lima into the church courts, litigants and defendants confronted the disjuncture between the ideal functioning of patriarchal authority and the more complex reality that colonial inhabitants lived every day.

Before delving into the evidence from colonial Lima, it seems appropriate to reflect briefly on the heuristic and theoretical value of 'patriarchy,' especially given the well-known scholarly controversy that has surrounded the concept in the last two decades. Feminist historians influenced by historical semiotics, including Joan Scott, have dismissed patriarchy as a concept that is ultimately meaningless, for it is too often portrayed as a changeless, cultureless phenomenon. In turn, other feminist historians have criticized gender scholars for abandoning the study of ordinary women and for replacing the question of what we know about women, men, and power with the epistemological question of how we know about gender in the past.[13]

While most feminist scholars in the field of Latin American history have taken the 'gender turn' along with Scott, they generally have sidestepped the debate surrounding the value of the concept of patriarchy.[14] That is, they have done so until very recently, when Kimberly Gauderman took Latin American historians to task for assuming patriarchy to be universal and blindly importing a concept drawn from absolutist European states to describe women's status in Spanish America's colonial era. In her study of Ecuador, Gauderman contends that women's legal rights within Spanish colonial law would be 'incomprehensible' in a patriarchal framework.[15]

Yet such a position assumes that the 'status of women' in Spanish colonial law and society was itself somehow fixed and unchanging, and that it developed in total isolation from broader European practices and norms. By exploring intergenerational conflict over marriage and monastery oaths from an Atlantic frame of reference, it becomes clear that patriarchal authority in colonial Lima was a mutable, conditional, and potentially combustible concept. This authority derived from the laws of European kings and popes, but it was practised in a way that often departed from the principles of male right enshrined in codes and canons. What is more, ordinary litigants debated and shaped its meaning every day in the city's church courts.

Prescription: Laws and Legal Opinion on Elder Right

Mothers' authority over children is an area of Spanish colonial legal history that has proved somewhat vexing for modern historians.[16] This is, I believe, because Spanish civil law avoided discussing maternal right except indirectly, while legal experts and intellectuals considered the matter more fully. Their injunctions against women's full participation in colonial public life have led some historians to claim that 'women and children were always minors under the tutelage of a senior male' and 'married women were legally minors.'[17] It is indisputable that Spanish law placed women under the protective and restrictive supervision of male relatives or court-appointed attorneys, who represented them in public transactions and whose authority theoretically would trump their own in family and public matters. Strictly speaking, women were not 'minors,' whether they were married or not. Despite men's tutelage of women in legal transactions, in certain instances women could manage their own assets, possess property if not usufruct, and even represent their elderly male relatives in court.[18] A husband's governance of his wife did share so much in common with his other powers that *potestad* came to be used in reference to marital relations. Juan Machado de Chávez y Mendoza, a bishop of Quito who wrote a treatise on canon and civil law in the seventeenth century, interpreted a husband's power as a kind of *potestad*. Yet he qualified his own usage of the term by claiming that 'this *potestad* is not like that over a slave, and [a husband] should not treat [a wife] as such, but as a companion and sister in his cares and life.'[19]

Despite the colonial practice of referring to all patriarchal authority – whether generational or gendered – as *potestad*, the distinction between different types of authority was crucial. As wives, women occupied a position within the household hierarchy that was legally distinct from that of minors of age and other dependants. And, as mothers, they sometimes could wield authority over their children and control their property.

When they did so, it simply was not classified in civil law as *potestad*.[20] For, as the *Siete Partidas* defined it, *patria potestad* was 'the power that fathers had over their children,' and 'the mother [does not] claim children in her power, even if they are legitimate.'[21]Women could not hold this authority because it was more than simply a right endowed by biology or generation; *patria potestad* was rooted in the management of finances and proprietary control. If a woman performed these functions for a minor, she was required to obtain the permission of a judge in order to do so. In short, women's authority over their children existed, but it was always contingent on the approval of a patriarch, whether public or private. ·

But, of course, the ideal functioning of relations between colonial Spanish American adults and children was not prescribed only in civil law, and secular courts were not the only institutions that mediated intergenerational relations. Colonials referred to the Catholic Church as 'our Holy Mother' and considered the institution an integral member of the family of political society. They marked the passage of hours by the church's bells, days by its saints, and time in their own lives by its sacraments, from baptism to the last rites. They also sought justice in its tribunals, turning to church magistrates to mediate disputes involving sacraments or conflicts with those who enjoyed ecclesiastical immunity.

Although lawyers from the Real Audiencia, or the royal high court, often represented Lima's minors of age before church tribunals, canon rather than civil law theoretically governed ecclesiastical legal proceedings. Canon law endowed priests with the power to reach deeply into the everyday lives of colonials, particularly in terms of regulating sexuality and marriage. Young children whose parents battled in annulment and other marital separation proceedings might find their futures resting squarely in the hands of church officials, especially when divorcing wives were placed 'on deposit' in private homes or institutions during the course of trials and wished to retain custody of children.[22] And often it was the very *fact* of children – that they had been conceived during a marriage at all – that ecclesiastical judges considered as critical for their judicial decisions. But the particulars concerning the obligations of fathers and mothers or details about children's lives typically did not deeply concern church authorities, who instead were intently focused on the relations between the adults involved.[23] Their goal was to keep parents married and living 'the married life' (*la vida maridable*) in order to protect the sacrament of matrimony by bringing extramarital affairs to a quick end and shepherding wandering spouses back to the hearth.[24]

Ecclesiastical judges displayed keener interest in generational matters when children had reached adolescence and prepared to 'take state' as adults in the colonial world. Several recent studies have exposed the multiple dimensions of parental authority in colonial Spanish America by examining *disensos*, or objections parents and other elders registered in order to halt their children's marriages.[25] As Patricia Seed has argued, until the Spanish monarch Charles III issued a watershed 1776 decree requiring parental consent for marriage, the church held jurisdiction over conflicts regarding marriage choice.[26] Buttressed by the doctrine of the Council of Trent (1545–63) on the sanctity of individual free will, church officials in Spanish America guarded children's rights to follow a religious vocation or choose a spouse, even against the protests of parents and other elders. In ruling on cases involving elder-child conflict over marriage, the church figured as a patriarchal legal entity that stood above both father and king in issues associated with youths' sacramental rites of passage.

There is scant record of parents rejecting their children's marriage choices in seventeenth-century Lima.[27] These cases simply may have been lost from the archdiocese archive, but their absence also may reflect a local tradition in Lima. *Limeños* (Lima's inhabitants) had long defended children's free will in marriage as a matter of local, customary law. At the end of the sixteenth century, elite inhabitants of the city responded to the monarch's attempt to impose an Aragonese version of civil law concerning parents' right to disinherit daughters for marrying against their wishes by stating that 'the custom used in this Kingdom [is that] those born here, men as well as women, marry whom they fancy without their parents' licence.'[28]

Even so, the customary recognition of Limeños' right to marry whom they 'fancied' did not mean that Lima's elders refrained from arranging marriages or from placing children in monastic houses in order to promote their families' economic and social standing.[29] Indeed, the elite in Lima had, by the end of the seventeenth century, become particularly concerned with the growing population of mixed-race inhabitants in the city, many of whom adopted the manners and practices of the 'Spanish' upper classes and who entered their religious institutions or married their sons and daughters.

Thus, elders' frequent intervention in children's life choices, often carried out to preserve family reputation or prevent downward mobility, clashed with the church's stance on free will, driving many of the city inhabitants into ecclesiastical courts. In the seventeenth century, church authorities often arbitrated cases that betrayed contentious interactions

between elders and children surrounding the decision to marry or enter
a regular order as a priest or nun. But children, not parents, were the
plaintiffs in these suits. Petitioners requested release from sacramental
vows taken when litigants were adolescents or young adults, often because they claimed they had professed marriage or holy orders under
duress from their elders. Litigants in these cases utilized a canonical condemnation of elder force to annul their vows and change the direction
of their lives. Yet children in Lima commonly protested the actions of elders only *after* they had complied with adults' wishes by becoming priests
and nuns or husbands and wives.

Spain possessed a long history of civil and ecclesiastical prohibitions
against forcing children to take sacramental vows.[30] Among the categories of force that could vitiate vows, the fear of authority, termed 'reverential fear' *(el miedo reverencial)* came to assume a privileged place during
the Middle Ages.[31] For fear to be 'reverential,' the person inflicting force
was required to be a hierarchal superior acting against a subordinate,
and the fear was to derive from an individual's natural dependence on
those who compelled them to take vows. Litigants in seventeenth-century Lima often described the nature of this kind of fear in the same way it
had been articulated by Pope Alexander III in the twelfth century: '*metus
qui posset in virum constantem,*' or the 'fear that would befall a constant
(steadfast, unshakable) male.'[32]

The concept of *miedo reverencial* had developed over centuries in a
lurching, piecemeal way and had never crystallized into a formal pro-
nouncement on who held the authority to inspire such trepidation. Most
Spanish medieval laws aimed to curb the power of princes, lords, and
seducers who compelled young people to marry or enter monastic institutions, rather than to curtail the power of parents.[33] At the Council
of Trent, which anathematized the use of force in all sacramental vows,
canonists separated the issue of seduction from instances where women
were compelled to enter convents.[34] But the council's decrees referred
to reverential fear only in its chapter on vows of profession to the regular orders, vaguely describing it as 'inflicted by a person vested with the
authority to do so.'[35] The respected sixteenth-century Spanish canon-
ist Tomás Sánchez pondered the issue in the post-Tridentine context,
and counted grandfathers, legal guardians, masters, patrons, and male
heads of households who were not fathers among those who could inspire reverential fear.[36] Yet his inclusion of men other than fathers as
valid authority figures was not completely accepted in Lima, either by
local moralists or by many defence attorneys in the ecclesiastical court

system.[37] Therefore, seventeenth-century jurists who wished to settle the matter of who was capable of inculcating the kind of terror that could nullify sacramental vows could not reliably base arguments on clear canonical pronouncements or popular theological treatises.

Neither did jurists find the question of who held sufficient authority to inspire reverential fear settled in Spanish civil law, which more pointedly favoured father's rights over children than did canon law. Secular laws denounced parents who forced daughters to marry against their will but permitted fathers to disinherit daughters who defied their parents' wishes in marrying.[38] In practice, then, it was difficult for colonials to balance laws protecting children from arranged marriages with those that provided fathers the right to use disinheritance to dissuade daughters from marrying spouses they deemed unacceptable. To reconcile this civil legal morass with the Tridentine doctrinal protection of children's free will would be delicate work.

Practice: Elder Right in the Courts

The complexity surrounding these civil and canon laws was more than an intellectual puzzle for scholars and moralists; it was a pressing issue for ordinary families in seventeenth-century Lima. Frequently, city inhabitants filed annulment suits arguing that they had taken sacramental vows as minors afflicted with reverential fear. In their petitions, these litigants accused a wide variety of elders of having forced them into marriage or monasteries, and in effect asked judges to determine whether the authority of adults other than fathers could vitiate vows.

In such cases, gender was particularly problematic for the church judges, who saw it as their responsibility to protect free will in sacramental vows. Throughout the seventeenth century, ecclesiastical judges read the petitions of litigants such as Josef Torres de Picón, who testified that, at the age of sixteen, he entered a Dominican monastery in Lima under the influence of his mother, who had treated him with 'a great deal of subjection' and for whom he 'possessed a lot of respect and fear' 'because she had imposed it upon me since I was of few years [of age.]'[39] Judges then turned their attention to the objections of defendants and their lawyers like the attorney who flatly stated that a woman 'is not one of those people who can incite fear,' since women were 'very weak and pusillanimous.'[40] Thus, litigants presented judges with the vexing problem of whether women, who were divested of *patria potestad* in civil law, held sufficient authority to inspire reverential fear in children.

In turn, gender also patterned the profile of litigants. Women and girls – most of whom bore the honorific title 'doña'– requested marital annulments at a rate between three and four times that of males through the period. Of 64 marital- annulment suits that involved issues of age and elder force in colonial Lima, only 9 per cent were male-initiated.[41] The tendency of women to initiate suits is also apparent in colonial Spanish American cases of *divorcio*, or the permanent separation of spouses who could never remarry. Noting this gendered disparity in his study of marriage in colonial Lima, historian Bernard Lavallé conjectures that men in colonial Lima took advantage of strategies other than litigation, such as abandonment, travel, and adultery, which allowed them to cope with unhappy marriages.[42] The female profile of litigants in marital suits also derived from the cultural dictates of masculine honour – or public esteem based on men's independence from the intervention of other men in their affairs, as well as on class and racial standing. Male honour proved a disincentive for many men to admit marital problems in the ecclesiastical court system. To illustrate, we need only to consider that, of a total of 927 surviving divorce cases, a mere seven petitions for divorce in colonial Lima were brought forward by men who could be identified as 'Spanish' (*españoles*), and only one of these was a member of the high elite of Lima's society.[43]

On the other hand, in annulments of religious professions, priests sued to trade their monastic existences for lives in the secular world far more often than did nuns.[44] In the records of the Dominicans and Franciscans, two major male monastic orders of the city, eighty-six petitions to annul vows of profession survive for the seventeenth century, whereas fewer than ten cases involving nuns remain in Lima's archives. In just under half of the priests' cases (forty), the grounds for annulment were reverential fear and elder force. Though these priests tended to be much older than the female litigants who sought marital annulments, all litigants had been under the age of twenty-five when they entered the orders, and a sizeable number (nine) of these cases were based on claims that those taking vows were younger than the age required to enter religious life. Still others explicitly referred to their youth as a factor that mitigated their free will when professing.

Whether young brides or priests instigated the suits, litigants accused a wide range of adults of forcing them to take sacramental vows. Especially in marriage- annulment cases, fear of fathers was rarely at issue. More often than not, female litigants blamed mothers or other elders who raised or financially supported them for pushing them into life de-

cisions. In over half the accusations of reverential fear in marriage annulments (57.8 per cent), litigants accused female elders of perpetrating
force, and mothers (as opposed to female guardians) were said to have
been solely responsible for inflicting reverential fear on their children
in no less than thirty of sixty-four suits. In contrast, litigants in marital-
annulment petitions named male elders as accessories in perpetrating
force in 32 per cent of suits, and named men as the sole perpetrators of
force in only six cases.

More frequently than young brides, priests accused male guardians
of using force and inspiring fear. Fathers were accused of acting alone
in perpetrating force against their sons in 22.5 per cent of *nulidades de
votos*. And in 62.5 per cent of the cases examined, priests named men as
one of the aggressors forcing them into the monastery, though many of
these men acted in concert with women. These figures suggest that male
elders might take a more active interest in the futures of male children,
whereas women were more concerned about the marriages of female
children. Nonetheless, most priests named women as the primary cul-
pable parties, and they often indicated that their mothers or other elders
had placed them in monasteries as a form of punishment for dallying
too long in taking on adult responsibilities. Juan de Espinoza, for one,
accused his mother of forcing him to take holy vows because she had
grown frustrated at his lack of concern for his studies. 'Look what you
have done,' he recalled her shouting. 'Now you will have no choice but
to continue your studies, because you are going to be a priest.'[45]

It is difficult to ascertain how accused women came to occupy the central position of authority over these youths. Some of the women were
widows, a few were women whose husbands were absent on voyages, and
still others seemed simply to have been unmarried. But, regardless of
how they came be single, for many of these women it was the financial
hardships associated with raising children alone that drove them to force
their children into marriages and professions. One single mother admitted that she had arranged her daughter's marriage to a suitor who
owned four thousand pesos in cash and real estate in the Plaza de Guadalupe. She compelled her daughter to marry because this suitor was
willing to take her daughter's hand even though the mother could not
afford a dowry.[46] Widow Doña María Francisca de Córdova even confessed that she had threatened to kill her daughter, Viviana, for refusing
to marry Juan Francisco de Boroqués, because, 'finding herself poor and
encumbered with many children, without anything to sustain them, she
had given [the suitor] her word' that Viviana would become his wife.[47]

Some single and widowed women married off their daughters perhaps
to garner a dowry, and many simply wanted to relieve themselves of a
mouth to feed. Some of the mothers who placed their adolescent sons
in monasteries were hoping for the same. Widow Luisa Moço admitted
she had used physical violence when placing her son in the Convento
Grande of Santo Domingo, because, 'being so poor that I had to wash
clothes with my own hands, I obliged him to be reduced to this state to
be relieved of this work.'[48]

Although single mothers often admitted that financial hardship had
compelled them to force their children to 'take state,' this was not the
sole reason that adults pushed children into monasteries and marriages.
Even wealthy married women living with husbands figured as principal
antagonists in the tales of reverential fear litigants told in ecclesiastical
court. In the seven marital-annulment cases in which litigants accused
both parents of pressuring them, most reported that their mothers took
the lead in making threats or meting out physical punishment. Such was
the situation of Doña María Teresa de Sáenz, whose mother meted out a
series of threats to force the girl to marry the suitor she had chosen. Only
when her threats failed to sway María Teresa did she seek her husband's
intervention as a last resort. In other instances, fathers attempted to dis-
engage from conflicts over marriage altogether, making it appear that
such matters were a primarily female concern. Doña María Francisca
de Báldez recalled how she went to her father for protection when her
mother attempted to force her to marry. Her father rebuffed her, she
said, telling her that 'he did not want to insert himself in a single thing
and that my mother would do as she wished and what seemed right to
her.'[49]

Litigants described filial obedience to both mothers and fathers by
suffusing notions of protection and subjugation into a single condition.
While they often began their testimony by describing their upbringing
with terms such as 'seclusion' (*recogimiento*), 'protection' (*amparo*), and
'shelter' (*abrigo*), they also referred to being raised under the 'dominion,' 'power,' and 'subjugation' of elders. For example, Doña Gerónima
de Piñeda de Santillán merged both descriptions of adult authority in
her opening statement: 'Say I, the past year 1635, being the age more or
less of twenty, and being under the subjection and shelter (*amparo*) of
... my parents ...'[50] According to litigants' testimony, women's authority
over children, just like men's authority, qualified as an authority based
on might rather than simply the ability to protect their children. Doña
Aldosa de Nuñes de Paredes explained in her petition that she was so 'af-

flicted' under the 'dominion and power' of her mother that she agreed to marry a man of her mother's choosing.[51]

As we have seen, a mother's authority was tacitly recognized in Spanish civil law as a kind of accessory authority over children, subsumed under the *patria potestad* of fathers. Thus, the expressions concerning mothers' authority should not be too surprising. But it is certainly striking that litigants in the ecclesiastical courts of Lima would use the term *potestad* – a concept generally reserved for the authority of fathers and kings and which was expressly denied to women – to refer to a mother's power.

Doña Juana de Herencia began her marriage-annulment case by describing herself as living under the *potestad* of her mother. Because she claimed to have been only eleven years old when she exchanged nuptials with her husband, and hence was under the canonical age for females to marry, her attorney compiled a questionnaire to be used for interviewing witnesses about Juana's age at marriage. He also set out to interrogate witnesses about the nature of her mother's authority. The second question he put to witnesses was 'if [the witnesses] know that, being under the *patria potestad* of Doña Ysabel de Vera, her mother, and being a girl of the mentioned age, her mother wanted her to marry Gabriel de Santillán, and that Doña Juana denounced [the marriage].'[52]

There seems to have been no correlation between Doña Isabela's social class and the fact that her mother was said to have possessed *patria potestad*. Even plebeian litigants who did not use the honorific 'doña' might refer to a mother's power by employing the term.[53] Crucially, however, litigants and lawyers reserved the term *potestad* for women who raised children without the presence or financial support of fathers or other male elders. Furthermore, the term appears only in marital-annulment suits brought forward by female litigants: no husband or priest ever referred to his mother's authority as *potestad*. Therefore, it was only in the absence of men that mothers' authority might become equivalent to masculine generational authority. That the prototype of adult authority was masculine was clear when Doña Ysabel de Miranda y Almeida levelled an accusation of force against her mother, whose actions she described as *varonil*, or 'manly.'[54]

Even such a restricted interpretation of women's power over children as *potestad* faced systemic opposition in the ecclesiastical court system. The task of church attorneys (*promotores fiscales*) and lawyers of the monastic orders (*promotores* or *procuradores*) was to block annulments in order to protect the indissolubility of sacramental vows. Given that litigants often accused adults other than fathers of force, these legal agents frequently attempted to win their cases by vehemently rejecting the implication that women held sufficient authority over their children to inspire reverential fear.

Church and monastic attorneys contended that no one other than fathers was capable of inspiring the degree of reverential fear necessary to invalidate marriages or religious professions. This was the key argument the Dominicans' lawyer put forward in the case of Gerónimo Solis, who had claimed that his mother had forced him into a monastery during his father's absence from the city. The procurador general of Santo Domingo maintained that, in order to invalidate vows, force 'had to [originate] from a person to whom the litigant is subject, and not just anyone but a superior like a father or judge or someone else of this quality.'[55]

Beyond arguing that women did not qualify as superiors, church and monastic attorneys also contended that women were too kind, or alternately too capricious, to elicit the kind of fear in children that could be classified as reverential. 'Experience demonstrates,' stated one monastic defence lawyer, 'that mothers are benevolent with children.'[56] Another *promotore fiscale* warned church judges against entertaining any claim to reverential fear that involved nuns accusing female elders, since ruling in women's favour would produce a tidal wave of annulment suits. Angelina del Niño brought suit to shed the habit she claimed her aunt had forced her to take in the Convento del Prado. The church attorney claimed that an aunt's authority was 'ineffective with respect to the fact that women do not have the violence, authority, or maturity [*mayoría*] that would cause the fear that would befall a constant man.' He went on to caution the judge that, were he to rule in favour of Angelina, 'it would open the door to unrest in the other convents,' because, since women 'believe anything, they will be persuaded of their defect of their [vows as] novitiates.'[57]

Even though the nature of women's authority over children ignited a special controversy in the church court system, litigants continued to accuse women, as well as a wide variety of elders who were not their parents, of forcing them to the altar or into the monastery. Parents and stepparents made up the majority of elders accused of forcing children into marriage or monasteries, but several litigants accused other adults who had raised or supported them, such as brothers, uncles, aunts, patrons, slave masters, and even priests.

Slave children fell subject to the authority of adults other than their parents by virtue of their very condition, yet the doctrine of free will theoretically extended to slaves as well as to free individuals. Spanish

American slave owners who either prevented their slaves from marrying or forced them into matrimony could be challenged before church authorities, although not always successfully.[58] In one successful case, the eleven-year-old slave Gertrudis de Jesús won her suit against the Jesuits who owned her when the priests compelled her to marry another slave. The judge dissolved Gertrudis's marriage in part because of her youth at the time of marriage (she was a month away from reaching the age of twelve) and in part because she recounted how on her wedding night she fled to sleep with her mother instead of in her new husband's bed.[59]

Gertrudis succeeded in annulling her marriage because her youth and failure to consummate the marriage diluted the strength of the vows she had taken. In cases such as hers, church attorneys could not argue that masters did not qualify as authority figures capable of inspiring reverential fear. Such an argument would have seemed illogical given masters' recognized authority over slaves, and since canonical prohibitions against force had long aimed at limiting the power of 'lords.' For free litigants, it was imperative to prove that their respect for and subordination to adults other than their parents was based on the debt of filial obedience they had incurred in their childhood homes.

Thus, litigants and their lawyers often stressed that they considered the adults who raised them to be 'fathers' or 'mothers.' Because Doña Leonor de Arebulo had been raised in the home of her brother, her lawyer contended that 'she respected him as a father, and thus had no way of refusing' his insistence that she marry Pedro Hurtado de Calmasseda.[60] The lawyer for Doña María de Arriaga pointed out that his client, who after birth was abandoned at the city's foundling home, had 'known no other mother' than Doña María de Bera, the woman who took her in as an infant. He therefore asserted that the fear this woman provoked when using violence to coerce his client to marry was sufficient to qualify as 'reverential.'[61] When a priest who had been raised in the same home as orphan Ynés de Rivera was interviewed for her marriage-annulment suit, he described how their guardian, scribe Juan Márquez de Toledo, had called Inés 'daughter' and how she had referred to him as 'father.'[62] These descriptions of the relations between children and adults breathe life into the patterns of childrearing found in other kinds of sources, such as city censuses and notary contracts. Children in colonial Lima were often raised outside biological families, and the time non-kin adults and children spent living together inspired filial feelings in children and endowed adults with parental prerogatives regardless of blood relations.

Church and monastic attorneys, ever vigilant to defend fathers as the sole individuals who exerted the kind of power that could incite reverential fear, refuted the accusations against these other adults just as they did accusations against mothers. Even the power of the priest Josef Martínez, who had raised Francisco de Córdova from infancy in his cell in the monastery of Santo Domingo, did not meet the procurator's criteria for an adult capable of filling a youth with fearful reverence. Francisco explained that he 'had lived on [the priest's] expenses and was subjected to him, seeing as how I had neither father nor mother in this city,' and witnesses corroborated that the fear and respect he held for Martínez was the same as if the priest had been his father. The attorney of the Dominican order protested that Josef's fear of the priest was 'in vain' since the priest was 'not one of the persons who, in conformity with law, can induce the just fear that would annul an action of this nature.' Nonetheless, the vicar of the archbishopric ruled on the case and declared Josef's profession invalid.[63]

As in the above instance, church and monastic lawyers frequently fought a losing battle in annulment suits. In the twenty-nine suits to annul monastic vows that contain judicial decisions, judges declared religious professions invalid fifteen times. In six of these cases, women acted alone in perpetrating force, and in three more both parents acted together. Church judges granted annulments in an even greater number of marriage suits. Judges' verdicts in favour of plaintiffs account for twenty-one of the twenty-eight cases involving reverential fear, and in fifteen of these twenty-one cases litigants had accused female elders of exerting force.

Verdicts in the unsuccessful marriage-annulment suits reveal that, rather than hinging on the relationship between the adult accused of using force and the litigant, judges' decisions pivoted primarily on the church's protection of sex as a procreative act. When it could be proved that the marriage had been freely consummated or when children had been conceived from the unions, judges flatly turned down petitioners' requests.[64] Litigants would win their suits only as long as litigants had not engaged in the procreative act that could make them parents themselves.

In sum, the Catholic Church of seventeenth-century Lima recognized a diverse array of adult authority over children as valid, precisely because there were simply too few ideal colonial patriarchs to go around. The very terms used to describe the authority and force of elders other than fathers revealed that even women unrelated to children were believed capable of exercising a kind of 'patriarchal' generational authority, a power based not on biology, legitimacy, or legal right but instead on the fact of rearing a child. One church attorney inadvertently admitted during the foundling Doña María de Arriaga's marital-annulment suit that authority could derive from childrearing. He argued that, because María had lived at a school rather than in the home of the woman who paid for her rearing, the plaintiff could 'not even claim *crianza*,' or rearing, as a basis for the woman's authority over her.[65]

Still, not even those Limeños who sought annulments contended that a wife's power over children sprang from legal authority on par with patria potestad. Take, for example, the case of Doña María Teresa de Saénz, who claimed that her mother was the parent who most exerted pressure on her to marry, even though her father was alive and living at home. The church attorney, in typical fashion, countered that the suit was groundless. Josef Ramírez, the lawyer representing María Teresa, argued the following on behalf of his client:

> It is wrong to say that we cannot call [the force exerted in this case] violence because the father, Domingo Bázquez, did not induce any fear (which is not the case, anyway, because that he did is certain.) The fear of her said mother is sufficient, for she had put herself upon [María Teresa], saying she would kill her and, at very least, take away everything she had, and imprison her ... [These are] threats sufficient to induce fear in a child of fourteen years [of age], and even more forceful are the threats of a mother than of a father, since, ordinarily, women, by their very nature, are more cruel than men, seeing as how normally the mother inflicts greater torment, than if the [fear] were [to be inflicted by] the father, because a man is not as relentless as a woman, and it is easier to convince him with reason.[66]

What is important here is that the lawyer constructed his legal argument from the cultural material of stereotypes about women's irrationality and cruelty rather than by building on canon or civil law. Though Lima's judges continually acknowledged that women could assert power over children, arguments and rulings ultimately denounced the exercise of this power as a violation of children's free will. Mother's authority over children was, ultimately, less of a right that could be exercised than a power that could be abused.

At the end of the seventeenth century, church officials outside the city decided that Lima's ecclesiastical judges had been overly generous in applying even this kind of negative definition of adult authority in defence of children's free will. Appeals of several cases involving Lima's Francis-

can priests – most of whom claimed that elders had forced them to enter
monasteries and that their reverential fear lasted for years, preventing
them from seeking annulments – had reached the Vatican. Following a
decision made by the congregation of cardinals who oversaw ecclesiastical appeals, Pope Innocent XI (1676–89) issued a papal brief on the
matter of Lima's annulments in 1683. The pontiff scornfully referred to
the 'abuse' of the precept of reverential fear in Peru's tribunals, and he
reiterated a Tridentine decree that required any priest of the regular orders who wished to annul his sacred vow to do so within five years of profession. Innocent XI overturned the rulings of Lima's church officials in
the cases of priests whose vows, he determined, were still valid. Included
among them were annulment suits in which priests alleged they had entered the order out of reverential fear of their mothers.[67]

The ruling from Rome made a delayed impact in Lima. References
to the papal brief did not appear in the city's ecclesiastical court system
until over a decade had passed. Even as late as 1698, a Franciscan priest
named in the papal brief claimed that he had not heard of the ruling
since it was never read aloud in the monastery.[68] But, by the turn of the
century, news of the pope's censure surely had reached the regular clergy in Lima's monasteries and had circulated through the city at large.
After 1701, the stream of monastic-annulment suits alleging force and
fear slowed to a trickle, and they almost disappeared after 1725.

Local church authorities also became reticent to grant marriage annulments based on the excuse of reverential fear after Innocent XI issued
his brief. In fact, the number of marital annulments and divorce cases
declined drastically during the early eighteenth century. The source of
this decline appears to have been an increasing unwillingness on the part
of judges to accept cases, rather than a decreasing litigiousness among
city inhabitants.[69] As the number of suits admitted dwindled, allegations
of fear and force all but completely vanished from the court record after
1715. On the rare occasion in which ecclesiastical courts heard annulment cases based on reverential fear, litigants proceeded with a new caution and the verdicts in their trials were decidedly less favourable than
they had been, for seldom were annulments granted.[70]

In addition to a waning willingness to hear cases of annulment and
divorce, church officials in Lima were dissuaded from intervening in domestic matters on behalf of children in other areas as well. In a 1741
papal encyclical, Benedict XVI attempted to halt priests from performing secret marriages against fathers' wishes, instructing them to inquire
as to whether the couple was exchanging vows in secret in order to hide

their marriage from 'a father who forbids it.'[71] By the middle of the eighteenth century, then, the church recoiled from intervening in intergenerational conflicts, including those surrounding reverential fear. As it retreated from its role as mediator between elders and children, the circle of adults who were legally recognized as possessing authority over children contracted, leaving in its wake only medieval civil laws emphasizing the power of the father.

Conclusion

A historian consulting the legal records of colonial Lima from 1650 to 1715 would find in royal courts or civil law little conflict or confusion concerning the definition of patriarchal right. When Limeños interacted with the secular state in matters surrounding their children, they regularly submerged daily practices of childrearing into the paperwork of patriarchal public dealings, masking the power that women privately exercised over children with suits filed in the name of male lawyers and guardians. Without attention to the debates over reverential fear that took place in Lima's church courts, it would be easy to conclude that Limeños smoothly adapted Spanish laws that favoured fathers in intergenerational matters to their socially complex lives in this colonial city, and it would be safe to assume that what was written in secular code was real.

But such a view could not fully explain how the mothers of María Teresa Saénz and Juan de Chavarre could force them into lives they had not chosen. Nor could it explain the final irony of the cases María and Juan brought forward: these litigants could triumph over their mothers only by forcing church judges to acknowledge that women held authority in colonial society.

This link between women and authority brings us to the feminist debates over patriarchy with which we began. The annulment cases that young brides and priests initiated against elders in colonial Lima suggest that the question of *what* we know about gender power in the past is, ultimately, inseparable from the question of *how* we know it. If patriarchy pervaded the exercise of authority in colonial Spanish America, it must be understood as more than a rule written in law. By considering the role of religious courts as an alternate space for the negotiation of intergenerational authority, we can see that, rather than words found in dusty Spanish codes, patriarchy in colonial Lima was a living practice of attempting to apply the civil laws that favoured fathers to a more complex colonial reality.

This does not mean that Lima's annulment cases are simply artifacts of competing secular and religious discourses of gendered authority. They are instead documents that give us a precious glimpse into the way that secular and religious discourses could frame, but not contain, the gendered experiences and understandings of the inhabitants of a colonial city. Limeños indeed attempted to make sense of the way that they lived, raised their children, and reproduced colonial power within a legal framework provided by Spanish civil law and Catholic doctrine. In both the ecclesiastical and secular courts, they pushed and prodded their lived experience into a normative ideology that emphasized the right of fathers.[72] But there existed a history of adult power that lay outside legally codified ideal family types and canonical prescriptions. Rearing children in this colonial city depended on the labours and authority of adults from diverse castes and classes, and, most pointedly, of women – not just ideal-typical fathers. In the end, it was this lived authority that Limeños, and the church judges who heard their cases, could not help but recognize as real. In these complex intersections between authority, age, and gender, we find evidence for political and legal history being played out in unexpected ways in the Catholic Atlantic.

Notes

1 Nulidad de matrimonio de doña María Teresa de Sáenz, Archivo Arzobispal de Lima (hereafter AAL), Nulidades matrimoniales (hereafter NM), Legajo (hereafter Leg.) 37, 1682.
2 A presidio was a garrisoned military base. Nulidad de voto de Juan de Chavarre, AAL, Convento de Santo Domingo, Leg. 6, no. 19, 1684.
3 See, for example, Renata Ago, 'Young Nobles in the Age of Absolutism: Paternal Authority and Freedom of Choice in Seventeenth-Century Italy,' in Giovanni Levi and Jean-Claude Schmitt, eds., *A History of Young People*, vol. 1 (Cambridge, Mass.: Harvard University Press, 1987), 283–322; Barbara B. Diefendorf, 'Give Us Back Our Children: Patriarchal Authority and Parental Consent to Religious Vocations in Counter-Reformation France,' *Journal of Modern History*, 68, no. 2 (1996): 265–307.
4 Joan Wallach Scott, *Gender and the Politics of History* (New York: Columbia University Press, 1988), 49.
5 For the caste diversity of living arrangements in colonial Lima, see Bianca Premo, *Children of the Father King: Youth, Authority, and Legal Minority in Colonial Lima* (Chapel Hill: University of North Carolina Press, 2005), 44–58;

Karen Graubart, *With Our Labor and Sweat: Indigenous Women and the Formation of Colonial Society in Peru, 1550–1700* (Stanford, Calif.: Stanford University Press, 2007), 15–17; Alejandra Osorio, 'El callejón de la soledad: Vectors of Hybridity in Seventeenth-Century Lima,' in Nicholas Griffiths and Fernando Cervantes, eds., *Spiritual Encounters: Interactions between Christianity and Native Religions in Colonial America* (Lincoln: University of Nebraska, 1999), 198–229.

6 For a description of the social implications of the predominance of women and the pressures on the colonial elite in seventeenth-century Lima, see Nancy van Deusen, *Between the Sacred and the Worldly: The Institutional and Cultural Practice of Recogimiento in Colonial Lima* (Stanford, Calif.: Stanford University Press, 2001), especially 11–12.

7 Noble David Cook, comp., *Numeración general de todas personas de ambos sexos, edades, y calidades que se [h]a hecho en esta Ciudad de Lima, año 1700* (Lima: COFIDE, 1985).

8 See van Deusen, *Between the Sacred and the Worldly,* 126.

9 Statistics are based on my sample of 658 households out of the 2,940 included in Cook, *Numeración general.* For comparative statistics demonstrating the high prevalence of female-headed households in Latin America, see van Deusen, *Between the Sacred and the Worldly,* 11–12; Silvia M. Arrom, *The Women of Mexico City, 1790–1857* (Stanford, Calif.: Stanford University Press, 1985), 130; and Guiomar Dueñas Vargas, *Los hijos del pecado: Ilegitimidad y vida familiar en la Santafé de Bogotá colonial* (Bogotá: Universidad Nacional de Colombia, 1997), 246–57.

10 Alfonso X, *Las Siete Partidas del sabio rey Alfonso el X, glosados por el Lic. Gregorio López* (12th century, repr.: Valencia: Imprenta de Benito Momfort, 1767), 2:10:2; 2:13:14.

11 This argument is based on an analysis of over 500 guardianship contracts and over 200 civil cases heard in Lima's colonial courts. For more on secular cases during the period, see Premo, *Children,* 68–77.

12 Again, statistics are based on my sample of 658 households out of the 2,940 included in Cook, comp. *Numeración general.*

13 See Judith Bennett, 'Feminism and History,' *Gender and History,* 1, no. 2 (1989): 251–72 (especially 256, 258); Bennett, 'Women's History: A Study in Continuity and Change,' *Women's History Review,* 2, no. 2 (1993): 173–82; Louise Tilly, 'Gender, Women's History and Social History,' *Social Science History,* 13 (1989): 439–62; Joan Hoff, 'Gender as a Postmodern Category of Paralysis,' *Women's History Review,* 3 (1994): 149–68, and the ensuing debate between Joan Hoff and other feminist historians in *Women's History Review* 5, no. 1 (1996). Also see Kathleen Canning, 'Feminist History after

the Linguistic Turn: Historicizing Discourse and Experience,' *Signs,* 19, no. 2 (1994): 368–404.

14 Sueann Caulfield, 'The History of Gender in the Historiography of Latin America,' *Hispanic American Historical Review,* 81, nos. 3–4 (2001): 449–90.

15 Kimberly Gauderman, *Women's Lives in Colonial Quito: Gender, Law and Economy in Spanish America* (Austin: University of Texas Press, 2003), 17.

16 Compare Arrom, *The Women of Mexico City,* 78; Susan M. Socolow, *The Women of Colonial Latin America* (Cambridge: Cambridge University Press, 2000), 9; and Elizabeth Dore, 'One Step Forward, Two Steps Back: Gender and the State in the Long Nineteenth Century,' in Maxine Molyneux and Elizabeth Dore, eds., *Hidden Histories of Gender and the State in Latin America* (Durham, N.C.: Duke University Press, 2000), 3–32, 10–13.

17 Richard Boyer, 'Women, *La mala vida* and the Politics of Marriage,' in Asunción Lavrin, ed., *Sexuality and Marriage in Colonial Latin America* (Lincoln: University of Nebraska Press, 1989), 252–86, 252–3; Irene Silverblatt, '"The Universe has turned inside out … There is no justice for us here": Andean Women under Spanish Rule,' in Mona Etienne and Eleanor Leacock, eds., *Women and Colonization: Anthropological Perspectives* (New York: Praeger, 1980), 149–60, 163.

18 Arrom aptly points out that the padre de familia's authority over his wife was 'clearly less' than his authority over slaves and minor children: *The Women of Mexico City,* 73. Also see Gauderman's detail of women's rights in ecclesiastical and criminal secular courts in *Women's Lives.*

19 Juan Machado de Chávez y Mendoza, *El Perfecto confesor y cura de almas,* vol. 2 (Madrid: Pedro de Cavalleria, 1646), 592.

20 Classic Roman *patria potestas* counted grandfathers as supreme patriarchs and endowed all patriarchs broad powers over their dependants, including over their lives. But, after the collapse of the Roman republic, Catholic moralists cast aside stricter forms of patriarchal authority. The new, tempered concept of *patria potestas* sustained throughout the Middle Ages was conceived of as both a right and a duty, and 'primarily, the fulfillment of the duty [of *patria potestad*] rests with the father, although it affects also *the mother as the associate* of the father.' See Rev. Joseph V. Sangmeister, *Force and Fear Precluding Matrimonial Consent: An Historical Synopsis and Commentary.* Catholic University of America Canon Law Series no. 80 (Washington, D.C.: Catholic University of America Press, 1932), 23.

21 Alfonso X, *Las Siete Partidas,* 4:8:2.

22 van Deusen, *Between the Sacred and the Worldly,* 93.

23 For similar arguments about the lack social historical information on children in colonial ecclesiastical cases before the late colonial period in Mexico,

see Sonya Lipsett-Rivera, 'Gender and Family Relations during the Transition from Colony to Republic in Mexico,' in Victor Uribe-Urán, ed., *State and Society in Spanish America during the Age of Revolution* (Wilmington, Del.: Scholarly Resources, 2001), 121–48, 138. Also see Richard Boyer, *Lives of the Bigamists: Marriage, Family, and Community in Colonial Mexico* (Albuquerque: University of New Mexico Press, 1995), 109–10.

24 Arrom, *The Women of Mexico City*, 211. Also see van Deusen, *Between the Sacred and the Worldly*, especially chapter 4; Alberto Flores Galindo and Magdalena Chocano, 'Los cargos del sacramento,' *Revista andina*, 2, no. 2 (1984): 403–23; and Ricardo Cicerchia, '*La vida maridable*: Ordinary Family, Buenos Aires, 1776–1850,' PhD thesis, Columbia University, 1995.

25 Verena Martínez-Alier (Stolcke), *Marriage Class, and Colour in Nineteenth-Century Cuba: A Study of Racial Attitudes and Sexual Values in a Slave Society* (Cambridge: Cambridge University Press, 1974); Daisy Rípodaz Ardanaz, *El matrimonio en Indias: Realidad social y regulación jurídica* (Buenos Aires: Fundación para la Educación, la Ciencia, y la Cultura, 1977); Ramón Gutiérrez, 'Honor, Ideology, Marriage Negotiation, and Class-Gender Domination in New Mexico, 1690–1846,' *Latin American Perspectives*,12, no. 1 (1985): 81–104, and *When Jesus Came, the Corn Mothers Went Away: Marriage, Sexuality and Power in New Mexico, 1500–1846* (Stanford, Calif.: Stanford University Press, 1991); Edith Couturier, 'Women and the Family in Eighteenth-Century Mexico: Law and Practice,' *Journal of Family History* 10, no. 3 (1985): 293–304; Robert McCaa, 'Gustos de los padres, inclinaciones de los novios y reglas de una feria nupcial colonial: Parral, 1770–1814,' *Historia Mexicana* 40, no. 4 (1991): 579–614; and Susan M. Socolow, 'Acceptable Partners: Marriage Choice in Argentina, 1778–1810,' in Lavrin, *Sexuality and Marriage*, 209–46.

26 Patricia Seed, *To Love, Honor and Obey: Conflicts over Marriage Choice in Colonial Mexico, 1574–1821* (Stanford, Calif.: Stanford University Press, 1988).

27 This is not to say that parental dissent never occurred. See, for example, Baltasar de Chamora Ginojossa Presbitero, AAL, Litigios Matrimoniales, Leg. 1 suelto, 1607; Da. Estefanía Rodríguez de la Gueva, AAL, NM, Leg. 37, 1683. However, I found few such cases in the Archivo Arzobispal de Lima or in the Archivo General de la Nación (hereafter AGN) until the end of the colonial period.

28 Quoted in Rípodaz Ardanaz, *El matrimonio*, 265.

29 For the elite placement of daughters in monastic orders as a spiritual and economic exchange in colonial Cuzco, see Kathryn Burns, *Colonial Habits: Convents and the Spiritual Economy of Cuzco, Peru* (Durham, N.C.: Duke University Press, 1999).

30 For the evolution of canon law on force, see Sangmeister, *Force and Fear*

Precluding Matrimonial Consent; Josiah G. Chatam, *Force and Fear as Invalidating Marriage: The Element of Injustice,* Catholic University Canon Law Series no. 310 (Washington, D.C.: Catholic University of America, 1950); and James Victor Brown, *The Invalidating Effects of Force, Fear and Fraud on the Canonical Noviciate,* Catholic University of America Canon Law Series no. 331 (Washington D.C.: Catholic University of America Press, 1951), 13–14. For Spain, note renowned jurist Francisco Suárez's position on free will in Caput 8, 'An ingressus religionis ex perfecta scentia et libertate fieri debeat,' in Carolo Berton, ed., *Opera Omni* (16th century, repr.: Paris: 1859). For colonial Spanish America and free will, see Asunción Lavrin, 'Sexuality in Colonial Mexico,' in Lavrin, *Sexuality and Marriage,* 54–6; Rípodas Ardanaz, *El matrimonio en Indias,* 97–101; and Socolow, 'Acceptable Partners,' 23n.5. Cf. Seed, who argues that Trent's decree on free will was primarily a response to the Reformation and that there was 'nothing in Catholic tradition that made this position [on free will in marriage choice] inevitable': *To Love, Honor and Obey,* 33.

31 See Brown, *The Invalidating Effects,* 339–66; Sangmeister, *Force and Fear Precluding,* 7–9; Chatam, *Force and Fear as Invalidating,* especially 84.
32 Sangmeister, *Force and Fear Precluding,* 62.
33 Ibid., 41–5.
34 Twenty-fifth Session, Reform of Regulars, chapters 15, 17, and 18, and Reform of Matrimony, chapter 9, *Canons and Decrees of the Council of Trent,* Rev. H.J Schroeder, trans. (St Louis: B. Herder, 1941).
35 Twenty-fifth session, Reform of Regular Orders, chapter 16, *Canons and Decrees of the Council of Trent,* 227.
36 Tomás Sánchez, *Disputaciones de sacro matrimonium sacramentum,* 3 vols. (Madrid: 1602–3); José Rodríguez González, *La nulidad de matrimonio por miedo en la Jurisprudencia Pontificia* (Vitoria: Editorial Este, 1962), 76–80.
37 Machado de Chávez, for example, limited his comments to royal oaths but, critically, affirmed the 'natural potestad that both the father and mother have over their children, in which both are equal': *El perfeto confessor,* 627.
38 *Siete Partidas,* 4:1:10.
39 Nulidad de voto de Josef Torres de Picón, AAL, Convento de Santo Domingo, Leg. 6, nos. 7, 9, and 13, 1671.
40 Nulidad de matrimonio de doña María de Arriaga, AAL, NM, Leg. 37, 1682, f.7.
41 Often in these cases men also mixed other claims – such as mistaken identity, 'errors' in knowing the caste of their brides, or accusations against their wives themselves – with the excuse of elder force and referential fear. See, for example, Nulidad de matrimonio de Diego Herrera, AAL, NM, Leg. 45, 1698; Nulidad de matrimonio de don Bartolomé del Beltrán, AAL, NM, Leg. 42, 1692.

In addition, men claimed to have been pressured by relatives of the bride. See Nulidad de matrimonio de Antonio González, AAL, NM, Leg. 20, 1658.

42 Bernard Lavallé, *Amor y opresión en los Andes coloniales* (Lima: Instituto de Estudios Peruanos, 1999), 29–30. For the preponderantly female profile of those seeking divorce in colonial Latin America, also see Arrom, *The Women of Mexico City*; Luis Martín, *Daughters of the Conquistadors: Women in the Viceroyalty of Peru* (Albuquerque: University of New Mexico Press, 1983), 141; van Deusen, *Between the Sacred and the Worldly*; Flores Galindo and Chocano, 'Los cargos'; and María Beatriz Nizza da Silva, 'Divorce in Colonial Brazil: The Case of São Paulo,' in Lavrin, *Sexuality and Marriage*, 313–40.

43 Lavallé, *Amor y opresión*, 30.

44 Bernard Lavallé, 'La population conventuelle de Lima (XVIè et XVIIè siècles): Approches et problemes,' in *Actes de 2è Colleque, Centre d'etudes et de rechereches sur le Péroue et les Pays Andins* (Grenoble: Université de Langues et Lettres de Grenoble, 1975), 167–95, 185.

45 Nulidad de voto de Juan de Espinoza, AAL, Covento de Santo Domingo, Leg. 6, no. 5, 1672.

46 Nulidad de matrimonio de doña Bárbara de Romero, AAL, NM. Leg. 37, 1683.

47 Nulidad de matrimonio de doña Viviana de Córdova, AAL, NM, Leg. 36, 1680. For other instances of financial collusion in arranged marriages, see Nulidad de matrimonio de Antonia de las Cuetas, AAL, NM, Leg. 18, 1653; Nulidad de matrimonio de Inés de Rivera, AAL, NM, Leg. 35, 1680; and Nulidad de matrimonio de Gerónimo García, AAL, NM, Leg. 49, 1713.

48 Nulidad de voto Nicolás de Espinoza, AAL, Convento de Santo Domingo, Leg. 4, nos. 12 and 14, 1664, and Leg. 4, no. 17, 1669. Also see Nulidad de voto de Juan de Loyaza, AAL, Convento de Santo Domingo, Leg. 4, no. 16, 1669; and Nulidad de voto de Luis de Osorio, AAL, Convento de Santo Domingo, Leg. 4, nos. 6 and 16, 1662.

49 Nulidad de matrimonio de doña María Francisca de Báldez AAL, NM, Leg. 37, 1683.

50 Nulidad de matrimonio de doña Gerónima de Piñeda y Santillán, AAL, NM, Leg. 19, 1656.

51 Nulidad de matrimonio de doña Aldosa Nuñes de Paredes, Leg 20, 1659.

52 Nulidad de matrimonio doña Juana de Herencia, AAL, NM, Legs. 35 and 36, 1711, ff.1 and 19. Also see Nulidad de matrimonio de doña Melchora de Sambrano, AAL, NM, Leg. 36, 1681, f.20.

53 Nulidad de matrimonio de Josefa de Albarez, AAL, NM, Leg. 37, 1682, f.1.

54 Nulidad de matrimonio de doña Ysabel de Miranda y Almeida, AAL, NM Leg. 18, 1653.

55 Nulidad de voto de Gerónimo de Solis, AAL, Convento de Santo Domingo, Leg. 6, no. 2, 1671, f.8.

56 Nulidad de voto de Juan de Chavarre, Convento de Santo Domingo, Leg. 6, no.19, 1684, f.15.

57 n/t, AGN, Ecclesiásticos, Conventos, Conventos y Ordenes, Leg. 53, 1680.

58 Seed, *To Love, Honor and Obey*, 58, 81–3.

59 Nulidad de matrimonio de Gertrudis de Jesús negra, AAL, NM, Leg. 48, Ex. 8, 1693.

60 Nulidad de matrimonio de doña Leonor de Arebulo Ballesteros, AAL, NM, Leg. 19, 1653.

61 Nulidad de matrimonio de doña María de Arriaga.

62 Nulidad de matrimonio de doña Ynés de Rivera, AAL, NM, Leg. 35, 1680. f.39.

63 Nulidad de voto de Francisco de Córdova, AAL, Convento de Santo Domingo, Leg. 6, no. 15, 1682.

64 See Nulidad de Flora Báldez, f.1, and Nulidad de Matrimonio de doña Antonia de Cuetas, AAL, NM, Leg. 37, 1683.

65 Nulidad de Doña María de Arriaga, f.9.

66 Nulidad de matrimonio de doña María Teresa de Sáenz, AAL, NM, Leg. 37, f.19.

67 A copy of the brief is contained in Nulidad de voto de Miguel Adame de Sotomayor, AAL, Convento de Santo Domingo, Leg. 5, no. 28, 1693. It cites two cases in which mothers inspired fear (*allegesset sibi a matre incussum metum*); both litigants had been priests for over a decade. Also see the statement issued specifically for the Franciscans contained in Nulidad de votos de Estevan Quiroz, Convento de San Francisco, Leg. 6, no. 24, 1701. For a description of the reform measures taken by Innocent XI to tighten control of the regular orders, see Freiherr Ludwig von Pastor, *The History of the Popes from the Close of the Middle Ages*, 33 vols., vol. 32, Dom Ernst Graf, trans. (London: Kean Paul, Threch, Trubner and Company, 1940).

68 Nulidad de voto de Diego de Torres, AAL, Convento de San Francisco, Leg. 6, C. 11, 1698.

69 Lavallé, *Amor y opresión*, 24.

70 An annulment was granted in a case in which a slave woman accused her master of forcing her into marriage: Juana Rivaneyra Negra de casta Terranova esclava contra Josef Yonofro, AAL, NM, Leg. 55, 1775. Also see Nulidad de Da. Ysabel María de Roxas, AAL, NM, Leg. 55, 1773; and Da. Gerónima Fernández. AAL, NM, Leg. 53, 1747. Note the caution with which the prosecution made its argument in the annulment case published as 'Breve apunte en el derecho sobre la causa de nulidad de Matrimonio de Doña María Belzunze con el Conde de Casa Davalos,' in Pedro Bravo de Lagunas y Castilla, *Colección*

legal de Cartas, Dictámenes y otros Papeles en Derecho (Lima: Casa de Niños Huérfanos, 1761), Duke University Special Collections.

71 On the eighteenth-century church 'retreat' in marriage cases, see Lavallé, *Amor
    y opresión*, 24; Seed, *To Love, Honor and Obey,* 192; Rípodaz Ardanaz, *Matrimonio
    en Indias*, 392.

72 My use of the term 'experience' here is self-conscious and reflects recent
    feminist scholarship on historical methodology after the linguistic turn. See
    Joan Scott, 'The Evidence of Experience,' *Critical Inquiry*, 17 (1991): 773–
    97; Canning, 'Feminist History after the Linguistic Turn'; and Shari Stone-
    Mediatore, 'Chandra Mohanty and the Revaluing of Experience,'*Hypatia*,
    13, no. 2 (1998): 116–33.

Works Cited

Ago, Renata. 'Young Nobles in the Age of Absolutism: Paternal Authority and Freedom of Choice in Seventeenth-Century Italy.' *A History of Young People*. Vol. 1. Ed. Giovanni Levi and Jean-Claude Schmitt. Cambridge, Mass.: Harvard University Press, 1987. 283–322.

Aguilera, Francisco. *Sermon.en que se da noticia de la vida ... de la Venerable Senora Catharina de San Joan*. Puebla: En la imprenta nueva de Diego Fernandez de Leon, 1688.

Ahlgren, Gillian T.W. *Teresa of Avila and the Politics of Sanctity*. Ithaca, N.Y.: Cornell University Press, 1996.

Alberro, Solange. 'Herejes, brujas y beatas: Mujeres ante el tribunal del Santo Oficio de la Inquisición en la Nueva España.' In *Presencia y transparencia: La mujer en la historia de México*. Ed. Carmen Ramos Escandón. Mexico City: Colegio de México, 1987. 79–94.

– *Inquisición y sociedad en México, 1571–1700*. 3rd ed. Mexico City: Fondo de Cultura Económica, 1998 [1988].

Alfonso X. *Las Siete Partidas del sabio rey Alfonso el X, glosados por el Lic. Gregorio López*. 12th century. Repr. Valencia: Imprenta de Benito Momfort, 1767.

Allestree, Richard. *The Ladies Calling*. London: n.p., 1673.

Altman, Ida. *Transatlantic Ties in the Spanish Empire: Brihuega, Spain, & Puebla, Mexico, 1560–1620*. Stanford, Calif.: Stanford University Press, 2000.

Ana de San Bartolomé. *Autobiography and Other Writings*. Ed. Darcy Donahue. The Other Voice in Early Modern Europe Series. Chicago, Ill.: University of Chicago Press, 2008.

Anastácio, Vanda. 'Cherchez la femme: À propos d'une forme de sociabilité littéraire à Lisbonne à la fin du XVIIe siècle.' *Arquivos do Centro Cultural Português*, special issue on *Sociabilités intellectuelles XVI–XX siècles*. Vol. 49. Paris: Centre Culturel C. Gulbenkian, 2005. 93–101.

– '"Mulheres varonis e interesses domésticos": Reflexões acerca do discurso
produzido pela História Literária acerca das mulheres escritoras da viragem
do século XVIII para o século XIX.' In *Cartographies. Mélanges offerts à Maria
Alzira Seixo.* Lisboa: Universidade Aberta, 2005. Accessed online 15 November
2008: http://www.vanda-anastacio.at/index_files/page0001.htm.

Anderson, Karen. *Chain Her by One Foot: The Subjugation of Native Women in Seventeenth-Century New France.* New York: Routledge, 1993.

Andrews, William L., ed. *Sisters of the Spirit: Three Black Women's Autobiographies of
the Nineteenth Century.* Bloomington: Indiana University Press, 1986.

Andrien, Kenneth J. *Andean Worlds: Indigenous History, Culture, and Consciousness
under Spanish Rule.* Albuquerque: University of New Mexico Press, 2001.

Arenal, Electa. 'The Convent as Catalyst for Autonomy: Two Hispanic Nuns of
the Seventeenth Century.' In *Women in Hispanic Literature: Icons and Fallen
Idols.* Ed. Beth Miller. Berkeley: University of California Press, 1983. 147–83.

– 'Monjas chocolateras: Contextualizaciones agridulces.' *Nictímene .... sacrílega:
Estudios coloniales en homenaje a Georgina Sabat-Rivers.* Ed. Mabel Moraña and
Yolanda Martínez-San Miguel. Mexico City: Universidad del Claustro de
Sor Juana, Instituto Internacional de Literatura Iberoamericana, 2003.
135–55.

– and Stacey Schlau, eds. and intro. *Untold Sisters: Hispanic Nuns in Their Own
Works.* Trans. Amanda Powell. Albuquerque: University of New Mexico Press,
1989.

Arrom, Silvia M. *The Women of Mexico City, 1790–1857.* Stanford, Calif.: Stanford
University Press, 1985.

Astell, Mary. *A Serious Proposal to the Ladies.* 4th ed. New York: Source Book Press,
1970 [1701].

Atwood, Craig. 'The Mother of God's People: The Adoration of the Holy Spirit
in the Eighteenth-Century Brüdergemeine.' *Church History,* 68 (December
1999): 886–909.

'Autobiography of Mrs. Alice Thornton of East Newton, co. York.' *Surtees Society,*
62. Durham: 1875.

Bach, Rebecca Ann. *Colonial Transformations: The Cultural Production of the New
Atlantic World, 1580–1640.* New York: Palgrave Macmillan, 2000.

Bade, Klaus. *Migration in European History.* Trans. Allison Brown. Malden, Mass.:
Blackwell, 2003.

Baernstein, P. Renée. *A Convent Tale: A Century of Sisterhood in Spanish Milan.*
New York and London: Routledge, 2002.

Bailey, Gauvin Alexander. 'A Mughal Princess in Baroque New Spain. Catarina
De San Juan (1606–1688), the *China Poblana.*' *Anales del Instituto de Investigaciones Estéticas,* 71 (1997): 37–73.

Bailyn, Bernard. *Atlantic History: Concept and Contours*. Cambridge, Mass.: Harvard University Press, 2005.

Bandelier Collection of Copies of Documents Relative to the History of New Mexico and Arizona. Microfilm edition on deposit at Perkins Library, Duke University.

Barbeito Carneiro, Isabel. *María de Orozco (1635–1709)*. Madrid: Ediciones del Orto, 1997.

– *Mujeres del Madrid barroco. Voces testimonials*. Madrid: Ediciones del Orto, 1992.

Barker, Francis, Peter Hulme, and Margaret Iverson, eds. *Cannibalism and the Colonial World*. New York: Cambridge University Press, 1998.

Barksdale, Clement. *A Letter Touching A Colledge of Maids, or, a Virgin Society*. London: 1675.

Bartoli, Daniello. *Missione al gran Mogol del Ridolfo Aquaviva della compagnia di Giesu, sua vita e morte*. Roma: Varese, 1663.

Beckwith, Sarah. 'A Very Material Mysticism: The Medieval Mysticism of Margery Kempe.' *Medieval Literature: Criticism, Ideology, and History*. Brighton, U.K.: Harvester, 1986. 34–57.

Behar, Ruth. 'Sex and Sin, Witchcraft and the Devil in Late-Colonial Mexico.' *American Ethnologist*, 14 (1987): 35–55.

– 'Sexual Witchcraft, Colonialism, and Women's Powers: Views from the Mexican Inquisition.' In Lavrin, *Sexuality and Marriage*. 178–206.

– 'The Visions of a Guachichil Witch in 1599: A Window on the Subjugation of Mexico's Hunter-Gatherers.' *Ethnohistory*, 34, no. 2 (1987): 115–38.

Beidler, Phillip, and Gary Taylor, eds. *Writing Race across the Atlantic World, 1492–1789*. New York: Palgrave Macmillan, 2002.

Benjamin, Thomas, Timothy D. Hall, and David E. Rutherford, eds. *The Atlantic World in the Age of Empire*. New York: Houghton Mifflin, 2001.

Bennett, Herman. *Africans in Colonial Mexico: Absolutism, Christianity, and Afro-Creole Consciousness, 1570–1640*. Bloomington: Indiana University Press, 2003.

Bennett, Judith M. 'Feminism and History.' *Gender and History*, 1, no. 2 (1989): 251–72.

– 'Women's History: A Study in Continuity and Change.' *Women's History Review*, 2, no. 2 (1993): 173–82.

– and Amy M. Froide, eds. *Singlewomen in the European Past, 1250–1800*. Philadelphia: University of Pennsylvania Press, 1999.

Benton, Lauren. *Law and Colonial Cultures: Legal Regimes in World History, 1400–1900*. Cambridge: Cambridge University Press, 2002.

Bergmann, Emilie. 1991. 'The Exclusion of the Feminine in the Cultural

Discourse of the Golden Age: Juan Luis Vives and Fray Luis de León.' In
  Religion, Body, and Gender in Early Modern Spain. Ed. Alain Saint-Saëns. San
  Francisco: Mellen Research University Press, 1991. 124–36.

Berlin, Ira. 'From Creoles to African: Atlantic Creoles and the Origins of African-American Society in Mainland North America.' *William and Mary Quarterly.* 3rd ser., 53 (1996): 251–88.

Berton, Carolo, ed. *Opera Omni.*16th century. Repr. Paris: 1859.

Bieñko de Peralta, Doris. 'Un camino de abrojos y espinas: mística, demonios
  y melancolía.' In *Transgresión y melancolía en el México colonial.* Ed. Roger
  Bartra. Mexico City: Universidad Nacional Autónoma de México, 2004.
  91–114.

Bilinkoff, Jodi. 'Confession, Gender, Life-Writing: Some Cases (Mainly) from
  Spain.' In *Penitence in the Age of Reformations.* Ed. Katharine Jackson Lualdi
  and Anne T. Thayer. Burlington, Vt.: Ashgate, 2000. 168–83.

– 'Confessors, Penitents, and the Construction of Identities in Early Modern
  Avila.' In *Culture and Identity in Early Modern Europe (1500–1800).* Ed. Barbara
  B. Diefendorf and Carla Hesse. Ann Arbor: Michigan University Press, 1993.
  83–102.

– 'Francisco Losa and Gregorio Lopez: Spiritual Friendship and Identity Formation on the New Spain Frontier.' In Greer and Bilinkoff, *Colonial Saints,*
  115–28.

– *Related Lives: Confessors and Their Female Penitents, 1450–1750.* Ithaca, N.Y.: Cornell University Press, 2005.

Blanco, Lourdes. 'Las Monjas de Santa Clara: el erotismo de la fe y la subversión de la autoridad sacerdotal.' *En el nombre del Señor: Shamanes, demonios
  y curanderos del norte del Perú.* Ed. Luis Millones and Moisés Lemlij. Lima:
  Biblioteca Peruana de Psicoanálisis. Seminario Interdisciplinario de Estudios
  Andinos, 1994. 184–98.

– 'Poder y pasión: espíritus entretejidos.' In *El monacato femenino en el Imperio Español: monasterios, beaterios, recogimientos y colegios.* Ed. Manuel Ramos Medina.
  Mexico City: Centro de Estudios de Historia de México CONDUMEX, 1995.
  369–80.

Block, Sharon. *Rape and Sexual Power in Early America.* Chapel Hill: University of
  North Carolina Press, 2006.

Bourne, Russell. *Gods of War, Gods of Peace: How the Meeting of Native and Colonial
  Religions Shaped Early America.* New York: Harcourt, 2002.

Boyer, Richard. *Lives of the Bigamists: Marriage, Family, and Community in Colonial
  Mexico.* Albuquerque: University of New Mexico Press, 1995.

– 'Women, *La mala vida* and the Politics of Marriage.' In Lavrin, *Sexuality and Marriage,* 252–86.

Brammwall, Kathryn N. 'Monstrous Metamorphosis: Nature, Morality and the Rhetoric of Monstrosity in Tudor England.' *Sixteenth Century Journal*, 27, no. 1 (1996): 3–21.

Brandt, E.A. 'The Role of Secrecy in a Pueblo Society.' *Flowers in the Wind: Papers on Ritual, Myth and Symbolism in California and the Southwest.* Ed. T.C. Blackburn. Socorro, N.M.: Ballena Press, 1977. 11–28.

Bravo de Lagunas y Castilla, Pedro. 'Breve apunte en el derecho sobre la causa de nulidad de Matrimonio de Doña María Belzunze con el Conde de Casa Davalos.' *Colección legal de Cartas, Dictámenes y otros Papeles en Derecho.* Lima: Casa de Niños Huérfanos, 1761.

Breen, T.H., and Timothy Hall. *Colonial America in an Atlantic World: A Story of Creative Interaction.* New York: Pearson Longman, 2004.

Bristol, Joan Cameron. *Christians, Blasphemers, and Witches.* Albuquerque: University of New Mexico Press, 2007.

Brodeur, Raymond, ed. *Femme, mystique et missionaire: Marie Guyart de l'Incarnation: Tours, 1599 – Québec, 1672.* Quebec: Les Presses de l'Université de Laval, 2001.

Brown, James Victor. *The Invalidating Effects of Force, Fear and Fraud on the Canonical Noviciate.* Catholic University of America Canon Law Series no. 331. Washington D.C.: Catholic University of America Press, 1951.

Brown, Kathleen. *Good Wives, Nasty Wenches, & Anxious Patriarchs: Gender, Race, and Power in Colonial Virginia.* Chapel Hill: Omohundro Institute of Early American History and Culture / University of North Carolina Press, 1996.

Brown, Vincent. 'Spiritual Terror and Sacred Authority in Jamaican Slave Society.' *Slavery & Abolition*, 24, no. 1 (2003): 24–53.

Bruneau, Marie-Florine. *Women Mystics Confront the Modern World: Marie de l'Incarnation (1599–1672) and Madame Guyon (1648–1717).* Albany: State University of New York Press, 1998.

Büdingische Sammlung. Vol. 4. Büdingen, 1741. In von Zinzendorf, *Ergänzungsband.* 483–7.

Burns, Kathryn. *Colonial Habits. Convents and the Spiritual Economy of Cuzco, Peru.* Durham, N.C., and London: Duke University Press, 1999.

Burschel, Peter. *Sterben und Unsterblichkeit. Zur Kultur des Martyriums in der frühen Neuzeit.* Munich: Oldenbourg, 2004.

Bynum, Caroline Walker. *Fragmentation and Redemption: Essays on Gender and the Human Body in Medieval Religion.* New York: Zone Books, 1991.

– *Holy Feast and Holy Fast: The Religious Significance of Food to Medieval Women.* Berkeley and Los Angeles: University of California Press, 1987.

Cañeque, Alejandro. *The King's Living Image: The Culture and Politics of Viceregal Power in Colonial Mexico.* New York: Routledge, 2004.

- 'Theater of Power: Writing and Representing the Auto de Fe in Colonial Mexico.' *Americas*, 52, no. 3 (1996): 321–44.
Cañizares-Esguerra, Jorge. *How to Write the History of the New World: Histories, Epistemologies, Identities in the Eighteenth-Century Atlantic World*. Stanford, Calif.: Stanford University Press, 2001.
- *Nature, Empire, and Nation: Explorations of the History of Science in the Iberian World*. Stanford, Calif.: Stanford University Press, 2006.
- 'New World, New Stars: Patriotic Astrology and the Invention of Indian and Creole Bodies in Colonial Spanish America, 1600–1650.' *American Historical Review*, 104, no. 1 (1999): 33–68.
- *Puritan Conquistadors: Iberianizing the Atlantic, 1550–1700*. Stanford, Calif.: Stanford University Press, 2006.
- and Erik Seeman, eds. *The Atlantic in Global History*. New York: Prentice Hall, 2006.
Canning, Kathleen. 'Feminist History after the Linguistic Turn: Historicizing Discourse and Experience.' *Signs*, 19, no. 2 (1994): 368–404.
Canny, Nicholas, ed. *Europeans on the Move: Studies on European Migration, 1500–1800*. Oxford: Oxford University Press, 1994.
- and Anthony Pagden, eds. *Colonial Identity in the Atlantic World, 1500–1800*. Princeton, N.J.: Princeton University Press, 1989.
Carmack, Robert M. *Quichean Civilization: The Ethnohistoric, Ethnographic, and Archaeological Sources*. Berkeley and Los Angeles: University of California Press, 1973.
Carrera, Magali M. *Imagining Identity in New Spain: Race, Lineage, and the Colonial Body in Portraiture and Casta Painting*. Austin: University of Texas Press, 2003.
Casey, James. *Early Modern Spain: A Social History*. New York and London: Routledge, 1999.
Castillo Graxeda, José del. *Compendio de la vida y virtudes de la venerable Catarina de San Juan*. Puebla: Gobierno del Estado de Puebla, 1987 [1692].
Cátedra, Pedro M., and Anastasio Rojo. *Bibliotecas y lecturas de mujeres. Siglo XVI*. Salamanca: Instituto de Historia del Libro y de la Lectura, 2004.
Caulfield, Sueann. 'The History of Gender in the Historiography of Latin America.' *Hispanic American Historical Review*, 81, nos. 3–4 (2001): 449–90.
Cervantes, Fernando. *The Devil in the New World: The Impact of Diabolism in New Spain*. New Haven, Conn.: Yale University Press, 1994.
Chamberlayne, Edward. *An Academy or Colledge, wherein Young Ladies and Gentlewomen May at a Very Moderate Expense Be Duly Instructed in the True Protestant Religion, and in All Vertuous Qualities That May Adorn That Sex*. London: 1671.
Chatam, Josiah G. *Force and Fear as Invalidating Marriage: The Element of Injustice*.

Catholic University Canon Law Series no. 310. Washington, D.C.: Catholic University of America, 1950.

Chávez y Mendoza, Juan Machado de. *El Perfecto confesor y cura de almas.* Vol. 2. Madrid: Pedro de Cavalleria, 1646.

Chojnacka, Monica. 'Singlewomen in Early Modern Venice: Communities and Opportunities.' In Bennett and Froide, *Singlewomen in the European Past,* 217–35.

– 'Women, Charity and Community in Early Modern Venice: The Casa delle Zitelle.' *Renaissance Quarterly,* 51 (1998): 68–91.

Cholenec, Pierre. *Catherine Tekakwitha: Her Life.* William Lone, S.J., trans. Hamilton, Ont.: William Lone, 2002.

Choquette, Leslie. '"Ces Amazones du Grand Dieu": Women and Mission in Seventeenth-Century Canada.' *French Historical Studies,* 17 (1992): 627–55.

Chowning, Margaret. *Rebellious Nuns: A Troubled History of a Mexican Convent (1752–1863).* New York and Oxford: Oxford University Press, 2006.

Cicerchia, Ricardo. '*La vida maridable.* Ordinary Family, Buenos Aires, 1776–1850.' PhD thesis, Columbia University, 1995.

Clark, Emily. *Masterless Mistresses: The New Orleans Ursulines and the Development of a New World Society, 1727–1834.* Chapel Hill: University of North Carolina Press / Omohundro Institute of Early American History and Culture, 2007.

Clossey, Luke. 'Distant Souls: Global Religion and the Jesuit Missions of Germany, Mexico and China, 1595–1705.' PhD thesis, University of California, Berkeley, 2004.

Cohen, Sherill. *The Evolution of Women's Asylums since 1500: From Refuges for Ex-Prostitutes to Shelters for Battered Women.* Oxford: Oxford University Press, 1992.

Coleridge, Henry James, ed. *St Mary's Convent Micklegate Bar York.* London: Burns and Oates, 1887.

Cook, Noble David, comp. *Numeración general de todas personas de ambos sexos, edades, y calidades que se [h]a hecho en esta Ciudad de Lima, año 1700.* Lima: COFIDE, 1985.

Cope, Douglas. *The Limits of Racial Domination: Plebeian Society in Colonial Mexico City, 1660–1720.* Madison: University of Wisconsin Press, 1994.

Cornelius, Janet Duitsman. *Slave Missions and the Black Church in the Antebellum South.* Columbia: University of South Carolina Press, 1999.

– *When I Can Read My Title Clear: Literacy, Slavery and Religion in the Antebellum South.* Columbia: University of South Carolina Press, 1992.

Corteguera, Luis. 'The Making of a Visionary Woman: The Life of Beatriz Ana Ruiz, 1666–1735.' *Women, Texts, and Authority in the Early Modern Span-*

ish World. Ed. Marta Vicente and Luis Corteguera. Aldershot, U.K.: Ashgate, 2003. 165–82.

Couturier, Edith. 'Women and the Family in Eighteenth-Century Mexico: Law and Practice.' *Journal of Family History*, 10, no. 3 (1985): 293–304.

Creel, Margaret Washington. *"A Peculiar People": Slave Religion and Community-Culture among the Gullahs.* New York: New York University Press, 1988.

Cruz, Anne J. 'Willing Desire: Luisa de Carvajal y Mendoza and Feminine Subjectivity.' In Nader, *The Mendoza Women: Gender and Power in Golden Age Spain,* 177–94.

– and Mary Elizabeth Perry, eds. *Culture and Control in Counter Reformation Spain.* Minneapolis: University of Minnesota Press, 1992.

Daniels, Christine, and Michael V. Kennedy, eds. *Negotiated Empires: Centers and Peripheries in the New World, 1500–1820.* New York: Routledge, 2002.

Darling, J. Andrew. 'Mass Inhumation and the Execution of Witches in the American Southwest.' *American Anthropologist*, 100, no. 3 (1999): 732–52.

Daston, Lorraine, and Katharine Park. *Wonders and the Order of Nature.* New York: Zone Books, 1998.

Davis, Natalie Zemon. *Fiction in the Archives: Pardon Tales and Their Tellers in Sixteenth-Century France.* Stanford, Calif.: Stanford University Press, 1987.

– 'Iroquois Women, European Women.' In *Women, 'Race,' and Writing.* Ed. Margo Hendricks and Patricia Parker. London: Routledge, 1994. 96–118.

– *Society and Culture in Early Modern France. Eight Essays.* Stanford, Calif.: Stanford University Press, 1975.

– *Women on the Margins. Three Seventeenth-Century Lives.* Cambridge, Mass.: Harvard University Press, 2005.

Deslandres, Dominique. *Croire et faire croire: Les missions françaises au XVIIe siècle.* Paris: Fayard, 2003.

Destefano, Michael Thomas. 'Miracles and Monasticism in Mid-Colonial Puebla, 1600–1750: Charismatic Religion in a Conservative Society.' PhD thesis, University of Florida, 1977.

Diefendorf, Barbara B. 'Discerning Spirits: Women and Spiritual Authority in Counter-Reformation France.' In *Culture and Change: Attending to Early Modern Women.* Ed. Margaret Mikesell and Adele Seeff. Newark: University of Delaware Press, 2003. 241–65.

– 'Franciser les carmélites espagnoles: la compétition entre Paris et Pontoise pour l'héritage thérésien.' Unpublished paper presented at the École des Hautes Études en Sciences Sociales, Paris, May 2006.

– *From Penitence to Charity: Pious Women and the Catholic Reformation in Paris.* New York and Oxford: Oxford University Press, 2004.

– 'Give Us Back Our Children: Patriarchal Authority and Parental Consent to

Religious Vocations in Counter-Reformation France.' *Journal of Modern History*, 68, no. 2 (1996): 265–307.

Dinan, Susan E. *Women and Poor Relief in Seventeenth-Century France: The Early History of the Daughters of Charity*. Aldershot, U.K.: Ashgate, 2006.

– and Debra Meyers, eds. *Women and Religion in Old and New Worlds*. New York: Routledge, 2001.

Dolan, Frances. *Whores of Babylon: Catholicism, Gender, and Seventeenth-Century Print Culture*. Ithaca, N.Y.: Cornell University Press, 1999.

Dompnier, Bernard. *Le venin de l'hérésie: Image du protestantisme et combat catholique au XVIIe siécle*. Paris: Editions du Centurion, 1985.

Dore, Elizabeth. 'One Step Forward, Two Steps Back: Gender and the State in the Long Nineteenth Century.' In *Hidden Histories of Gender and the State in Latin America*. Ed. Maxine Molyneux and Elizabeth Dore. Durham, N.C.: Duke University Press, 2000. 3–32.

Downs, Laura Lee. *Writing Gender History*. Oxford: Oxford University Press, 2005.

Dueñas Vargas, Guiomar. *Los hijos del pecado: ilegitimidad y vida familiar en la Santafé de Bogotá colonial*. Bogotá: Editorial Universidad Nacional de Columbia, 1997.

Duhr, Bernard. *Deutsche Auslandssehnsucht im 18. Jahrhundert: Aus der überseeischen Missionsarbeit deutscher Jesuiten*. Stuttgart: Ausland und Heimatverlags-Aktiengesellschaft, 1928.

Dunn, Marilyn. 'Nuns as Art Patrons: The Decoration of S. Marta al Collegio Romano.' *Art Bulletin*, 70 (1988): 451–77.

– 'Piety and Patronage in Seicento Rome: Two Noblewomen and Their Convents.' *Art Bulletin*, 76 (1994): 644–63.

Ebright, Malcolm, and Rick Hendricks. *The Witches of Abiquiu: The Governor, the Priest, the Genízaro Indians, and the Devil*. Albuquerque: University of New Mexico Press, 2006.

Elliott, John Huxtable. *Empires of the Atlantic World: Britain and Spain in America, 1492–1830*. New Haven, Conn.: Yale University Press, 2006.

– *Spain and its World: 1500–1700*. New Haven, Conn., and London: Yale University Press, 1989.

Erauso, Catalina de. *Memoir of a Basque Lieutenant Nun: Transvestite in the New World*. Trans. Michelle and Gabriel Stepto. Foreword by Marjorie Garber. Boston: Beacon, 1996.

Evans, William and Thomas, eds. 'A Memoir of Mary Capper, Late of Birmingham. A Minister of the Society of Friends.' *The Friends Library*. Vol. 12. Philadelphia: 1848.

– 'Memoirs of the Life of Catharine Philips.' *The Friends Library*. Vol. 11. Philadelphia: 1847.

Eze, Katherine Faull. 'Self-Encounters: Two Eighteenth-Century African Memoirs from Moravian Bethlehem.' In *Crosscurrents: African Americans, Africa, and Germany in the Modern World.* Ed. David McBride, Leroy Hopkins, and C. Aisha Blackshire-Belay. Columbia: University of South Carolina Press, 1998. 29–52.

Farmer, Sharon. '"It is Not Good That [Wo]man Should be Alone": Elite Responses to Singlewomen in High Medieval Paris.' In Bennett and Froide, *Singlewomen in the European Past.* 82–105.

Fernández Fernández, Amaya, Lourdes Leiva Viacava, Margarita Guerra Martinière, and Lidia Martínez Alcande. *La mujer en la conquista y la evangelización en el Perú (Lima 1550–1650).* Lima: Pontificia Universidad Católica del Perú, 1997.

Ferrazzi, Cecilia. *Autobiography of an Aspiring Saint.* Ed. and trans. Anne Jacobson Schutte. Chicago: University of Chicago Press, 1996.

Ferry, Robert J. 'Don't Drink the Chocolate: Domestic Slavery and the Exigencies of Fasting for Crypto-Jews in Seventeenth-Century Mexico.' *Nuevo Mundo Mundos Nuevos,* 5 (2005). http://nuevomundo.revues.org/documento934.html.

Few, Martha. 'Indian Autopsy and Epidemic Disease in Early Colonial Mexico.' In *Invasion and Transformation: Interdisciplinary Perspectives on the Conquest of Mexico.* Ed. Rebecca Brienen and Margaret Jackson. Mesoamerica Worlds Series. Boulder, Colo.: University Press of Colorado, 2007. 153–65.

– *Women Who Live Evil Lives: Gender, Religion and the Politics of Power in Colonial Guatemala.* Austin: University of Texas Press, 2002.

Finucci, Valeria. 'Genealogical Pleasures, Genealogical Disruptions.' In Finucci and Brownlee, *Generation and Degeneration,* 1–14.

– 'Maternal Imagination and Monstrous Birth: Tasso's *Gerusalemme liberate.*' In Finucci and Brownlee, *Generation and Degeneration,* 41–80.

– and Kevin Brownlee, eds. *Generation and Degeneration: Tropes of Reproduction in Literature and History from Antiquity to Early Modern Europe.* Durham, N.C.: Duke University Press, 2001.

Fischer, Kirsten. *Suspect Relations: Sex, Race, and Resistance in Colonial North Carolina.* Ithaca, N.Y.: Cornell University Press, 2002.

Flores Galindo, Alberto, and Magdalena Chocano. 'Los cargos del sacramento.' *Revista andina,* 2, no. 2 (1984): 403–23.

Foote, Cheryl, and Sandra Schackel. 'Indian Women of New Mexico, 1535–1680.' In *New Mexico Women: Intercultural Perspectives.* Ed. J. Jensen and D. Miller. Albuquerque: University of New Mexico Press, 1986. 17–40.

Francisca de los Apóstoles. *The Inquisition of Francisca: A Sixteenth-Century Visionary on Trial.* Ed. and trans. Gillian T.W. Ahlgren. The Other Voice in Early Modern Europe Series. Chicago: University of Chicago Press, 2005.

Frey, Sylvia R. *Water from the Rock: Black Resistance in a Revolutionary Era.* Princeton, N.J.: Princeton University Press, 1991.

– and Betty Wood. *Come Shouting to Zion: African-American Protestantism in the American South and British Caribbean to 1830.* Chapel Hill: University of North Carolina Press, 1998.

– and Betty Woods, eds. *From Slavery to Emancipation in the Atlantic World.* New York: Frank Cass, 1999.

Froide, Amy M. *Never Married: Singlewomen in Early Modern England.* Oxford: Oxford University Press, 2005.

Fuentes y Guzmán, Francisco Antonio de. *Historia de Guatemala ó Recordación Florida.* Madrid: L. Navarro, 1882–3.

– *Recordación Flórida. Discurso Historial y Demostración Natural, Material, Militar, y Política del Reyno de Guatemala.* 2 vols. Guatemala: Tipografía Nacional, 1932–3.

Gabbacia, Donna. 'A Long Atlantic in a Wider World.' *Atlantic Studies: Literary, Cultural, and Historical Perspectives,* 1, no. 1 (2004): 1–27.

García, Genaro. *Autos de fe de la Inquisición de México con extractos de sus causas, 1646–48. Documentos inéditos o muy raros para la historia de México 28.* Mexico City: Viuda de Charles Bouret, 1910.

Gaspar, David Barry, and Darlene Clark Hine. *Beyond Bondage: Free Women of Color in the Americas.* Urbana and Chicago: University of Illinois Press, 2004.

Gates, Henry Louis. *The Signifying Monkey: Towards a Theory of Afro-American Literary Criticism.* Oxford: Oxford University Press, 1988.

Gauderman, Kimberly. *Women's Lives in Colonial Quito: Gender, Law, and Economy in Spanish America.* Austin: University of Texas Press, 2003.

Gerona, Carla. *Night Journeys: The Power of Dreams in Transatlantic Quaker Culture.* Charleston: University of Virginia Press, 2004.

Giles, Mary E. *The Book of Prayer of Sor María of Santo Domingo.* Albany: State University of New York Press, 1990.

– ed. *Women in the Inquisition: Spain and the New World.* Baltimore and London: Johns Hopkins University Press, 1999.

Gillis, John. *Islands of the Mind: How the Human Imagination Created the Atlantic World.* New York: Palgrave Macmillan, 2004.

Gitlitz, David M. *Secrecy and Deceit: The Religion of the Crypto-Jews.* Jewish Publication Society, 1996. Albuquerque: University of New Mexico Press, 2002.

Golden, Richard. 'Satan in Europe: The Geography of Witch Hunts.' In *New Perspectives on Witchcraft, Magic, and Demonology: Witchcraft in Continental Europe.* Ed. Brian P. Levack. New York: Routledge, 2001. 2–33.

González, Deena J. 'Juanotilla of Cochiti, Vecina and Coyota: Nuevomexicanas in the Eighteenth Century.' *New Mexican Lives: Profiles and Historical Stories.*

Ed. Richard Etulain. Albuquerque: University of New Mexico Press, 2002. 78–105.

Goodich, Michael. *Other Middle Ages: Witnesses at the Margins of Medieval Society.* Philadelphia: University of Pennsylvania Press, 1998.

Graubart, Karen. *With Our Labor and Sweat: Indigenous Women and the Formation of Colonial Society in Peru, 1500–1700.* Stanford, Calif.: Stanford University Press, 2007.

Graziano, Frank. *Wounds of Love: The Mystical Marriage of Saint Rose of Lima.* Oxford: Oxford University Press, 2004.

Greenleaf, Richard. 'The Inquisition and the Indians of New Spain: A Study in Jurisdictional Confusion.' *The Americas,* 22, no. 2 (1965): 138–66.

– 'The Inquisition in Eighteenth-Century New Mexico.' *New Mexico Historical Review,* 60, no. 1 (1985): 29–60.

Greer, Allan. 'Iroquois Virgin: The Story of Catherine Tekakwitha in New France and New Spain.' In Greer and Bilinkoff, *Colonial Saints,* 235–51.

– *Mohawk Saint: Catherine Tekakwitha and the Jesuits.* Oxford: Oxford University Press, 2005.

– and Jodi Bilinkoff, eds. *Colonial Saints: Discovering the Holy in the Americas, 1500–1800.* New York: Routledge, 2003.

Griffiths, Nicholas, and Fernando Cervantes, eds. *Spiritual Encounters: Interactions between Christianity and Native Religions in Colonial America.* Lincoln: University of Nebraska Press, 1999.

– and Sue Peabody. *Slavery, Freedom, and the Law in the Atlantic World: A Brief History with Documents.* New York: Bedford St. Martin's Press, 2007.

Grulich, Rudolf. *Der Beitrag der böhmischen Länder yur Weltmission des 17. und 18. Jahrhunderts.* Königstein: Institut für Kirchengeschichte von Böhmen, Mähren, Schlesien, 1981.

Gruzinski, Serge. *Man-Gods in the Mexican Highlands: Indian Power and Colonial Society, 1520–1800.* Trans. Eileen Corrigan. Stanford, Calif.: Stanford University Press, 1989.

Guevara, María de. *Warnings to the Kings and Advice on Restoring Spain: A Bilingual Edition.* Ed. and trans. Nieves Romero-Díaz. The Other Voice in Early Modern Europe Series. Chicago: University of Chicago Press, 2007.

Gunnarsdóttir, Ellen. *Mexican Karismata: The Baroque Vocation of Francisca de los Ángeles 1674–1744.* Lincoln: University of Nebraska Press, 2004.

Gutiérrez, Ramón A. 'Honor, Ideology, Marriage Negotiation, and Class-Gender Domination in New Mexico, 1690–1846.' *Latin American Perspectives,* 12, no.1 (1985): 81–104.

– *When Jesus Came, the Corn Mothers Went Away: Marriage, Sexuality and Power in New Mexico, 1500–1846.* Stanford, Calif.: Stanford University Press, 1991.

Guy, Donna J., and Thomas E. Sheridan, eds. *Contested Ground: Comparative Frontiers on the Northern and Southern Edges of the Spanish Empire.* Tucson: University of Arizona Press, 1998.

Haggerty, Sheryllynne. *The British-Atlantic Trading Community, 1760–1810: Men, Women, and the Distribution of Goods.* London: Brill, 2006.

Haliczer, Stephen, ed. 'The First Holocaust: The Inquisition and the Converted Jews of Spain and Portugal.' In *Inquisition and Society in Early Modern Europe.* London and Sydney: Croom Helm, 1987. 7–18.

Hall, Neville A.T. *Slave Society in the Danish West Indies: St. Thomas, St. John, and St. Croix.* Ed. B.W. Higman. Mona, Jamaica: University of the West Indies Press, 1992.

Hamilton, Kenneth G., and J. Taylor Hamilton. *History of the Moravian Church: The Renewed Unitas Fratrum, 1722–1957.* Bethlehem, Penn.: Interprovincial Board of Christian Education, Moravian Church in America, 1967.

Hansom, J. S. 'The Nuns of the Institute of Mary at York from 1677 to 1825.' *Catholic Record Society,* 4 (London: 1907): 353–67.

Harline, Craig. 'Actives and Contemplatives: The Female Religious of the Low Countries before and after Trent.' *Catholic Historical Review,* 81 (1995): 541–68.

– *The Burdens of Sister Margaret.* New York: Doubleday, 1994.

– and Eddy Put. *A Bishop's Tale: Mathias Hovius among his Flock in Seventeenth-Century Flanders.* New Haven, Conn., and London: Yale University Press, 2000.

Harness, Kelley. *Echoes of Women's Voices: Music, Art, and Female Patronage in Early Modern France.* Chicago: University of Chicago Press, 2005.

Harting, Johanna. 'Catholic Registers of Hammersmith, Middlesex, 1710–1838.' *Catholic Record Society,* 26 (London: 1926): 58–130.

Harvey, L.P. *Muslims in Spain, 1500 to 1614.* Chicago and London: University of Chicago Press, 2005.

Hausberger, Bernd. *Jesuiten aus Mitteleuropa im kolonialen Mexiko: Eine Bio-Bibliographie.* Munich: Oldenbourg, 1995.

Herbermann, Charles G. 'Der Neue Welt-Bott: Introduction.' *Historical Records and Studies,* 8 (1915): 157–67.

Herzog, Tamar. *Defining Nations: Immigrants and Citizens in Early Modern Spain and Spanish America.* New Haven, Conn.: Yale University Press, 2003.

Highfield, Arnold R. 'The Danish Atlantic and West Indian Slave Trade.' In *The Danish West Indian Slave Trade: Virgin Islands Perspectives.* Ed. George F. Tyson and Arnold R. Highfield. St Croix: Virgin Islands Humanities Council, 1994. 11–32.

– 'Patterns of Accommodation and Resistance: The Moravian Witness to Slavery in the Danish West Indies.' *Journal of Caribbean History,* 28 (1994): 138–64.

Hill, Bridget. 'A Refuge from Men: The Idea of a Protestant Nunnery,' *Past and Present*, 117 (1987): 107–30.

– ed. *The First English Feminist: Reflections upon Marriage and Other Writings by Mary Astell.* New York: St Martin's Press, 1986.

Hills, Helen. *Invisible City: The Architecture of Devotion in Seventeenth-Century Neapolitan Convents.* Oxford and New York: Oxford University Press, 2004.

Hoff, Joan. 'Gender as a Postmodern Category of Paralysis.' *Women's History Review*, 3 (1994): 149–68.

Holler, Jacqueline. *Escogidas Plantas: Nuns and Beatas in Mexico City, 1531–1601.* New York: Columbia University Press, 2002.

Howe, Elizabeth. *Education and Women in the Early Modern Hispanic World.* Aldershot, U.K.: Ashgate, 2008.

Huerga Criado, Pilar. 'El problema de la comunidad judeoconversa.' *Historia de la Inquisición en España y América.* Vol. 3: Temas y problemas. Ed. Joaquín Pérez Villanueva and Bartolomé Escandell Bonet. 2nd ed. Madrid: Biblioteca de Autores Cristianos, Centro de Estudios Inquisitoriales, 2000. 441–97.

Hulme, Peter. 'Introduction: The Cannibal Scene.' In Barker, Hulme, and Iverson, *Cannibalism and the Colonial World*, 1–38.

Humez, Jean M., ed. *Gifts of Power: The Writings of Rebecca Cox Jackson, Black Visionary, Shaker Eldress.* Amherst, Mass.: University of Massachusetts Press, 1981.

Huonder, Anton. *Deutsche Jesuitenmissionäre des 17. und 18. Jahrhunderts.* Freiburg im Breisgau: Herder'sche Verlagsbuchhandlung, 1899.

Ibsen, Kristen. *Women's Spiritual Autobiography in Colonial Spanish America.* Gainseville: University Press of Florida, 1999.

Jaffary, Nora. *False Mystics: Deviant Orthodoxy in Colonial Mexico.* Lincoln: University of Nebraska Press, 2004.

– 'Virtue and Transgression: The Certification of Authentic Mysticism in the Mexican Inquisition.' *Catholic Southwest*, 10 (1999): 9–28.

– ed. and intro. *Gender, Race, and Religion in the Colonization of the Americas.* Aldershot, U.K.: Ashgate, 2007.

Johnson, Lyman L., and Sonya Lipsett-Rivera, eds. 'Introduction.' In *Faces of Honor: Sex, Shame, and Violence in Colonial Latin America.* Albuquerque: University of New Mexico Press, 1998. 1–17.

Johnson, Walter. *Soul by Soul: Life inside the Antebellum Slave Market.* Cambridge, Mass.: Harvard University Press, 1999.

Juana Inés de la Cruz (Sor). *Enigmas ofrecidos a la Casa del Placer.* Ed. Antonio Alatorre. Mexico: Colegio de México, 1994.

– *La respuesta / The Answer.* Ed. and trans. Electa Arenal and Amanda Powell. New York: Feminist Press / City University of New York, 1994.

Kagan, Richard, and Geoffrey Parker, eds. *Spain, Europe, and the Atlantic World:*

Essays in Honour of John H. Elliott. Cambridge: Cambridge University Press, 1995.

Kamen, Henry. *Empire. How Spain Became a World Power, 1492–1763.* New York: HarperCollins, 2003.

– *Inquisition and Society in Spain in the Sixteenth and Seventeenth Centuries.* Bloomington: Indiana University Press, 1985.

– *The Spanish Inquisition: A Historical Revision.* New Haven, Conn.: Yale University Press, 1997.

Kaminsky, Amy Katz. 'María de Zayas and the Invention of a Women's Writing Community.' *Revista de Estudios Hispánicos,* 35 (2001): 487–509.

– *Water Lilies / Flores del agua: An Anthology of Spanish Women Writers from the Fifteenth through the Nineteenth Century.* Minneapolis: University of Minnesota Press, 1996.

Karasch, Mary. *Slave Life in Rio de Janeiro, 1808–1850.* Princeton, N.J.: Princeton University Press, 1987.

Keitt, Andrew. *Inventing the Sacred: Imposture, Inquisition, and the Boundaries of the Supernatural in Golden Age Spain.* Leiden: Brill, 2005.

Kelly-Gadol, Joan. 'Did Women Have a Renaissance?' In *Becoming Visible: Women in European History.* Ed. Renate Bridenthal and Claudia Koonz. Boston: Houghton Mifflin, 1977. 148–52.

Kidd, Colin. *The Forging of Races: Race and Scripture in the Protestant Atlantic World, 1600–2000.* Cambridge: Cambridge University Press, 2006.

Kiddy, Elizabeth W. *Blacks of the Rosary: Memory and History in Minas Gerais, Brazil.* College Station: Penn State University Press, 2005.

– 'Ethnic and Racial Identity in the Brotherhoods of the Rosary of Minas Gerais, 1700–1830.' *The Americas,* 56 (1999): 221–52.

Kinkel, Gary. *Our Dear Mother the Spirit: An Investigation of Count Zinzendorf's Theology and Praxis.* Lanham, Md.: University Press of America, 1990.

Kirk, Stephanie. *Convent Life in Colonial Mexico: A Tale of Two Communities.* Gainesville: University Press of Florida, 2007.

Kirkus, Sister M. Gregory. 'The History of Bar Convent.' Unpublished pamphlet. Bar Convent Archives, York, U.K.

– 'The Institute after 1645.' Unpublished pamphlet. Bar Convent Archives, York, U.K.

Klein, Cecilia F. 'Wild Woman in Colonial Mexico: An Encounter of European and Aztec Concepts of Other.' In *Reframing the Renaissance.* Ed. Claire Farrago. New Haven, Conn.: Yale University Press, 1995. 244–64.

Klepp, Susan E., Farley Grubb, and Anne Pfaelzer de Ortiz, eds. *Souls for Sale: Two German Redemptioners Come to Revolutionary America.* College Station: Penn State University Press, 2006.

Klooster, Wim, and Alfred Padula, eds. *The Atlantic World: Essays on Slavery,*

Migration, and Imagination. Upper Saddle River, N.J.: Pearson/Prentice Hall, 2005.

Kostroun, Daniella. 'A Formula for Disobedience: Jansenism, Gender and the Feminist Paradox.' *Journal of Modern History,* 75 (September 2003): 483–522.

Kristal, Efraín, ed. and intro. *The Cambridge Companion to the Latin American Novel.* Cambridge: Cambridge University Press, 2005.

Landers, Jane, and Barry M. Robinson, eds. *Slaves, Subjects, and Subversives: Blacks in Colonial Latin America.* Albuquerque: University of New Mexico Press, 2006.

Larson, Rebecca. *Daughters of Light: Quaker Women Preaching and Prophesying in the Colonies and Abroad 1700–1775.* New York: Alfred A. Knopf, 1999.

Lauret, Maria, Bill Marshall, and David Murray. 'The French Atlantic.' Editorial. *Atlantic Studies,* 4, no. 1 (2007): 1–4.

Lavallé, Bernard. *Amor y opresión en los Andes coloniales.* Lima: Instituto de Estudios Peruanos, 1999.

– 'La population conventuelle de Lima (XVIè et XVIIè siècles): Approches et problemes.' *Actes de 2è Colloque. Centre d'etudes et de rechereches sur le Péroue et les Pays Andins.* Grenoble: Université de Langues et Lettres de Grenoble, 1975. 167–95.

Laven, Mary. *Virgins of Venice: Broken Vows and Cloistered Lives in the Renaissance Convent.* New York: Viking, 2003.

Lavrin, Asunción. *Brides of Christ: Conventual Life in Colonial Mexico.* Stanford, Calif.: Stanford University Press, 2008.

– 'Indian Brides of Christ: Creating New Spaces for Indigenous Women in New Spain.' *Mexican Studies / Estudios Mexicanos,* 15 (1999): 225–60.

– 'In Search of the Colonial Woman in Mexico: The Seventeenth and Eighteenth Centuries.' In *Latin American Women: Historical Perspectives.* Ed. Ascunció Lavrin. Westport, Conn.: Greenwood Press, 1978. 23–59.

– 'Sexuality in Colonial Mexico: A Church Dilemma.' In Lavrin, *Sexuality and Marriage,* 47–95.

– ed. *Sexuality and Marriage in Colonial Latin America.* Lincoln: University of Nebraska Press, 1989.

– and Rosalva Loreto L., eds. *Monjas y beatas: la escritura femenina en la espiritualidad barroca novohispana: siglos XVII y XVIII.* Mexico City: Archivo General de la Nación / Universidad de las Américas, 2002.

Legnani, Nicole Delia. *Titu Cusi: A 16th Century Account of the Conquest.* Cambridge, Mass.: Harvard University Press, 2006.

Lehfeldt, Elizabeth A. *Religious Women in Golden Age Spain: The Permeable Cloister.* Aldershot, U.K.: Ashgate, 2005.

León, Nicolás. *Catarina de San Juan y la china poblana. Estudio etnográfico crítico.* Mexico City: Biblioteca Aportación Histórica, 1946.

Leonard, Amy. *Nails in the Wall. Catholic Nuns in Reformation Germany*. Chicago: University of Chicago Press, 2005.

Lerner, Gerda. *The Creation of Patriarchy*. New York: Oxford University Press, 1986.

Lewin, Boleslao. *Los criptojudíos: Un fenómeno religioso y social*. Buenos Aires: Editorial Milá, 1987.

– *La inquisición en México: Racismo inquisitorial. El singular caso de María de Zárate*. Puebla: J.M. Caijca, Jr, 1971.

Lewis, Laura. *Hall of Mirrors: Power, Witchcraft, and Caste in Colonial Mexico*. Durham, N.C.: Duke University Press, 2003.

Liebowitz, Ruth. 'Virgins in the Service of Christ: The Dispute over an Active Apostolate for Women during the Counter-Reformation.' In *Women of Spirit: Female Leadership in the Jewish and Christian Traditions*. Ed. Rosemary Ruether and Eleanor McLaughlin. New York: Simon and Schuster, 1979. 131–52.

Lierheimer, Linda. 'Preaching or Teaching: Defining the Ursuline Mission in Seventeenth-Century France.' In *Women Preachers and Prophets through Two Millennia of Christianity*. Ed. Beverly Mayne Kienzle and Pamela J. Walker. Berkeley and Los Angeles: University of California Press, 1998. 212–26.

Lipsett-Rivera, Sonya. 'Gender and Family Relations during the Transition from Colony to Republic in Mexico.' In *State and Society in Spanish America during the Age of Revolution*. Ed. Víctor Uribe-Urán. Wilmington, Del.: Scholarly Resources, 2001. 121–48.

– '"Mira lo que hace el diablo": The Devil in Mexican Popular Culture, 1750–1856.' *The Americas*, 59, no. 2 (2002): 201–20.

Little, Ann M. *Abraham in Arms: War and Gender in Colonial New England*. Philadelphia: University of Pennsylvania Press, 2006.

Loreto López, Rosalva. 'The Devil, Women, and the Body in Seventeenth Century Puebla Convents.' *The Americas*, 59, no. 2 (2002): 181–99.

Luria, Keith. *Sacred Boundaries: Religious Coexistence and Conflict in Early-Modern France*. Washington, D.C.: Catholic University of America Press, 2005.

– *Territories of Grace: Cultural Change in the Seventeenth-Century Diocese of Grenoble*. Berkeley: University of California Press, 1991.

Lux-Sterritt, Laurence. *Redefining Female Religious Life: French Ursulines and English Ladies in Seventeenth-Century Catholicism*. Aldershot, U.K.: Ashgate, 2005.

MacCormack, Sabine. *On the Wings of Time: Rome, the Incas, Spain, and Peru*. Princeton, N.J.: Princeton University Press, 2006.

Mack, Phyllis. *Visionary Women: Ecstatic Prophesy in Seventeenth-Century England*. Berkeley: University of California Press, 1992.

Mali, Anya. *Mystic in the New World: Marie de l'Incarnation (1599–1672)*. Leiden: E.J. Brill, 1996.

Malvido, Elsa, and Carlos Viesca. 'La epidemia de cocolitzli de 1576.' *Historias*, 11 (1985): 27–33.

Mangan, Jane E. *Trading Roles: Gender, Ethnicity, and the Urban Economy in Colonial Potosí.* Durham, N.C.: Duke University Press, 2005.

María Rosa (Madre). *Atlantic Nuns: Journey of Five Capuchin Nuns (1722)* [originally titled *Account of the Journey of Five Capuchin Nuns Who Travelled from Their Convent in Madrid to Found the Convent of Jesus, Mary, and Joseph in Lima*]. Ed. and trans. Sarah Owens. The Other Voice in Early Modern Europe Series. Toronto: University of Toronto Press, 2009.

María de San José (Madre). *A Wild Country out in the Garden: The Spiritual Journals of a Colonial Mexican Nun.* Ed. and trans. Kathleen Myers and Amanda Powell. Bloomington: Indiana University Press, 1999.

– *Word from New Spain: The Spiritual Autobiography of Madre María de San José (1656–1719).* Ed. Kathleen Myers. Liverpool: Liverpool University Press, 1993.

María de San José Salazar. *Book for the Hour of Recreation.* Ed. Alison Weber. Trans. Amanda Powell. The Other Voice in Early Modern Europe Series. Chicago: University of Chicago Press, 2002.

Marshman, Michelle. 'Exorcism as Empowerment: A New Idiom.' *Journal of Religious History*, 23, no. 3 (1999): 265–81.

Martín, Luis. *Daughters of the Conquistadors: Women in the Viceroyalty of Peru.* Albuquerque: University of New Mexico Press, 1983.

Martínez, María Elena. 'The Black Blood of New Spain: *Limpieza de Sangre*, Racial Violence, and Gendered Power in Early Colonial Mexico.' *William and Mary Quarterly*, 61, no. 3 (2004): 479–520.

Martínez-Alier (Stolcke), Verena. *Marriage, Class and Colour in Nineteenth-Century Cuba: A Study of Racial Attitudes and Sexual Values in a Slave Society.* Cambridge: Cambridge University Press, 1974.

Matter, E. Ann. 'The Personal and the Paradigm: The Book of Maria Domitilla Galluzzi.' In Monson, *The Crannied Wall*, 87–102.

Maza, Francisco de la. *Catarina de San Juan: Princesa de la India y visionaria de Puebla.* Mexico City: Cien de México, 1990.

Mazzonis, Querciolo. *Spirituality, Gender, and the Self in Renaissance Italy: Angela Merici and the Company of St. Ursula (1474–1650).* Washington, D.C.: Catholic University of America Press, 2007.

M'Call, Hardy B. *Story of the Family of Wandesforde of Kirklington and Castlecomer.* London: 1904.

McCaa, Robert. 'Calidad, Clase, and Marriage in Colonial Mexico: The Case of Parral, 1788–1790.' *Hispanic American Historical Review*, 64, no. 3 (1984): 477–501.

- 'Gustos de los padres, inclinaciones de los novios y reglas de una feria nupcial colonial: Parral, 1770–1814.' *Historia Mexicana,* 40, no. 4 (1991): 579–614.

McKnight, Kathryn Joy. 'Blasphemy as Resistance: An African Slave Woman before the Mexican Inquisition.' In Giles, *Women in the Inquisition,* 229–53.

- *The Mystic of Tunja. The Writings of Madre Castillo 1671–1742.* Amherst: University of Massachusetts Press, 1997.

Melammed, Renée Levine. *Heretics or Daughters of Israel?: The Crypto-Jewish Women of Castile.* New York: Oxford University Press, 1999.

Mello e Souza, Laura de. *The Devil and the Land of the Holy Cross: Witchcraft, Slavery, and Popular Religion in Colonial Brazil.* Austin: University of Texas Press, 2003 [1986].

Merediz, Eyda M., and Nina Gerassi-Navarro, eds. 'Introducción: Confluencias de lo transatlántico y lo latinoamericano.' *Otros estudios transatlánticos. Lecturas desde lo latinoamericano. Revista Iberoamericana,* 75, no. 228 (2009).

Merrim, Stephanie. *Early Modern Women's Writing and Sor Juana Inés de la Cruz.* Nashville, Tenn.: Vanderbilt University Press, 1999.

Merritt, Jane. T. 'Cultural Encounters along a Gender Frontier: Mahican, Delaware, and German Women in Eighteenth-Century Pennsylvania.' *Pennsylvania History,* 67 (autumn 2000): 503–32.

Miller, Mary, and Simon Martin. *Courtly Art of the Ancient Maya.* New York: Thames on Hudson, 2004.

Mills, Kenneth. *Idolatry and Its Enemies: Colonial Andean Religion and Extirpation, 1640–1750.* Princeton, N.J.: Princeton University Press, 1997.

- and Anthony Grafton, eds. *Conversion: Old Worlds and New.* Rochester, N.Y.: University of Rochester Press, 2003.

Moch, Leslie Page. *Moving Europeans: Migration in Western Europe since 1650.* 2nd ed. Bloomington: Indiana University Press, 2003.

Moitt, Bernard. *Women and Slavery in the French Antilles, 1635–1848.* Bloomington: Indiana University Press, 2001.

Molina, J. Michelle. 'True Lies: Athanasius Kircher's *China Illustrata* and the Life Story of a Mexican Mystic.' In *Athanasius Kircher: The Last Man Who Knew Everything.* Ed. Paula Findlen. New York: Routledge, 2004. 365–81.

Monson, Craig A., ed. *The Crannied Wall: Women, Religion, and the Arts in Early Modern Europe.* Ann Arbor: University of Michigan Press, 1992.

Monter, William. 'Toads and Eucharists: The Male Witches of Normandy, 1564–1660.' *French Historical Studies,* 20, no. 4 (1997): 563–95.

Morgan, Ronald. 'Saints, Biographers, and Creole Identity Formation in Colonial Spanish America.' PhD thesis, University of California at Santa Barbara, 1998.

- *Spanish American Saints and the Rhetoric of Identity 1600–1810.* Tucson: University of Arizona Press, 2002.

Mott, Luiz. 'Crypto-Sodomites in Colonial Brazil.' In *Infamous Desire: Male Homosexuality in Colonial Latin America*. Ed. Pete Sigal. Chicago: University of Chicago Press, 2003. 168–96.

Mujica, Bárbara. *Women Writers of Early Modern Spain. Sophia's Daughters*. New Haven, Conn.: Yale University Press, 2004.

Muriel, Josefina. *Cultura femenina novohispana*. Mexico City: Universidad Nacional Autónoma de México, 1982.

– ed. *Las Indias caciques de Corpus Christi*. Mexico City: Universidad Nacional Autónoma de México, 1963.

Myers, Kathleen Ann. 'Introduction.' In María de San José, *Word from New Spain*, 1–76.

– 'The Mystic Triad in Colonial Mexican Nuns' Discourse: Divine Author, Visionary Scribe, and Clerical Mediator.' *Colonial Latin American Historical Review*, 6, no. 4 (1997): 479–524.

– *Neither Saints Nor Sinners: Writing the Lives of Women in Spanish America*. New York and Oxford: Oxford University Press, 2003.

– 'Testimony for Canonization or Proof of Blasphemy? The New Spanish Inquisition and the Hagiographic Biography of Catarina De San Juan.' In Giles, *Women in the Inquisition*, 270–95.

– and Amanda Powell, eds. and trans. *A Wild Country out in the Garden: The Spiritual Journals of a Colonial Mexican Nun*. Bloomington: Indiana University Press, 1999.

Nader, Helen, ed. and intro. *Power and Gender in Renaissance Spain. Eight Women of the Mendoza Family, 1450–1650*. Urbana and Chicago: University of Illinois Press, 2003.

Nalle, Sara. 'Literacy and Culture in Early Modern Castile.' *Past and Present*, 125 (November 1989): 65–96.

Nash, Mary. 'Two Decades of Women's History in Spain: A Reappraisal.' In *Writing Women's History: International Perspectives*. Ed. Karen Offen et al. Bloomington: Indiana University Press, 1991. 381–415.

Niccoli, Ottavia. *Prophecy and People in Renaissance Italy*. Trans. Lydia G. Cochrane. Princeton, N.J.: Princeton University Press, 1990.

Nirenberg, David. 'Conversion, Sex, and Segregation: Jews and Christians in Medieval Spain.' *American Historical Review*, 107, no. 4 (2002): 1065–93.

Norris, Jim. *After "The Year Eighty": The Demise of Franciscan Power in Spanish New Mexico*. Albuquerque: University of New Mexico Press, 2000.

Núñez de Miranda, Antonio. 'Carta y discuros preocupativo, de algunas dificultades, que pueden resaltar luego a la primera vista de esta historia.' In Ramos, *Primera parte*.

Oldendorp, C.G.A. *History of the Mission of the Evangelical Brethren on the Caribbean*

Islands of St. Thomas, St. Croix, and St. John. Ed. Johann Jakob Bossard. Trans. Arnold R. Highfield and Vladimir Barac. Ann Arbor: Karome Publishers, 1987 [Barby, 1777].

Olivares, Julián, and Elizabeth S. Boyce, eds. *Tras el espejo la musa escribe. Lírica femenina de los siglos de oro*. Madrid: Siglo Veintiuno, 1993.

Olivereau, Christian, ed. *Les collections du Carmel de Pontoise: Un patrimoine spirituel à découvrir*. Paris: Éditions Créaphis, 2004.

Olwig, Karen Fog. 'African Cultural Principles in Caribbean Slave Societies: A View from the Danish West Indies.' In *Slave Cultures and the Cultures of Slavery*. Ed. Stephan Palmié. Knoxville, Tenn.: University of Tennessee Press, 1995. 23–39.

– *Cultural Adaptation and Resistance on St. John: Three Centures of Afro-Caribbean Life*. Gainesville: University Press of Florida, 1985.

O'Reilly, William. 'Genealogies of Atlantic History.' *Atlantic Studies*, 1, no. 1 (2004): 66–84.

Osorio, Alejandra. 'El callejón de la soledad: Vectors of Hybridity in Seventeenth-Century Lima.' In Griffiths and Cervantes, *Spiritual Encounters*, 198–229.

O'Toole, Rachel Sarah. 'Danger in the Convent: Colonial Demons, Idolatrous *Indias*, and Bewitching *Negras* in Santa Clara (Trujillo del Perú).' *Journal of Colonialism and Colonial History*, 7, no. 1 (2006), http://www.muse.jhu.edu/journals/journal_of_colonialism_and_colonial_history/v007/7.1otoole.html.

Pagden, Anthony. *European Encounters with the New World: From Renaissance to Romanticism*. New Haven, Conn.: Yale University Press, 1993.

– *The Fall of Natural Man: The American Indian and the Origins of Comparative Ethnology*. Cambridge and New York: Cambridge University Press, 1986.

Painter, Nell Irvin. *Sojourner Truth: A Life, a Symbol*. New York: W.W. Norton, 1996.

Palmer, Colin. *Slaves of the White God: Blacks in Mexico, 1570–1650*. Cambridge, Mass.: Harvard University Press, 1976.

Paz, Octavio. *Sor Juana, or the Traps of Faith*. Trans. Margaret Sayers Peden. Cambridge: Belknap Press of Harvard University, 1988.

Pérez Villanueva, Joaquín, and Bartolomé Escandell Bonet, eds. *Historia de la Inquisición en España y América*. Vol. 3: Temas y problemas. 2nd ed. Madrid: Biblioteca de Autores Cristianos, Centro de Estudios Inquisitoriales, 2000.

Perry, Mary Elizabeth. 'Beatas and the Inquisition in Early Modern Seville.' *Inquisition and Society in Early Modern Europe*. Ed. and trans. Stephen Haliczer. Totowa, N.J.: Barnes and Noble, 1987. 147–68.

– *Gender and Disorder in Early Modern Seville*. Princeton, N.J.: Princeton University Press, 1990.

– *The Handless Maiden: Moriscos and the Politics of Religion in Early Modern Spain.*
  Princeton, N.J.: Princeton University Press, 2005.
Perry, Ruth. *The Celebrated Mary Astell: An Early English Feminist.* Chicago: Univer-
  sity of Chicago Press, 1986.
Pestana, Carla Gardina. *The English Atlantic in an Age of Revolution, 1640–1661.*
  Cambridge, Mass.: Harvard University Press, 2004.
Plane, Ann Marie. *Colonial Intimacies: Indian Marriage in Early New England.* Ith-
  aca, N.Y.: Cornell University Press, 2000.
*Popul Vuh: The Definitive Edition of the Mayan Book of the Dawn of Life and the Glor-
  ies of Gods and Kings.* Trans. Dennis Tedlock. New York: Touchstone, 1985.
Poska, Allyson M. *Regulating the People: The Catholic Reformation in Seventeenth-
  Century Spain.* Boston and Leiden: Brill, 1998.
– *Women and Authority in Early Modern Spain. The Peasants of Galicia.* Oxford and
  New York: Oxford University Press, 2005.
– and Elizabeth A. Lehfeldt. 'Redefining Expectations: Women and the
  Church in Early Modern Spain.' In Dinan and Meyers, *Women and Religion,*
  21–42.
Powers, Karen Vieira. *Women in the Crucible of Conquest: The Gendered Genesis of
  Latin American Society, 1500–1600.* Albuquerque: University of New Mexico
  Press, 2005.
Prem, Hanns J. 'Disease Outbreaks in Central Mexico during the Sixteenth
  Century.' In *Secret Judgments of God: Old World Disease in New World Contexts.* Ed.
  Noble David Cook and W. George Lovell. Norman: University of Oklahoma
  Press, 1991. 20–48.
Premo, Bianca. *Children of the Father King: Youth, Authority, and Legal Minority in
  Colonial Lima.* Chapel Hill: University of North Carolina Press, 2005.
Proctor, Frank T. 'Slavery, Identity, and Culture: An Afro-Mexican Counter-
  point, 1640–1763.' PhD thesis, Emory University, 2003.
Putnam, Lara. 'To Study the Fragments/Whole: Microhistory and the Atlantic
  World.' *Journal of Social History,* 39, no. 3 (2006): 615–30.
Raboteau, Albert S. *Slave Religion: The "Invisible Institution" in the Antebellum
  South.* New York: Oxford University Press, 1978.
Ramos, Alonso. *Primera parte de los prodigios de la omnipotencia, y milagros de la
  gracia en la vida de la venerable sierva de dios Catharina De S. Joan; natural del
  gran Mogor, difunta en esta imperial ciudad de la Puebla de los Angeles en la Nueva
  Espana.* Puebla: Imprenta de Diego Fernández de León, 1689.
Ramos Medina, Manuel. *Místicas y descalzas: Fundaciones femeninas carmelitas en la
  Nueva España.* Mexico City: CONDUMEX, 1997.
Ranft, Patricia. *A Woman's Way: The Forgotten History of Women Spiritual Directors.*
  New York: Palgrave, 2001.

Rapley, Elizabeth. *The Dévotes: Women and Church in Seventeenth-Century France.* Montreal and Kingston: McGill-Queen's University Press, 1990.

– *A Social History of the Cloister: Daily Life in the Teaching Monasteries of the Old Regime.* Montreal and Kingston: McGill-Queen's University Press, 2001.

Razovsky, Helaine. 'Early Popular Hermeneutics: Monstrous Children in English Renaissance Broadside Ballads.' *Early Modern Literary Studies*, 2, no. 3 (1996): 1–34.

Restall, Matthew, ed. *Beyond Black and Red: African-Native Relations in Colonial Latin America.* Albuquerque: University of New Mexico Press, 2005.

Reyes, Angelita. *Mothering across Cultures: Postcolonial Representations.* Minneapolis: University of Minnesota Press, 2002.

Rhodes, Elizabeth. 'Join the Jesuits, See the World: Early Modern Women in Spain and the Society of Jesus.' In *The Jesuits, II: Cultures, Sciences, and the Arts, 1540–1773.* Ed. John W. O'Malley, Gauvin Alexander Bailey, Steven J. Harris, and T. Frank Kennedy. Toronto: University of Toronto Press, 2005. 33–47.

– *This Tight Embrace: Luisa de Carvajal y Mendoza (1566–1614).* Milwaukee, Wis.: Marquette University Press, 2000.

– '"Y yo dije, sí, señor": Ana Domenge and the Barcelona Inquisition.' In Giles, *Women and the Inquisition*, 134–54.

Rípodaz Ardanaz, Daisy. *El matrimonio en Indias: Realidad social y regulación jurídica.* Buenos Aires: Fundación para la Educación, la Ciencia, y la Cultura, 1977.

Rodríguez González, José. *La nulidad de matrimonio por miedo en la Jurisprudencia Pontificia.* Vitoria: Editorial Este, 1962.

Rodríguez de la Gueva, Da. Estefanía. Archivo arzobispal de Lima. Nulidades de Matrimonios, Legajo 37, 1683.

Rosa, Susan, and Dale Van Kley. 'Religion and the Historical Discipline: A Reply to Mack Holt and Henry Heller.' *French Historical Studies*, 21, no. 4 (1998): 611–29.

Rountree, Helen C. *Pocahontas, Powhatan, Opechancanough: Three Indian Lives Changed by Jamestown.* Charleston: University of Virginia Press, 2005.

Rubial García, Antonio. *La santidad controvertida. Hagiografía y conciencia criolla aldrededor de los venerables no canonizados de Neuva España.* Mexico City: UNAM/FCE, 1999.

Ruiz, Teófilo. *Spanish Society (1400–1600).* Harlow, U.K., and New York: Longman, 2000.

Ruiz de Montoya, Antonio. *The Spiritual Conquest: Accomplished by the Religious of the Society of Jesus in the Provinces of Paraguay, Paraná, Uruguay and Tape. Written by Father Antonio Ruiz de Montoya (1639).* Trans. C.J. McNaspy, S.J. St Louis: Institute of Jesuit Sources, 1993.

Sahagún, Bernardino de. *General History of the Things of New Spain: Florentine Codex.* Trans. Arthur J.O. Anderson and Charles E. Dribble. Santa Fe, N.M.: School of American Research, 1975.

Salomon, Frank. 'Shamanism and Politics in Late-Colonial Ecuador.' *American Ethnologist,* 10, no. 3 (1983): 413–28.

Sampson Vera Tudela, Elsa. *Colonial Angels: Narratives of Gender and Spirituality in Mexico, 1580–1750.* Austin: University of Texas Press, 2000.

Sánchez, Magdalena. *The Empress, the Queen, and the Nun: Women and Power at the Court of Philip III of Spain.* Baltimore and London: Johns Hopkins University Press, 1998.

Sánchez, Tomás. *Disputaciones de sacro matrimonium sacramentum.* 3 vols. Madrid: Josephum Pationem, 1602–3.

Sánchez Lora, José Luis. *Mujeres, conventos y formas de la religiosidad barroca.* Madrid: Fundación Universitaria Española, 1988.

Sangmeister, Rev. Joseph V. *Force and Fear Precluding Matrimonial Consent: An Historical Synopsis and Commentary.* Catholic University of America Canon Law Series no. 80. Washington, D.C.: Catholic University of America Press, 1932.

Scaraffia, Lucetta, and Gabriella Zarri, eds. *Women and Faith: Catholic Religious Life in Italy from Late Antiquity to the Present.* Cambridge, Mass.: Harvard University Press, 1999.

Schlau, Stacey. 'Following Saint Teresa: Early Modern Women and Religious Authority.' *Modern Language Notes,* 117, no. 2 (2002): 286–309.

– 'Gendered Crime and Punishment in New Spain: Inquisitional Cases against *ilusas.*' In *Colonialism Past and Present.* Ed. Félix Alvaro Bolaños and Gustavo Verdesio. Albany: State University of New York Press, 2001. 151–73.

– *Spanish American Women's Use of the Word: Colonial through Contemporary Narratives.* Tucson: University of Arizona Press, 2001.

– '"Yo no tengo necesidad que me lleven a la inquisición": Las Ilusas María Rita Vargas y María Lucía Celis.' In *Mujer y Cultura en la Colonia Hispanoamericana.* Ed. Mabel Moraña. Pittsburgh: Instituto Internacional de Literatura Iberoamericana, University of Pittsburgh, 1996. 183–93.

– ed., intro., and trans. *Viva al Siglo, Muerta al Mundo. Selected Works / Obras escogidas by / de María de San Alberto (1568–1640).* New Orleans: University Press of the South, 1998.

Schlegel, Alice. 'Sexual Antagonism among the Sexually Egalitarian Hopi.' *Ethos,* 7 (1979): 124–41.

Schorsch, Jonathan. 'Blacks, Jews and the Racial Imagination in the Writings of Sephardim in the Long Seventeenth Century.' *Jewish History,* 19, no. 109 (2005): 109–35.

Schreiber, Markus. 'Cristianos nuevos de Madrid ante la Inquisición de Cuenca

(1650–1670).' In *Historia de la Inquisición en España y América.* Vol. 3: Temas y problemas. Ed. Joaquín Pérez Villanueva and Bartolomé Escandell Bonet. 2nd ed. Madrid: Biblioteca de Autores Cristianos, Centro de Estudios Inquisitoriales, 2000. 531–56.

Schroeder, Rev. H.J., ed. and trans. *Canons and Decrees of the Council of Trent.* St Louis: B. Herder, 1941.

Schutte, Anne Jacobson. *Aspiring Saints: Pretense of Holiness, Inquisition, and Gender in the Republic of Venice, 1618–1750.* Baltimore: Johns Hopkins University Press, 2001.

– 'Inquisition and Female Autobiography: The Case of Cecelia Ferrazzi.' In Monson, *The Crannied Wall,* 105–18.

– '"Such Monstrous Births": A Neglected Aspect of the Antinomian Controversy.' *Renaissance Quarterly,* 38, no. 1 (1985): 85–106.

Scott, Joan Wallach. 'The Evidence of Experience.' *Critical Inquiry,* 17 (1991): 773–97.

– *Gender and the Politics of History.* Rev. ed. New York: Columbia University Press, 1999 [1988].

Scully, Pamela, and Diana Paton. *Gender and Slave Emancipation in the Atlantic World.* Durham, N.C.: Duke University Press, 2005.

Seed, Patricia. *To Love, Honor and Obey in Colonial Mexico: Conflicts over Marriage Choice, 1574–1821.* Stanford, Calif.: Stanford University Press, 1988.

Séguier, Jeanne de Jésus. *Lettres à son frère, chancelier de France (1643–1668).* Ed. Bernard Hours. Lyons: Centre André Latreille, 1992.

Sensbach, Jon. *Rebecca's Revival: Creating Black Christianity in the Atlantic World.* Cambridge, Mass.: Harvard University Press, 2005.

– *A Separate Canaan: The Making of an Afro-Moravian World in North Carolina, 1763–1840.* Chapel Hill: University of North Carolina Press, 1998.

Shannon, Timothy J. *Atlantic Lives: A Comparative Approach to Early America.* New York: Pearson Longman, 2004.

Silva, María Beatriz Nizza da. 'Divorce in Colonial Brazil: The Case of São Paulo.' In Lavrin, *Sexuality and Marriage,* 313–40.

Silverblatt, Irene. *Modern Inquisitions: Peru and the Colonial Origins of the Civilized World.* Durham, N.C.: Duke University Press, 2004.

– *Moon, Sun and Witches: Gender Ideologies and Class in Inca and Colonial Peru.* Princeton, N.J.: Princeton University Press, 1987.

– '"The Universe has turned inside out ...There is no justice for us here": Andean Women under Spanish Rule.' In *Women and Colonization: Anthropological Perspectives.* Ed. Mona Etienne and Eleanor Leacock. New York: Praeger, 1980. 149–60.

Silverman, David J. *Faith and Boundaries: Colonists, Christianity, and Community among the Wampanoug Indians of Martha's Vineyard, 1600–1871.* Cambridge: Cambridge University Press, 2005.

Slade, Carole. *St. Teresa of Avila: Author of a Heroic Life.* Berkeley: University of California Press, 1995.

– 'St. Teresa of Avila as a Social Reformer.' In *Mysticism and Social Transformation.* Ed. Janet K. Ruffing. Syracuse, N.Y.: Syracuse University Press, 2001. 91–103.

Sleeper-Smith, Susan. *Indian Women and French Men: Rethinking Cultural Encounter in the Western Great Lakes.* Amherst: University of Massachusetts Press, 2001.

Sluhovsky, Moshe. *Believe Not Every Spirit: Possession: Mysticism, & Discernment in Early Modern Catholicism.* Chicago: University of Chicago Press, 2007.

Smolenski, John, and Thomas J. Humphrey, eds. *New World Orders: Violence, Sanction, and Authority in the Colonial Americas.* Philadelphia: University of Pennsylvania Press, 2005.

Sobel, Mechal. *Trabelin' On: The Slave Journey to an Afro-Baptist Past.* Princeton, N.J.: Princeton University Press, 1988.

Socolow, Susan Migden. 'Acceptable Partners: Marriage Choice in Argentina, 1778–1810.' In Lavrin, *Sexuality and Marriage,* 209–46.

– *The Women of Colonial Latin America.* Cambridge: Cambridge University Press, 2000.

Soufas, Teresa S., ed. *Women's Acts. Plays by Women Dramatists of Spain's Golden Age.* Lexington: University of Kentucky Press, 1997.

'Spanish Archives of New Mexico.' Microfilm edition on deposit at the Center for Southwest Research, University of New Mexico, Zimmerman Library.

Sperling, Jutta Gisela. *Convents and the Body Politic in Late Renaissance Venice.* Chicago: University of Chicago Press, 1999.

Splendiani, Anna María, José Sánchez Bohórquez, and Emma Cecilia Luque de Salazar. *Cincuenta años de inquisición en el Tribunal de Cartagena de Indias. 1610–1660.* 4 vols. Bogotá: Centro Editorial Javieriano CEJA, Instituto Colombiano de Cultura Hispánica, 1997.

Starr-LeBeau, Gretchen. 'Mari Sánchez and Inés González: Conflict and Cooperation among Crypto-Jews.' In Giles, *Women in the Inquisition,* 19–41.

– *In the Shadow of the Virgin: Inquisitors, Friars, and Conversos in Guadalupe, Spain.* Princeton, N.J.: Princeton University Press, 2003.

Stern, Steve J. *Peru's Indian Peoples and the Challenge of Spanish Conquest: Huamanga to 1640.* 2nd ed. Madison: University of Wisconsin Press, 1993. 113–47.

– *The Secret History of Gender: Women, Men, and Power in Late Colonial Mexico.* Chapel Hill: University of North Carolina Press, 1995.

Stöcklein, Joseph. *Allerhand so lehr- als geistreiche Brief, Schrifften und Reis-beschrei-*

bungen, welchen von denen Missionariis der Gesellschaft Jesu aus beyden Indien, und andern über Meer gelegenen Ländern seit An. 1642 biss auf das Jahr 1726 in Europa angelangt seynd. Erster Bund oder die 8. Erste Teil. Augsburg und Grätz: Verlag Philip, Martins und Joh. Veith seel. Erben, 1726.

Stone-Mediatore, Shari. 'Chandra Mohanty and the Revaluing of Experience.' *Hypatia,* 13, no. 2 (1998): 116–33.

Strasser, Ulrike. 'Bones of Contention: Cloistered Nuns, Decorated Relics, and the Contest over Women's Place in the Public Sphere of Counter-Reformation Munich.' *Archïv für Reformationsgeschichte / Archive for Reformation History,* 90 (1999): 254–88.

– '"The First Form and Grace": Ignatius of Loyola and the Reformation of Masculinity.' In *Masculinity in the Reformation Era.* Ed. Scott Hendrix and Susan Karant-Nunn. Sixteenth Century Essays and Studies Series. Ed.-in-chief Ray Mentzer. Kirksville, Mo.: Truman State University Press, 2008. 45–70.

– *State of Virginity: Gender, Religion and Politics in an Early Modern Catholic State.* Ann Arbor: University of Michigan Press, 2004.

Sturtz, Linda. *Within Her Power: Propertied Women in Colonial Virginia.* New York: Routledge, 2002.

Sunzin de Herrera, Francisco. *Consulta práctico-moral en que se pregunta si los fetos abortivos se podrán bautizar a lo menos debaxo de condición, a los primeros días de concebidos.* Guatemala: Imprenta nueva de Sebastián de Arébalo, 1756.

Surtz, Ronald. *The Guitar of God: Gender, Power, and Authority in the Visionary World of Mother Juana de la Cruz (1481–1534).* Philadelphia: University of Pennsylvania Press, 1990.

– *Writing Women in Late Medieval and Early Modern Spain.* Philadelphia: University of Pennsylvania Press, 1995.

Sweet, James H. *Recreating Africa: Culture, Kinship, and Religion in the African-Portuguese World.* Chapel Hill: University of North Carolina Press, 2003.

Tarbin, Stephanie, and Susan Broomhall, eds. *Women, Identities, and Communities in Early Modern Europe.* Burlington, Vt.: Ashgate, 2008.

Tate, Carolyn, and Gordon Bendersky. 'Olmec Sculptures of the Human Fetus.' *Perspectives in Biology and Medicine,* 42, no. 3 (1999): 303–32.

Teresa of Jesus. *The Complete Works of Saint Teresa of Jesus.* Trans. and ed. E. Allison Peers. London: Sheed and Ward, 1946.

Terpstra, Nicholas. 'Mothers, Sisters, and Daughters: Girls and Conservatory Guardianship in Late Renaissance Florence.' *Renaissance Studies,* 17 (2003): 201–29.

Thornton, John. *Africa and Africans in the Making of the Atlantic World, 1400–1680.* Cambridge: Cambridge University Press, 1998.

– 'On the Trail of Voodoo: African Christianity in Africa and the Americas.' *The Americas*, 44 (1988): 261–78.

Tillot, P.M., ed. *The Victoria History of the Counties of England. A History of Yorkshire. The City of York*. London: Oxford University Press, 1961.

Tilly, Louise. 'Gender, Women's History and Social History.' *Social Science History*, 13 (1989): 439–62.

Twinam, Ann. *Public Lives, Private Secrets: Gender, Honor, Sexuality, and Illegitimacy in Colonial Spanish America*. Stanford, Calif.: Stanford University Press, 1999.

Twitchell, Ralph. *The Spanish Archives of New Mexico*. 2 vols. Cedar Rapids, Iowa: Torch Press, 1914.

Uchmany, Eva Alexandra. *La vida entre el judaísmo y el cristianismo en la Nueva España, 1580–1606*. Mexico City: Archivo General de la Nación, Fondo de Cultura Económica, 1992.

Valis, Noël M. 'Mariana de Carvajal: The Spanish Storyteller.' In *Women Writers of the Seventeenth Century*. Ed. Katharina M. Wilson and Frank J. Warnke. Athens and London: University of Georgia Press, 1989. 251–82.

Valone, Carolyn. 'Architecture as a Public Voice for Women in Sixteenth-Century Rome.' *Renaissance Studies*, 15 (2001): 301–27.

– 'Roman Matrons as Patrons: Various Views of the Cloister Wall.' In Monson, *The Crannied Wall*, 49–72.

– 'Women on the Quirinal Hill: Patronage in Rome, 1560–1630.' *Art Bulletin*, 76 (1994): 129–46.

van Deusen, Nancy. *Between the Sacred and the Worldly: The Institutional and Cultural Practice of Recogimiento in Colonial Lima*. Stanford, Calif.: Stanford University Press, 2001.

Velasco, Sherry. *Demons, Nausea, and Resistance in the Autobiography of Isabel de Jesús, 1611–1682*. Albuquerque: University of New Mexico Press, 1996.

Veyna, Angelina. '"It Is My Last Wish That …": A Look at Colonial Nuevo Mexicanas through Their Testaments.' In *Building with Our Hands: New Directions in Chicana Studies*. Ed. Adela de la Torre and Beatriz Pesquera. Berkeley: University of California Press, 1993. 91–109.

Vicente, Marta V. *Clothing the Spanish Empire: Families and the Calico Trade in the Early Modern Atlantic World*. New York: Palgrave Macmillan, 2006.

Villa-Flores, Javier. '"To Lose One's Soul": Blasphemy and Slavery in New Spain, 1596–1669.' *Hispanic American Historical Review*, 82, no. 3 (2002): 435–68.

– 'Talking through the Chest: Divination and Ventriloquism among African Slave Women in Seventeenth-Century Mexico.' *Colonial Latin American Review*, 14, no. 2 (2005): 299–321.

Vogt, Peter. 'A Voice for Themselves: Women as Participants in Congregational Discourse in the Eighteenth-Century Moravian Movement.' In *Women Preach-*

ers and Prophets through Two Millennia of Christianity. Ed. Beverly Mayne Kienzle and Pamela J. Walker. Berkeley: University of California Press, 1998. 227–47.

Vollendorf, Lisa. 'Across the Atlantic: Sor Juana, *La respuesta,* and the Hispanic Women's Writing Community.' In *Approaches to Teaching the Works of Sor Juana Inés de la Cruz.* Ed. Emilie L. Bergmann and Stacey Schlau. New York: Modern Language Association, 2007. 95–102.

– *The Lives of Women: A New History of Inquisitional Spain.* Nashville, Tenn.: Vanderbilt University Press, 2005.

– 'Women Writers of Sixteenth-Century Spain.' *Dictionary of Literary Biography: Sixteenth-Century Spain.* Ed. Gregory Kaplan. Farmington Hills, Mich.: Gale Group, 2005. 334–41.

– ed. *Recovering Spain's Feminist Tradition.* New York: Publications of the Modern Language Association, 2001.

von Pastor, Freiherr Ludwig. *The History of the Popes from the Close of the Middle Ages.* 33 vols. Trans. Dom Ernst Graf. London: Kean Paul, Threch, Trubner, 1940.

von Zinzendorf, Nikolaus Ludwig. *Ergänzungsband.* Vol. 7. Hildesheim: Olms, 1965.

Walker, Claire. *Gender and Politics in Early Modern Europe: English Convents in France and the Low Countries.* New York: Palgrave, 2003.

Ward, W.R. *The Protestant Evangelical Awakening.* Cambridge: Cambridge University Press, 1992.

Weber, Alison. 'Between Ecstasy and Exorcism: Religious Negotiation in Sixteenth-Century Spain.' *Journal of Medieval and Renaissance Studies,* 23, no. 2 (1993): 221–34.

– 'Gender and Mysticism.' In *Cambridge Companion to Christian Mysticism.* Ed. Amy Hollywood and Patricia Beckman. Cambridge: Cambridge University Press, forthcoming 2009.

– 'Locating Holiness in Early Modern Spain: Convents, Caves, and Houses.' In *Structures and Subjectivities: Attending to Early Modern Women.* Ed. Joan E. Hartman and Adele Seeff. Newark, Del.: University of Delaware Press, 2007. 52–74.

– 'The Partial Feminism of Ana de San Bartolomé.' In Vollendorf, *Recovering Spain's Feminist Tradition,* 69–87.

– 'Spiritual Administration: Gender and Discernment in the Carmelite Reform.' *Sixteenth Century Journal,* 31 (2000): 123–46.

– *Teresa of Avila and the Rhetoric of Femininity.* Princeton, N.J.: Princeton University Press, 1990.

Weissberger, Barbara. 'The Critics and Florencia Pinar: The Problem with Assigning Feminism to a Medieval Court Poet.' In Vollendorf, *Recovering Spain's Feminist Tradition,* 31–47.

— *Isabel Rules: Constructing Queenship, Wielding Power.* Minneapolis: University of Minnesota Press, 2003.

Westergaard, Waldemar. *The Danish West Indies under Company Rule, 1671–1754.* New York: Macmillan, 1917.

Wheler, George. *A Protestant Monastery.* London: 1698.

Whiteley, Peter. 'The Interpretation of Politics: A Hopi Conundrum.' *Man,* 22 (1987): 696–714.

Wiesner-Hanks, Merry. *Christianity and Sexuality in the Early Modern World: Regulating Desire, Reforming Practice.* New York: Routledge, 2000.

— *Gender in History.* London: Blackwell, 2001.

— 'The Voyages of Christine Columbus.' *World History Connected,* July 2006. Accessed online 9 November 2008: http://www.worldhistoryconnected.press. uiuc.edu/3.3/wiesner-hanks.html.

— *Women and Gender in Early Modern Europe.* Cambridge: Cambridge University Press, 1993.

Wiznitzer, Arnold. 'Crypto-Jews in Mexico during the Seventeenth Century.' *American Jewish Historical Quarterly,* 51 (1961): 222–68.

Wollstadt, Hanns-Joachim. *Geordnetes Dienen in der christlichen Gemeinde.* Goettingen: Vandenhoeck and Ruprecht, 1966.

Women Writers: Reception of their Work Database. Dir. Suzan van Dijk. University of Utrecht. http://www.databasewomenwriters.nl/.

Wood, Stephanie. *Transcending Conquest: Nahua Views of Spanish Colonial Mexico.* Oklahoma City: University of Oklahoma Press, 2003.

Woodson, Carter G. *The History of the Negro Church.* 2nd ed. Washington, D.C.: Associated Publishers, 1945 [1921].

Woollacott, Angela. *Gender and Empire.* New York: Palgrave Macmillan, 2006.

Wray, Grady. *The Devotional Exercises / Los Ejercicios Devotos of Sor Juana Inés de la Cruz, Mexico's Prodigious Nun (1648/51–1695).* Lewiston, N.Y.: Edwin Mellen Press, 2005.

Young, M. Jane. 'Women, Reproduction, and Religion in Western Puebloan Society.' *Journal of American Folklore,* 100 (1987): 436–45.

Zantop, Susanne. *Colonial Fantasies: Conquest, Family, and Nation in Precolonial Germany, 1770–1870.* Durham, N.C.: Duke University Press, 1997.

Zarri, Gabriella. 'From Prophecy to Discipline, 1450–1650.' Trans. Keith Botsford. In *Women and Faith: Catholic Religious Life in Italy from Late Antiquity to the Present.* Ed. Lucetta Scaraffia and Gabriella Zarri. Cambridge, Mass.: Harvard University Press, 1999. 83–112.

Zayas y Sotomayor, María de. *Desengaños amorosos.* 2nd ed. Ed. Alicia Yllera. Madrid: Cátedra, 1993.

— *The Disenchantments of Love.* Trans. H. Patsy Boyer. Binghamton, N.Y.: SUNY Press, 1997.

— *The Enchantments of Love.* Trans. H. Patsy Boyer. Berkeley: University of California Press, 1990.

— *Novelas amorosas y ejemplares.* Ed. Julián Olivares. Madrid: Cátedra, 2000.

Zupanov, Ines G. *Missionary Tropics: The Catholic Frontier in India (16th-17th Centuries).* Ann Arbor: University of Michigan Press.

Index

Abarca de Bolea, Ana Francisca, 85, 101
Acarie, Barbe, 42
African American Christianity, 115–35; fear of slave revolts and, 119-20; Great Awakening in, 117–18; Methodist, 131–2; Moravian missionaries and, 119–31; planter resistance to, 120, 124, 126–7; prophecy in, 123–4; secret societies and, 125; self-confidence and, 123–4; on St Thomas, 119–32; transnational sisterhood in, 129–31; women in, 118–19, 128–31
Ago, Renata, 294n3
Agreda, María de Jesús de, 85, 100
Aguilera, Francisco, 167
Agustina de Saint Teresa, 95
Ahlgren, Gillian, 105n1, 108n22
Akbar, 162–3
Alberro, Solange, 199n4, 201n14, 241–2, 248n52, 249n98, 249n100, 250n101, 250n111, 250n113, 250n122, 251n125
Albrecht V, 35
Alexander III (Pope), 282
Alfonso X, 295n10, 296n21

Allestree, Richard, 60–1, 64, 71, 75
alliances, 13, 19, 253. *See also* community
Altman, Ida, 21n3
Ana de Jesús, 86
Ana de San Bartolomé, 57n46, 86, 109n24, 152n35
Anastácio, Vanda, 106n4, 107n14
Anderson, Karen, 24n14
Andrews, William M., 133n5
Andrien, Kenneth J., 24n14
Angela María de la Concepción, 86
Angelics (Milan), 35–6, 49
Anna Maria (Moravian), 129–30
annulments, 3, 18, 277–94, 300; decline in, 291–2; plaintiffs in, 282–3, 283–4; rate of requests for, 284; verdicts in, 290
Antigua, 120, 128, 32
Antonia, Paola, 49
Antonia Lucía de Espíritu Santo, 95
Apodaca, Juana de, 254, 260–1, 273n40
Apolonia de la Santísima Trinidad, 95
Aquaviva, Rudolfo, 162
Arebulo, Leonor de, 289, 300

40; property rights and, 37–9; women's reactions to, 32, 39–40. *See also* convents and monasteries

Clossey, Luke, 158, 175n4

cocolitzli, 211–12

Cohen, Sherill, 78n17

Coimagea, Lorenzo, 252, 254, 262–4

Coleridge, Henry James, 78n19, 78nn21–3

colonialism: anxiety over indigenous healers in, 217–18; authority in, 182–5; Christianity among African Americans and, 115–22; German, 173–4; hagiography and, 158–9; landmark studies on, 7–8; medicine and, 16–17; missionaries in, 120–6, 166; religion and, 11, 16–17; on St Thomas, 115–35; women's contributions in, 3–20, 80–2; women's economic participation in, 81; writing about, 83–4

Columbian exchange, 4

community, 13, 19; Jewish, 242–3; among Pueblo women, 256–61; religion, 61–78

confession and confessors, 8, 46, 156, 175n7. *See also* spiritual auto/biography

conjoined twins, 212–14

control, 112n47

convents and monasteries, 11; active vs. contemplative, 39, 40–1, 76; annulments of religious professions and, 284; asceticism in, 43–6; cloistering in, 11, 31–59; covert, 71–75; demonic possession in, 44–5; diversity in, 95; dowry requirements in, 40, 99; education in, 74–5, 84–5; elites and, 33, 35–6; English exceptionalism in, 12; female founders

of, 50–1; forced placement in, 275–7, 282–6; indigenous people in, 33, 36–7; informally organized, 37; lay retreats and, 50–1; leadership in, 99; literature from, 84–94; mysticism in, 40, 43; New World vs. Old World, 33; orthodox spirituality in, 39–43; personal luxuries in, 35–6; property rights and, 51; race and leadership of, 81–2; relation of with larger society, 48–52; retreat houses and, 37; reverential fear and, 282–3; in Spanish American literature, 95–100; spiritual directors in, 45–7; spirituality and authority in, 39–48

conversos, 11, 81, 91–2, 107n10, 237–8, 247n31. *See also* New Christians

Conyers, Esther, 74

Cook, Noble David, 22n29, 295n7, 295n9, 295n12

Cope, Douglas, 270n9

Córdova, Francisco de, 290

Córdova, María Francisca de, 285

Cornelius, Janet Duitsman, 134n9, 135n20

Cornwallis, Cecilia, 72, 73

Corteguera, Luis, 154n84

Council of Trent, 11, 31–59, 83-4, 281, 298n30, 298nn34–5

Counter-Reformation, 11, 31–59; prophetic cultures in, 207–8; women's literature influenced by, 82–3; women's patronage in, 50–1

Couturier, Edith, 297n25

Creel, Margaret Washington, 133n4, 135n18

Cruz, Anne J., 106n5, 108n22

Cruz, Felipa de la, 254, 260–1

Cruz, Magdalena de la, 185, 188–9

Cueva y Silva, Leonor de la, 87

227–8, 230–1, 232–3, 245; torture
    of, 232–3
Zarri, Gabriella, 34, 53n5
Zayas y Sotomayor, María de, 91–4,
    100–1, 110n24, 110n31, 110n33,
    112n42

Zinzendorf, Nikolaus Ludwig von,
    119, 126–8
Zúñiga y Sandoval, Catalina de, 91